Clocktower Books, San Diego
❧ Bonus 120th Anniversary Double Edition ☙

Coronado Mystery

by John T. Cullen

First Time Together under One Cover, the Full Text of Two Fascinating Books about the Famous Ghost at the Hotel del Coronado.

Dead Move

Dead Move: Kate Morgan & The Haunting Mystery of Coronado, Fourth Edition (Nonfiction)—A Scholarly Analysis of Known Historical Facts Hidden in Plain Sight for over 120 Years Due to an Expert Cover-up by the Spreckels Machine.

Plus:
A Dramatization Closely Based on the True Crime Story:

Lethal Journey

A Noir 1892 Thriller (Fiction - Novel)

~ 1892 Coronado, California ~

The heart-breaking tragedy of a beautiful but poor shop girl from Detroit (a true Victorian Fallen Angel, 'ruined' and desperate), of a blackmail conspiracy against a fabulously wealthy hotel owner (John D. Spreckels) by a ruthless grifter named Kate Morgan, and of the 'cad' and 'bounder' John Longfield, father of three children and husband, who brought poor Lizzie low in fortunes, until she perished violently and mysteriously at the Hotel del Coronado, near San Diego, on 28-9 November 1892.

Coronado Mystery by John T. Cullen. Copyright © 2016 by John T. Cullen. All Rights Reserved.

Dead Move: Kate Morgan and The Haunting Mystery of Coronado By John T. Cullen Copyright © 2008 by John T. Cullen. All Rights Reserved.

Lethal Journey By John T. Cullen. Copyright © 2009 by John T. Cullen. All Rights Reserved.

Available online and in bookstores—print and digital Editions

Graphics (except maps), both on the covers and inside the text, are the creations and property of John T. Cullen. Maps are the licensed property of John T. Cullen and may not be reused without the author's permission.

Photograph (title page) of the Hotel del Coronado around 1892 is in the public domain. Same for Grand Union Depot, Hotel Brewster, and other period photographs.

Clocktower Books, Publisher
P.O. Box 600973
Grantville Station
San Diego, California 92160-0973

www.clocktowerbooks.com—-editorial@clocktowerbooks.com

Dedication
Of the 125th Anniversary Double Edition
Coronado Mystery
(*Dead Move* and *Lethal Journey*):

To
Carolyn and Andrew
As always

And to
Elizabeth 'Lizzie' Wyllie
(c1868-1892)
The quintessentially classic and tragic
Victorian Fallen Angel

Special Thanks to our intrepid, detail-oriented editor, Sarah Dawson, for a great job on every line of this manuscript. Contact Mrs. Dawson at **WordPlay Editing** by email at **sdawson@wordplayediting.com**. The editorial website is

www.wordplayediting.com.

Special thanks to 1SG Richard Agler, USMC-Ret. for invaluable information regarding hand guns, ballistics, and related issues about the gun found near the violently and mysteriously deceased Elizabeth 'Lizzie' Wyllie's hand.

Elizabeth 'Lizzie' Wyllie was the Beautiful Stranger, who has ever since gained fame as the ghost of the Hotel del Coronado under various false or wrongly attributed names including 'Kate Morgan' and 'Lottie A. Bernard.' When her unexplained death became a national sensation in 1892, the press called her 'The Beautiful Stranger,' a name still used in official publications of the Hotel del Coronado in the twenty-first century. Based on the most famous, contradictory feminine ideal and nadir of her age, she is the incarnation of Thomas Hardy's Tess of the D'Urbervilles, and other Victorian Fallen Angels.

About the Author: John T. Cullen

Visit the Clocktower Books publisher website at www.clocktowerbooks.com

or the author's website at www.johntcullen.com

for more information, see also the back (*About*) pages of this volume.

John T. Cullen (also Jean-Thomas Cullen and John Argo) has been an Internet publishing and e-book pioneer since he first started publishing full novels online in 1996. Full information available at the Clocktower Books website - see the museum pages. In nonfiction, he specializes in history and science writing at a high level of scholarly rigor without losing his entertaining and personable style.

Degrees, scholarship: John T. Cullen holds a B.A. in English (University of Connecticut, Storrs); a B.B.A. in Computer Information Systems (National University, San Diego); and an M.S. in Business Administration (Boston University). He writes both fiction and nonfiction, and has authored over thirty books plus articles and shorter fiction. He lives in San Diego with his wife, son, and cat.

The author worked at the Hotel del Coronado part-time for several years after retiring from the aerospace and computer systems development industries. As a driver, he became intimately familiar with the hotel and transportation industries in general, and in particular the history of Coronado and its U.S. National Landmark hotel (the Del). He read the hotel's official history of the 1892 true crime and ghost legend (*Beautiful Stranger: the Ghost of Kate Morgan and the Hotel del Coronado*). As an avid researcher, he became deeply interested in what remains essentially a cold case—an unsolved crime from long ago in the Victorian gaslamp era. Using his considerable understanding of history (San Diego and world; macrohistory), he was able—in these books—to present the first plausible and comprehensive explanation of the true crime mystery of 1892 that gave rise to San Diego's most famous ghost legend associated with the Hotel del Coronado.

Dead Move: Kate Morgan and the Haunting Mystery of Coronado is his nonfiction, scholarly analysis of the true crime in its 1892 context. He removed the dramatized time line originally in the nonfiction book, rewrote it, and produced the riveting noir period novel **Lethal Journey**. Both books are included in this volume, titled **Coronado Mystery**.

❧ Bonus 125th Anniversary Double Edition ❧

General Table of Contents

1st Book (Nonfiction—True History Analysis):
Dead Move
Kate Morgan & the Haunting Mystery of Coronado, 4th Edition
☞ Page 19

2nd Book (Fiction—Novel)
Lethal Journey
A Noir 1892 Thriller Closely Based on True History
☞ Page 169

❧ **Both Books in One Volume** ❦

Detailed Table of Contents

First Book: Dead Move:
Kate Morgan & the Haunting Mystery of Coronado, 3rd Ed.

Table of Contents

Preface to the 2017 Double Edition 12
Preface to the 2012 Third Edition of Dead Move 14
Book One: 19
Prologue: 21
   A TRUE STORY THAT WILL NOT DIE 21
      Ghost by Gaslight 21
Part I. Mystery Story 27
   THE MYSTERY IN A NUTSHELL 27
      Gunshot, by Gaslight, with Sea Storm and Ghost 27
Part II. Ghost Story 33
   SOME LIKE IT SPOOKY 33
      Haunted Hotel 33
Part III. What We Know For Sure 37
   LOTTIE A. BERNARD TIMELINE 37
      Day 0—Wednesday, Nov. 23, 1892 (Katie Logan in L.A.) 37
      Day 1—Thursday, Nov. 24, 1892 (Lottie Bernard Checks In) 39
      Day 2—Friday, Nov. 25, 1892 46
      Day 3—Saturday, Nov. 26, 1892 46
      Day 4—Sunday, Nov. 27, 1892 47
      Day 5—Monday, Nov. 28, 1892 47
      Day 6—Tuesday, Nov. 29, 1892 (Body Found) 50
      Day 7—Wednesday, Nov. 30, 1892 (Coroner's Inquest) 51
   NEWSPAPER ACCOUNTS DEC. 1-DEC. 14 56
      Day 8—Thursday, Dec. 1, 1892 56
      Day 9—Friday, Dec. 2, 1892 58
      Day 10—Saturday, Dec. 3, 1892 60
      Day 11—Sunday, Dec. 4, 1892 60
      Day 12—Monday, Dec. 5, 1892 62

    Day 13—Tuesday, Dec. 6, 1892 .... *62*
    Day 14—Wednesday, Dec. 7, 1892 .... *64*
    Day 15—Thursday, Dec. 8, 1892 .... *65*
    Day 16—Friday, Dec. 9, 1892 .... *67*
    Day 17—Saturday, Dec. 10, 1892 .... *69*
    Day 18—Sunday, Dec. 11, 1892 .... *69*
    Day 19—Monday, Dec. 12, 1892 .... *70*
    Day 20—Tuesday, Dec. 13, 1892 .... *70*
    Day 21—Wednesday, Dec. 14, 1892 (Funeral and Burial) *71*

Part IV. Solved! 73

THE CORE OF MY THEORY 73
    Key Points *73*
    Web of Indirect Evidence *74*
REWINDING THE TAPE 75
    Day 0—Wednesday, Nov. 23, 1892 (Katie Logan in L.A.) *75*
    Day 0 ½—The Missing Day *82*
    Day 1—Thursday, Nov. 24, 1892 (Lottie Bernard Checks In) *85*
    Day 2—Friday, Nov. 25, 1892 .... *89*
    Day 3—Saturday, Nov. 26, 1892 .... *90*
    Day 4—Sunday, Nov. 27, 1892 .... *90*
    Day 5—Monday, Nov. 28, 1892 .... *91*
    Day 6—Tuesday, Nov. 29, 1892 (Body Found) *93*
    Day 7—Wednesday Nov. 30, 1892 (Coroner's Inquest) *98*
NEWSPAPER ACCOUNTS DEC. 1-DEC. 14 104
    Day 8—Thursday, Dec. 1, 1892 .... *104*
    Day 9—Friday, Dec. 2, 1892 .... *105*
    Day 10—Saturday, Dec. 3, 1892 .... *106*
    Day 11—Sunday, Dec. 4, 1892 .... *107*
    Day 12—Monday, Dec. 5, 1892 .... *110*
    Day 13—Tuesday, Dec. 6, 1892 .... *111*
    Day 14—Wednesday, Dec. 7, 1892 .... *112*
    Day 15—Thursday, Dec. 8, 1892 .... *114*
    Day 16—Friday, Dec. 9, 1892 .... *116*
    Day 17—Saturday, Dec. 10, 1892 .... *117*
    Day 18—Sunday, Dec. 11, 1892 .... *117*
    Day 19—Monday, Dec. 12, 1892 .... *119*
    Day 20—Tuesday, Dec. 13, 1892 .... *119*
    Day 21—Wednesday, Dec. 14, 1892 (Funeral and Burial) *119*

Part V. Lottiepedia 121

(CONCORDANCE A-Z) 121
    Guide to the Concordance: *121*
    Anderson: *121*
    Bernard: *122*
    brother: *122*

    Brown, Josie: *123*
    doctor: *123*
    embalming: *123*
    Detroit: *124*
    gun: *125*
    husband: *126*
    Fibs: *126*
    Friends: *127*
    hankies: *127*
    Jones, Joseph: *129*
    Kate Morgan: *131*
    Katie Logan: *131*
    Missing Day: *132*
    Pregnancy *133*
    Sponge *134*
    Stingaree *134*
    Trunks: *134*
    Victorian culture: *136*
    Victorian sentimentalism: *139*
    women, two: *142*

Epilog: **145**
   THE BIG PICTURE 145
    Of Sugar Barons and Pineapple Kings *145*

Appendix: Maps **151**
    Map 1: Transcontinental Rail System *152*
    Map 2: San Diego and Peninsula with Coronado *155*
    Map 3: San Diego Overview *161*
    Map 4: San Diego and Coronado (3 Inset—Detail) ... *163*
    Map 5: San Diego and Coronado (Inset, Detail 2) *164*

Book Two: Lethal Journey **169**

2012 Preface to Lethal Journey **173**

1. Kate & Tom Morgan, 1888 .... **177**

2. Lizzie & John–Late Summer 1892 .... **202**

3. Kate Morgan–Late Summer 1892 .... **213**

4. Detroit—Early Fall 1892 .... **221**

5. Knocked Up & Ruined **224**

6. Detroit—Kate, Lizzie, & John **230**

7. Los Angeles—Mid-Autumn 1892 .... **243**

8. Conspiracy—Late Autumn 1892 255
9. San Diego—November 1892 261
10. Coronado—Thanksgiving 1892 271
11. Conspiracy's End—Legend's Start 312
Author's Notes~Lethal Journey 316
Selected Reading: 329
Notes: 329
About Clocktower Books: 331
We Made History 341
End Notes for Dead Move 344

For End Notes to <u>Dead Move</u>, see end pages of this volume.

See Page 175 for Table of Contents of the novel (second book, titled <u>Lethal Journey</u>).

Preface to the 2017 Double Edition

It has been a decade since I seriously began to study the enigmatic case of the Beautiful Stranger, an elegant and refined young woman who died violently and mysteriously at the Hotel del Coronado near San Diego in November 1892.

This story is a true crime investigation, with no paranormal aspects. If you do not believe in ghosts, you can treat this as it is—a historical, scientific analysis with no supernatural elements. If you believe the ghost legend, this true crime analysis will explain who she was, and how she became the hotel's famous ghost.

This new double edition of 2017 (on the 125th anniversary of Elizabeth 'Lizzie' Wyllie's tragic death) eliminates the dramatization formerly contained in Dead Move, and substitutes the rousing, dark thriller Lethal Journey in its stead. The day by day, hour by hour detail in the obsolete narrative is adequately traced in *Lethal Journey*, which is a smoother flowing, more dramatic read. Separate prefaces for each edition are included in this book.

Over these years, my convictions have deepened—first, that my careful and painstaking analysis about a blackmail plot was correct in the first place; secondly, that the expert agents and security operatives of the Spreckels family created a highly successful cover-up to protect John Spreckels' reputation at a critical moment. He was in Washington, D.C., negotiating with family friend President Benjamin Harrison, and a hostile, partisan Congress, over the future of Hawai'ian sovereignty, the Monarchy, and the fate of Claus Spreckels' vast sugar cane plantations in Hawai'i.

The dead woman was not Kate Morgan, as muddled and disembodied local legends would have us believe, but Elizabeth 'Lizzie' Wyllie of Detroit. She was, in fact, the first major I.D. on the corpse after it was established that Lottie A. Bernard was a fake persona; missing Los Angeles maid Katie Logan was a dead end.

In fact, while legend sometimes confuses Kate Morgan with the fake alias 'Katie Logan,' evidence clearly hidden in plain sight for well over a century proves that Katie Logan and Lizzie Wyllie were one and the same person.

The owner of the Hotel Del at the time was the wealthy and politically connected John D. Spreckels. The basis for the events of 1892 was a blackmail plot by Kate Morgan, using Lizzie Wyllie and John Longfield. The target was the hotel's owner, John Spreckels, who was innocent of Lizzie's out of wedlock pregnancy.

I have by now firmly concluded—reluctantly, because I am not a conspiracy minded person—that there was a cover-up. The reason for the muddled legends can be traced to a very successful cover-up by the expert security agents protecting the Spreckels family from assassination, blackmail, and other predictable plots hatched against any of the leading families in the United States. My research, revealed in these books, tangentially (and relevantly) relates the well-known history of the fall of the Hawai'ian monarchy, the annexation of that sovereign nation as a U.S. territory, and the tragedy of HRM Crown Princess Ka'iulani of the Kalakaua Dynasty.

On a smaller scale, contained within the scandals of the Yellow Press, and the cover-ups of Spreckels' agents and newspapers in San Diego, is the heart-breaking tragedy of an ordinary young shop girl from Detroit, who fancied herself to be in a league with the great actresses (Louise Leslie Carter, Lillian Russell) of her time, as well as the eminent playwright Denham Thompson.

Ironically, Thompson's stage play *The Old Homestead*, which sold out nationally to raves and packed theaters, is emblematic of the young nation's growing pains from an agrarian to an urban society. Lizzie, no less than any of the play's millions of other fans, no doubt felt a visceral longing for simpler times and purer morays. She became the incarnation of that Victorian ideal, the Fallen Angel—a pure woman, laid low through no fault of her own, by a hostile and uncaring world. Her fancy funeral and unmarked burial symbolize the cruelties and contradictions of her world, and constitute a moral lesson for people of all times and places, including our own.

Preface to the 2012 Third Edition of Dead Move

Time and reflection have only deepened the conclusions I drew in my original, painstaking research that led to the 2008 First and Second Editions of this scholarly, nonfictional analysis of the famous Hotel del Coronado 1892 true crime and ghost story.

The entire enigmatic true crime case was the result of a blackmail attempt against the fabulously wealthy but imperiled John D. Spreckels, scion of a vast Hawai'i based sugar cane fortune. All of what I discovered, and my conclusions from it, have been hidden in plain sight for over 120 years.

There is nothing paranormal, conspiratorial, or invented about the facts as I lay them out. This is, to be sure, a very old, brittle, long-cold police case with missing pieces. As is the case in all history researches, it is amazing how much we know, yet heartbreaking what has been lost. Luckily, a complete, plausible scenario can be deduced from what has come down to us, recorded both in local San Diego sources and in our national histories.

What is new in this Third Edition primarily consists of two things.

❧ 1 ☙

I have replaced the dramatized reenactment of Lottie A. Bernard's life and death at the Hotel del Coronado with the complete text of my dark 1892 thriller Lethal Journey.

Lethal Journey conforms to my historical research, except Tom Morgan is dramatically embellished. These revelations would have been obvious 120+ years ago, with honest, and objective scrutiny.

A historian's dilemma confounds the choice of either narrative. On the one hand, Lethal Journey is fiction, though closely based on true fact. On the other hand, the original dramatization was based on hour by hour, day by day known facts as gathered in the Hotel del Coronado Heritage Department's official book Beautiful Stranger (see Bibliography in End Notes). The problem is one of granularity, for lack of a better way to describe it. Even in the dramatization, I often had to transition from one moment to the next with an imagined gesture or conversation, because we do not have a running film of the dead woman's five final, agonizing days.

The hourly events are pretty well captured in the carefully detailed account of her passage, as recorded mainly in news stories and interviews from the time. To include both the dramatization and Lethal Journey would be redundant. I made a Solomonic choice of Lethal Journey, with only the following caveat.

I have independently concluded that the myths and legends about Kate Morgan's husband, Tom Morgan, have no discernible basis in fact. Their marriage was real, they did lose a baby son (Edward), and they lived in Iowa until their apparent separation for reasons that have nothing to do with this story.

In Lethal Journey (as in the earlier dramatization) I did not entirely cast aside the legend of Tom Morgan as a gambler and, with the publication of an unfortunate book in 1987, possibly a murderer.

In my novel Lethal Journey, written from a noirish screenplay suggested by a play producer, I used the most rousing elements of the legend (Tom Morgan as a violent and dangerous cardsharp), together with my scholarly analysis. Readers are asked simply to remember that the conclusion of Dead Move is that Lizzie most likely committed suicide out of despair and sickness (murder is unlikely, though not 100% ruled out).

❧ 2 ☙

My earlier suspicions of a cover-up have, for me, become firmly entrenched in logic and conviction. The hastily convened and absurdly brief Coroner's Inquest are too blatantly improbable to not have been engineered for purposes of getting things over with, and shielding John D. Spreckels. The forbidding of an autopsy, which would have revealed her pregnancy and thus cast a shadow of doubt on Spreckels, is another blatant factor—in fact, shifting the identity of the victim to Kate Morgan further obfuscated the issue. If the dead woman was not pregnant (as Dr. B. F. Mertzman said she was), then there could be no blackmail. Without a cogent reason for the entire affair, the shadowy issue of blackmail would be permanently covered up. The cover-up is still working quite well to this very day.

The logic for a massive cover-up is impeccable. John Spreckels was the scion of a fabulously wealthy, by then old-money family of the Gilded Age. The better known 'Robber Baron' names (Astor, Vanderbilt, Carnegie, Rockefeller, *et al*.) were primarily national in character, whereas the stories of John Spreckels and James and Sanford Dole were international. The story of the blackmail at the Hotel del Coronado, therefore, has national and international ramifications. These have been painfully evident all along, but are only now revealed to be firmly linked to global events at the time.

The better known Robber Barons (as historians often call the mega-wealthy U.S. aristocracy of the Gilded Age) derive their pedigree from industries within the vastness of the 48 contiguous states. On pragmatic terms, they acquired vast wealth and tended to marry their daughters to bankrupt but titled British aristocrats to blatantly affirm their loyalties to foreign monarchy rather than the strict anti-monarchist traditions of the U.S. Founding Fathers, and indeed of the British North American colonies (which made the War of Independence possible from a U.S. perspective, within global superpower politics of the late 18th Century). The century-long drive to expand U.S. boundaries west to the Pacific Ocean is called Manifest Destiny. Its racist, sectarian, and related bigotries made an irresistible fuel whose combustion consumed all that stood in its way—be it the Native North American, the Spanish or Russian empires, or the boundaries of sovereign Mexico. The drive westward was all but over by the 1880s.

Without pause, a new class of internationalist power brokers and corporate moguls—e.g., Claus Spreckels, John Spreckels, Sanford Dole, and James Dole (the 'Pineapple King')—continued the Gilded Age's wealth-driven, quasi-religious fervor masked in the slogan of Manifest Destiny, which brooked no opposition.

The 1890 U.S. Census included the declaration that the Frontier was closed. However, expansionary U.S. political, religious, and economic forces pressed on beyond Continental borders. Men like Dole and Spreckels created trans-oceanic fortunes that seem, in retrospect, a continuation of Manifest Destiny by other means.

In the 1840s, it had taken many months, or several years, to laboriously cross the United States on foot or on horseback, via the famous Conestoga Wagons or Prairie Schooners. Just half a century later, the modern person of the 1890s could cross the continent in luxury, in a week or less, aboard the vast arterial and capillary network of the Transcontinental Railroad system.

Likewise, John Spreckels in Washington, D. C. and his father Claus in San Francisco could communicate within hours, coast to coast via telegraph network amid delicate, doomed negotiations over the fate of Hawai'i, and of Spreckels' vast sugar cane plantations.

The telegraph was the 'Internet' of its time, which gave rise to national news coverage by Yellow Press moguls like Joseph Pulitzer and William Randolph Hearst. Scandal, lies, and political-corporate propaganda would be a better term than 'news' for what came out of the Yellow Press. For much of the U.S. public, such coverage was all the exposure they would ever have to national or international events. They had nothing else to go on, so they believed wholeheartedly that the Hawai'ian people were pagan savages deserving of conquest and domination, and that the beautiful, cultured, Anglican-Hawai'ian (and Scottish) Crown Princess Victoria Ka'iulani was a brutal and ugly cannibal with a bone through her nose.

The national scandal of the Beautiful Stranger at the Hotel del Coronado was merely an early dry run for the excesses and propaganda of the Yellow Press. Spreckels' newspapers and agents in Coronado and San Diego succeeded in covering up the worst of his exposure. The Yellow Press relied on half-truths and innuendo to darkly hint of the Beautiful Stranger's alleged liaisons with men in the highest places. In the tightly and cruelly repressed Victorian world, that alone was enough to sell oceans of newsprint to gullible and titillated men and women across the United States.

The Yellow Press' alignment with the corporate-led coup in Honolulu, January 1893, and their defamation of the Hawai'ian people, were prelude to the United States' 1898 acquisition of the Spanish Empire. This is no longer current events, but substantiated and commonly understood history.

The War with Spain came upon a constant drumbeat to war in the Yellow Press, fueled by feverish allegations that an accidental boiler room explosion aboard the U.S.S. Maine in Havana, Cuba Harbor was a deliberate act by Spanish saboteurs. Cuba was a fertile island producing huge quantities of sugar, tobacco, and other goods on the back of an impoverished, near-slave class of human beings who were, due to their race and religion, not covered by the grandiose promises and short deliveries of Manifest Destiny.

❦ 3 ❦

Brief Publication History. I conducted my initial, substantial research on this case in 2006-2008, using my own resources and the Internet, while relying heavily on the excellent groundwork laid by the official Hotel del Coronado Heritage Department historian in their publication Beautiful Stranger: the Ghost of Kate Morgan and the Hotel del Coronado (Heritage Dept., 2002, 2005).

Moving with what proved to be an excess of caution, I initially released the book as a novel of historical fiction. This is a time-honored way of advancing a historical hypothesis. As I soon discovered, this put my research into an unintended limbo between fact and fiction, only in terms of how it was perceived. Within a few weeks, still in 2008, I released the same text in a more boldly stated theory format (nonfiction, history) under the same title, as a 2nd Ed.

In 2009, at the suggestion of an interested play producer from out of state, who had been stationed in Coronado during his Navy days and loved the Hotel Del and the ghost story, I wrote a dark, noirish novel which I published under the title Lethal Journey. The Second Edition of *Dead Move* contained a dramatization of events involving Lizzie Wyllie (the true Beautiful Stranger, who died at the hotel and gave rise to the famous ghost legend). Lethal Journey allowed me to take a few liberties, incorporating the best elements of the legend (cover-up) as received for over a century, along with my careful, scholarly analysis in Dead Move.

In 2012 (120th Anniversary Edition of the Beautiful Stranger's death), bowing to the strong demand for Dead Move, and the fact that Lethal Journey was often lost in the shuffle among the constant outpouring of New York-hyped thrillers, I decided to drop the somewhat creaky and obsolete dramatization from Dead Move, and instead include the full text of Lethal Journey in the current edition that you are reading.

For the 2017 (125th Anniversary Edition) I am retitling the duet as Coronado Mystery, to include both Dead Move and Lethal Journey. Each of those two books also is to appear separately to offer more choices to interested readers. See www.coronadomystery.com.

Book One:

Dead Move:
Kate Morgan & The Haunting Mystery of Coronado, Fourth Edition
To the 125th Anniversary of her Death 1892-2017
First Book of Two

By
John T. Cullen

~ 1892 Coronado, California ~
A True Crime and Ghost Legend Investigation
Clocktower Books, San Diego

Dead Move: Kate Morgan and The Haunting Mystery of Coronado By John T. Cullen. Copyright © 2008, 2012, 2016 by John T. Cullen. All Rights Reserved.

www.sandiegoauthor.com

Available online and in bookstores—print and digital Editions

Graphics (except maps), both on the covers and inside the text, are the creations and property of John T. Cullen. Maps are the licensed property of John T. Cullen and may not be reused without the author's permission.

Photograph (title page) of the Hotel del Coronado around 1892 is in the public domain. Same for Grand Union Depot, Hotel Brewster, and other period photographs.

Clocktower Books, Publisher
P.O. Box 600973
Grantville Station
San Diego, California 92160-0973
www.clocktowerbooks.com

Prologue:

A True Story That Will Not Die

Ghost by Gaslight

The story you are about to read is true on two counts—as a mystery story, and as a ghost story. The real-life mystery story in 1892 became an instant national sensation, laced with beauty, passion, and hope—but also conspiracy, betrayal, and ultimately violent death. This mystery (murder or suicide?) spawned a famous ghost saga that has endured over a century. Whether or not you believe in ghosts, the story of the 'Beautiful Stranger' is a living piece of Hotel del Coronado lore—and even skeptics may at times get goose bumps.

To capture the atmosphere, it is worth dwelling a moment on how I came upon this story. Being an author, semi-retired from the computer systems development industry, and in search of some fresh experiences, I took a part-time job several years ago as a shuttle van driver with the Hotel del Coronado near San Diego.

The Hotel del Coronado (or the Hotel Del to local residents, sometimes just 'the Del') is an official U.S. National Landmark and a San Diego icon. It is usually portrayed on book covers, in all of its splendor, as a white Victorian lady with her famous brick-red roofs. It sits on the Peninsula of San Diego, on a Pacific Ocean beach in the City of Coronado, facing away from the City of San Diego.

The Pacific Ocean laps at sugar-white beaches, just a tennis ball's throw from the rear stairs where the Beautiful Stranger died—who became the famous ghost who is said to still haunt the great resort to this day. Visible along that shore, to the southeast, is the southwestern corner of the contiguous United States—including Imperial Beach and Nestor—before you reach Tijuana, Baja California del Norte, Mexico.

The weather in Coronado is usually balmy and sunny, as tall fan palms rustle in a slight breeze under clear blue skies. Visible to the west (the shore runs east-west at the Hotel Del) is the looming ridge of Point Cabrillo, which overlooks the San Diego Harbor entrance where the first Spanish expedition dropped anchor more than four centuries ago. The view from the barren, wind-blown site of his future hotel toward Point Cabrillo must have reminded mega-rich developer John Spreckels of gorgeous South Pacific beaches in Hawai'i, where his father owned vast sugar cane plantations. That was back in 1887, when Spreckels first visited San Diego and fell in love with the place. He would go on to own much of the area, and leave a lasting impression on its history.

Millions of visitors come to the area every year. But there is another side to the image—dark, atmospheric, spooky. As this book will show, John Spreckels was a key player in the mysterious events of Thanksgiving Week 1892 that led to the Beautiful Stranger's violent, mysterious death, and her incarnation as the hotel's most famous ghost.

My two years at the hotel were fascinating—new things to learn, nice people, great surroundings, interesting history, sunshine, fresh air, rustling palm trees, crashing surf…topped off by the fact that I believe I have solved a great mystery of the Hotel del Coronado: The legend of an unknown woman who died violently and mysteriously on the hotel's back steps during a huge sea storm; and of her ghost, which thousands of visitors and some staff claim to have seen. I personally have met a number of people who claim to have witnessed ghostly manifestations, though I myself can't make that claim. Then again, maybe I missed something. After all, if there is a ghost, it's clear that she would be trying to tell us something, and I unwittingly stepped into the role of oracle to deliver her message: She is not Kate Morgan, as is commonly thought, but a beautiful young woman who was betrayed and abandoned in the midst of a cruel blackmail conspiracy. Her name was Elizabeth 'Lizzie' Wyllie. Lizzie was pregnant when she took her life out of despair—a fallen Victorian angel, in the true sense and sentiment of that age. I will explain it all in this book.

On many an evening when business was slow, we drivers in our black suits would sit in our vans waiting for passengers, by turns either in the dark, starlit parking lot below, or under the softly gleaming coach lights around the front entrance of the hotel. A good deal of our traffic was taking guests to or from Lindbergh

International Airport, ten miles away. The ride included an enjoyable two mile jaunt nearly 300 feet in the air across the Coronado Bay Bridge (another San Diego icon).

Another substantial part of our evening traffic was bringing guests to or from eating and entertainment venues in the Gaslamp Quarter of San Diego. This is a modern salvage and gentrification of the long-decaying Victorian city and its infamous red light district, through which Kate Morgan and her accomplices moved. Today's Gaslamp Quarter (Fourth to Sixth Avenues east-west, and K Street to Broadway north-south) was the heart of downtown San Diego in the 1890s, with the notorious Stingaree district partially overlapping to the south. The Stingaree, which was one of the most violent and dangerous red light districts on the West Coast, took its name from the stingrays that are common on San Diego area shores, and have a poisonous stinger that causes agonizing pain, and can (rarely) kill. The saying about the red light district was: "You get stung as badly in the Stingaree as in San Diego Bay."

On many nights during the winter months as I sat waiting in the van, fog would roll in off the Pacific Ocean, and a chill would run up and down my spine in the cold, damp air. Sometimes you could hear the booming of naval guns out at sea (the Navy's Special Warfare Command has its headquarters a block away, housing the Navy SEALs). On a breezy night, you could hear the clasps on the main flag pole banging as if shaken by a crazed spirit desperate for attention. There are always stray sounds of someone laughing, or people talking, and snatches of music, or even the distant night cargo train blaring as it slowly rumbles through downtown San Diego. For the most part, though, the atmosphere is softly lit and quiet. On some nights, a dense sea fog (marine layer) percolates silently among the streets, buildings, and palm trees of Coronado. On other nights the air is clear, and calm, smelling sweetly of night-blooming jasmine and other scents.

A strange, almost eerie silence descends around the Hotel Del with dusk, amid those jutting turrets and many-angled white walls that overlook pine trees and luscious lawns. In the winter months, it gets dark as early as 4:30 in the afternoon. Fog creeps up from the sea, and dampness brings with it a chill that crawls up your back and touches skeletal fingers along your spine. The valets and doormen stand about talking when things are slow. Some evenings are incredibly busy, and a constant stream of taxis and vans and cars presses through the narrow, circular driveway. Men and women in evening wear move leisurely up the front stairway and through the wide entrance. On other evenings, the entrance has a ghostly calm about it—when the census is down, or during the interstice of the dinner hour, between the rush of arrivals and the rush of departures. A balmy glow of coach lamps bathes the area. Soft light in rich hues emanates from a large stained glass picture window above, which portrays the Amazon queen Califia (or Calafia) amid all the splendors of her realm. Calafia was, in a Spanish novel of 1510, a fictional queen ruling a mythical island named California, to be found on the route westward from Europe, which Christopher Columbus took in search of a sea passage to India. From this, our state derived its romantic name. As you stand facing the hotel about 50 feet from the main entry, you see the curving windows of the Crown Room to your right. This contains a number of large chandeliers with light bulbs (high tech over a century ago) allegedly designed by L. Frank Baum, who often stayed at the Del after he published *The Wizard of Oz* in 1900. The Crown Room, at 23,500 square feet, is one of the largest all-wood halls of its kind in the United States. Its pine-vaulted ceiling is beautiful to behold, and has overarched the dinner table of many a president, king, movie star, and billionaire. The first royalty to dine in this room, in fact—and important to this book—was King David Kalakaua, the last King of Hawai'i, who came as a guest of John Spreckels for Christmas dinner in 1890, and died a few weeks later in San Francisco as a guest of Spreckels' Sugar Baron father, Claus Spreckels. John Spreckels, as we will see, was most likely the object of a blackmail conspiracy that puts the entire mystery of the 'Beautiful Stranger' in perspective. If Lizzie Wyllie is the key to the tragic mystery of the

'Beautiful Stranger,' the hotel's owner, John Spreckels, is the hinge upon which this tale turns.

One night, having gone to our office to warm up, I found a copy of the Heritage Department's beautifully written, illustrated, and designed book.[1] I started reading it in the Transportation Department's small office, upstairs in the same row of brick buildings as the original 1880s power plant. As I sat reading amid the odors of rotting carpets, decaying documents, and stale coffee, I was pretty quickly hooked on this captivating story. As is usually the case with history, it is amazing how much we actually know about the story—and yet, equally frustrating is the loss of information and artifacts that could help us resolve the many loose threads, baffling clues, and chilling dead ends.

The challenge I set myself was to see if I could figure out what really happened, using the copious details in the hotel's book and my own research at the library and online. Although I regaled thousands of visitors to San Diego with tales of the famous ghost—how the maids won't go in her room alone; how they go in to clean and make up beds in teams and get out as soon as possible; how a security officer I know was one of many people who have seen the outline of a Victorian woman on the bed, and if you smooth the blankets, the outline reappears as if by magic; how books fly off the shelves in the downstairs gallery; a whole set of ghostly doings like that—I was less interested in the haunted aspect of the story as I was in the mystery of her life and violent death. All that follows grows out of my analysis of evidence that has been hidden in plain sight for well over a century. I offer many fine little points of reference and detail, most of which are important to the solution of the mystery, while a few will help visitors to the Hotel Del appreciate the history and local color of this national landmark.

☙ ❧

Part I. Mystery Story

The Mystery in a Nutshell

Gunshot, by Gaslight, with Sea Storm and Ghost

On Thanksgiving Day, 1892, a beautiful and elegantly dressed young woman appeared at the Hotel del Coronado—the most luxurious resort in the region, whose doors had opened just a few years earlier in February 1888. Signing in as Mrs. Lottie A. Bernard, the woman attracted attention to herself from the start. She was traveling alone—frowned upon by Victorian society—and without luggage. She kept anxiously inquiring at the desk—not about her 'husband,' the missing Mr. Bernard, but a man she said was her 'brother.' Her brother, Dr. M.C. Anderson, was supposedly due at any time to help her with a vague but serious ailment. She never mentioned the husband. Both men would prove to be as fictional as Lottie A. Bernard herself. Both were part of the haunting mystery of Coronado that would endure for generations, and still today.

Over the next few days, she made odd requests of hotel staff (some of them downright chilling when reviewed in the light of new theories). Her health deteriorated rapidly, so that by Monday, November 28, four days after her arrival, she had difficulty walking. Nevertheless, she made an arduous journey—on foot, by trolley, and by ferry boat—to downtown San Diego, where she bought a gun and some ammunition. She returned to the hotel and was last seen on a balcony with other guests, staring westward at the impending arrival of a great sea storm. The next morning, an electrician found her dead on the back steps, a gunshot wound to her head, and that same gun lying by her side. The Deputy Coroner and his men took the body across the bay to San Diego, where she lay in state for at least two weeks. Thousands of Victorians—mostly women—came to view her embalmed and well-dressed body as if she were a dead princess or, more to the point, a fallen Victorian angel in the best sentimental traditions of the age. The story became an instant national sensation in the scandal-mongering Yellow Press. Daily telegraph dispatches crossed the wires with the latest breathless news, gossip, and innuendoes. What had she been up to? Why had she died? The mystery deepened as people started to realize she wasn't who she said she was. But who was she really?

Even as the police were looking for the illusory Dr. Anderson and a presumed Mr. Bernard, the corpse's identification shifted to that of Elizabeth 'Lizzie' Wyllie, a pregnant and troubled young beauty from Detroit.

That identification was clouded by the allegation that she was really a missing housemaid named Katie Logan from Los Angeles.

Briefly, she was thought to be a renter from Anaheim named Josie Brown. She was also thought to be the wife of a gambler named L. A. Bernard from Iowa.

Except Lizzie Wyllie, all of these women turned out to be fictions, and part of the pattern was that each had a mysterious doctor-brother orbiting unseen somewhere on the periphery, exerting some dark authoritative force that gave Kate Morgan's schemes some ephemeral credibility. Finally, the dead woman was reported to be Kate Morgan of Hamburg, Iowa, a shady lady of many false identities, unknown but dark secrets, and a pungent aura of sexual disgrace that electrified the Victorian imagination. The Kate Morgan legend persists to this day. Nobody has figured out why she came to the hotel, what really went on while she stayed there, or why she shot herself. Some even claim she was murdered.

I suggest in this book that the dead woman was not Kate Morgan but Lizzie Wyllie. If there is a ghost at the Hotel del Coronado, it is that of Lizzie Wyllie, who wants us to know it is she who is buried in a lonely grave up on Market Street, at that time outside town, in Mount Hope Cemetery. I think the mystery of why she appeared under a false name at this great resort was a blackmail plot gone horribly wrong. The owner of the hotel was the only man left standing financially after San Diego's terrible financial collapse of 1889—John Spreckels, heir to a fabulous Hawai'i sugar fortune, and one of the richest men in the United States. Kate Morgan was a ruthless schemer who dreamed up this blackmail scheme. She draped herself in false names with the same ease that Mata Hari tossed scarves about. Kate's target was Spreckels, the place of execution was his grand hotel, and her tool was a pregnant and desperate young Lizzie Wyllie. There were at least two men involved. One was John G. Longfield, Lizzie's lover and former book bindery foreman, a married man with several children, who had been fired from his job along with Lizzie and her sister May when word of their affair became known. The other was a shadowy figure, possibly Kate's husband Tom Morgan, or some lover of hers, who appeared briefly in a bank in Hamburg to help deliver a letter of credit for the alleged wife of 'a friend' in California—a woman named Lottie A. Bernard who was staying at the great hotel halfway across the country in Coronado.

I do not quite have a smoking gun, like a blackmail note. In fact, the woman at the Del was seen urgently burning a stack of papers in her hotel room, the day before she killed herself—and those probably included such documents. What convinces me of my case is how my theory solves every one of the dozens of loose ends that have dangled for over a century. It is an old and brittle case—a true cold case, in police parlance—that begins to make sense when you put all these many little pieces together in a way that every last detail makes sense. There are, in fact, several bits of evidence that are so egregious that it is almost laughable not to think that (a) the dead woman was Lizzie; (b) Kate Morgan was the planner who almost literally got away with murder; (c) Spreckels was the victim of a blackmail plot gone bad; and (d) there was a highly effective cover-up to protect John Spreckels. Those are highlights of the evidence I sort through in this book.

I believe I am the first to analyze the situation in its global context. The key to the analysis is John Spreckels. He owned the Hotel del Coronado. Though still based in San Francisco, he had bought or was buying up much of financially devastated greater San Diego, including Coronado. At the moment that Kate Morgan chose to strike with her ill-considered plan, John Spreckels was in Washington, D.C., lobbying with President Benjamin Harrison and Congress to prevent the overthrow of the Hawai'ian monarchy. The monarchy's fall would mean the loss of the Spreckels family's vast sugar plantations in the Hawai'ian kingdom, which the elder Claus Spreckels managed by controlling the monarchy and its royal cabinet appointments. Claus Spreckels was at that very same time doing desperate shuttle diplomacy between San Francisco and Honolulu. It is impossible to imagine that John Spreckels did not have an army of accountants, bankers, reporters, and other workers in San Diego to mind his affairs. That would include the local police and private security agents, possibly Pinkerton people. Spreckels owned the banks, the newspapers, all of Coronado, much of downtown San Diego, the light rail company, the utilities, the water flume, and anything else that could be bought and sold. Kate Morgan not only had an ill-conceived plan, but picked a bad time to put it into effect. As I will point out, there are moments when we can glimpse the dark hand of what I call the Spreckels Machine at work, shielding John Spreckels and his reputation at a time when his enemies would have been glad to smear him. As it would turn out, the corporate and missionary interests bent on ending Hawai'ian sovereignty—and getting it annexed as a U.S. territory—would win a huge victory less than a month after Lottie A. Bernard's death in Coronado. U.S. military and local militia deposed Queen Lili'uokalani at bayonet point on January 17, 1893, and a transitional government (followed by a short-lived republic ruled by Sanford Dole, cousin of the soon-to-be 'Pineapple King' James Dole) was established in preparation for annexation in 1897. On the hundredth anniversary of the annexation, in 1997, President Clinton and Congress would issue an official joint, bi-partisan apology to the Hawaiian people.

To fully understand what happened in the life and death of the 'Mysterious Stranger' at the Hotel del Coronado, it is necessary to understand both the local facts on the ground—outside the doors of the Hotel Del, and beyond what the official book covers—and the context, both national and global—in which those events took place.

And in the end, again, it comes down to the tragedy of Lizzie Wyllie—a beautiful woman, a fallen angel, a betrayed lover, and perhaps a grieving mother—who took her life when she saw no other recourse.

The Heritage Department's book is filled with more questions and mysteries than answers. My book picks up where the Heritage Department's book stops—at the border of speculation, where a weird scatter of myriad and ill-fitting facts lies like objects abandoned on the beach after a storm. With some daring, I thought my way through—from fact to puzzling fact, from mischievous clue to frustrating dead end, from loose end to logical trap—until I could finally make sense of it all. There was such a profusion of people's names and place names that I ended up drawing charts and maps, on which I connected people and places with variously colored pencil lines. When I published the first edition of my book in mid-2007, I decided to release it as historical fiction. After much deliberation and more insights—like about the sponge and medicine bottle that Lizzie ordered during her stay, of whose chilling implications I have more to say in this book—I am now confidently releasing this as nonfiction, true crime and history. It is the most comprehensive and coherent theory anyone has yet developed to explain a truly complex and tangled web of—yes—sex, violence, deceit, ruthless cunning, greed, and something approaching murder.

Some readers will find the ghost story more intriguing. Others will find that the ghost story pales in the shadow of an 1890s gaslamp true crime mystery that is contemporaneous with the world of Sherlock Holmes and Queen Victoria. Both realms will intrigue you.

There are actually two layers of conspiracy. The inner conspiracy (in which Kate Morgan was the driving force) stretch from Coronado to other cities around the U.S. We can begin organizing the endless profusion of named cities into several clusters of interest: Lake Ontario (Toronto, Cleveland, Detroit, Grand Rapids); Iowa/Nebraska (Hamburg, Iowa); San Francisco (San Francisco, Hanford, Visalia); Los Angeles (Los Angeles, Orange, Anaheim); and of course San Diego (San Diego and Coronado).

Independent but relevant is the global conspiracy in which the Spreckels family played their historic and losing defense. Those tentacles of conspiracy (framing the smaller conspiracy at the Hotel del Coronado) reached around the globe, from Honolulu to London, from San Francisco to Washington, D.C. They involved the last King and Queen of Hawai'i; a beautiful and tragic Crown Princess of Hawai'ian-Scottish origin; and indirectly the Empress of India herself, Queen Victoria, after whom Crown Princess Victoria Ka'iulani was named.

Part II. Ghost Story

Some Like It Spooky

Haunted Hotel

The Hotel del Coronado is a U.S. National Landmark, floating like a vast white fairy castle with brick-red turrets over a remarkable vista under clear blue skies. She sits on a long white beach overlooking the Pacific Ocean's placid expanse—framed to her west by palm-encrusted cliffs, and to the south by Mexican beaches. The view could be straight out of the South Sea Islands described by Robert Louis Stevenson in his pirate adventures (a topic not as far removed from the conversation of this book as you'd think—more on that in the Epilog, where we discuss another beautiful and tragic woman, young Crown Princess Victoria Ka'iulani).

The Hotel del Coronado is a great rambling sugar-white confection, whose design makes up in beauty what she omits in symmetry. She is one of the only surviving Victorian structures of her size and genre in the world. The grounds sprawl over about 31 acres of prime seascape property along the Pacific Ocean in the exclusive City of Coronado (pop. 26,600), which lies across the bay from the City of San Diego (metropolitan pop. 1.3 million). The original hotel contains over 330 rooms. The modern Ocean Towers and Cabanas add yet another 330 or more rooms, for a total of 679.[2] She holds over 1,000 guests when fully occupied, most of the year. At least one of those guests, it has long been rumored, is a ghost.

📚 📖

Arguably, the most enduring guest and legend in the Hotel Del's history is its famous ghost.[3] There are at least two ghost stories associated with the Hotel Del, actually. The dead woman stayed in Room 302 (now 3327) overlooking Orange Avenue. As you approach the hotel, heading east on Orange Avenue coming from the

Bay side, look toward the hotel approaching on your right at the intersection of Orange Avenue and R. H. Dana Place (which turns into Adella Avenue on the left side of Orange Avenue). Look straight from the street corner over the fence, at the square white tower with the miter-shaped dark red roof. From there, look down to the right at the curving corner of the building, which at that point is convex pointing toward you. You see two low roofs, atop thin white pillars, and the second floor windows behind those. On the next floor up, the third floor of four stories, is the triple set of windows through which Lottie A. Bernard gazed over Victorian Coronado.

The list of reported ghostly incidents surrounding that room, and other areas of the hotel, is legion. Some are documented at length in the Heritage Department's book. I will relate a few in this book. If the ghost is real, what would be the purpose of her haunting and her capricious activities? I believe it would be to try and communicate the truth about who she really was (Lizzie Wyllie, not Kate Morgan) and what really happened. One hears that ghosts live in the moment. Usually it is the moment of their sudden and often violent death. Perhaps, in that moment, she is still trying to reach out to her grieving mother, Elizabeth, and her sister, May, in Detroit. Everyone else in her life had betrayed her, especially her lover, John G. Longfield—and Kate Morgan, whom she had trusted, but who probably stole Longfield from her, and used her and the baby growing within her to commit a crime against John Spreckels. Lizzie was, to put it bluntly, a beautiful airhead without much common sense, but she never harmed anyone, and she clearly showed regret and remorse at involving herself in Kate Morgan's conspiracies. She was the only person in the saga with any genuine, admirable emotions. That makes her victimhood and cruel, lonely death all the more tragic. She really was that Victorian ideal of the Pre-Raphaelites and of Dickens' readership—the good angel, brought low by the machinations of evil people in a cruel and senseless world.

                        ❧ ☙

Ghosts and ghost stories have been with us since the beginning of the human race. Many primitive peoples burned or crushed their dead out of fear that otherwise they might walk again at night. Ghost stories have been told around campfires since Paleolithic times, as some of the ancient cave paintings around the world suggest. Most cultures believe in the survival of the soul beyond death, and that not all souls wander off into some reward, but a few wayward ones get stuck for one reason or another and stay behind to frighten the living. Ancient Roman and Greek culture was rife with ghost stories. Among the Romans, it was more common for the ghost to be described as wearing a black toga while scaring the daylights out of people. In fact, the Romans were animists who believed in a profusion of spirits living in a parallel shamanistic world. They believed in countless *numina* (from *numen*, a nod or gesture) who inhabited every nook and cranny of the world. In the household, it was the ancestor spirits, or *lares*, and they had their altar in the entrance of the house. The father and sons of the household were the priests of the *lares*, and tended their shrine or *lararium*, which occupied a closet-like structure along with the death masks of the ancestors—and these ancestors haunted every house. The mother and daughters were priestesses of the kitchen part of the house, which was haunted by the *penates*, literally 'cupboard gods.' The custom was to throw a crust into the fire at each meal, and a few drops of wine on the floor, to appease them. These ancient customs are just a few that have survived into modern Italy in the form of *stregheria*, or witchcraft. Since Rome occupied most of Europe for centuries, something of the Roman culture survives in both northern and southern Europe as well as North Africa, the Middle East, and Britain. Every culture has its wealth of scary stories, and ours is no exception. One only needs to look at the popularity of books and films like William Blatty's 1973 story *The Exorcist* to realize the power of these ideas in modern society. What's remarkable about that movie is not only that people were badly affected while viewing it—a whole urban lore also sprang up about deaths among those who worked on the film, fire on the set, and so forth. Some of this lore parallels the 'Curse of the Pharaohs' legends that followed discovery of the XIII Dynasty Egyptian Pharaoh Tut-Ankh-Amun's tomb in 1922 by Howard Carter.

In contrast with all the black tales and nightmares since ancient and medieval times, including *succubi* that torment people in their sleep, and vampires who drink our blood, the ghost at the Hotel del

Coronado is a very light touch. That doesn't mean she won't scare you out of your wits.

A friend of mine moved into management at the hotel, and a few weeks later I asked him if he was aware of any ghostly doings. He told me, with a bemused expression, that he had only a few days earlier received notice of a 'dead move' during the night. The expression 'dead move,' from which this book gets its name, is a hotel industry term for moving someone's belongings from one room to another. The case my friend referred to is one that often happens at the Del—in Room 3327 in particular (though 3519 is said to be heavily haunted also). There is little lore attached to Room 3519, except that a maid is said to have hung herself long ago in there. This maid is sometimes associated with the housekeeper mentioned in connection with Lottie A. Bernard, although the maid's name is not known and the story may be entirely urban lore. The hotel's official policy is not to rent out Room 3327 unless it is the only room available or a guest specifically requests it. The story my friend related is fairly common. Often, a guest will light-heartedly and skeptically ask for Room 3327, and then become so frightened during the night that they call the front desk downstairs in a panic and demand to be moved immediately—a dead move, in the dead of night.

Part III. What We Know For Sure

Lottie A. Bernard Timeline

Day 0—Wednesday, Nov. 23, 1892 (Katie Logan in L.A.)

We'll call this Day Zero because it is the last day of one daring fraud, and the transition into another daring fraud that starts the next day.

Day Zero—the day before Thanksgiving, 1892—was last day of an imaginary person named Mrs. Katie Logan. Katie Logan worked for several weeks in Los Angeles, as a domestic servant for at least three wealthy families, the last of whom was the family of contractor L. A. Grant. This Katie Logan would, the following afternoon (Day 1), wink out of existence. She would transition into yet another fraudulent persona—Mrs. Lottie Anderson Bernard, baptized with the ink flowing from a desk clerk's dipping pen in the softly lit Hotel del Coronado lobby. Lottie A. Bernard was fated for a brief, five-day life whose termination resulted in the death of a real and unknown person.

The twenty-four hour period from sometime in the middle of Day Zero, when Katie Logan said goodbye to the L. A. Grant family in Los Angeles, to the signing-in of Lottie A. Bernard at the Hotel del Coronado during the next afternoon, is also known as 'The Missing Day.' The Missing Day addresses the question of why the two-hour train trip from Los Angeles took her a whole day. Does it matter? What if she just went shopping, or goofed off? But she didn't. As we will see, she was heading south on a train from Los Angeles to San Diego, at the same time that a witness placed her on a train from Denver headed to Orange (halfway between Los Angeles and San Diego). On that train, she had a heart-wrenching argument with a cruel-seeming man—possibly her lover.

> **HOTEL DEL CORONADO,**
> E. S. BABCOCK, Manager.   Coronado, California.
>
> Money, Jewels, and other valuable Packages, must be placed in the Safe in the office, otherwise the Proprietor will not be responsible for any loss.
>
> | NAMES. | RESIDENCE. | ROOMS. | |
> |---|---|---|---|
> | *Thursday Nov. 24th 1892* | | | |
> | Mark J. Williams | NY City | 30x | |
> | Henry Pereire | Pawtucket R.I. | 15x | |
> | Mr R M Gage | Pawtucket R.I. | 153 | |
> | Mrs M E French | Pawtucket R.I. | 153 | |
> | Geo Nester | Detroit M | 113 | |
> | Mrs R. Irwin | Denver Colo | 315 | |
> | Grace Irwin | Denver Colo | 315 | |
> | Miss Lottie A Bernard | Detroit | 30x | |
> | J A Jones | Boston | 371 | |
> | I A Clark + wife | Coronado | | |
> | Fran E Clark | | | |
> | H C Moon | New Mex | 196 | |

So the Missing Day will be very interesting for us to figure out. It is one of several mysteries within a mystery that has long festered in the soul of the Lottie Bernard saga. When I present my theory in the next section, I will propose an answer for this, and all other questions in this complex saga. Even the names Lottie and Charlotte have special significance.

Bear in mind, none of what happened on Day Zero became known until well after Lottie Bernard's death. On the day of the Coroner's Inquest, November 30, 1892, six days after she signed in at the Hotel Del, it was assumed she really was Mrs. Lottie Anderson Bernard. As far as the nine men on the Coroner's jury were concerned, she appeared out of nowhere on November 24, our Day One.

From Day Zero, we now follow the known facts in chronological sequence. Katie Logan was well-liked by the L. A. Grants, and they fully expected her to return the next day to help with Thanksgiving dinner. She would never be seen again. Stored at the L. A. Grants' home was a trunk that would be opened many days later by Los Angeles police—revealing startling clues that nobody has really examined in context until now. The solution to the Lottie Bernard mystery (or Kate Morgan mystery) begins taking shape at the L. A. Grants' house—in that trunk, which we'll examine in greater detail soon.

Day 1—Thursday, Nov. 24, 1892 (Lottie Bernard Checks In)

An attractive young woman stepped from the train sometime in the late morning hours of Thanksgiving Day. She was traveling alone—a fact frowned upon in Victorian times—with only a hand satchel and the clothes on her back.

The original San Diego train station was built 1887 during the same economic boom that saw the Hotel del Coronado constructed. The station was an ornate, one-story wooden Victorian structure[4] with a short but imposing clock tower. It was demolished in 1915, and replaced by today's Union Station or Santa Fe Depot.

She went to the baggage office near the old train station and spoke with a clerk at a window. She told him she needed to check out her three trunks. The clerk asked her for the baggage claim checks ('checks') or tickets. She told him her 'brother'[5] had them, and she had gotten separated from him. This is the 'brother' of whom we shall hear time and again. The clerk refused to turn over the luggage, and the woman left with only her hand satchel.

She did not immediately head to the ferry landing to cross over to Coronado. Instead, witnesses would later state that she walked some ten blocks east on C Street to the Hotel Brewster.[6] The Hotel Brewster was a large new hotel on the corner of 4th and C Streets. Created during the 1880s boom years, it was designed to be efficient, clean, and safe for traveling businessmen. The purpose of the woman's detour has remained unknown until now, but I will offer an explanation. Witnesses claimed she asked about her brother (the sometime 'doctor') and his wife. Hotel staff told her they were not known at the Brewster.

From the Hotel Brewster, she walked or rode to the Coronado ferry landing on the San Diego side. Today's ferry landing is at the foot of West Broadway (then D Street) in San Diego. At that time, the ferry landing was near the foot of H Street (today's Market Street, on the waterfront near what is today the area around Tuna Lane by the Aircraft Carrier Midway Museum).

That's approximately one mile as the crow flies, or a walk equivalent to about fifteen city blocks. She might have walked through the Stingaree, one of the most notorious red light districts on the West Coast. More likely, she traveled back down C Street to the rail depot, and then turned left to walk south along the harbor shore some five or six blocks to the ferry landing. She was known to be in robust health at this time, and the walk would hardly have strained her.

It is possible, but not very likely, that she could have traveled to Coronado on the Belt Line,[7] which circled the Bay from San Diego to Coronado, via National City and what are today Chula Vista and Imperial Beach. The ferry ride was the shortest way to cross the Bay, and one is inclined to think she used this route. She boarded one of the large metal ferries then operating, collectively known as the 'Nickel Snatcher' because the fare was five cents. These vessels were large enough to carry horses and buggies—unlike today's ferry, which is moderate in size, and can accommodate bicycles. She may well have ridden on the side-wheeler *Coronado*, 208 tons and built of steel, commissioned 1886. Another ferry boat in service was the large steamer *Ramona*.[8]

The crossing was about a quarter mile. She disembarked some fifteen minutes later at the Coronado ferry terminal, a few hundred feet north (at today's Centennial Park) of today's Ferry Landing Marketplace in the City of Coronado. Bits of the old concrete wharf are still visible along the Centennial Park shoreline.

Coronado (incorporated as a city in 1891) sits on a portion of the Peninsula of San Diego.[9] As with much of the background detail given here, it is helpful information in understanding the Lottie Bernard saga.

From the ferry landing, she walked three or four minutes to First and Orange, where she boarded the little Coronado trolley for the 1.3 mile ride to the Hotel del Coronado.

&&

So it came to be that the 'Beautiful Stranger' checked into the lobby of the Hotel del Coronado, using the name Lottie A. Bernard. It was early to mid-afternoon on Thanksgiving Day, Thursday, November 24, 1892.[10] She immediately attracted attention, not only because of her charm and beauty, but because she was traveling alone and without any luggage except her small handbag. Clerks thought her 'peculiar.'[11] Victorians felt it reflected badly on a woman's moral character to travel alone, without her husband, a male family member, or an older female chaperone.

She stepped up to the dark wood counter (at a special side window reserved for women) and asked the clerk to sign her in. Most people signed the guest register themselves, but it was not unheard-of for a clerk to provide that courtesy. She gave her name as Mrs. Lottie A. Bernard of Detroit, Michigan.

A few things are notable about the guest register, whose page has come down to us as a historical artifact.[12] It appears that twelve persons signed in that day (there is a termination line at the bottom of the page, and there are various check marks that suggest the page was proofed by the chief clerk or an auditor, as a matter of daily routine). A nicely rounded dot above the scrawled word 'Mrs.' on her line suggests that she may have first said "Miss" and then changed it to 'Mrs.' In fact, a close examination suggests the confused clerk perhaps wrote 'Mis.' In the upper left hand corner, the name 'E. S. Babcock, Manager' is given. That was Elisha Babcock, who conceived and executed a breathtaking plan to develop a magnificent resort across the bay from San Diego, on a section of the barren Peninsula of San Diego known as South Island (also known as Coronado Island, no relationship to the Coronado Islands some miles off shore that are owned by the municipality of

Tijuana, Mexico). Together with his friend, Chicago piano fortune heir Hampton Story, and Jacob Gruendike, president of the First National Bank of San Diego, Babcock founded the Coronado Beach Company and developed what would soon become the City of Coronado. With the proceeds from the land sales, Babcock built the sprawling sugar-baker palace of white walls and brick-red turrets called the Hotel del Coronado in 1887. It opened February 1888 to receive its first guest. In the meantime, San Francisco sugar fortune heir John Spreckels (1853-1926), who had discovered the beauty and mild climate of San Diego during an 1887 yacht visit, bought out Story and Gruendike's interests in the Coronado Beach Company, and thus became co-owner of the Del with Elisha Babcock. In 1889, the worst economic collapse in San Diego history caused the population to plummet from (an estimated) 44,000 to about 16,000 people—roughly the population before the boom. During the economic downturn, Babcock had to borrow money to keep the operation afloat, and he turned to John Spreckels.

John Spreckels was one of the sons of a remarkable, self-made man named Claus Spreckels (1828-1908), a German immigrant who arrived penniless in the U.S. in the 1840s and built several fortunes involving groceries. Claus Spreckels had several sons, of whom oldest son John appears to have been his right-hand man. Claus Spreckels became known as the Sugar Baron, because he owned huge cane sugar plantations in Hawai'i, and, along with a small group of cronies, virtually controlled the islands' economy and much of the Pacific sugar trade. He also shaped the Hawai'ian political landscape by controlling appointments to the king's cabinet. This was bitterly resented by a group of primarily conservative U.S. Protestant missionaries who had tried to ban Hawai'ian traditions they found offensive, like hula dancing, singing, and scant clothing. The missionary faction was allied with a coterie of armed Whites known as the Honolulu Rifles, and with U.S. corporations led by a cousin (James Ballard Dole) of the soon to be 'Pineapple King,' Sanford Dole. Together, they formed a secret society called the Hawai'ian League, which strongly militated toward Hawai'i's annexation by the United States. This faction held a near-coup in 1887, imposing the so-called Bayonet Constitution. They removed most of the king's powers, and took voting and property rights from nearly all Asians in favor of wealthy U.S. and European whites.

After the overthrow of the monarchy (January 17, 1893, just seven weeks after Lottie A. Bernard's death), James Dole was on his way to become president of a republic.

By the time Lottie Bernard checked in at the Hotel del Coronado, the balance of powers in Hawai'i had become very shaky. At that very moment, John Spreckels, owner of the Hotel del Coronado, was in Washington lobbying President Benjamin Harrison and the Congress to prevent a takeover of Hawai'i. At the same time, the elder Claus Spreckels was en route to Honolulu for desperate, last-minute shuttle diplomacy to try and save the dynasty of Queen Lili'uokalani. By this time, John Spreckels' financial holdings in San Diego were already vast. He owned most of Coronado, much of downtown San Diego, the local newspaper, the utilities, the light rails, the telegraph, and just about anything else. When Elisha Babcock was deep in debt, John Spreckels called his loans. Babcock was unable to produce payment, so Spreckels offered him a deal in lieu of foreclosure. Spreckels became the sole owner of the Hotel. He forgave Babcock's debts, paid him a large sum of money, and kept him on as General Manager. Hence, the heading at top left in the guest register, which identified Babcock as General Manager.

I believe here lies the key to the entire mystery: John Spreckels was the target of Kate Morgan's blackmail plot, using a gullible, naïve, and very attractive young girl from Detroit—Lizzie Wyllie, pregnant, in love, in trouble, and increasingly desperate as she began to realize she was being betrayed by the very two persons she needed and trusted most: Kate Morgan, and Lizzie's lover John G. Longfield.

Lottie appears to have paid on a day by day basis, the only one checking in that day who did. This is judging by the notation in the rightmost column of the guest register,[13] where a "D" is written on her line. The other guests are either indicated by an "S" (presumably short term, or weekly) or an "L" (long term, or monthly). Lottie took Room 302, on the third floor, a reasonably spacious room (about 12 by 15 feet) with three windows in an angled or curved configuration, overlooking the intersection of Orange Avenue (Coronado's main street) and Richard Henry Dana Place. From that intersection, a half a block south along Dana Place takes you to the beach and Ocean Boulevard.

If one stands in that room today (now Room 3327), one looks kitty-corner across a parking lot toward the intersection, with Orange Avenue on the right, and R. H. Dana Place coming into view on the left as an extension of Ocean Boulevard (not visible). In other words, the room faces away from the sea. As one drives along the Pacific shore on Ocean Boulevard, the boulevard turns into R. H. Dana Place along the western side of the hotel, crosses Orange Avenue, and turns into tiny Adella Avenue. This is today probably Coronado's busiest pedestrian intersection, with heavy foot traffic coming from the beach and the Hotel del Coronado, and many little shops along either side of Orange Avenue.

During Lottie Bernard's day, the Coronado Beach Rail Road trolley line ran between the Hotel Del and the Ferry Landing, and Lottie took that trolley several times, including on her final, deadly errand to buy the gun that killed her. The trolley was at that time a two-car affair, the one being a little steam engine (or 'steam dummy') disguised as a trolley car to avoid scaring horses, and the driver sat in there; the other car was a light rail platform with four completely open bays, each containing two wooden seats capable of holding about three persons, so that the trailer could probably hold two dozen people when full. Orange Avenue is so called because, when the trolley was eliminated, a long stand of orange trees was planted where the tracks had been. The oranges, however, were a favorite food of the jack rabbits that still infested the peninsula, so the orange trees were removed in favor of a manicured grassy strip running the entire 1.3 mile distance of Orange Avenue from the Hotel Del on the Pacific coast side (south, because the beach there runs east-west). Orange Avenue briefly runs west, then curves northeastward through Spreckels Park in the center of Coronado, to Centennial Park and the Ferry Landing and Market Place overlooking the beautiful San Diego skyline on the Bay side in a northeasterly direction.

Looking out from Lottie's room toward the intersection of Dana/Orange/Adella, one sees a low, Spanish-style building (now the Hotel El Cordoba and various shops and restaurants, built in 1902 as a mansion for Elisha Babcock). Moving one's eyes toward the right along Orange Avenue, one sees several hotels, including the upscale Glorietta Bay Inn, named after the street and the bay east of there. This white mansion was constructed after the 1906 San

Francisco earthquake disaster, when John Spreckels permanently moved his family to San Diego and ensconced them in this palatial estate overlooking Glorietta Bay (now housing the Coronado Yacht Club) on the east, and Spreckels' grand hotel across the street looking south.

When Lottie took up residence in Room 302, third floor rooms were traditionally cheapest. The best rooms were on the ground floor, in this age before widespread elevators, because wealthy guests did not expect to walk up and down flights of stairs. The Hotel actually has one of the oldest functioning elevators anywhere—Otis Number 61, dating from at or around the Hotel's opening in 1888. Each room had its own little fireplace, with a vent to the roof. During renovations over the years, the fireplaces were removed and replaced with central heating. When the Cabanas and Ocean Towers were constructed in the late 20th Century, men digging along the beach property east of the original hotel uncovered a mass of brick wreckage where the old fireplaces had been buried. Today's Room 3327 has a full bath where the fireplace was at one time. In her day, Lottie used a communal bathroom (and tub for bathing) down the hall.

Lottie befriended a bellman (or 'bellboy') named Harry West on her first evening.[14] She told Harry she suffered from neuralgia—not today's more specific neurological disorder by the same name, but a vague nervous ailment commonly diagnosed in that era, covering all sorts of psychological and neurological disorders (and no small amount of hypochondria). She also told Harry that she was waiting for her 'brother,' who by now had acquired a name—Dr. M. C. Anderson of Indianapolis. This is now the second 'man' in her life. She would want us to assume the first 'man' was a putative 'husband' (since she signed in as Mrs. Lottie A. Bernard)—the presumed Mr. Bernard, for whom police across the country searched vainly after her death. Like Lottie herself, both of the men were fictions.

She was vigorous and healthy when she checked in. A young fellow employed by Star Stables, Charlie Stevens, took her on a long ride around town,[15] and he later told people that she seemed in good health, though he implied she seemed a bit preoccupied or sad.

Day 2—Friday, Nov. 25, 1892

Early in the day, she spoke with Chief Clerk A. S. Gomer. She explained that her luggage was locked up in the baggage depot near the train station in downtown San Diego. This was the same story she told others at the hotel, and which was repeated in the Coroner's Inquest—and mutated after her death into quite a different story by the apocryphal testimony of a train traveler from Denver, Joseph A. or Joseph E. Jones of Boston. Jones' comments to a bellman throw light on the notorious 'Missing Day' of this saga, as we shall see. Lottie A. Bernard told Gomer that she had been traveling with her brother, but that they became separated on the trains at Orange, California (about an hour north, near today's Disneyland at Anaheim, and roughly halfway between San Diego and Los Angeles). She said that her brother had the tickets in his pocket, that she didn't know where her brother was, and that the baggage clerks would not release her trunks without the tickets. According to Gomer (at the Coroner's Inquest) she asked daily, with growing anxiety, if word had come from her 'brother' (neither Kate Morgan nor Lizzie Wyllie is known to have had a brother, but Kate Morgan often used the 'brother' and 'doctor' ruse during what can only have been scams).

Day 3—Saturday, Nov. 26, 1892

On the third day at the Hotel del Coronado, real estate agent T. J. Fisher testifies she came into the hotel drugstore, where he shared an office with the druggist. Fisher says she wandered about 'slowly' and apparently 'in pain.' She asked for medicine to ease her pain (described as 'intense suffering'). Fosdick suggested she consult a doctor, and she brushed this aside, telling him that her brother, a physician, would be arriving any day to care for her—the elusive 'Dr. Anderson,' who would never show up nor send word.

Later in the day, Harry West rather vaguely remembered that she asked him to get her an empty pint bottle and a sponge from the hotel drugstore. No reason is known why she wanted these items, but, like so many tiny details, they are significant, and downright chilling, in my theory—as I will explain in the next section, *Part IV: Solved!*.

Day 4—Sunday, Nov. 27, 1892

No activity known.

Day 5—Monday, Nov. 28, 1892

During the morning on the fifth day, Lottie had Harry West bring her a glass of wine from the bar, and later a whiskey cocktail. Harry prepared a bath for her (down the hall from her room), and brought her a pitcher of ice water she requested. She told him she would be in the bath for an hour or two.

Around noon, Lottie returned to her room and rang for Harry West. He would later testify that he found her suffering and groaning a great deal, and sleeping much of the day. She told him she had fallen in the tub and gotten her hair wet, and she asked him to dry it for her. It appears that she fell because she was weak, that she felt her wet hair would worsen her illness, and that she was too weak to dry it. Harry toweled her hair dry. He would later tell investigators that she seemed to sleep a while, wake up, spend time groaning in pain, and then fall back to sleep. He said she again mentioned that Dr. Anderson, who would soon join her.

Between noon and 1:00 p.m., Harry told Gomer, his superior, that he had brought Lottie a whiskey. Gomer testified that he had suggested, through a female housekeeper, that Lottie have a doctor see her.

Gomer went to the room to inquire about her health, and also about her finances. Apparently she was paying her room charge daily, but she was running up an expense tab on the side, which a guest would customarily pay when checking out. Gomer was keeping a worried eye on this tab.

It was a cold, dreary, gloomy day—a huge sea storm was approaching, which would lash the region fiercely all night, and then subside by morning. Barometric pressure was falling, and there was a growing air of dreadful anticipation as the violent storm approached. This storm would set the mood for events that followed. Gomer found her as Harry had described her—sick, in bed, suffering. Gomer suggested she light a fire in her fireplace, but she refused. She then told him a story that she was near death from stomach cancer (which Dr. Mertzman would later deride as virtually impossible). Whereas before she had said Dr. Anderson would take care of her when he arrived, now she said the doctors had given up on her and death was just around the corner. It sounds as though she was simply trying to get rid of Gomer, who appears to have been a somewhat fussy and inquisitive man, concerned about guests and goings-on at the hotel where he held some responsibility.

Gomer—no doubt because of her 'peculiarity' and alarming condition—was concerned whether she would be able to pay her tab. Lottie urged Gomer to telegraph a Mr. G. L. Allen in Hamburg, Iowa, who would wire the needed funds.

During the afternoon, Lottie rang for some matches. Harry West offered to bring a whole box, but she said she only needed a few matches (he had some in his pocket, which he gave her) to burn a stack of papers (possibly including letters) in the fireplace. Neither Gomer nor Harry got a good look at what these papers might be. From notes she wrote, which the coroner found in her room, it seems she had much on her mind.

That afternoon, Lottie went downstairs to the pharmacy. Real estate agent T. J. Fisher described her as walking very slowly, and appearing to be in great pain. During their conversation, she indicated she planned to go across the Bay to San Diego, and he warned her against doing so—because of her condition and the coming storm. Lottie replied that she had to go, and then made a statement that appears somewhat unfocused and out of kilter with already established facts (or fibs).[16] From what Fisher quoted at the Coroner's Inquest, she said that she must make the trip. She said that she forgot her baggage 'checks' [claim tickets], and that she must go across the Bay "to identify my trunks, personally."

Between 4:00 and 5:00 p.m. (there is confusion about whether she was in San Diego as early as 3:00 p.m., or later) Lottie journeyed to downtown San Diego. She rode the little Coronado Beach R.R. trolley mentioned earlier, with its steam dummy and trailer, to the ferry landing. Witnesses said she appeared so weak that, as she left the Hotel del Coronado, she had to be helped onto the little streetcar by the conductor.

She took the ferry across the bay, a 15 minute ride to cross a quarter mile of water. She stepped ashore near G Street in the City of San Diego, and walked several blocks to Fifth Avenue (in the heart of today's Gaslamp Quarter). She probably skirted the violent, noisy

Stingaree district at the southern end of Fifth Street (today's Fifth Avenue near the baseball stadium).

She walked into a store called the Ship Chandlery at 624 Fifth Street,[17] and asked clerk Frank Heath if he sold revolver cartridges. He testified she seemed 'nervous or excited.' She spoke in a very low (or soft) voice and appeared to be sick. She walked slowly and looked 'very bad.' Heath, who noted she was very well dressed, told her he did not sell cartridges, and directed her to Chick's Gun Shop at 1663 Sixth Street.

M. Chick testified that Lottie walked into the store and asked if he had a gun she could buy for a friend as a Christmas present. He sold her a revolver and cartridges, and showed her how to load and fire the weapon. A witness, W. P. Walters, observed this, and remarked to another bystander that that woman was going to "hurt herself with that pistol."

Lottie left Chick's Gun Shop and walked south on Fifth Street toward the store of Schiller & Murtha's at Fifth Street and D Avenue.[18] Her movements from there are unknowns, but the general direction seems to have been toward the ferry landing.

At 6:30 p.m., says bellman Harry West at the inquest, he saw Lottie on a hotel veranda overlooking the ocean. It was dark by then, and an air of dread and excitement hung in the air as the atmospheric monster approached. It was the last time Harry would see Lottie alive.

Lottie made one more stop at the front desk to ask Gomer if there was any word from Dr. Anderson. That was between 7:00 and 8:00 p.m., and Gomer said there was not yet any word from her 'brother.' This was the last time anyone saw her alive.

People stood on balconies all around the Hotel, looking south and west over the Pacific Ocean. They watched in awe as the black clouds of the storm rolled closer, and raged and thundered. It is likely that some guests may have requested relocation to the landward side of the Hotel, because nobody heard a gunshot fired during the night, on the beach just behind the hotel.

Day 6—Tuesday, Nov. 29, 1892 (Body Found)

Electrician David Cone discovered her body at 8:20 a.m. Cone was walking his daily rounds, 'trimming the lights,' which probably meant manually turning off some (especially outdoor) lights.

      ぞ ぐ

As is typical of the San Diego region, the storm vented its fury during the night, and quickly passed, leaving a mild and foggy silence. By daylight, the storm was long gone. The electrician David Cone came across the grotesque scene of a mannequin-like body lying on the concrete steps overlooking the beach, which was not far from the sea in those days. When he realized it was a woman's dead body, he saw that her clothing was all wet, and the body "seemed to have been lying there quite a while, to have been dead quite a while."[19]

The body lay in something like a sitting position on the concrete steps, with its feet toward the ocean. There was a gun by its side, and blood on the steps. A 'large pistol' lay to her right. Her clothes were soaked. Cone was utterly shaken, and hurried to report the find to his superiors. Along the way, he encountered a gardener named F. W. Koeppen, with whom he returned to the crime scene. The two men separated and ran in opposite directions around the Hotel. Koeppen ran to inform the assistant manager, Mr. Rossier, while Cone ran to tell the chief clerk. Cone eventually went back to his duties of 'trimming' the lights. Koeppen brought Rossier to the steps, where the two men covered the body with a tarp. Koeppen stayed with the corpse until the coroner's men arrived.

That morning, when chief clerk A.S. Gomer opened his office, he received a telegram from a Hamburg, Iowa bank, in which $25 credit was extended to one Lottie A. Bernard. This was the credit she had promised, though it is not clear whether it satisfied her debt. US$25 in 1892 would be worth over $500 in early 21st Century U.S. dollars.[20] Compared to a laborer's estimated $1 a day at the time (hence 'another day, another dollar'), that should cover any services billed to her room, since there is no indication she did anything extravagant—she did tip Harry West a dollar for a trivial service at one point. Gomer wired back that the woman had died, and instructed the bank to contact the San Diego Coroner's office.

Between 9:30 and 10:00 a.m., Deputy Coroner H. J. Stetson arrived from the mainland with a crew to remove the body. Stetson estimated Lottie had been dead about six or seven hours, meaning she shot herself (or was murdered, by some urban lore) between 2:00 and 3:00 a.m. That would mean the body lay on the steps for up to seven hours as the storm abated. From the time of discovery to the time Stetson and his crew arrived, two hours passed—a remarkable short time. There was rudimentary telephone service to the mainland from the hotel itself, and there was always the telegraph. Stetson would then gather his men, walk or ride several blocks from the police headquarters on Fifth Street to the waterfront, and then ride the ferry ('the next boat'[21]) across to Coronado. The crossing took 15 minutes on the steam-powered ferry. Stetson and his men would then cross the island—1.3 miles to the Hotel del Coronado from the ferry landing—which can be walked in a leisurely twenty to thirty minutes. Stetson's crew took the body to Johnson & Company Mortuary, 907 Sixth Street. The same day, Stetson searched Lottie's room. He found several items of puzzling and tantalizing interest, which he was to describe at the Coroner's Inquest.

Day 7—Wednesday, Nov. 30, 1892 (Coroner's Inquest)

Newspaper Accounts

The Daily Bee (San Diego) reports[22] dramatically that Mrs. Lottie A. Bernard died at the Hotel del Coronado "...last night alone and desperate...on the stone stairs at the west end of the ocean terrace leading to the beach...the surf wrapped and then re-wrapped her with its spray, and the pitiless rain fell upon her bared head and young white face."

☙ ❧

The San Diego Union, Wednesday, November 30, the day of the coroner's inquest, gushingly and excitedly reports the finding of a body at the Hotel del Coronado the previous day at 8:20 a.m. by the electrician David Cone.

Hotel staff, who saw her when she was alive, described the woman as "attractive, prepossessing, and highly educated..."[23]

She wore black the night she died, with a lace shawl over her head when Harry West last saw her on a seaward veranda late Monday (between 9:00 and 10:00 p.m. Monday, Nov. 28).

The article describes a lashing "tempest that is sweeping over the whole coast" and says she ventured "within fifteen feet of the ocean's edge."[24]

Her body was cold and stiff. According to the article in the paper, the storm obliterated any blood stains.[25]

She checked in Thursday, Nov. 24, carrying only a small handbag.[26]

She was "frequently attended by a housekeeper," but this person was not called to testify at the inquest.

By November 28, she was so weak that she fell in the bath and had to have bellman Harry West dry her hair in her room. She is described as "nervous and unstrung." There are references to her being 'lonely' because she continually asked about her 'brother,' who never did show up (no doubt another alias for John Longfield.)

The article mentions that she had over $20 cash in her purse, or well over $240 in today's dollars (assuming a differential of 12 to 1 between 1892 vs. 2008 U.S. Dollars).

According to the article, telegrams about Lottie's death were sent to a bank officer in Hamburg, Iowa (who had extended $25 credit on Lottie's behalf to the Hotel del Coronado, as reported by chief clerk Gomer) and possible Bernard family members in Detroit (the city listed as Lottie's home at registration). In other words, it is clear at this point that the deceased is believed to truly be one Lottie A. Bernard.

ಲ ೂ

The Coroner's Inquest

Shortly before the Coroner's Inquest was gaveled into session, the leading physician and surgeon in town, Dr. B. F. Mertzman, did a half-hour examination of the body. He was not permitted to autopsy her. He would testify at the inquest.

On November 30, the day after her death, per order of Deputy San Diego Coroner H. J. Stetson, a nine man jury gathers for a formal inquest. Justice of the Peace and Acting Coroner W. A. Sloane, Esq., gavels the session to order and calls witnesses to the stand.

David Cone, the electrician who first spotted the body, testifies that, around seven the previous morning, he was trimming the lights around the hotel after the great storm, when he came upon the dead woman's body. He testifies that she lay face up, near the top of the stairs and facing the ocean. He saw blood on the steps to the right of the body, and the body appeared to have lain there for some time. A 'large pistol' lay on the right beside the body.

Next, Sloane interrogates gardener F. W. Koeppen, who fetched the assistant manager, Rossier. They covered the body with a tarpaulin. The pistol lay untouched under the tarpaulin.

Next, Frank Heath of the Ship's Chandlery, 624 Fifth Street, testifies. He saw the dead woman in the store, and she asked for cartridges. She spoke in a low voice, nervously, and he had trouble understanding her. She was well dressed, and walked slowly and looked bad, as if she were sick.

Next, Dr. B. F. Mertzman, physician and surgeon, testifies. He was called in this morning, a half hour before the inquest (more than a day after David Cone's discovery of he body), to examine the corpse at Johnson & Company. He was not permitted to autopsy her. He has found an entry wound in the right temple, and no exit wound. The bullet traveled a little bit forward and a little bit upward. Mertzman estimates the caliber to be 'about .38 or .40.' There was no exit wound. The bullet stayed in the brain, despite the considerable caliber of the cartridge.

Next, real estate agent J. Fisher testifies. His existence at the Hotel Del is a direct, but anachronistic, result of the real estate boom of the late 1880s buoyed by Elisha Babcock's auctioneering of lots in Coronado before building the Del. Fisher testifies that he first saw the woman the previous Saturday, when she appeared to be suffering as she paced up and down in the arcade. Fisher says he sent her to Fosdick, the pharmacist. She ventured in again on Monday, and Fosdick advised her not to travel on account of her neuralgia and the coming storm, but she said she must look after her missing luggage.

Next, Harry West is asked to testify. He lives with his parents at 2519 I Street between 16th and 17th Streets. He says he saw her often. The last time he saw her was at half past six on Monday evening. She appeared to be in great pain, slept a great deal, and would wake up groaning.

Next, A. S. Gomer testifies. He says he can only identify her by the name she gave—Mrs. Lottie A. Bernard (or Barnard), Detroit. He says she arrived by way of Orange, and apparently lost her brother along the way—Dr. M. C. Anderson. Gomer noticed letters or documents in her room, that she intended to burn in the fireplace [but in no hurry, since she didn't want them to light a fire]. Says he saw two or three letters addressed by her, to herself, at a Detroit address. Says that a telegram arrived from Hamburg, IA, covering $25 funds.

Next, M. Chick, the gun shop owner, testifies. The woman wanted a gun for a Christmas present. She purchased a .44 American Bulldog. He looks at the pistol as the coroner holds it, and states that he cannot positively testify if that is the gun he sold the dead woman, but he seems to recognize a bit of rust on it. He describes how he showed her to load and fire it.

Next, W.P. Walters testifies. He had been a customer at Chick's Gun Shop. He saw the woman walk in very slowly, 'straight out' as if stiffly, and speak with Chick. She asked Chick to verify that the gun would be easy to operate. Chick showed her that the "pull" (on the trigger) was easy, and showed her how to load it. She had him put it in a box and wrapped. As she left, Walters heard another man say that the woman was 'going to hurt herself with that pistol.' Walters and another man followed her to the door, and determined that she went into at least two other retail establishments—Schiller & Murtha's, and The Combination.

Next, Deputy Coroner H. J. Stetson testifies that he was summoned (by telephone) to the hotel on the peninsula. He arrived to find the woman's body lying on the steps, covered by a tarpaulin. The undertakers followed on the next ferry, put it in a receiving box (a temporary coffin), and removed it to Johnson & Company in the city. He says that she was stiff and cold after lying there perhaps six or seven hours. He testifies that "the pistol was lying on the next step, the stone steps that go down to the surf, and her hand rested on the lower edge of one, and it had fallen out on to the edge of the next one below, and there was blood around it and underneath it."

Stetson further testifies that, while examining her room, he found a valise. He also found an envelope she had addressed to *Denman Thompson, The Old Homestead.* This refers to one of the most famous actors of the day, Denman Thompson of New Hampshire. According to a contemporary critic, "Thompson interpreted America to itself in the core persona of the solid New England farmer."

Stetson also found a piece of paper on which was written the word Frank four times: *Frank Frank Frank Frank.*

Stetson found another scrap of paper on which she had written: "I merely heard of that man. I do not know him." As with the rest of the artifacts in her room, we have no guess at an explanation, but we can imagine they elicited stunned silence and wonderment in the courtroom.

Stetson found an invitation, by Louise Leslie Carter and Lillian Russell, for Lottie to join them at the Hotel del Coronado. Carter and Russell were two of the most famous stage actresses of the day.

Stetson mentions another innocent little detail about yet another piece of critical evidence. In the room were several embroidered hankies. Some of them clearly had the name Louisa Anderson embroidered on them. Stetson stumbles over the name on some evidently more faded hankies, where the last name is clearly Anderson, but he says he can't read the first name—which he says looks like 'Little.'

Under further questioning, Stetson says that he examined the grate in the room, and found some papers that had burned entirely to ashes. A nightgown hung on a hook. On the mantel were a hat, a bottle, and a penknife. Among the other bottles in the room were one with camphor (a topical anesthetic) and alcohol—a considerable quantity of brandy. There were some quinine pills, and a bottle of some kind that had a notice wrapped around it: "If it does not relieve you, you better send for the doctor." The notice was signed "Druggist," without address.

Stetson testifies that when he came to the hotel, clerk A. S. Gomer informed him that a telegram had been received just that morning from a bank in Iowa, confirming that Mrs. Bernard's expense account would be honored to the amount of $25.00. Stetson asked Gomer to inform the bank of Mrs. Bernard's suicide, which Gomer did, but there has been no reply—in itself not surprising, since it has only been one day.

Stetson has not gone to inquire at the baggage office, but says he didn't bother "because she had no checks or anything put away, to know." Stetson says he knows nothing of her brother.

The coroner states that the court has received all the testimony it can get, and asks the jury to issue its finding. It is afternoon, and the entire proceeding has taken less than one day.

Newspaper Accounts Dec. 1-Dec. 14

Day 8—Thursday, Dec. 1, 1892

The San Diego Union reports that Kate traveled into San Diego just after noon Monday, Nov. 28, to buy a handgun.[27]

It is now established she traveled on the streetcar in Coronado, and both ways was with the same conductor (who, like so many other potential witnesses, was not called to testify at the inquest). According to the article, she went straight to buy a gun, and then returned immediately to Coronado.[28]

While riding on the trolley, she apparently asked for a hardware store (she most likely did not ask about a gun shop, which would have attracted more attention) and was referred to Todd & Hawley's hardware store.

At 6:30 p.m., Lottie once more checked with hotel staff[29] to see if they had received any letters or telegrams for her, or if her brother had come.

The article reports that handkerchiefs were found in her room, after her death, with the name 'Lottie Anderson' embroidered on them. They were said to be "of the finest linen."[30]

The article suggests that people are starting to wonder if there was more to the relationship between Lottie Bernard and her purported 'brother' than she had let on. If he was truly her brother, the reasoning went, he would have contacted authorities already, because news of her suicide had been telegraphed all over the country, and was being avidly followed by the Yellow Press. Already, there is speculation that the mysterious 'brother' was actually her lover. So quickly, the story in the Yellow Press took on a salacious tone that must have sold many newspapers, because her case overnight became a national sensation.

The San Diego Union, December 1: A second article speculates that she was ruined by a man, betrayed, and abandoned—after which, in despair, she committed suicide.

The reporter interviewed a prominent physician (presumably Dr. B. F. Mertzman, who had examined the body the previous morning, Nov. 30, a half hour before the coroner's inquest, and testified later). Mertzman tells the reporter that the girl was 24 or 25 (a close age for either Lizzie Wyllie, 24, or Kate Morgan, 26). Merman states she seemed healthy, and he dismisses as 'nonsense' the idea that she was so near death from cancer that doctors had pronounced her case hopeless, as she had told Gomer[31] when the latter came to her room on Monday, Nov. 28.

Mertzman tells the reporter that the first symptoms of stomach cancer (which rarely develops under age 40, and he's never heard of one before age 35) are almost identical with the symptoms of pregnancy—pain, sourness, vomiting, as well as sallow skin. Mertzman states he cannot say for sure, but the signs point to pregnancy. He states that she appears to have been taking 'strong medicine'[32] (or 'violent medicine') to produce a miscarriage. He attributes the sallowness of her complexion and the dark rings under her eyes (mentioned by the Coronado pharmacist) as typical of such a course of self-medication.

Mertzman states "The indications are that she has already borne a child, and was [pregnant] when she died, but this cannot be definitely proven without a post-mortem examination."[33] He opines that she shot herself over "some love affair."

Mertzman references a three-hour horseback ride Lottie was said to have taken sometime after her arrival. Charles Stevens, of Star Stables, apparently saw her trying to deal with a 'fractious' horse she couldn't well control. Stevens offered to help, and she accepted, so he took her for a three-hour tour (on horseback or in a carriage). During this time she appeared to be "pleasant and companionable, if not in high spirits." In other words, for a woman suffering the terminal stage of stomach cancer, this seemed utterly out of line.

The article mentions that Lottie stopped at the Hotel Brewster after arriving in San Diego—before she ventured to Coronado and signed in at the Hotel del Coronado. At the Brewster, Lottie asked about the arrival of her presumable brother and his wife, 'Mr. and Mrs. Anderson.' Nobody by that name had signed in at the Brewster. Interestingly, she apparently did not refer to her 'brother' as Dr. Anderson, if this account is correct, but as Mr. Anderson.

ಊ ಊ

The San Francisco Chronicle reports[34] that "the [coroner's inquest] verdict was undoubtedly correct, but fails utterly to give satisfaction to the public mind since the identity of the woman is not positively fixed, and the cause of the suicide is left enveloped in mystery." The article cites "the contradictory stories told by the victim." The article dwells upon the many contradictions and inconsistencies of the saga.

Day 9—Friday, Dec. 2, 1892

The San Diego Union[35] now reports that the question of her identity is still unresolved. The paper speculates with increasing fervor that "the beautiful and mysterious stranger" killed herself over "love-trouble."

A bellman reported that Joseph E. (or A.) Jones of Boston had seen Lottie Bernard on a train, in the same car he was riding from Denver to Orange. He later recognized her in the Hotel del Coronado—in fact, he signed in after she did the afternoon of November 24. Jones' strange story highlights a mystery within a mystery: the Case of the Missing Day. Why did it take the woman a full day to make the two-hour train trip from Los Angeles to San Diego?

Jones was never called to testify at the coroner's inquest. He told the unspecified bellman that he had not mentioned the sighting on the train before, because he was loath to testify before the coroner's jury. According to Jones, he started becoming aware of the woman he would later know as Lottie Bernard, in the company of a well-dressed gentleman. People in the car began to notice "high words and bitter quarreling." This went on for some time, rising and falling. In the final minutes of the quarrel, she repeatedly begged him to forgive her for something. He adamantly and angrily refused, and stormed off the train. Jones thought nothing more of it until he saw her at the Hotel del Coronado, and he recognized her as the woman on the train. [The article uses the language "saw her at Hotel del Coronado day or so afterward"—thus, this incident could have happened either on the afternoon of November 23 after she said goodbye to the L.A. Grants in Los Angeles, or on November 24, presumably in the morning, before she completed the trip to San Diego.]

The article goes on to say that people felt her trip to San Diego was "an escapade," because she arrived without baggage. [Those people may not have been aware of the three trunks she said were being kept for her at the baggage office of the train terminal.] People noted the familiarity with which she spoke of Los Angeles hotels, which made it sound as if she were from the region.

[Employees at the Hotel del Coronado were quoted in an article in *The San Francisco Chronicle*, Dec. 6., as saying she seemed to be quite familiar with hotels in San Francisco (the Palace) and Los Angeles (the Nadeau, the Westminster) than would be expected from a common bookbindery worker only a few weeks out of Detroit.[36]]

Lottie stated that her mother and father lived in Detroit, and that G. L. Allen—the Iowa bank officer she told Gomer to wire for funds—was in charge of her finances.

The article cites puzzlement at the many contradictions in her story. It mentions that, at one point, she tipped a bellman a dollar (a day's wages) and waved it off, saying she had plenty of money—yet she had only $20 in her purse.

At this point there is speculation that G. L. Allen (who never did reply to the information about her suicide) was romantically involved with her, and had possibly "sent her away."

The article offers another speculation—that the man on the train was not her 'brother,' as she had claimed, but her lover, and that he deserted her at Orange.

The article reiterates that she gave her 'brother's' name as W. C. or M. C. Anderson of Minneapolis [in another account it was Indianapolis], but the Minneapolis directory contains no such person.

As of December 2, the 'Beautiful Stranger' remained unidentified. She was still known only as Mrs. Lottie Anderson Bernard.

Day 10—Saturday, Dec. 3, 1892

The San Diego Union reports a significant break. San Diego Police Chief Joseph W. Brenning[37] received a telegram from Miss May Wyllie of Detroit. Miss Wyllie requested a full description of the body, and asked if she had short hair, a black corset, large black hat, and gold buckle. Deputy Coroner Stetson said it was not an exact match, but it was the only communication the city had so far received about the decedent.

San Diego police, on a separate note, had telegraphed the Farmers' and Merchants' Bank in Hamburg, Iowa, for information about the elusive Mr. G. L. Allen who had wired $25 credit to Gomer on Lottie's behalf the day she died.

Police also located three trunks at the D Street baggage depot. The trunks had come from Omaha, via Denver—Denver being, we recall, the point of departure of James Jones, who told a bellman he had seen Lottie in an argument with a well-dressed man on that train. The trunks could not be opened without authorization from higher-ups in the baggage hierarchy.

Day 11—Sunday, Dec. 4, 1892

The San Diego Union identifies the dead woman as Lizzie Wyllie of Detroit. Lizzie's mother, Elizabeth Wyllie, states she is certain that the dead woman is her daughter Elizabeth 'Lizzie' Wyllie (sister of the Miss May Wyllie who the previous day telegraphed Chief Brenning to ask for details about the body).

Lizzie has relatives in San Diego, but they have not seen her since she was a child, and cannot be asked to identify her. Other relatives, it is claimed, would soon arrive from Pasadena [which never happened, as far as the history reveals] to identify her and "take care of her remains" [which also ended up not happening].

It is thus learned that Lizzie and her sister May had worked at Winn & Hammond Bookbindery in Detroit. The company was located at 12-156 Wayne Street, Tel. 220. Their foreman was a married man with children, named John G. Longfield.[38] Longfield resided at 606 12th Street, while the Wyllies (mother and two daughters; pronounced like 'Willy' or *Why-lee*) lived nearby.

Apparently, Lizzie had an affair with Longfield. Soon, Lizzie, her sister May, and Longfield were all fired.

On another front, the newspaper reports that the president of the Hamburg, Iowa, bank finally responded to the telegram from San Diego Police, saying that "neither Allen nor myself know of the relatives of Mrs. Bernard. Her husband [is] supposed to be in Wichita, Kansas."

The Los Angeles Herald reports[39] that Mrs. Elizabeth Wyllie of Detroit, upon receiving the exact description of the body as requested by her daughter May, claimed it was an exact description of Lizzie, and requested that her niece travel from Pasadena to San Diego to see the body. [No record that the niece actually did this.]

The body was described by San Diego authorities as being that of a woman five and a half feet tall, with a fair but sallow complexion. She had medium-length black hair. She had two small moles on the left cheek, broad features, high cheekbones, and brown eyes. She weighed 150 pounds, was about 26, had good teeth. She wore: a plain gold ring on the third finger of the left hand; a pure gold ring with four pearls and blue stone in its center; black corsets; and a large black hat.

The San Francisco Chronicle reports[40] that "Driven almost to distraction by worry and shame, Mrs. Elizabeth Wyllie of Detroit admitted this afternoon that it was her daughter Lizzie who was found dead..."

Mrs. Wyllie says her daughter eloped a month earlier with [John G. Longfield] of Detroit. Neither she nor Longfield had any money. She pins the date of Lizzie's disappearance at "five weeks ago last Monday [on or about Monday, Oct. 24] she went...downtown on an errand. She never returned." She had apparently said she was going to look for work, and did not go alone.

The article reports a somewhat disjointed story that on the Saturday before Lizzie's disappearance, one afternoon a man called at the Wyllie house to tell everyone goodbye. He said he was going south, likely to California, and he 'jocosely' told May Wyllie "I will be picking roses in California while your feet are freezing in Detroit."

Mrs. Wyllie is described as 'prepossessing' and Lizzie was 'an attractive girl.'

Apparently the name L. Anderson Bernard reminded her of her lost daughter. The initial L could stand for Lizzie, while Anderson is the name of her married sister in Grand Rapids.

Regarding her receipt of the telegram describing the dead woman in Coronado, the article reads: "Mrs. Wyllie read the telegram as far as the mention of the two moles and then the paper dropped from her hands. 'My Lizzie; it's my Lizzie,' she sobbed repeatedly. 'What will become of me?' Not a word of reproach came from her lips upon the name of the dead girl."

John Longfield, her supervisor at the bookbindery, has a wife and two children. Mrs. Longfield says her husband has found work in Cleveland, and that is why he has not been home in five weeks.

Day 12—Monday, Dec. 5, 1892

The San Diego Union reports that the body is now lying in state at Johnson & Company funeral home. Many curious people are coming to look at it, "including many ladies."

The bank president in Hamburg, Iowa telegraphed to say he thought Mrs. Bernard's husband was named John. He had personally never met this John.

The paper says that a relative of Lizzie Wyllie was due to arrive on the night train from Pasadena to identify the body. [There is no indication whether or not this came to pass].

Day 13—Tuesday, Dec. 6, 1892

The San Diego Union claims[41] that it is now for certain that the dead girl is 'pretty Lizzie Wyllie' of Detroit.

The article claims that she 'disappeared' from her home 'some six weeks ago' [which would put it in October or even as far back as September, depending on how reliable the reporter's story was].

The paper notes that Lizzie's Pasadena relative "has not yet materialized."

Authorities contacted a Mr. John Bernard of Wichita to inform him his wife "had suicided," to which he chose not to respond.

The love affair of Lizzie Wyllie and John G. Longfield is being fleshed out in the voracious press. Apparently, the two lovers were so obvious that it caused a scandal. Despite knowing he was married, Lizzie continued going with him.

After being fired, Lizzie visited her married sister, Mrs. [Louisa] Anderson, in Grand Rapids, Michigan for a time, and then returned home [to her mother and sister] for a short time six weeks earlier, before then 'disappearing.' It is assumed this accounts for the dead woman having several handkerchiefs marked 'Lottie Anderson.'

Mrs. Elizabeth Wyllie was certain the dead girl was her daughter Lizzie. For one thing, the dead girl had two moles on her left cheek, as did Lizzie.

Speculation has it that "Longfield was at Hamburg under an assumed name, and sent Lizzie the $25. If this be the case, who came to California with her, with whom did she have a quarrel at Orange, and who as the man that left her at that point? Who was the dead girl expecting at Hotel del Coronado? Not a brother, but one Longfield, if the truth were known, Allen of Hamburg may have played a leading part in the dastardly affair himself. Longfield is known at Detroit as a sport, and a rounder of not the best reputation even for one of his class."

The paper mentions that Lizzie continues lying in the funeral home, looking peaceful as if sleeping at home. Mrs. Wyllie is expected to send word on what to do with the body. The three trunks at the San Diego baggage depot remain unclaimed.

The San Francisco Chronicle reports[42] that staff at the Hotel del Coronado were impressed with the charm, education, and class of the woman who died at the hotel. They feel her knowledge of the fine hotels of San Francisco and Los Angeles could not be forthcoming from a factory girl only recently run away from Detroit.

In a separate article, the same paper reports that Mrs. Longfield sent her husband a letter in Cleveland on Saturday [Dec. 3]. Not knowing his address, she sent it General Delivery. She had a reply from him this morning, saying "I received a letter from Miss Wyllie last Wednesday [Nov. 30]. Will send it on at once. There is no truth in it."

Day 14—Wednesday, Dec. 7, 1892

The San Diego Union reports[43] that the undertaker has sent a photograph of the dead woman's face to Mrs. Wyllie in Detroit. In so doing, the mortuary noted an apparent discrepancy that Lizzie had pierced ears, whereas the corpse did not.

It was reported that the handkerchiefs did not read 'Lottie Anderson,' as previously reported, but 'Louisa Anderson'—the name of Lizzie's aunt [previously referenced as her married sister] in Grand Rapids, Michigan.

The article mentions that a telegram had come [sender not named] the previous day, Dec. 6, swinging the weight back into the Bernard camp. Evidently, a professional gambler named L. A. Bernard had come through Hamburg recently. This man was now thought to be the deceased's husband. Bernard was said to have left Hamburg November 7 for Topeka, Kansas. He had said his wife was sick in California, and he was going to bring her back to Iowa. He tried to borrow money for the trip, but could not get a loan and has not been heard from since. G. L. Allen of Hamburg, who wired the $25 credit, is said to have been a roommate of Bernard in Illinois. Allen never met Bernard's wife, but contributed the $25 out of charity. The message concludes by restating a strong belief that the identification of the body as Lizzie Wyllie's is wrong, implying that she was, after all, Mrs. Bernard.

In San Diego, the Bernard story is being discredited by the newspapers. The papers follow an even more confusing track. They imply that Allen was romantically linked with the dead woman, and invented the sick wife story 'as a blind.' They claim that a San Diego man, who knows Allen, says Allen is a wealthy cattleman and ladies' man. The papers opine that "either Allen is a consummate liar and had dealings with Miss Lizzie Wyllie, which he is trying to conceal, or the girl...is Mrs. L. A. Bernard" [presumably the wife of the L. A. Bernard reported by G. L. Allen].

The San Francisco Chronicle opines[44] that Miss Lizzie Wyllie of Detroit and Mrs. L. Anderson Bernard "were not the same person. The Wyllie girl is alive and well in Toronto and Mrs. Bernard is supposed to have been the wife of a Hamburg, Iowa gambler..."

"...As he promised in his dispatch of yesterday, Longfield, whose name has been associated with Miss Wyllie's disappearance, enclosed to his wife a letter from Miss Wyllie, dated Toronto, in which she says that she is not coming home... and indicates that Lizzie left home on account of trouble with her family."

Day 15—Thursday, Dec. 8, 1892

The San Diego Union reports[45] that, based on the issue of the pierced ears, the dead woman was not Lizzie Wyllie. Lizzie had pierced ears and wore silver earrings, while the dead woman's ears were not pierced.

G. L. Allen of Hamburg, Iowa, is again reported as saying he had been a schoolmate of a gambler named L. A. Bernard, whose wife lay ill in California. At her request [i.e., Gomer's] he wired $25 credit, without ever having met her. The San Diego papers, however, tend to be suspicious of Allen and not believe his story because of details that in themselves are convoluted and questionable.

A Mrs. Florence S. Howard, of Orange, California, writes that the dead woman is one Josie Brown, 24, of Detroit. Josie Brown had stayed with Mrs. Howard during the previous summer. She said Josie Brown had a sister named Mrs. Anderson. A young man claiming to be her brother, and calling himself Dr. Brown, of Detroit, had spent some time there, but claimed to have come from Minneapolis."

The paper reports that the three trunks remain as yet unopened at the baggage depot.

୬ ୭

The Los Angeles Times reports[46] that "young woman's trunk and baggage are...at Mrs. [L.A.] Grant's, No. 917 South Hill Street, where she was last seen. When she left, on the 23rd...she stated that she would be back in time for Thanksgiving dinner, but not a word has been heard from her since."

The story relates that she arrived from Omaha about two months earlier [September or October]. She said her husband was a gambler, and she did not know what had become of him.

She applied at several employment agencies. She first found work as a domestic at the R. M. Widneys', and then at the T. H. Hughes'. Lastly, she found employment at the L. A. Grants'.

The day before she left Los Angeles, she was anxious to get some papers signed, and appeared to be very worried about something.

She wore the ring and the black underclothes found on the body in Coronado. She had two moles on her left cheek.

"She told several persons that her name was Lizzie, but that she liked the name of Kittie better, and that was the reason she adopted it."

The paper reported that she came to Los Angeles from San Francisco. She was "well posted" in San Francisco, and knew all about the public places and the hotels, which shows she must have lived there.

While in Los Angeles, she maintained an excellent reputation. She kept to her duties, never went out at night, and had no men about. She seemed to be in good spirits on the day she left for San Diego, and "promised faithfully that she would be home next day in time to cook the Thanksgiving dinner."

She appeared to be 'fairly well educated' and had traveled much, since her husband was a gambler.

The Evening Express (Los Angeles) reports that "The woman, whose husband was a gambler, was described as being very pretty."

The San Francisco Chronicle reports[47] that it is believed the suicide is Mrs. Katie Logan, a domestic for several families in Los Angeles. She came from Omaha about two months ago [late September or early October]. The description of the dead woman fits her exactly. "It is believed that Mrs. Logan also lived in San Francisco, since she was well informed about that city."

Day 16—Friday, Dec. 9, 1892

The San Diego Union reports[48] that the dead woman is still unidentified. The feeling now is that she was not Lizzie Wyllie, who is said to be living with her lover John G. Longfield in Ontario, Canada. She is now thought to be the wife of Iowa gambler L. A. Bernard.

Los Angeles Police Chief Glass has informed San Diego Police Chief Brenning that the dead woman was probably a missing housemaid from Los Angeles, named Katie Logan.

The newspaper also raises, perhaps for the first time, the name Kate Morgan that will receive most of the press attention in the case spanning at least three centuries. The paper connects the dots thus: "...Mrs. Bernard is really the woman's name...she was at Orange last year under the name of Josie Brown...she was at Omaha two months ago, where she perhaps met Allen of Hamburg...came to Los Angeles under the name of Kate Morgan, and appeared [in San Diego] under her real name [Lottie A. Bernard]."

The Los Angeles Times reports[49] that the trunk of Kate Morgan was moved, on order of Los Angeles Police Chief Glass, to the central police station from Contractor Grant's house.

The trunk was opened there, and it was found that her home was in Hamburg, Iowa. This was the town from which the Hotel del Coronado received the wire of $25 credit.

A marriage certificate indicated she was married to Thomas E. Morgan by Rev. W. H. Howes, on 30 December 1885. Her maiden name was Miss Katie K. Farmer.

Telegrams between Chief Glass in Los Angeles and Chief Brenning in San Diego indicated the body still lay unclaimed at Johnson & Company mortuary on Fifth Street in San Diego.

Mr. Grant stated he never had a better servant in his house. When she went missing, he immediately reported it to police.

The Los Angeles Herald reports[50] that the trunk marked 'Mrs. Kate Morgan' was taken from the L. A. Grants' home to the Los Angeles police station.

The box contained a tin box marked 'Louise' [or 'Louisa'?].

There was a photograph of a man about 50 years old, with a full beard, tinged with gray. On the reverse side of this picture was a name (scratched out) but the word Visalia left visible.

There was a photograph of a man about 35 years old, with a black mustache, black hair, and thick skull, "who looked something like a sporting character." The reporter speculates that this might be "her husband, who had deserted her."

There were photographs of two boys, about 9 and 10; a girl about 2; and a baby.

On several photos, names had been "carefully erased."

There was a paper containing a lock of blonde hair. On the paper someone had written in a coarse hand, "Elizabeth A. Morgan's hair."

A letter from W. J. [W.T.] Farmer, Hanford, recommended Mrs. Morgan as an honorable and trustworthy woman.

The trunk contained the cards of several ladies and their addresses, where most likely Kate Morgan [Katie Logan] had worked: Mrs. J. H. McDonough of San Rafael; Mrs. M. R. Abbott of San Francisco; and Mrs. Ottinger of San Francisco.

A 'cabinet size photo' shows Mrs. Morgan "as a woman about 26, with black eyes, large ears, a rather large, open face, and somewhat coarse features." It seemed to be a recent picture. In the reporter's judgment, the photo doesn't represent a woman accustomed to staying in fine hotels, or wears lace shawls. She doesn't seem pretty, and her features don't look like those of an educated woman.

The San Francisco Chronicle reports[51] that the dead woman was undoubtedly Kate Morgan...

"Her maiden name was Katie K. Farmer. She had only been on the coast for two months, and, as near as can be learned, she worked for W. T. Farmer, a supposed relative, at Hanford, Tulare County."

Day 17—Saturday, Dec. 10, 1892

The San Diego Union reports that the trunk of the woman in Los Angeles [Katie Logan, a pseudonym] was opened. The owner of the trunk has been identified, based on papers and photos inside, as Kate Morgan. She and Lottie A. Bernard are thought to be one and the same.

Inside the trunk was found a tin box with the name 'Louisa Anderson' on it. That name matches the name embroidered on the handkerchiefs found in the dead woman's room at the Hotel del Coronado. The effects include a lock of hair. *The Los Angeles Herald* says that a photograph of Mrs. Morgan does not match the description of the Coronado suicide. This is contradicted by other evidence, including a marriage certificate dated December 30, 1885, for Thomas E. Morgan and Kate K. Farmer, united in matrimony by Rev. W. E. Howe in Hamburg, Iowa.

This article states that [Katie Logan] had been a domestic servant in the home of the L. A. Grants, a family of Los Angeles. Her employers and co-workers described her as 'reticent' about her life, saying only she was married to a gambler and was unhappy about it.

Echoing a report in *The Los Angeles Times*, *The San Diego Union* says [Katie Logan] had been in California for two months. She had previously worked for a W. T. Farmer [Kate Morgan's uncle, in Hanford, California, near Visalia]. Police believe Kate Morgan had gone from Chicago to Omaha, and from there to Cheyenne, Ogden, Sacramento, and then Hanford. In Hanford, she had gotten a letter of recommendation from W. T. Farmer. Then she had traveled to Los Angeles.

The paper opines that the contents of the trunk—in which all names, addresses, and other personal information had been destroyed—made it evident that she wanted to conceal her identity.[52]

Mr. Farmer has been contacted for information.

Day 18—Sunday, Dec. 11, 1892

The San Diego Union reports[53] that a Mr. A. D. Swarts of Los Angeles had contacted the coroner's office in San Diego to say that he had known her since 1869. He says she is [Kate Morgan], the granddaughter of a miller named Joe Chandler in Riverton, Iowa [near Hamburg]. Swarts says that Tom Morgan, Sr., her husband's rich uncle, lives in that area, along with other wealthy relatives, all of whom would help her have a decent burial. Accordingly, San Diego authorities sent telegrams to several of these persons.

The paper reports that large numbers of visitors, mostly female, daily throng to Johnson & Company funeral parlor to view the body.

The three trunks at the San Diego baggage depot have been claimed "by the owners" and this removes "any remaining doubt" that the dead woman was Mrs. Kate Morgan.

Day 19—Monday, Dec. 12, 1892

The San Diego Union reports[54] that Kate's grandfather, Joe Chandler, of Riverton, Iowa, sent a telegram to the undertaker, Johnson & Company of San Diego. "Your telegram received regarding Kate Morgan, *née* Farmer. Bury her and send me statement.—J. W. Chandler."

The newspaper says that "none of her other relatives have uttered a word." The cause of her suicide is still unknown.

The paper says "she will be buried today." [In fact, her funeral was not held until two days later, Dec. 14, followed by her burial].

༶ ༶

The Los Angeles Times on [date uncertain, but after Dec. 10] comments[55] on the report from W. T. Farmer, Kate Morgan's uncle at Hanford, California, that she had considerable money with her when she arrived at his residence. Kate said she intended to deposit the money in a bank. Farmer opined that Kate was frugal, and had employment while in Los Angeles, and thus would not have spent her money. This was in reaction to comments that she died with only $16 in her purse.

Day 20—Tuesday, Dec. 13, 1892

No news.

Day 21—Wednesday, Dec. 14, 1892 (Funeral and Burial)

According to *The San Diego Union*,[56] the funeral was held at 10:00 a.m. at Johnson & Company. A Rev. H. B. Restarick officiated with prayers and Bible verses. Members of the Brotherhood of St. Andrew, along with ladies of the Episcopal Church, made responses during the service. The funeral was well attended. After the funeral, the casket was put in a hearse and carried to Mount Hope Cemetery for burial.

The Daily Bee, San Diego [story apparently dated Dec. 13] reports that there were "many women" at the funeral. "Prominent ladies sent flowers for the casket, but no one followed the remains to the cemetery."

☙ ❧

The Los Angeles Times reports[57] that W. T. Farmer, Kate Morgan's uncle in Hanford, California, finally responded to Los Angeles Police Chief Glass' inquiries. Farmer says Kate had no cause for suicide, and implies that, if the body was indeed hers, something else caused her death. He wrote that her husband, Thomas E. Morgan (Tom Morgan) was traveling[58] on business for a manufacturing company, and his home is in Hamburg, Iowa. Farmer had known them for many years. Kate wrote to Farmer from Los Angeles, saying she had secured work with the Whitney family. She had a good sum of money with her when she stayed with Farmer in Hanford. She had one flat-top trunk, two leather satchels, and a lady's gold watch, and said she would deposit the money in a bank.

Farmer enumerates some of her relatives—Henry Broomback and Thomas Morgan of Hamburg, Iowa; her grandfather, Joe W. Chandler, and John Samuella, of Riverton, Iowa—and continues to protest he does not believe Kate Morgan would have committed suicide, and perhaps there is a mistake about the identity pinned on the corpse.

The reporter presses his own conviction that there can be no doubt it was Kate Morgan, and that she did commit suicide, and in fact left the L.A. Grants with that intention already in mind. However, the reporter goes on to say that a number of mysteries about the case may never be answered—what happened to the considerable sum of money Farmer said she left Hanford with; what papers she was so anxious to have signed; and why she killed herself. The article affirms that Kate Morgan's relatives paid for the burial in San Diego.

☙ ❧

The body of the unknown woman—Lottie A. Bernard? Josie Brown? Katie Logan? Kate Morgan? Lizzie Wyllie?—lay in state several weeks at the mortuary. The funeral was variously reported as having been held either Tuesday, December 13, or the 9th, or even the 15th. Many ladies attended the funeral. Many people sent flowers, but none accompanied the casket to Mount Hope Cemetery. Pious, overwrought ladies in Sunday finery trooped daily from dawn to dusk to the funeral parlor, with its smells of flowers and candle wax. A High-Church funeral followed, in the best Episcopalian tradition. The simple coffin was loaded on a donkey cart, and the dead woman rumbled off without a single pall bearer or mourner, outside town to a forgotten grave at Mt. Hope Cemetery, Market Street. Neither the relatives of Lizzie Wyllie, nor those of Kate Morgan, ever showed up. Kate Morgan's grandfather paid the bill, with only the telegraphed words: "Bury her and send me the bill." He knew his granddaughter all too well.

Her uncle, W. T. Farmer of Hanford, the last family member to see Kate Morgan, said she was happy, had no cause for suicide, and was married to Thomas Morgan who "has been traveling in the interest of some manufacturing company." Kate must have really pulled the wool over her uncle's eyes. Joe Chandler must have been ashamed of her, and kept the truth from Farmer—that Kate was a source of constant trouble. Farmer says Kate was traveling with a single trunk—not three trunks, as reported in Los Angeles. The three trunks belonged to Lizzie, and were part of the switch the two women pulled. Farmer stated he thought authorities were mistaken in identifying the corpse as Kate's—as I believe they were.

Part IV. Solved!

The Core of My Theory

Key Points

In a moment, we are going to rewind the timeline traced in "Part III: What We Know For Sure," and re-examine the details in a new light. First, let me summarize my theory.

Blackmail was the real reason: Traditionally, no reason is usually offered for Lottie A. Bernard's appearance at the Hotel del Coronado. Less often, the story goes that she had been abandoned by her partner in crime—allegedly her husband, Tom Morgan who used her charms to lure men in to card games on trains, only to get them drunk and rob them—and that Tom had no use for her anymore when she got pregnant. In the latter scenario, Tom would be the 'brother,' a 'Dr. Anderson,' about whom she frequently and desperately inquired at the hotel's front desk. Supposedly, then, she killed herself out of despair. Even more rarely, the story goes that she was murdered, either by Tom, or by shadowy and powerful men of the region—one thinks immediately of John Spreckels, one of the wealthiest men in the United States, and the most powerful by far in the San Diego region. While the facts do not support any of these theories, John Spreckels is in fact the key to the entire saga. He is the biggest puzzle piece, and all the pieces start to neatly and logically snap into place when we consider one huge detail: John Spreckels had recently become sole owner of the Hotel del Coronado.

I believe John Spreckels was the target of a blackmail plot to extort money from him in a false claim of paternity.

Two women, not one: The traditional story has it that only one person was involved—Kate Morgan, a con artist and grifter from Hamburg, Iowa. The evidence clearly shows there were two women and up to two men involved.

Lizzie Wyllie, not Kate Morgan: Where the traditional story has it that the woman who died was Kate Morgan, I believe the dead woman was Elizabeth 'Lizzie' Wyllie (pronounced like Wylie, of which it is a variant. The body was first identified as being that of Lottie A. Bernard, the fictitious name under which she registered. Days later, the body was identified as that of Lizzie Wyllie. A few days after that, based on an anonymous tip, police shifted their attention to a woman named Kate Morgan. The change in IDs was arbitrary and based largely on the flimsy factor of pierced ears.

Two men, not one: The traditional story has it that a man was in the background, usually considered to be Kate's husband Tom Morgan. I believe there were two men in the background—one of them John G. Longfield, Lizzie's married lover with whom she fled Detroit after she became pregnant; and probably Kate's husband or a male lover.

Web of Indirect Evidence

I don't have direct proof or a smoking gun to prove my theory that it was blackmail, being perpetrated by Kate Morgan and three accomplices (Lizzie Wyllie, John G. Longfield, and possibly Tom Morgan or another lover of Kate's). There is not, for example, let us say, a hypothetical telegram from Kate Morgan to John Spreckels, threatening him and demanding money. There is currently no such document, nor is there even known to have been one, though I suspect it was how Kate Morgan conveyed her message to Spreckels as she got Lizzie ('Lottie A. Bernard') situated at Spreckels' hotel. Logically, the timing may have been that Spreckels knew of her on or before the day she checked in.

Once we start sifting through all the clues, they form a network of corroborating and circumstantial evidence so strong that one begins to approach certainty. Every piece of the puzzle makes sense once the whole thing is assembled. There are no loose ends left, and that makes this at least a strong theory—and it may well be possible to find other stray granules of fact that have drifted around in the wind, disconnected, for over a century, once people know where to look.

We have here what could be called a brittle case. It is a cold case in the truest sense—the Victorian era is long gone, all the witnesses are dead, key evidence was tampered with and lost, and even the official transcript of the coroner's inquest was lost for a time (its integrity therefore compromised). Still, using the voluminous evidence compiled by the Heritage Department, and other facts gathered from library and internet sources, it is possible to formulate a theory or strong conjecture that is compelling in how all of its myriad pieces fit together.

It is a complicated story—some would say far-fetched, but one has only to look at the contorted and amazing manner in which Kate Morgan lived her life to lay aside all disbelief and doubt. Here was a woman who traveled throughout the Central and Western United States leaving a trail of aliases. Her life itself, and that of the fictitious 'brother' who keeps shadowing her in parallel under ever-changing names, is like a huge fantasy story that she wove, using the transcontinental railroad and her dark and hyper-active imagination as a loom.

Rewinding the Tape

Day 0—Wednesday, Nov. 23, 1892 (Katie Logan in L.A.)

It may seem strange that I did not choose to start the timeline on Thanksgiving Day, Nov. 24, when Lottie A. Bernard sprang into life. Day Zero may seem like an odd choice also, but it is a ghostly nod to the last day in the short life of an imaginary person named Mrs. Katie Logan. And this is a highly important part of our story, because Los Angeles Police unearthed some startling, major clues in her trunk during the nationwide search for the phantom housemaid. Katie Logan appeared out of Omaha (coincidentally the capital of the state in which Tom Morgan would live most of his life; and also about fifty miles from Kate Morgan's home town of Hamburg, Iowa). Katie existed for thirty to sixty days, during which she worked as a domestic temp in three prominent Los Angeles households. She was attractive, efficient, and well-liked. Her last employers, the civil contractor L. A. Grant and his wife, heartily invited her to return from some unspecified errands that afternoon, and to assist the family with their Thanksgiving dinner. We know, of course, that she vanished, never to be seen again, and the Grants missed her enough to report her disappearance almost immediately to Los Angeles Police. Thus, even as a new fictional person (Lottie A. Bernard) sprang to life in the Cities of Coronado and San Diego some two hours south as the train chugs, the LAPD was already developing a missing person's case on Katie Logan.

LAPD's case pursued the usual lawful ends, but was headed on a trajectory that would soon coincide with the Lottie A. Bernard suicide investigation in the San Diego area. The critical element at the end of that trajectory, a critical element in the case—and in this theory—was a single trunk containing the possessions of the missing domestic. The Grants said Katie Logan had brought the trunk with her from Omaha, her reputed last residence. At the end of the trajectory, that trunk would be taken to police headquarters in Los Angeles. Until the police had reasonable cause, they could not lawfully open the trunk—anymore than San Diego Police were able to open Lottie's three trunks at the baggage depot there. However, when the missing Katie Logan of Los Angeles was connected to the dead Lottie A. Bernard of Coronado, police did open the trunk. Inside, they found a wealth of artifacts that baffled them, and have continued to baffle analysts until now. The contents of that trunk are remarkable, because they contain artifacts belonging to both Kate Morgan and Lizzie Wyllie. This trunk connects the two women. It connects them not only in some vague manner, but *in situ*, in the location of one of Kate Morgan's notorious and enigmatic false identities. The trunk is not the only connection—Deputy Coroner Stetson found hankies belonging to Lizzie's aunt in the dead woman's room at the Hotel Del.

As we noted in the previous part, Katie Logan made that strange statement to another domestic—a statement so baffling that it can only be truthful, amid the often dubious claims and reports of the Yellow Press. Katie Logan was described as being quiet and keeping to herself. She was worried about several things. She was unhappily married to a gambler, and did not know his whereabouts. She was anxious to have some unspecified papers signed, but nobody learned what these were about. Then, another woman working as a domestic stated that Katie Logan informed her that her name was Lizzie, but that she preferred Kittie or Katie. Katie Logan (who is usually suspected of being Kate Morgan) actually tells another domestic that her name is Lizzie. This, like the trunk, ties the two women together. And if Katie Logan was really Lizzie Wyllie, this supports my theory (borne out by other evidence) that Lottie Bernard was Lizzie.

One can imagine a brief conversation—later reported to Los Angeles police detectives—between two domestics in the shadowed halls of the wealthy Grant home. One can imagine how the pseudonymous Katie Logan lets her guard down and blurts out, "My name is really Lizzie," and then she catches herself, realizing her *faux pas*, and quickly recovers by adding: "...but I prefer Kittie...err, Katie...so I go by that name."

Finally, some hankies belonging to Lizzie Wyllie (actually, her Aunt Louisa) turned up in that same trunk.

Lizzie Wyllie was an attractive but air-headed young Detroit woman in serious trouble. She had gotten pregnant by her married lover, John Longfield, with whom she ran away to California after they were both fired from the bookbinding plant (Bin & Hammond) where they worked. She had relatives in San Diego, but did not visit with them.[59]

Now why would Katie Logan's trunk show up in the L.A. Grants' house, with articles in them belonging to both Kate Morgan and Lizzie Wyllie? Remember that Lottie A. Bernard at the Hotel del Coronado was telling people she had three trunks sitting at the freight depot in San Diego. She could not check those trunks out, because her 'brother' (most people until now have thought that was Tom Morgan; I believe it was John Longfield) stormed off the train with the tickets in his pocket at Orange. Those three trunks disappeared—which appeared to resolve yet another issue. But it seems far-fetched to think of the coincidence that (a) Lottie Bernard said she couldn't get her three trunks out and (b) the police actually determined there were three trunks at the depot but, as with the trunk in Los Angeles, they couldn't open them. This simple element is a good example of the tissue of fine details that combine to form a tenable theory in this old, brittle, cold case. We have Lottie in Coronado, stating repeatedly to various persons that she had three trunks in the depot in San Diego, but she didn't have the claim checks (with numbers on them); and there actually were exactly three trunks (not two, not four) sitting unclaimed at the depot during that precise time period—with tags on them, but no name and no matching claim checks with numbers to redeem the trunks. This tends to corroborate Lottie's story.

By the time the San Diego Police felt free to open the trunks, the trunks had vanished. The police felt the owner had picked them up. I suspect they were taken away under false pretenses by either the Spreckels Machine or by Kate Morgan and her accomplices. Since John Spreckels' agents controlled San Diego by then (he owned most of Coronado, much of downtown San Diego, the newspapers, the utilities, the rail system, the water flume, and anything else that was for sale) it is more likely that the Spreckels Machine removed the three trunks from play. The Spreckels Machine would have seen its core interest as protecting their master from scandal, at a critical time when he and his father were lobbying the President and Congress to prevent the overthrow of the Hawai'ian monarchy and therefore the loss of Spreckels' vast sugar fortune. We must remember, too, that San Diego had only a rudimentary police force at this time. Chief Brenning was a recent successor to the first chief, Coyne, who took office in 1889. San Diego had no detective force, and it is almost a given that a man as powerful and connected as Spreckels would be using Pinkertons or a similar agency, perhaps even his own private detective force. Thus Spreckels' private law enforcement arm would be far more sophisticated than Chief Branding's uniformed patrol.

If we believe that the three trunks in San Diego were really those of the woman at the Hotel del Coronado (Lottie Bernard), and if we believe, as I do, that Lottie Bernard was really Lizzie Wyllie, then we may presume that Lizzie brought three trunks out of Detroit. We know Lizzie was a snappy and stylish dresser, so it's hard to imagine she did not travel with a wardrobe. As much as the three trunks were Lizzie's, the single trunk at the L.A. Grants' house was Kate Morgan's trunk.

But if we believe that Lizzie first played Katie Logan in Los Angeles, and then played Lottie Bernard in Coronado, what is the meaning of this? How did Lizzie Wyllie, pretending to be the fictitious Katie Logan, have in her possession Kate Morgan's single trunk? Because Kate Morgan and her lover—presumably her husband, Tom Morgan, though there is room to believe she had abandoned her husband at that point and had another lover, who was the second man in Hamburg, setting up a $25 credit line for Lottie Bernard at the Hotel del Coronado—were training Lizzie for the hoped-for big coup in Coronado. Helping out was Lizzie's lover, John Longfield, who must have traveled to Hamburg with the other man to set up the credit line that came through on the day of Lottie Bernard's death.

On the topic of the trunks for one more moment: it makes sense that Kate Morgan had one trunk, because she was a frequent traveler and (as evidenced from the photos inside the trunk in Los Angeles) not a very good looking woman, nor a snappy dresser. On the other hand, Lizzie was a beautiful young woman with fine clothing, as witnesses said of Lottie A. Bernard. Lizzie had fine tastes in clothes, and it makes sense she would have eloped with three trunks—probably full of fine dresses and hats and purses and so forth. She may have been poor after losing her job, and she probably pawned her silver earrings, as we'll see later, but a woman like this would give her life to avoid being ill-dressed.

Kate Morgan is known to have spent time in San Francisco, where the Spreckels family had their estates and business headquarters. LAPD found, in her trunk, calling cards of a number of wealthy ladies there, although not of any Spreckels family members that we know of. I believe Kate Morgan was in the business of traveling around the country, finding temporary domestic work in wealthy homes, and setting up all manner of scams, as one can deduce from her many aliases. While in San Francisco, she would most certainly have learned all the gossip and inside news about wealthy families there from her fellow domestics. Ever one to exploit any possibility for a con job or a blackmail opportunity, it seems she came to focus on John Spreckels as the perfect target for the largest and most daring scam of her life. All this is conjecture, in itself, and would not stand up to the light of day on its own, but follows from many other fine details known for certain, and from minute conjectures that can be more solidly drawn. An example is that of Katie Logan blurting out that her real name is Lizzie, but she quickly catches herself and says that she goes by Kittie or Katie because she likes that name better—probably stammering, the poor airhead, at that moment unable to remember even her fake name.

I believe that Kate Morgan probably learned of some true life dalliance of John Spreckels, and embroidered it to fit her plan. The distance from San Francisco to San Diego would be enough to gain her the breathing space, in that age before rapid transit, to threaten Spreckels, and to collect the hush money and disappear before anyone could come down to investigate. She also knew Spreckels owned the Hotel del Coronado, the most remote of his possessions, on an island off the coast yet. That is why she chose his hotel to stage her crime.

We know that Detroit is mentioned in the travels of Kate and Tom. At one point, she refers to her 'brother' as being Doctor So-and-So of Detroit. It is logical to think she met Lizzie Wyllie either in Detroit, or immediately after Lizzie and John Longfield left Detroit for California—in the latter case, most likely on a train. Lizzie was pregnant—for the second time, again out of wedlock (because Dr. Mertzman was to testify at the Coroner's Inquest that the dead woman was most likely pregnant, that she had borne a child before, and that she was taking extreme measures to induce a miscarriage). It is easy to fit together the pieces logically then. If Kate Morgan could create the impression that a domestic servant or other lover had become pregnant by him—if she could even imply that—and the threat was staged in a locale far removed from San Francisco, then Kate was gambling that Spreckels or his agents would accept some kind of written release in return for hush money.

I mentioned earlier that Katie Logan came from Omaha, Nebraska, which is about fifty miles from Kate's home town of Hamburg, Iowa. It seems that Kate, in training the rather slow Lizzie, had to use aliases and details the poor girl could remember. Thus, 'Katie' was easy to remember as a version of Kate, the experienced name-changer, and Logan was similar to Morgan. She might have drilled Lizzie and helped her to remember her fictitious name—*if you forget, just think of my name,* Kate Morgan probably told her, *and you'll easily remember your name is Katie Logan.* We know from the other pseudonyms that Kate always had a doctor-brother floating around, from some city picked at a whim. This time, the fictitious doctor-brother was going to be Dr. M.C. or M.E. Anderson (Lizzie's aunt Louisa's last name) of Detroit (Lizzie's home town). Kate probably picked a city from her own reference (Omaha) for Katie Logan's home town. There was no doctor-brother for Katie, as far as we know—keeping things simple during the training wheels stage. And when it came to Lottie A. Bernard, one has to suspect that the very name Kate Morgan chose for Lizzie to bear must have some trigger effect on Spreckels. Kate had worked among the wealthy homes of San Francisco, and could easily have heard gossip of any extramarital liaisons John Spreckels might have had with his servants. Kate might even have purchased some telltale letters from a fellow servant who had such an affair with her employer—all guesswork—and this could have been the stack of letters or papers Lottie A. Bernard was burning in her fireplace in Room 302 the day before her death. Maybe Spreckels' real lover was a woman with a name like Charlotte Bernard, as I have it in the dramatization later in this book. A blackmail note from Lottie Bernard, couched in just the right wording, would have gone over the heads of Spreckels' secretaries, but would surely have shot his eyebrows up and sent shivers up and down his spine. We will never know exactly how Kate Morgan planned to pull off her scheme. Most likely, the incriminating letters were all burned in Room 302 on November 28, 1892, and the blackmail message soon after conveniently destroyed by Spreckels' unknown chief of private security.

Kate Morgan did not understand into what a hornet's nest, what a nightmare, she was leading her accomplices. Spreckels was at that moment in Washington, lobbying with the President and Congress, and hardly in a position to respond to a rather absurd threat. Kate would not have realized the power of the institution Spreckels had put together in San Diego. He controlled thousands of lives, thousands of acres of land, many millions of dollars of real estate and capital equipment, and he would need an army of accountants and other functionaries to manage all this *in absentia*. Moreover, Allan Pinkerton (1819-1884) had created a unique detective and spy service. Pinkerton had served Lincoln during the Civil War, and he served many wealthy masters afterward as a strike-breaker and corporate advocate. It would be logical for a family as wealthy as the Speckles to be on intimate terms with such services. Kate Morgan had never really gone up against people of the power and wealth the Spreckels family possessed. John Spreckels was his father's trusted right-hand man, and a brilliant, ruthless businessman in his own right, with predatory instincts—see how he helped Elisha Babcock slide into debt as the economy worsened after 1888, and called the loans when it was clear Babcock could not repay them. Spreckels, although an absentee landlord (he didn't permanently move to San Diego until after the devastating San Francisco Earthquake of 1906), would have protected his San Diego possessions with a formidable array of security and intelligence—what I call the Spreckels Machine.

Kate Morgan saw the opportunity to use a pregnant and desperate Lizzie Wyllie in her scheme to blackmail Spreckels. From events that followed later, I surmise that John Longfield—a ladies' man, though he had several children and was married to a seemingly tolerant and gullible woman—had removed Lizzie from Detroit to dump her off somewhere. By Victorian standards, Lizzie was a totally ruined woman. Even her mother had reached the brink of despair over her daughter.

Kate Morgan brought Lizzie to Los Angeles and trained her in the art of impersonation. She taught her to use a false name—Katie Logan—and to accept short temp assignments (three in the month of October-November 1892 alone)—to get used to pseudonyms and falsifications. At the chosen moment—which happened to be Thanksgiving Day—Kate had Lizzie travel to San Diego to check into the Hotel del Coronado.

Day 0 ½—The Missing Day

Before we go to Day 1, we must address another major part of the mystery—'The Missing Day.' From Los Angeles to San Diego is now, and was then, about a two hour train ride. We know that Lizzie ('Katie Logan') bade the Grants farewell sometime during the daylight hours of Wednesday, November 23, and signed in at the Hotel del Coronado in the afternoon of Thursday, November 24. What did she do during these approximately twenty-four hours? A remarkable and convoluted story surfaced after her death, which opens up a breath-taking explanation.

When we examine the guest register at the Hotel del Coronado for November 24, we see that Lottie A. Bernard signs in as the eighth person on the page, of a total of twelve persons. The ninth person to sign in is one Joseph A. Jones of Boston. Jones is assigned a room on the same floor (the third floor, or top floor, which is a cheaper flight of rooms normally taken by staff and the less well-heeled, because in the era before elevators, first floor rooms were usually the more expensive and convenient). Remarkably, it comes to light in the newspapers after the Coroner's Inquest, that Jones had told an unnamed bellman he had recognized Lottie A. Bernard as a woman he saw having an argument with a man on the train from Denver.

Now consider this. If Lizzie ('Katie Logan'/'Lottie Bernard') traveled from Los Angeles to San Diego, how could she simultaneously be on a train heading west from Denver at that same exact time?

There can really only be one explanation. Lizzie was said to be very anxious during her time in Los Angeles. She was pregnant, and time was running out. The only person in the world who could help her was John Longfield—who she undoubtedly wished would leave his wife and children and marry her, which would explain the papers she was anxious to take care of in Los Angeles (probably having to do with his proposed divorce; just as likely, a ruse planted by Kate Morgan as a carrot to keep Lizzie devoted to her dangerous impersonation). We know that someone—a man—physically walked into a bank in Hamburg, Iowa, and told the bank officer he wanted to extend credit to a woman at the Hotel del Coronado. Presumably, that would have to be John Longfield, posing as G. L. Allen to pull off this feat, since Tom Morgan could not have done it without being recognized.

Now the evidence suggests that John Longfield was not anxious to leave his family. He kept up a correspondence with his wife, in which he claimed to be in Cleveland, looking for work. There is reason to think, however, that John Longfield was having an affair with Kate Morgan by now. A compelling fact is that Kate's husband, Tom Morgan, shows up in autumn 1893—less than a year after his wife's purported death—in his boyhood home in Nebraska, and marries a new bride. Tom Morgan becomes a town constable, a mail carrier, the devoted father of a daughter and lifelong spouse of his new wife, and a deacon in his church. This hardly describes a man who was a cardsharp on trains—which in itself was not a likely possibility anyway, since railroad police and detectives would soon have started recognizing such repeat petty criminals and barring them from the trains. It has been suggested that Tom Morgan never even came along on the Coronado caper, because Kate had abandoned him and run away with a new lover. That seems in keeping with Kate's character. In any event, if John Longfield was having an affair with Kate, and we know he was telling his wife he was in Cleveland, there is every reason to think he would be on a train back to California. It is very likely that he and Kate were stringing poor Lizzie along, judging from Lizzie's actions. Longfield was probably bringing Lizzie's three trunks along (on his way to spend time with Kate Morgan) and had the claim checks in his pocket.

Lizzie somehow found out the love of her life was coming west. She took a train south to Anaheim, transferred to an east-west train to Orange or another station even further east. This would be the train John Longfield was on—and, coincidentally, Joseph A. Jones. The train was coming from Denver, where Jones must have had business, and John may have been traveling on this line from as far east as Cleveland or Hamburg, or both, having accomplished his business—sending his wife letters from General Delivery in Cleveland (she had no idea where her husband was staying), and setting up the credit for Lottie A. Bernard in Hamburg. Kate Morgan had the two men running around the country on errands, helping to set up her ruse, while she stayed close to Lizzie in Los Angeles. Kate was thus stringing John Longfield along, telling him she was going to fix his problem (getting rid of Lizzie), while she and he were both stringing Lizzie along (which reached its breaking point in the argument on the train, and no doubt precipitated Lizzie's growing doubts and her suicide a few days later).

Jones was to tell the bellman that he started becoming aware of a man and a woman—the woman he saw at the Hotel Del, Lottie A. Bernard (Lizzie)—having a heated discussion on the train as the train was approaching the (West) coast. This suggests he was not aware of them before that, and had no idea when she actually boarded the train. She might have done this during the evening of November 23, spent the night shivering in some train station a few hours east of Los Angeles, boarded the train he was on, gone from car to car, found him, and confronted him with a plea to divorce his wife and marry her, since he'd ruined her. Jones describes her tone as 'pleading.' This conjures a heart-rending and pathetic scenario. Jones says that her tone became more and more pleading, and then she repeatedly apologized to the man. The man, however, kept denying whatever she wanted, and finally stormed furiously off the train. Jones then took no further notice of her until he coincidentally spotted her in the lobby of the Hotel del Coronado later that day. The man—John Longfield—disappeared into the crowds with her baggage checks in his pocket, and Lizzie continued on her journey south to her final fate.

We can now roll the film forward to Day One.

Day 1—Thursday, Nov. 24, 1892 (Lottie Bernard Checks In)

It appears that Lottie A. Bernard ('A' as in Anderson, her aunt Louisa's name, and the name of the fictitious Mr. or Dr. M.C. Anderson) checked into the Hotel del Coronado in the afternoon of Thanksgiving Day. We don't know exactly what time she left Los Angeles the previous day, or when the episode on the train happened the next morning, but we know she made at least two stops in San Diego after leaving the train—and it would take several hours for her to reach the Hotel del Coronado, which is located at the far end of Coronado, across the bay from San Diego—so she couldn't have checked in at the Del much before mid-afternoon.

Lottie Bernard (Lizzie) got off the train at the old train station (long ago demolished) near today's Santa Fe Depot on Kettner Street and West Broadway (then D Street).

As her first stop, she went to the baggage depot nearby to claim her three trunks, but was refused because the tickets were (she said) in the pocket of her 'brother' and she had no idea where he was. The clerks refused to turn over the trunks to her without claim checks.

Now she made her second stop. From the baggage depot, she walked several blocks up C Street to the corner of C Street and 4th Street (today's Fourth Avenue), where she spent a short amount of time (for mysterious reasons, to which I think I know the answer) at the Hotel Brewster. It was a novel idea of the 1890s—a hotel designed for businessmen (businesswomen were as yet a thought of the future), clean and efficient in every way. So why not just stay at the Brewster rather than go all the way to the most expensive resort in the area, the Hotel Del? She had little money, and no possessions but the clothes on her body and a little satchel or purse—so why would this doomed and beautiful young woman choose to bypass so many less pricey hotels and rooming houses? Why did she purposefully walk back down to the waterfront, take the ferry across to Coronado, and then take the trolley to the opposite end of the island to the Hotel del Coronado? Why pick the most expensive place in the area, and one located so far away? Because she was on a mission that must be accomplished at that very place, whose owner was the wealthy John Spreckels.

◈ ◈

Why did Lizzie make the detour to the Hotel Brewster? According to eyewitnesses, she inquired there about her 'brother' and his wife, Mr. (Dr.?) and Mrs. Anderson. This fictitious doctor-brother was someone about whom she would repeatedly and anxiously keep asking the clerks at the Hotel Del in days to come.

I believe that there were two reasons for her going to the Hotel Brewster. One was to meet Kate Morgan, who would be hovering out of sight throughout this scenario. Kate Morgan would have already instructed her to refer to her lover as her 'brother,' as Kate was in the habit of referring to her husband and/or lover. It would add dignity and credibility if this 'brother' happened to be an accomplished man of stature and authority—a medical doctor. I believe Kate had lied to Lizzie, and Lizzie expected to meet Kate Morgan and either Tom Morgan or John Longfield at the Hotel Brewster.

The second reason for going to the Brewster was to pick up the medicines she would need to terminate her pregnancy. That much she surely received, perhaps from Kate Morgan directly, or from a desk clerk whom Kate had bribed a dollar to make a discreet handover.

In any case, somehow Kate Morgan had sent a message to Spreckels in San Francisco, telling him she was Charlotte Barnard (or some similar name, semi-disguised as Lottie Bernard) and he had gotten her pregnant. Now, to stay out of his hair, she needed a sum of money to take care of herself and her baby, or there would be trouble for Spreckels. The plan was for her to create a public spectacle to embarrass Spreckels before the world—and what better way than to have a messy, bloody, noisy, panic-inducing miscarriage right in the main lobby of Spreckels' hotel?

That in itself would solve nothing for Kate Morgan—would potentially kill Lizzie, and bring in no money—but the idea was that it wouldn't get to that. The idea was that Spreckels would quickly cave, and that Kate and John and Tom would remove Lizzie to the care of a doctor while they divided the money—how many ways is anyone's guess. Lizzie did not have the brains to think up such a complex scheme, however whacko it certainly was. Kate Morgan did possess the brains and the imagination, but it shows her ruthlessness and her detachment from reality and from human feelings. When Lizzie shot herself, it was out of very human, humane feelings—remorse, and a sense of betrayal. She had remorse not just for what she was doing ("I hardly know that man, I have only heard of him," she writes in a note found after hear death, most likely in reference to the man she was trying to harm, Spreckels). We can infer that she had been pregnant out of wedlock on a previous occasion, that she bore the baby, and that she was forced to give it up for adoption—a great hardship for many women today, but a social death sentence in Victorian times. We know that she was a handful for her mother, Elizabeth, and her loving sister, May. We know that she had to go into exile for a short while with her Aunt Louisa Anderson across the Michigan Panhandle in Grand Rapids, to escape her mother's wrath. We know that John Longfield's later letter to his wife refers to bad feelings between Lizzie and her mother. All of this is to say that, as she neared her suicide, Lizzie felt terrible not only about the blackmail scheme against a man she did not know, who had done her no harm; but also about having disappointed her mother and sister again by getting pregnant with a married man in an openly and irresponsibly flaunted relationship that got Lizzie, John, and sister May all fired from Bin & Hammond; and no doubt about the fact that she was killing (destroying, if you will) her unborn child. Whatever views one takes on abortion, if we put ourselves in the head of this beautiful, and in some ways childlike, woman, we can well suppose that she felt the unborn child was being subjected to the same horrific pain that was beginning to seize Lizzie herself ("she was groaning," one witness said of her. "She appeared to be suffering intensely," said Harry West). The pain of an extramarital pregnancy was nothing new to Lizzie—and something she could not bear to endure again. Nor would Victorian society forgive her. Without marriage to John Longfield, she was a ruined woman, and might as well dramatically throw herself off a cliff. Or shoot herself, as she did.

Lizzie, who arrived in sparkling good health on Thursday, started taking these medicines and her condition rapidly deteriorated until, within a day or two, she could hardly walk or stand by Monday. Dr. Mertzman testified to this effect at the Coroner's Inquest, adding that he was sure she was pregnant, had borne a child before, and that she was taking 'terrible medicines' to induce a miscarriage. Let's examine the ominous signs of what Lizzie was doing (on Kate's instructions).

Among the artifacts found in the dead woman's hotel room was a bottle of pills (most likely laudanum) with instructions "If this does not relieve you, you better send for the doctor" (signed, 'Druggist')."[60]

಄ ಄

From the Hotel Brewster, she makes her way back down to the harbor, across the bay, and across Coronado to the Hotel del Coronado. There, she has the clerk sign her in. At some point, the man who signs in after her (Joseph Jones) recognizes her as the woman he saw arguing and pleading with the angry man on the train near Orange and Anaheim. Then she goes upstairs to Room 302, where she locks the door and prepares to start taking her medicines.

಄ ಄

An interesting question occurs in regard to this scenario. If it is a blackmail plot, and Spreckels is now aware of the threat, we must assume that the Spreckels Machine is in high gear. Spreckels is busy in Washington, so he has people locally hard at work (the Spreckels Machine, my term for the shadowy underside of the official Spreckels Company), blunting this situation as best they can. Now normally, even today, if an attractive young woman arrives to check in out of a clear blue sky at a hotel, traveling alone and without luggage, it is natural for a hotel clerk to at least momentarily think of prostitution if there is something somehow odd or salacious about her behavior on top of the rest. It isn't the first thought, but it hovers in the periphery. If you work at a hotel, there is always a certain small amount of illegal traffic that managers do their best to root out, and which doormen and valets (and shuttle drivers) talk about.

When Elisha Babcock laid out the master plan for Coronado, he stipulated it would be a dry city—with one exception, the bar at the Hotel Del. Coronado was to be a health resort, and this was the time of Kellogg's corn flakes and health nuts and the temperance movement. Also, he most certainly did not wish for his town to become another Stingaree, like the venue across the Bay, from which one could hear distant gunshots, laughter, and screams by day or night.

It seems remarkable that Lottie A. Bernard was allowed to sign in at all—in an era when it was frowned upon for a woman to travel alone.[61] Now this is just gratuitous speculation, but it occurs to me that, maybe, the chief clerk (A.S. Gomer) was tipped off to let her register. What better location to have her, than directly under Spreckels' roof, for his detectives to observe if she was really acting alone (an aggrieved, desperate girl) or if she was a crook aided by accomplices?

Day 2—Friday, Nov. 25, 1892

She starts asking Chief Clerk A.S. Gomer if her 'brother' has left any messages, and mentions the problem about the claim checks and her three trunks—which are still stuck at the baggage depot, and will remain there until they disappear. She tells Gomer that she is expecting her 'brother,' 'Dr. Anderson,' to arrive at any time to take care of her because she is ill. She claims to be suffering from a vague and over-diagnosed contemporary ailment called 'neuralgia' (Gr. *Neuron,* 'tendon, nerve' + *algesis,* 'pain'). There is a more specific modern ailment with this name—an inflamed nerve or tendon—but in Lizzie's time, the word covered a host of psychological and psychosomatic as well as physiological illnesses. The only known cure was to send you to the seashore, so nobody was surprised that a young woman suffering from neuralgia would show up to recuperate at the Hotel Del.

లు ఌ

Day 3—Saturday, Nov. 26, 1892

On the third day at the Hotel del Coronado, real estate agent T. J. Fisher says she came into the hotel drugstore, where he shared an office with the druggist. Fisher says she wandered about 'slowly' and apparently 'in pain.' She asked for medicine to ease her pain (described as 'intense suffering'). Fosdick suggested she consult a doctor, and she told him that her brother, a physician, would be arriving any day. The elusive 'Dr. Anderson' would never show up nor send word. We can be sure the only man she felt so strongly about was John Longfield.

Later in the day, Harry West would rather vaguely remember, she asked him to get her an empty pint bottle and a sponge from the hotel drugstore. This request seems innocent and enigmatic until one really considers what it was about—something I had not yet considered while writing the first edition of this book.

One ancient method of inducing an abortion or a miscarriage was to insert a medically treated sponge, called a pessary, into the vaginal canal as close to the womb as possible. Pessaries, from the Greek *pessos*, 'pebble' or 'stone,' could be used for various other local applications—for example, as a suppository. This procedure for aborting was known as far back as in ancient Egypt. The empty bottle she requested would be for mixing and storing her medicine for repeated applications. She used the sponge as a pessary. The occasional requests for wine or whiskey were as palliatives to ease her pain and discomfort, along with the laudanum she was taking. Bit by bit, as we interpret the minute little known facts that have come down to us, the story begins to swim into focus like a photograph in a fixative bath. What we should carry away from this is a sense of horror at the suffering of this poor, lovely, befuddled woman—and the heartlessness of the people around her, except kind and compliant Harry West and an unnamed housekeeping woman who occasionally helped her.[62]

Day 4—Sunday, Nov. 27, 1892

No activity known. We can surmise that she ate little, and spent most of the time in her room feeling sicker and sicker. She had time to reflect, also, that she was being betrayed. Nevertheless, we know that as shortly before her death as Monday evening she still asked about the elusive Dr. Anderson one last time. But think about this. Compare her behavior on Saturday, when she started the pessary, with her behavior on Monday, when she had difficulty walking. And on Monday, she would already be drinking alcohol in the morning—to ease her acute pain. It is possible we know nothing of her activities Sunday because she may have been in bed, semi-conscious, as her 'terrible medicines' (as Dr. Mertzman called them) started to take hold of her and ravage her—even as it became clear she had been betrayed and abandoned, and had little room for hope. We can only imagine her suffering that day, alone in her room.

Day 5—Monday, Nov. 28, 1892

In the morning on the fifth day, Lottie had Harry West bring her a glass of wine from the bar, and later a whiskey cocktail. She had him bring a pitcher of ice water—she drank these alcoholic beverages early in the day—to dull her pain, we can be sure.

Around noon, she had Harry West dry her hair after she'd fallen in the bath. He would later testify that he found her suffering and groaning a great deal, and sleeping much of the day. He would tell investigators that she seemed to sleep a while, wake up, spend time groaning in pain, and then fall back to sleep. He said she again mentioned her brother, Dr. Anderson, who would soon join her.

Between noon and 1:00 p.m., Harry West and Gomer went to visit her in Room 302 to inquire about her health. Gomer grilled her about her finances. She told Gomer she had stomach cancer, obviously a fib. She also assured him that credit would be available to cover her expense tab. She suggested he telegraph a G. L. Allen in Hamburg, Iowa (Kate Morgan's home town) for the needed funds—and a credit for $25 arrived from a Hamburg bank on Tuesday morning, just after Lottie or Lizzie was found dead.

A great sea storm was approaching, making her room gloomy and cold. She had thus far refused to light the fireplace. Perhaps she was burning up with fever, as the expression goes. During the afternoon, Harry West gave her a few matches, and she began to burn a stack of papers (possibly including letters) in the fireplace. Neither Gomer nor Harry got a good look at what these papers might be.

That afternoon, Lottie went downstairs to the pharmacy. Real estate agent T. J Fisher described her as walking very slowly, and appearing to be in great pain. During their conversation, she indicated she planned to go across the Bay to San Diego, and he warned her against doing so, because of her condition, and the coming storm. Lottie replied that she had to go, and then made a statement that appears somewhat unfocused and out of kilter with already established facts (or fibs).[63] From what Fisher quoted at the Coroner's Inquest, she said that she must make the trip. She said that she forgot her baggage claim [tickets], and that she must go over (the Bay) "to identify my trunks, personally." Earlier, she said she knew where the tickets (checks) were—her brother had taken them when they were separated at Orange the past Thursday. The clerks refused to hand the trunks over on that day, and there is no reason to think that anything had changed since then. It is more likely that Lottie had at least one very different reason [to buy a gun], maybe two [to see someone, like maybe Kate Morgan, conjecturally staying at the Hotel Brewster?], to make what must be an extremely painful and difficult journey, and that she concocted this story to throw him off the trail. There are lots of little bits of evidence like this that Lottie liked to fib, like a somewhat air-headed young girl, and her fibs tended to be somewhat clumsy, like when she told Gomer she was dying of stomach cancer,[64] blurting that out to get rid of him.

Between 4:00 and 5:00 p.m. (there is confusion about whether she was in San Diego as early as 3:00 p.m., or later) Lottie journeyed to downtown San Diego. Crossing the bay, she went to Fifth Avenue and bought a gun and cartridges, as mentioned in Part III.

There is a time, after she left the last known store, when her movements are unaccounted for. Could she have gone back to the Hotel Brewster to seek out Kate Morgan one last time and tell her the show was off, she wanted out, and where was John Longfield? Chances are Kate Morgan understood by then that Spreckels' agents were not about to pay her off, and that she and Longfield had already skipped town.

Lizzie on the other hand, wracked with pain and guilt, may have considered killing Kate Morgan and John Longfield. We'll never know. She made the painful journey back to Coronado because that's where her only possessions were—in that handbag—and because she had no recourse left but to return to where her fate would play out its final act.

At 6:30 p.m., bellman Harry West says he saw Lottie on a hotel veranda overlooking the ocean. It was dark by then, and there was an air of dread and excitement as the atmospheric monster approached. It was the last time Harry would see Lottie alive.

Lottie made one more stop at the front desk to ask Gomer if there was any word from Dr. Anderson. That was between 7:00 and 8:00 p.m., and she was told there had not yet been any word from her 'brother.' This was the last time anyone saw her alive.

People stood on balconies around the Hotel, looking southwest over the Pacific Ocean. They watched in awe as the black clouds of the storm rolled closer, and raged and thundered. Some guests may have requested relocation to the landward side of the Hotel. Nobody heard a gunshot fired, during the night, on the beach just behind the hotel.

Day 6—Tuesday, Nov. 29, 1892 (Body Found)

Electrician David Cone found Lottie's body at 8:20 a.m.. Cone found (my words) a mannequin-like body lying on the concrete steps overlooking the beach, which was not far from the sea in those days. When he realized it was a woman's dead body, he saw that her clothing was all wet, and "the body seemed to have been lying there quite a while; to have been dead quite a while."[65]

ૡ ૱

There is a fine detail here that calls for some remedial conjecture. The next day, at the Coroner's Inquest, witnesses say that there was blood on the steps, along with the large gun. The question is: how could there be blood on the steps when the area, and the body, had been inundated by a violent rain and possibly the thundering surf during the night's storm?

This is an important question because there has circulated some urban lore that she was murdered or that something else happened rather than a straightforward suicide—a hypothesis discounted by official sources, and I concur. A more complex interpretation requires yet more conjecture, so I prefer to navigate the simplest course among the many baffling clues. If she had died in the morning, after the storm, does that somehow open the door to other possibilities? Who knows. Because there was blood on the steps, does this mean that she died after the rain storm? We don't know what time the worst of the rain ended, but we can surmise that, even if the downpour ended between 2:00 and 3:00 a.m. (which Stetson pegged as the time of death), there would have been drizzle for a time. The blood would have been watery, and one finds it hard to imagine this not being mentioned; but then the coroner's inquest does not mention the copious black powder residue that suicide would have left on her hand and face—did the rain wash this away, or was she shot by another person from a distance, with a slightly different-caliber handgun? I don't know. I can only show it is possible she did kill herself during the storm.

Regarding powder residue, it is possible that might have washed away in a severe downpour—which would also have washed any blood away; so how could there be blood on the steps? It's possible that, when she shot herself, she fell backward in something like a sitting position (as Cone attested). The gun had a trigger guard, and would have stayed on her hand until she lay still, and it dropped down a step from her finger. From the impact and entry wound on her right temple, her head was turned slightly to the left, tilted to one side. That meant some amount of blood could not escape from the entry wound (there was no exit wound). Blood clots formed in the entry wound. When Cone found her, he may have slapped her face in a hysterical and unthinking attempt to revive her. The majority of people are right-handed, so that probably makes sense. A right-handed slap to the left cheek might have turned her head to the right (despite rigor mortis). Cone, as we know, ran off as fast as he could to get Gomer, but returned with the gardener for another look, and then the two men were caught up in such a dither that each ran a different way around the hotel to get Gomer. One or more slaps would loosen any blood clots in the entry wound. Cone left, came back with Koeppen, and they both ran off again. Meanwhile, residual blood and fluids could have leaked from the open skull, down the arm, puddling under her finger and around the gun. There was said to be blood 'under' the gun, but that could just as well mean 'around' the gun. This suggests that there no problem between the fact that blood was found, and the fact that there was a rain storm. In other words, I do not see this as ruling out suicide during the storm. While I do not rule out the murder hypothesis, I feel that hypothesis requires a lot more conjectural stretches, and the suicide hypothesis is entirely reasonable.

※ ※

What about the credit from Hamburg, Iowa? It seems likely, for whatever reason—maybe as simple as the fact that she knew the place, or it was convenient for some other reason, like there was a trusted accomplice—Kate Morgan chose that place to establish a credit alibi or cover, that she sent John Longfield to deliver $25 to the bank manager, and explain it was to be sent if someone from California asked for it on behalf of an old school friend's wife. It would have been impossible for anyone from that area (Kate or Tom Morgan) to pull this off, because everyone would have recognized them. It could have been done by telegram, but the bank officer specifically said a man came to see him.

A conjectural scenario to cover all this is that (a) Kate Morgan sent John Longfield to set up the credit scenario for use later, as transpired; (b) John Longfield traveled on to Cleveland to set up a General Delivery address at the main post office to cover his tracks with his wife—note that Cleveland is part of a cluster of cities around Lake Ontario that become important in the story, and it's not far from Hamburg; (c) Kate Morgan and John Longfield had become an item, unbeknownst to Lizzie or probably to Tom, if the latter was still on the scene, and this would motivate John to make the trip back to California to see Kate—as well as deliver Lizzie's three trunks from wherever they had been stashed, and possibly to lie to Lizzie— although he then told Lizzie on the train that he didn't intend to divorce his wife. What he probably told Lizzie was that he would think about it, and that she should think about how rich they were all going to be (after blackmailing Spreckels) and how her pregnancy problem was about to be solved. When Lizzie pressed him, he became angry, and she apologized, but he stormed off the train, forgetting to give her the baggage claim checks. She rode on to San Diego, and tried to redeem the trunks at the baggage terminal. It is not clear whether the baggage claim scene happened before or after her walk to the Hotel Brewster. It would have taken a little time, after the train arrived, to unload the baggage car and wheel loads of suitcases and trunks to the baggage depot.

I do think Lizzie remained convinced he would come to help her at the Hotel Del, under the guise of being her 'brother,' the doctor, for whom she kept anxiously asking at the desk. When she kept pressing him to divorce his wife, he grew angry and stormed off the train, never to see her again.

I mentioned above that it is possible that Tom Morgan and Kate had separated already. The reason we suspect there was yet another man involved is because the testimony from the bank manager in Hamburg, Iowa, suggests there were two men who set up the credit scheme. It is possible that Kate (who was alone when she visited her uncle in Hanford) was at that point alone, and that she somehow encountered John and Lizzie in Detroit and enmeshed them in her scheme. The second man, little more than a phantom, might have been an old friend of Kate's in Hamburg. There is also mention of a 'professional gambler' being in the Hamburg area—but this could be anybody. It is sometimes assumed this was Tom, but there is nothing conclusive.

&

Sometime between 9:30 and 10:00 a.m., on Tuesday, Nov. 29, after the body had been found, Deputy Coroner H. J. Stetson arrived from the mainland with a crew to remove the body. Given the critical juncture a few days hence, when the identification changed from Lizzie Wyllie to Kate Morgan, we wonder how the body was handled, and what changes might have occurred before and after embalming.

Stetson estimated Lottie had been dead about six or seven hours, meaning she shot herself (or was murdered, by some persistent rumors) between 2:00 and 3:00 a.m. That would mean that from about (splitting the difference) 2:30 a.m. to 7:30 a.m., the body lay on the steps for five hours while the storm abated. From the time of discovery to the time Stetson and his crew arrived, about two hours passed—remarkable in that they had to be summoned. There was rudimentary, early telephone service to the mainland from the hotel itself, and there was always the telegraph. Stetson would then gather his men, walk or ride several blocks from the police headquarters on

Fifth Street to the waterfront, and then ride the ferry ("the next boat")[66] across to Coronado. The crossing would take 15 minutes on the steam-powered ferry, or up to 30 minutes rowing, or sailing and tacking, depending on the winds; and we can presume the Bay was still a little rough, in the aftermath of the storm. Stetson and his men would then cross the island, a distance of 1.3 miles to the Hotel del Coronado from the ferry landing, which can be walked in a leisurely twenty to thirty minutes. Stetson's crew took the body to Johnson & Company Mortuary at 907 Sixth Street.

Given the high mortality rate in the Stingaree, in addition to normal coverage for a city of then 16,000 souls, it is likely that a coroner's crew could easily be assembled on short notice—in fact, this segues into a parallel question: how did the Coroner managed to assemble nine jurors for the inquest the next day? And yet another question—if there was a formal inquest, literally a jury trial, why was there no autopsy?

Two hours from the time of notification to the time of removal is a remarkable efficiency, which in itself raises some questions. It makes one wonder if it was an anticipated event. This is not the same as suggesting she may have been murdered. It is quite likely, in the blackmail scenario, the Spreckels Machine had numerous operatives attentively monitoring events surrounding the Beautiful Stranger.

How much did the body deteriorate before it was embalmed at least half a day after her death? We don't know if it was packed in ice, but we can be sure it was embalmed, because she lay in state. The matter of the pierced ears will come up in the days to follow, as the I.D. shifts from Lottie Bernard to Katie Logan to Lizzie Wyllie, and finally to Kate Morgan. This final change was made on the basis of a flimsy matter—the body did not have pierced ears, and neither did Kate Morgan, but Lizzie did. I don't feel this discrepancy is enough to shift the I.D. away from Lizzie. First of all, her mother said she was broke after being fired from her job. She and Longfield had no money. Would she not have pawned her silver earrings? If she had her ears pierced recently, it is possible that the holes would have closed up. If the body lay exposed for hours, and then was packed in sawdust or canvas without benefit of ice, and then embalmed at Johnson Company, what physical deterioration can we expect, particularly in peripheral soft tissue like the ear lobes? Far more important to the identification would be the two small moles on the left cheek, which both the corpse and Lizzie Wyllie had—and Lizzie's mother was bereaved and convinced the dead woman was her daughter.

Day 7—Wednesday Nov. 30, 1892 (Coroner's Inquest)

The next morning, before the Coroner's Inquest, the leading physician and surgeon in town, Dr. B. F. Mertzman, did a half-hour examination of the body. He was not permitted to autopsy her, but he would testify briefly at the inquest. He is undoubtedly the medical authority later quoted off-record in the newspapers as saying she did not have stomach cancer but most likely shot herself "over some love affair." That same medical authority said he felt she had borne a child before, was now pregnant, and was taking 'terrible medicines' to induce a miscarriage.

☙ ❧

In recent times, much has been made of an alleged discrepancy between the caliber of the gun and the caliber of the bullet. Dr. B. F. Mertzman estimates the caliber to be "about .38 or .40." There was no exit wound. The bullet stayed in the brain, despite the considerable caliber of the cartridge, and murder proponents have suggested that a second person (possibly Tom Morgan or, following my presentation, agents of the Spreckels Machine) used a smaller caliber gun, maybe a .38, with a lesser charge of gunpowder. Such arguments are not persuasive at all, in my opinion.

An expert on guns (Mr. Richard Agler; see "Acknowledgement" at front of this volume) told me the gun would have used black powder, and the charge was probably weakened by dampness in the rain. In fact, remembering the discussion of blood on the steps, this expert said (and I have since confirmed by further research) that people who commit suicide by shooting themselves using black powder propellants always have a thick coating of oily black residue in two places—on the shooting hand, and around the entry wound. That means the dead woman should have had significant traces of black powder residue all over her right hand and all over the right side of her head. Strangely, there is no mention of this—which suggests the residue was washed away by rain, and that in turn tends to confirm that she died before the storm ended—which leaves us with the slapping hypothesis to explain the blood on the steps.

Chick testifies he recognizes the gun he sold her by the rust on it, which supports information on the Internet that this particular weapon was essentially a throwaway or a 'suicide special.' This gun was not a brand name or a model, but a generic ('American Bulldog') which itself was a variant on a generic ('Bulldog') copied from a copy of a standard 1887 British Army revolver, the .455 caliber Webley Mark II. First, this army weapon was made commercially available in the United Kingdom as the British Bulldog. A variant across the Channel was called the Belgian Bulldog. The U.S. variant was produced by a number of manufacturers, with a number of calibers, under the name American Bulldog. Compared to most handguns, it was a relatively dainty piece at the standard .32 caliber. The gun sold to Lottie Bernard was a .45 variant, with a grotesquely enlarged and re-engineered five-bullet cylinder that made it seem larger than it was, because the grip and the barrel maintained the same relative smallness as on the .32. Suffice it to say, when the bystander said "She is going to hurt herself with that gun," most likely he echoed the sort of comments usually made in regard to cheap Saturday Night Specials. He was not commenting on her mannerisms, but on the rusty and untrustworthy weapon Chick sold her.

☙ ❧

Stetson testifies that, while examining her room, he found a valise. He also found an envelope she had addressed to *Denman Thompson, The Old Homestead*. This refers to one of the most famous actors of the day, Denman Thompson of New Hampshire. According to a contemporary critic, "Thompson interpreted America to itself in the core persona of the solid New England farmer." Thompson's play is, essentially, about a New England rustic who journeys to a big city, is the victim of many misadventures, and returns happily to the simple and honest country life. It seems Lizzie had seen the great thespian's play, and wanted to write a fan letter while she was sitting in her lonely room at the Hotel Del, waiting for the medicine to wreak its painful changes, and still hoping for a signal from 'Dr. M.C.

Anderson' (Kate? John?) that Spreckels had paid, and that she could get out.

There is another theater reference of interest. It seems the poor, benighted girl left behind an invitation by Louise Leslie Carter and Lillian Russell to the Hotel del Coronado. Carter and Russell were two of the most famous stage actresses of the day. Like all the items surrounding the late Mr. Bernard, each of these items elicits stunned and silent puzzlement in the courtroom. Was the girl hallucinating? Did she concoct fantasies about being asked to this great hotel by two famous actresses? She whiled her time away in fantasies like this, composing dreamy letters from great actresses who, in her imagination, invited her to this famous resort.

❧ ☙

Stetson found a piece of paper on which was written the word Frank four times: *Frank Frank Frank Frank*. Who knows what to make of that? In Chapter 10 of my novel <u>Lethal Journey</u>, I playfully make this a reference to a frequent later visitor to the Hotel Del, none other than L. Frank Baum, the author of *The Wizard of Oz*. While that book was not published until 1900, it is known that Baum came to San Diego and presumably Coronado during the 1890s to scout out health resort possibilities, and the Theosophical Society at Point Loma. I do not positively suggest this was the Frank of whom she wrote. Maybe she'd had an old boyfriend named Frank in Detroit. Maybe he was the first lout who got her pregnant and helped her lose her innocence—clearly, she was terribly traumatized and alone in the growing fog of pain, drugs, fear, remorse, and despair. Whoever Frank was, she obviously wished he were there to comfort her.

❧ ☙

Stetson found another scrap of paper on which she had written: "I merely heard of that man. I do not know him." I take this to be a clear reference to the owner of the Hotel del Coronado, John Spreckels, whose reputation she was helping Kate Morgan besmirch. It sounds like the beginning of a written confession. It sounds as if she is full of remorse at being the vehicle to accuse a man she had never met of making her pregnant. Unlike Kate Morgan—who seems sociopathically incapable of doubt or remorse, and John Longfield not much better ('a rounder,' as the newspapers cited his low reputation around Detroit[67])—Lizzie is really the only actor in this drama with real, human feelings. That makes her situation all the more tragic and pathetic.

※ ※

Stetson mentions another innocent little detail that is yet one more piece of critical evidence. In the room were several embroidered hankies. Some of them clearly had the name Louisa Anderson on them—which was the name of Lizzie Wyllie's aunt in Grand Rapids, where Lizzie fled after her mother discovered Lizzie was once again pregnant out of wedlock, this time by the married John Longfield.

Remarkably, a similar set of hankies, with 'Louisa Anderson' embroidered on them, will shortly appear in a trunk owned by Kate Morgan, at the L.A. Grants' house in Los Angeles, where the pseudonymous Katie Logan worked. More than anything (except Katie Logan blurting out that her name was really Lizzie), the objects in that Los Angeles trunk tie the two women together—we'll get to that shortly.

Somehow, at the Coroner's Inquest, the detail of the hankies got lost in the shuffle, despite the fact that the middle name used by the fictitious Lottie A. Bernard was 'Anderson.'

More stunning is the fact that Stetson stumbles over a name on some faded hankies, clearly embroidered with the last name Anderson; but but he says he can't read the first name—which he says looks like 'Little,' but is almost certainly name Lizzie.

The find of these hankies is one of the most important in the entire case. The hankies in the hotel room point to Lottie Bernard being Lizzie Wyllie. The hankies in Los Angeles tie Kate Morgan and Lizzie Wyllie together. Kate was training Lizzie to be an impersonator, under the name Katie Logan. Kate parked her trunk with Lizzie, because Kate was busy traveling around setting up the caper in Coronado. As part of her manipulation, she had to keep dangling the carrot of John Longfield before Lizzie, which is why the poor girl was running around in Los Angeles during her off-hours, presumably trying to get some sort of papers put together pertaining to the divorce she wanted John to get so he could marry her. She may have confronted Longfield on the train with those very papers—first rather pushy about it, which made him angry, and then pleading and apologetic as she began to realize it would not be so easy for him. Lizzie undoubtedly had a set of her own hankies (and it is possible they were her mother's since they were so faded; maybe 'Little' or 'Lizzie' was actually Elizabeth, the mother, who had a set in common with her sister, Louisa; and Louisa gave poor Lizzie some of her own hankies to cry into while Lizzie was staying with her in Grand Rapids).

Under further questioning, Stetson says that he examined the grate in the room, and found some papers that had burned entirely to ashes. A nightgown hung on a hook. On the mantel were a hat, a bottle, and a penknife. One wonders if that was the bottle she used to imbue her pessary. And where had the sponge gone? Had she finished her doses (the bottle was empty) and thrown the sponge away? Was it still inside her? It was a common contraceptive device, so the doctor might not have mentioned it in court out of Victorian modesty. If the undertakers found it, they might not have thought much of it for the same reason.

Among the other bottles in the room were one with camphor (a topical anesthetic) and alcohol—a considerably quantity of brandy. Lizzie was most likely somewhat inebriated on Sunday as the medicine clawed her in its grip. There were some quinine pills, and a bottle of some kind that had a notice wrapped around it: "If it does not relieve you, you better send for the doctor." The notice was signed "Druggist," without a name or address. This type of medicine was not something you bought in a pharmacy without a prescription and a lot of questions, so this could be one reason for Lizzie's side trip to the Hotel Brewster upon her arrival. And the 'druggist' was probably not a licensed practitioner, but a quack of the same variety who performed back-alley abortions.

The coroner states that the court has received all the testimony it can get, and asks the jury to issue its finding. It is afternoon, and the entire proceeding has taken less than one day. Why was Dr. Mertzman not permitted to do an autopsy? Why were some potentially important witnesses, like Joseph A. Jones of Boston, not subpoenaed? It is not clear that Jones' comment had been passed along to the press by this time. The haste of the proceeding—selecting nine jurors, albeit probably from a ready roll—and the brevity of the inquest suggest that the city, which was heavily in thrall to Spreckels, was in a hurry to get things over with.

It is remarkable that the woman's real identity had not been established by the end of the day and this hasty trial. Granted, they thought she really was Mrs. Lottie A. Bernard, whose husband or whose doctor brother were expected to soon inquire after her. Still, without knowing anything about her, it is difficult to see that they could firmly discount murder and opt for suicide, when there was no clear motive.

And then, the official transcript of the inquest is 'lost' for some time, and then restored with a handwritten note by a city clerk to the effect that it was misplaced.[68] By modern standards, the chain of property on the document was thus lost, and it could potentially have been tampered with. It has been suggested that perhaps the official transcript was 'held up' until her identity could be firmly established, but government entities do not 'misplace' an official transcript for such reasons.

Finally, also, the way the I.D. of the body would soon change several times on the flimsiest of grounds, ultimately to a woman (Kate Morgan) whose character was questionable, makes one wonder if there was not some manipulation going on by the Spreckels Machine to cast aspersion on the character of the (we presume) blackmailers (Tom and Kate Morgan) in a further effort to inoculate John Spreckels' good name. The County issued a death certificate, naming her as 'Lottie A. Bernard, a.k.a. Kate Morgan,' and—remarkably—gave the wrong date for her death. The given date is Monday, November 28, when the Coroner stated she died in the early hours of Tuesday, November 29. If they misplaced the transcript and then found it again, and if they got the date of death wrong, then what other blunders (or cover-ups) are there in this case?

Newspaper Accounts Dec. 1-Dec. 14

Day 8—Thursday, Dec. 1, 1892

Newspapers are beginning to wonder if there was something more to the relationship between Lottie Bernard and her purported 'brother.' If he were truly her brother, the reasoning went, he would have contacted authorities. News of her suicide was telegraphed all over the country, avidly followed by the Yellow Press. Speculation was immediately rife (couched in Victorian circumlocution) that the mysterious 'brother' was her lover—the man who ruined, betrayed, and abandoned her. This scent of scandal is known to have promoted the story to overnight national sensation in the Yellow Press. Press reports also speculated that her lover was 'highly placed.'

A leading medical authority (presumably Dr. B. F. Mertzman) affirms that she seemed healthy, and he dismisses as 'nonsense' the idea that she was so near death from cancer that doctors had pronounced her case hopeless. Mertzman states "The indications are that she has already borne a child, and was [pregnant] when she died, but this cannot be definitely proven without a post-mortem examination."[69] In the official haste to close the case, in a city effectively owned by John Spreckels, and lacking much of a police department, there was inordinate haste to get the coroner's inquest over and done. The doctor opines that she shot herself over "some love affair." He references her three-hour horseback ride with Charles Stevens on her first day at the Hotel del Coronado. Young Charlie said the woman was in good spirits, but seemed troubled.

Now we see the first mention that Lottie stopped at the Hotel Brewster after arriving in San Diego but before venturing to Coronado and signing in at the Hotel del Coronado. At the Brewster, Lottie asked about the arrival of her presumable brother and his wife, Mr. and Mrs. Anderson." Nobody by that name had signed in at the Brewster. Interestingly, she apparently did not refer to her 'brother' as Dr. Anderson, if this account is correct, but as Mr. Anderson.

Newspaper stories are beginning to question her identity, citing 'contradictory stories told by the victim' and the many contradictions and inconsistencies of the entire episode.

Day 9—Friday, Dec. 2, 1892

Newspapers speculate with increasing fervor that "the beautiful and mysterious stranger" killed herself over "love-trouble." A bellman reports the comments of Joseph E. (or A.) Jones regarding the argument on the train. The papers report that people feel her trip to San Diego was 'an escapade,' because she arrived without baggage. [Those people may not have been aware of the three trunks she said were being kept for her at the baggage office of the train terminal.] People noted the familiarity with which she spoke of Los Angeles hotels, which made it sound as if she had traveled much.

Employees at the Hotel del Coronado made comments indicating that the woman had been well-dressed and elegant, unlike the unattractive features associated with Kate Morgan from the photos that would soon be found in Kate's trunk in Los Angeles.

As the days are going by, doubts and loose ends proliferate. I believe it is logical to assume that the Spreckels Machine was not passive. Logically, having deflected the main element of the threat, now that Lottie was dead and her companions had disappeared, the Spreckels Machine continued manipulating behind the scenes. Remember, these people were nation-builders. They had, in effect, taken over the sovereign nation of Hawai'i by manipulating its royal cabinet, and now they were at war with a rival corporate gang set upon toppling them and their monarch, and putting Dole's faction in charge of the nation. Although the Spreckels family were shaken, and were about to lose Hawai'i, they still had vast resources and political power. Claus Spreckels, even as he was conducting shuttle diplomacy in Honolulu, and had his son John lobbying the President and Congress in Washington, was already plotting an alternative course, just in case. Spreckels had been experimenting in California with sugar beets since the 1870s. Now he easily switched sugar production to the area around Monterey, California, in the Salinas Valley.[70] Instead of sugar cane, his raw material became sugar beets. He would be fully operational by 1899, and the tiny town of Spreckels would be named after him. Immediately, his factory would be the world's largest refiner of sugar beets. These were people who had enormous resources, tens of thousands of employees in many places, and a vested interest in preventing John Spreckels' name from being besmirched by petty crooks at this critical time. For these reasons, I think it is reasonable to look for the unseen and dark hand of the Spreckels Machine in *l'affaire Lottie*.

Day 10—Saturday, Dec. 3, 1892

The identity shifts toward Lizzie, while the Hamburg, Iowa, bank and G. L. Allen come into play. Police confirm there are three trunks at the D Street baggage depot, which had shipped from Omaha, via Denver—Denver being, we recall, the point of departure of James Jones, who told a bellman he had seen Lottie in an argument with a well-dressed man on that train. The trunks could not be opened without authorization from higher-ups in the baggage hierarchy.

Take note, again, that the Spreckels Company controlled much of Greater San Diego, including Coronado. There were actually two companies in San Diego with the Spreckels name, one run by John Spreckels, the other owned by John's brother Adolph, who would gain notoriety as a young man of 27, when in 1884, in public view, he shot the publisher of The San Francisco Chronicle over an editorial critical of Claus Spreckels. The publisher, Michael de Young, lived, and Spreckels was acquitted after pleading insanity. Adolph would die in 1924 from pneumonia, after being weakened by decades of syphilis. His flamboyant wife, Alma, was famous for both her philanthropies and her extravagant lifestyle.[71] Spreckels is a sacred name in both San Francisco and San Diego, but the reality is that they were a family of real people, endowed with greatness on one hand, and equally grandiose foible on the other hand. So it is not a leap of imagination to suppose that there was a dark side to it all. The fact that John Spreckels owned the major newspapers in San Diego, and lavished the city with endowments, ensured that his legacy would be a bright one. In this book, we want to dispassionately look at the nimbus of mystery surrounding the Lottie A. Bernard affair, and try to make sense of the muddle—including a recognition that John Spreckels had a vested interest in covering his good name. The fact that Lottie Bernard was allowed to check into the Hotel Del in the first place, despite her traveling alone and without baggage, showing up as a dusty and attractive young woman without visible means, could have aroused enough suspicion to call for a check of her means and connections, and a refusal to allow her to check in. The haste with which the Coroner's men arrived, and the haste of the jury trial the next day, and its inconclusive result, suggest that the Spreckels Machine that virtually ran the city wanted this affair put behind. The 'loss' and 'rediscovery' of the official transcript of the jury trial opens the possibility that the permanent record was tampered with by the Spreckels Machine. It would probably have been enough to let it go there. However, just in case the blackmail story did leak, it was an effective touch to make the dead woman be Kate Morgan. She was essentially an unsavory person, who was now cast in the Yellow Press (with input from the Spreckels Machine, funded by the Spreckels fortune) as a grifter and a gambler's wife. There is no doubt that the Yellow Press had a lurid momentum all its own, but it is quite possible that the Spreckels Machine seeded the kernels of various scandalous threads to obfuscate the issue as well as set up a pair of villains at the heart of the story. As the record tells us, sources both anonymous and named (e.g., Swarts) popped up out of nowhere and chimed in with distracting leads that create ambiguities. As it turned out, the underlying story was effectively squelched, and the result is the tantalizing and salacious mystery story we are endeavoring to finally resolve today, in this book, after more than a century of mythology and a world-class ghost story.

Day 11—Sunday, Dec. 4, 1892

The San Diego Union identifies the dead woman as Lizzie Wyllie of Detroit, and we learn that Lizzie and May had worked for Binn & Hammond in Detroit, where Lizzie had an affair with her foreman, and both sisters and John Longfield had been fired.

The Los Angeles Herald reports[72] that Mrs. Elizabeth Wyllie of Detroit positively identified the body as her daughter's, based on pictures and descriptions sent to her from San Diego. Among the effects were jewelry, which arouses our curiosity. Elizabeth Wyllie stated Longfield and her daughter were broke when they fled Detroit. I have guessed that Lizzie may have sold her silver earrings. It is possible that Kate Morgan bribed Lizzie with jewelry and clothes, but that is pure speculation. However, Mrs. Wyllie provides us with a substantial timeline for her daughter's activities. We know she went to stay with her Aunt Louisa, whose hankies showed up in Kate Morgan's trunk in Los Angeles. The reason for this follows from Mertzman's opinion that the dead woman had borne a child before. In the family crisis of 1892, Lizzie and her mother were at loggerheads. Elizabeth was obviously upset by Lizzie's affair which had led to the firing. However, since Lizzie had been pregnant before, and never married, this opens up a whole new scenario that is universal in nature, a tragedy that has recurred for countless young women throughout human history. She had gotten pregnant out of wedlock, and we know she bore the child—we have Mertzman's authority on that. That means she most likely gave the child up for adoption, which is biologically and psychologically very traumatic for an already shaken young woman. The hormonal changes in the young mother's body are all-pervasive, and continue past delivery in the form of lactation and other changes. When the child is then abruptly torn from her, in the midst of a vast societal wave of disapproval, the young woman is traumatized. There is no mention of a father in the Wyllie household, which suggests the possibility of previous troubles (either Mr. Wyllie left his family, or perhaps he died, but there is no way this could not also have been traumatic). When Lizzie apparently again stumbled into the same error, we can understand how distraught Mrs. Wyllie would have been—enough to cause Lizzie to flee into exile with her aunt. It is undoubtedly this rift that John Longfield's letter refers to when he claims Lizzie is in Toronto and wants nothing more to do with her family. That is in a letter he sent from Cleveland to his wife. This indirectly and purposefully telegraphed a message to Mrs. Wyllie. This weird and unbelievable message also reached a Yellow Press eager for scandal.

The San Francisco Chronicle reports:[73] "Driven almost to distraction by worry and shame, Mrs. Elizabeth Wyllie of Detroit admitted this afternoon that it was her daughter Lizzie who was found dead..."

Mrs. Wyllie says her daughter eloped a month earlier with [John G. Longfield] of Detroit. Neither Lizzie nor Longfield had any money. She pins the date of Lizzie's disappearance at "five weeks ago last Monday [on or about Monday, Oct. 24] she went...downtown on an errand. She never returned." She had apparently said she was going to look for work, which one would expect on a Monday, and did not go alone. We need not take the hiatus as exactly thirty days, because it changes with plasticity from a month to five weeks, and might be a little longer. In Mrs. Wyllie's distraught frame of mind, exactitude would not be likely.

The article reports a somewhat disjointed story that on the Saturday before Lizzie's disappearance, a man called at the Wyllie house one afternoon to visit with Lizzie and her family, and to tell everyone goodbye. He said he was going south, likely to California, and he 'jocosely' told May Wyllie "I will be picking roses in California while your feet are freezing in Detroit." That man cannot have been Longfield, because he would have been thrown on his ear by May and Mrs. Wyllie. Much of Detroit probably knew the story of the three being fired from the bookbindery, except maybe Longfield's patient and gullible wife. More likely, the visitor was just an acquaintance of May Wyllie, and the reference to California was merely coincidence. However, the tone of the paper makes it sound as if there is more to the story (the man "also disappeared")[74] so there is a remote possibility it might have been the other man in the story—a lover or accomplice of Kate's who also appeared at the bank in Hamburg to help set up the $25 credit.

Mrs. Wyllie is described as 'prepossessing' and Lizzie was 'an attractive girl.' Kate Morgan's unappealing photograph suggested to contemporaries that she was not the same person, as we'll see.

Apparently the name L. Anderson Bernard reminded Mrs. Wyllie of her lost daughter. The initial L would stand for Lizzie, while Anderson is the name of her married sister in Grand Rapids. Just as the invented name must have sent signals to Spreckels, so it sent signals to Mrs. Wyllie in her mother's instinct that the worst had come to pass.

Regarding her receipt of the telegram describing the dead woman in Coronado, the article reads: "Mrs. Wyllie read the telegram as far as the mention of the two moles and then the paper dropped from her hands. 'My Lizzie; it's my Lizzie,' she sobbed repeatedly. 'What will become of me?' Not a word of reproach came from her lips upon the name of the dead girl." We of today must give enormous credence to this woman's belief that the dead person was her daughter.

We can construct a loose timeline for events from the clues here. Lizzie was in Los Angeles in October and November, and finally in San Diego during late November. Nobody noticed or mentioned she was pregnant, so she was probably not past the middle of her term. That means she was less than four or five months pregnant (at most). In turn, that suggests she became pregnant in either July or August. She would have noticed a missed period in, let's say, September, and at some point maybe some morning sickness. Having had a child before, the symptoms would be quite unmistakable to her. She would have noticed a second missed period in October. That was approximately the time when she, May, and Longfield were all fired from their jobs. It is possible that Lizzie (just before being fired) both logically argued with Longfield from the desperate situation in which she found herself, and emotionally harangued him because of strong hormonal surges. One can imagine the scandal and titillation that disrupted the strict Victorian work ethic, perhaps with all three persons storming back and forth with accusations, denials, demands, and angry refusals, and in the end they were all sacked.

So again…if Lizzie had been pregnant out of wedlock before, by her own irresponsibility, and had to give the child up for adoption, this would have been traumatic for her, as well as for her mother and sister. Mrs. Wyllie could not have failed to notice the signs that Lizzie was pregnant again. Lizzie took off for at least a week or two to stay with her Aunt Louisa on the other side of the Michigan peninsula. Mrs. Wyllie was no doubt on her war horse, and Longfield was setting up his own alibi in Cleveland or elsewhere, looking for work out of town and out of his wife's reach. Lizzie had a cooling off period, during which she probably cried a great deal, and Aunt Louisa gave her a stack of hankies to dry her tears. This is how Lizzie ended up with two sets of hankies—some embroidered Lizzie Anderson, others Louisa Anderson. Deputy Coroner Stetson found the Lizzie hankies in Room 302 at the Del after her death, while Los Angeles Police found the Louisa hankies in the trunk from the L.A. Grants' house where Katie Logan had worked.

Day 12—Monday, Dec. 5, 1892

As the body lay in state in San Diego, the bank president in Hamburg, Iowa telegraphed to say he thought Mrs. Bernard's husband was named John. He had personally never met this John. Can this be a reference to John Longfield? Did Longfield or someone interacting with him make a slip of the tongue and give his real name, much as Lizzie blurted out hers in Los Angeles? It seems that the only really talented liar among the conspirators was Kate Morgan.

Day 13—Tuesday, Dec. 6, 1892

The San Diego Union claims[75] that it is now for certain that the dead girl is 'pretty Lizzie Wyllie' of Detroit.

Speculation has it that "Longfield was at Hamburg under an assumed name, and sent Lizzie the $25. As I have assumed here, the press back in 1892 already fastened on the theory that John Longfield was still in the picture. It seems fairly clear that he really wanted to get back to his wife and children, or he would not have continued the charade of searching for work in Cleveland. It almost has to be that Kate Morgan was stringing him along, in order to dangle him as a carrot before Lizzie. Kate had to get Lizzie to stay with the program, both at the L. A. Grants' and in Coronado. We know that Lizzie was under considerable duress (e.g., she was anxious to get papers signed in Los Angeles; she was unhappy about her husband, a gambler whose whereabouts she didn't know; and in Coronado she kept asking about her 'brother,' who could be none other than John Longfield, upon whom her life and her future hung, not to mention the fate of her unborn child).[76] To keep the attention of a sporting fellow like Longfield, who had been reckless enough to gamble his family and his job, which he lost, amid a reputation for unsavory activities, Kate Morgan had only two weapons (or carrots) in her arsenal. The first was the promise of great wealth to flow from her scheme against John Spreckels. The second was her undoubtedly equine sexual appetite, which obviously captivated John Longfield. I think Longfield went back East at least twice—the first time, to retrieve Lizzie's trunks and to plant the $25 credit in Hamburg; later, to pick up his job hunting charade, placate his wife from afar, and plant the disinformation his manipulative lover Kate Morgan wanted to target at Elizabeth Wyllie (that she would never see her daughter again, not because she lay dead in San Diego, but because somehow her pregnancy, insolvency, and lack of work skills or references had been solved, and she was living a life of bliss in Toronto—utterly absurd). When Lizzie met John on the train from Denver, he was no doubt returning from the East, with her trunks on board. He had no intention of seeing Lizzie, and was surprised when she boarded the train. Longfield's goal was to rejoin Kate Morgan and receive his rewards. In the heat of his disavowal of Lizzie, he stormed off the train and forgot to give her the three baggage claim checks.

                              ❧

The San Francisco Chronicle reports[77] that staff at the Hotel del Coronado were impressed with the charm, education, and class of the woman who died at the hotel. They feel her knowledge of the fine hotels of San Francisco and Los Angeles could not be forthcoming from a factory girl only recently run away from Detroit.

In a separate article, the same paper reports that Mrs. Longfield sent her husband a letter in Cleveland on Saturday [Dec. 3]. As noted in the previous passages, John Longfield at this point was enamored of Kate Morgan, and would do anything for her; hence, the absurd letter saying Lizzie was alive and well in Toronto (across Lake Ontario from Detroit) and never wanted to see or contact her loving mother and sister again. This spurious letter alone puts a huge and irreparable crack into the entire mythos of the Kate Morgan saga as it has been commonly received.

Day 14—Wednesday, Dec. 7, 1892

The San Diego Union reports[78] that the undertaker has sent a photograph of the dead woman's face to Mrs. Wyllie in Detroit.

The mortuary noted the discrepancy that Lizzie had pierced ears, whereas the corpse did not.

The handkerchiefs did not read 'Lottie Anderson,' as previously reported, but 'Louisa Anderson'—the exact name of Lizzie's aunt in Grand Rapids, Michigan. This is no coincidence.

The article mentions that a telegram had come from [sender not named] the previous day, Dec. 6, swinging the weight back into the Bernard camp. Allegedly, a professional gambler named L. A. Bernard had recently come through Hamburg. It is remarkable that this man, who was for a time thought to be the deceased's husband, shared the same initials with his wife. Could they both be L. A. Bernard? The papers become entangled in the contradictions of this L.A. Bernard/G.L. Allen story, but the simple answer would be that an unknown outsider [Longfield?] posing as L. A. Bernard came to town, spoke with the bank manager (while accidentally blurting out his name was John), and set up the $25 credit with help from G. L. Allen (who may have been a real resident of the area). The bottom line to it is that the Hamburg bank reference would have lent credibility to Lottie A. Bernard's machinations in Coronado, had she not been dead by the time the money arrived. It seems quite possible that the Spreckels Machine were spreading rumors via the Yellow Press to set up the discredited Morgans as villains, just in case the true story of the blackmail were to leak out. Spreckels' agents clearly built a powerful defensive position, now that their nemesis was dead; its effectiveness is evident from history, and the fact that even in the twenty-first century, the smokescreen ghost story survives stronger than ever (a good marketing play for the local tourist trade). Spreckels owned the major newspapers in San Diego, *The San Diego Union* and *The Herald-Tribune*, which had the lead for most of the time in how this story was fed to national news media. These two papers had boots on the ground, and reporting resources in place, to do legwork no other paper could do, even assuming *The Los Angeles Times*, let's say, had sent a reporter down the coast for a few days.

❧⚜

The San Francisco Chronicle opines that Miss Lizzie Wyllie of Detroit and Mrs. L. Anderson Bernard "were not the same person. The Wyllie girl is alive and well in Toronto and Mrs. Bernard is supposed to have been the wife of a Hamburg, Iowa gambler..." and "...As he promised in his dispatch of yesterday, Longfield, whose name has been associated with Miss Wyllie's disappearance, enclosed to his wife a letter from Miss Wyllie, dated Toronto, in which she says that she is not coming home... and indicates that Lizzie left home on account of trouble with her family."[79] So there we have it, again—a transparent ruse, but *cui bono*?

Is it Kate Morgan, working through John Longfield, to deflect attention from herself and onto the unidentified dead woman (Lizzie)? Or is it the Spreckels Machine, continuing to deflect attention away from the discarded Lizzie identification, to further bolster the Kate Morgan schema? The County Coroner's finding is that the dead woman is 'Lottie Anderson Bernard, a.k.a. Kate Morgan' once the 'lost' official transcript has been 'recovered' by clerk W. W. Whitson. [Again, if the county's intention had been to wait for release until the dead woman's identity was certain, they would not have 'lost' or 'misplaced' the document for that purpose, as has been suggested. They would have stated: "We are withholding release of the official transcript, pending final certainty about the dead woman's identity."]

If Kate Morgan were behind the letter, one benefit to her would be if she were to actually assume the dead girl's identity. This seems like a stretch, until we consider that aliases were Kate Morgan's stock in trade. In any case, it would benefit her if the dead woman were confirmed to be Kate Morgan, since her name had been dragged through the mud nationally and would be of no further use to her. Kate Morgan, as such, was ruined. She would have to assume an entirely new identity—but that was one of her major talents.

Day 15—Thursday, Dec. 8, 1892

The San Diego Union reports[80] that, based on the issue of the pierced ears, the dead woman was not Lizzie Wyllie. Lizzie had pierced ears and wore silver earrings, while the dead woman's ears were not pierced. As I have elaborated in the discussion of the pierced earlobes versus twin moles on the left cheek (see Nov. 29 in *Part IV: Solved!*), the twin moles must win out over the pierced earlobes. She was Lizzie, not Kate.

The only halfway viable story at this point is that told by G. L. Allen of Hamburg, Iowa. Allen says he was a schoolmate of a gambler named L. A. Bernard, whose wife lay ill in California. At her request [Gomer's] he wired $25 credit, without ever having met her. The San Diego papers, however, tend to be suspicious of Allen and not believe his story because of details that in themselves are convoluted and dubious. Odd, too, is the fact that then both husband and wife would have the same initials—LAB. Sounds like two imaginary rabbits pulled from the same cocked hat.

A Mrs. Florence S. Howard, of Orange, California, writes that the dead woman is one Josie Brown, 24, of Detroit—another of Kate Morgan's many aliases.

ஒ~ஒ

A new theory now raises its head, that the dead woman was the missing Katie Logan of Los Angeles. *The Los Angeles Times* reports[81] that "young woman's trunk and baggage are...at Mrs. [L.A.] Grant's, No. 917 South Hill Street, where she was last seen. When she left, on the 23rd...she stated that she would be back in time for Thanksgiving dinner, but not a word has been heard from her since." The story relates that she arrived from Omaha about two months earlier [September or October]. She said her husband was a gambler, and she did not know what had become of him. She applied at several employment agencies. She first found work as a domestic at the R. M. Widneys', and then at the T. H. Hughes'. Lastly, she found employment at the L. A. Grants'.

The day before she left Los Angeles, she was anxious to get some papers signed, and appeared to be very worried about something. Those papers most likely had something to do with her campaign to help John Longfield divorce his wife and marry Lizzie.

She wore the ring and the black underclothes described as being on the body found in Coronado. She had two moles on her left cheek.

"She told several persons that her name was Lizzie, but that she liked the name of Kittie better, and that was the reason she adopted it."

So, newspapers are now leaning toward the theory that Lottie A. Bernard was really a domestic named Katie Logan, who had disappeared from Los Angeles the day before Lottie A. Bernard appeared in Coronado. The descriptions of the two women ("attractive," etc.) match, and we note again that 'Katie Logan' blurted out that her real name was Lizzie. We know that Lizzie came from Detroit, but Katie Logan was "well posted" in San Francisco, and knew all about the public places and the hotels, which shows she must have lived there—in other words, Kate Morgan had grilled her well on the long train ride from Detroit to Los Angeles. Lizzie, who—unlike Kate Morgan—was attractive and a stylish dresser, would easily have passed for an urbane and sophisticated woman with a little prepping. Witnesses said Katie Logan was "fairly well educated" and had traveled much, since her husband was a gambler.

Day 16—Friday, Dec. 9, 1892

The San Diego Union reports[82] that the dead woman is still unidentified. The feeling now is that she was not Lizzie Wyllie, who is said to be living with her lover John G. Longfield in Ontario, Canada. She is now thought to be the wife of Iowa gambler L. A. Bernard.

Actually, at this moment in time, as the Lottie A. Bernard and Lizzie personas fade from popular attention, three new personas are in play—Katie Logan, Josie Brown, and Mrs. L. A. Bernard (wife of L.A. Bernard, somewhat absurdly). But the game of identities is moving to its final gambit: Kate Morgan.

Los Angeles police open Katie Logan's trunk and find a number of artifacts. The trunk contains objects and papers belonging primarily to Kate Morgan, but also the Louisa Anderson hankies that could only have come from Lizzie Wyllie's aunt in Grand Rapids.

May we suppose that Kate Morgan, in order to keep her muddled understudy straight on names, gave her her own name (Katie, as in Katie Logan, from Kate Morgan) in the hope she wouldn't blurt out that her name was Lizzie, but she preferred to go by Kitty…er, make that Katie?

The trunk also contained a tin box marked 'Louise' or 'Louisa.'[83] There again is Lizzie's Aunt Louisa.

There are a number of photos, locks of hair, etc. all probably from Kate Morgan's family. Oddly, on the backs of several photos, names had been "carefully erased."

A letter from W. J. [W.T.] Farmer, Hanford, recommended Mrs. Morgan as an honorable and trustworthy woman. I would suggest that Kate Morgan made a forgery of this letter, addressed to Katie Logan, and had Lizzie use that copy to gain her first temp job in Los Angeles. This was her training period for the caper in Coronado a month later.

The trunk contained the cards of several ladies and their addresses, where most likely Kate Morgan [Katie Logan] had worked: Mrs. J. H. McDonough of San Rafael; Mrs. M. R. Abbott of San Francisco; and Mrs. Ottinger of San Francisco. I would suggest that Kate

Morgan spent some time working under who knows what fake name in San Francisco. There is no evidence she ever worked in the Spreckels household, but she would have heard stories from women who had, and quite possibly met a woman who had had an affair with Spreckels and had a packet of love letters—or the whole thing may have been at yet more of a remove—for example, a servant might have come across a packet of love letters while working at the Spreckels home, and stolen them for a lark—until Kate Morgan got her mitts on them and hatched a blackmail scheme.

The reporter questions whether the 'cabinet size photo' of a rather plain, even gross Mrs. Morgan could match the description of the 'Beautiful Stranger.' Whatever her sexual prowess that enslaved the already randy John Longfield, Kate Morgan and the dead woman were not the same person. Nevertheless, the identification now became the final one that appeared on the death certificate and would remain attached to the story until the 21st Century: Kate Morgan.

Day 17—Saturday, Dec. 10, 1892

The San Diego Union throws doubt on the Kate Morgan identification, affirming that the photograph of Mrs. Morgan in Los Angeles cannot fit the description of the Coronado suicide. The paper opines that the contents of the trunk—in which all names, addresses, and other personal information had been destroyed—proved that she wanted to conceal her identity.[84] How very much is the devious and scheming hand of Kate Morgan evident in all this!

Day 18—Sunday, Dec. 11, 1892

The San Diego Union reports[85] that a Mr. A. D. Swarts of Los Angeles had contacted the coroner's office in San Diego to affirm the Kate Morgan identification. Mr. Swarts may be on the level, or he may be a plant of the Spreckels Machine, which has an interest in tarnishing the dead woman's reputation to further defuse the threat to John Spreckels.

The three trunks at the San Diego baggage depot (image: Grand Union depot, demolished 1914, replaced by Santa Fe Depot) have been claimed "by the owners" and this removes "any remaining doubt" that the dead woman was Mrs. Kate Morgan. Indeed, John Spreckels probably did not own the baggage depot outright, or Lizzie's three trunks would already have disappeared. Most likely the Santa Fe Railroad owned the depot, and was under injunction by local police to leave the trunks locked until there could be a legal writ. For local authorities to open the trunks—and find a trail of effects leading backward to Lizzie and Detroit—would have opened the possibility of reviving elements of Kate Morgan's blackmail scheme, thereby putting John Spreckels once again at risk. The three trunks were a loose end. It's possible that Kate Morgan got the claim checks from John, and paid a man with a donkey cart to pick them up so they could be disposed of—burned, thrown into the ocean, buried in a distant canyon. More likely, the Spreckels Machine created some fake checks and hauled the trunks off, again for disposal. Likewise, the telegram or letter, or however else Kate communicated the Lottie A. Bernard threat to John Spreckels, ended up in oblivion. The end result is that history has been handed an enigmatic and meaningless Swiss cheese of disjointed clues pointing to a supposedly disreputable couple of petty criminals from Iowa, who cheated card players on trains…and a ghost story that lives on in opaque mystery at the Hotel del Coronado.

Day 19—Monday, Dec. 12, 1892

The San Diego Union reports[86] that Kate's grandfather, Joe Chandler, of Riverton, Iowa, sent a telegram to the undertaker, Johnson & Company of San Diego. "Your telegram received regarding Kate Morgan, nee Farmer. Bury her and send me statement.—J. W. Chandler." It is clear Mr. Chandler was at the end of his rope with his niece, and with good reason. Nobody would be in a better position than Chandler to know what a dark spirit she really was. Although Kate's relatives and acquaintances concurred that she was definitely not the type to commit suicide, the world now accepts the story that the dead woman was Kate Morgan. Nobody even raises the issue that the owner of the Hotel del Coronado was John Spreckels, and that there actually might be a reasonable explanation, however far-fetched.

Day 20—Tuesday, Dec. 13, 1892

No news.

Day 21—Wednesday, Dec. 14, 1892 (Funeral and Burial)

After the funeral, police finally hear from Kate's uncle in Hanford, W. T. Farmer, who says Kate had no cause for suicide. Farmer implies that, if the body was indeed hers (so there is still doubt), something else caused her death. He wrote that her husband, Thomas E. Morgan (Tom Morgan) was traveling on business for a manufacturing company, and his home was in Hamburg, Iowa. Farmer knew them for many years, and protested he did not believe Kate Morgan would have committed suicide—so there must be a mistake about the identity pinned on the corpse. The reporter (employed by *The San Diego Union*, one of John Spreckels' newspapers) presses his conviction that it was Kate Morgan, and that she did commit suicide. The reporter does (conveniently) allow that a number of mysteries about the case may never be answered.

Part V. Lottiepedia

(Concordance A-Z)

Guide to the Concordance:

This alphabetic concordance is an encyclopedic reference for some of the salient people, places, and topics in my book. My principal source is the Hotel del Coronado's official and well-researched Heritage Department book (Beautiful Stranger: The Ghost of Kate Morgan and the Hotel del Coronado, ISBN 091625173X and ISBN 9780916251737, edition of 2002, available in bookstores and online). Usually, I reference at least the first page ('[page number]') on which a word occurs, but some words occur several times in the book. To really understand my conjecture in full, please read both my book and the Hotel Del's official book, and see the multitude of clues buried in plain sight in the latter. The hotel's book, however, does not offer a sufficient contextual framework of events beyond the Lottie A. Bernard story, showing the connections with Spreckels and the Hawai'ian monarchy, among the many contemporaneous factors so important to the story. I frequently use the acronym LAB (Lottie Anderson Bernard) in reference to the woman who died. Page numbers for Beautiful Stranger (HD for Heritage Department or Hotel Del) may be accompanied by closer reference for either Upper Left, Middle Left, Lower Left, Upper Right, Middle Right, or Lower Right—e.g., [HD63UL] would mean 'Heritage Dept. page 63 upper left;' similarly: [HD5ML] [HD9LL] [HD13MR] [HD22UR] [HD79LR]. References within this book (Dead Move: Kate Morgan and the Haunting Mystery of Coronado, Fourth Edition) are noted [DM], followed by a page number if practicable.

Anderson:

Lizzie's aunt in Grand Rapids was Louisa Anderson. The name Lottie Anderson Bernard gave as her alleged brother's was Dr.

Anderson, 'a practicing physician in Indianapolis' [HD31UL]. LAB may have told Gomer her 'brother's' name was Dr. M. C. Anderson [HD29UL]. Hankies with the name (Louise or) Louisa Anderson [HD70LL] were found in Kate Morgan's trunk at the L.A. Grants' home in Los Angeles, where Katie Logan (another fake name) worked briefly as a temporary housemaid. The contents of this trunk tie the two women (Lizzie Wyllie and Kate Morgan) together, along with 'Katie Logan' blurting out that her real name was Lizzie.

Bernard:

Fake name given by the Beautiful Stranger while staying at the Hotel del Coronado [HD1UL]. Full name: Lottie Anderson Bernard. Anderson was the name of Lizzie's aunt in Grand Rapids [HD].

NOTE: (6/25/2012) Increasingly, I have to wonder if the choice of names (Lottie or Charlotte Bernard) was random, or if it actually was the name of a woman Spreckels would recognize as a potential blackmail candidate. The Anderson middle name most likely relates to Lizzie's Aunt Louisa Anderson in Grand Rapids, Michigan. Like Katie Logan, it sounds like a name Kate Morgan made up to comfort and reassure poor Lizzie. Will future research determine that there was a domestic or other woman in the orbit of John D. Spreckels (or his brother Adolph?) in San Francisco, who could be a potential source of embarrassment and, in Kate Morgan's hopes, lead to a payoff to avoid scandal?

brother:

Neither Kate Morgan nor Lizzie Wyllie had a brother in real life. Kate had no siblings, and Lizzie had one sister named May who lived with Lizzie and her mother (Elizabeth) in Detroit, possibly at an address given in the 1890 census (237 Fifth Street, Detroit [DM]). Kate Morgan, while pulling her scams, always claimed to have a brother who was a doctor, hovering somewhere nearby. I believe she taught Lizzie how to be an impersonator, and the fake 'Dr. Anderson' (Lottie A. Bernard's alleged brother) fit the bill. LAB was clearly obsessed with his contacting her, which he never did. He was probably either her lover (John Longfield, who had split angrily from her in the train incident at Orange) or possibly even a local abortion specialist being secretly retained to help her if anything went wrong, per Stetson's quote [HD35LL] "...send for the doctor..." (my italics). Could this even have been the house physician [HD29LL,UR], who had gone hunting early that day [HD31UL], presumably on North Island, despite the previous night's storm? She does make reference to the man on the train as her 'brother' [HD2LL], so most likely it was John Longfield—the man who had 'ruined' her, and who she desperately hoped would leave his wife and children to marry her—which shows again how air-headed poor Lizzie really was, and how Kate Morgan probably had strung her along with such fantasies.

Brown, Josie:

One of Kate Morgan's aliases. Reported by a lady in Anaheim.

doctor:

Kate Morgan had a history of using aliases in various cities, and stating that she had a brother who was a doctor, practicing in various other cities, who was however hovering somewhere nearby, apparently ready to come to her rescue if needed. This appears to have been partly a claim to some respectability (being of a family that produced a respected physician) and a veiled threat (that she had a concerned and capable man ready to come to her aid if needed).

embalming:

It can be inferred that the body was embalmed,[87] for she lay in state in a public room at Johnson & Company for about two weeks, during which she became a national *cause célèbre* of the Yellow Press, with breathless daily or even hourly telegraph reports emanating from San Diego.

The body's hair was cropped, and a police sketch was sent abroad in an effort to get someone to identify her.

Detroit:

Lizzie's home city [HD1]. Given by Lottie A. Bernard as her home city signing in to the hotel register [HD54]. Home of John Longfield, and the Wyllie family (Lizzie's mother Elizabeth and sister May).

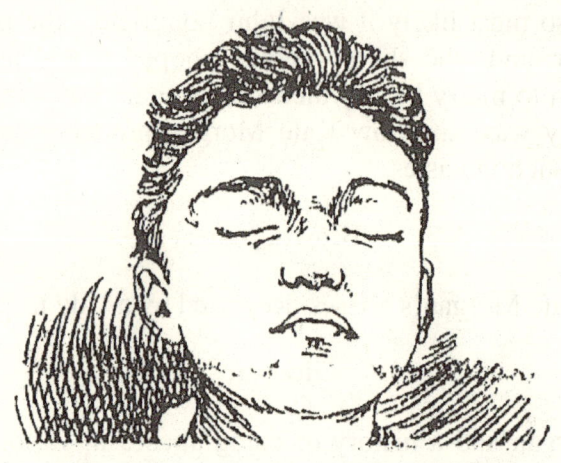

Since it was at first assumed she was Mrs. Lottie Bernard, and there was only a matter of locating Mr. Bernard (who did not exist, because the name was a false alias), the sketch probably was not made until several days after her death. After lying on the frigid steps for hours, then being carried across to the city (was she packed in ice? Nobody today knows for sure how the body was handled), the cadaver was treated at Johnson & Company. The embalming process is performed in various ways, but generally serves to preserve the body in as lifelike a condition as possible. Some of the body's processes disappear with death and the removal of inner organs. Other processes, pertaining to the skin, like hair growth and nail growth, may continue for a time. Common chemicals used by morticians in Lottie Bernard's time included arsenic and formaldehyde.[88] While these chemicals have slightly different effects, in common they cause the death of bacteria that cause flesh to break down. Among the most noticeable changes in the body after death is rigor mortis, the stiffening of the muscles that may cause contortions, accompanied by a loss of water that causes the body to shrink. Decomposition and putrefaction cause the breakdown of proteins through hydrolysis and anaerobic bacterial processes, resulting in foul-smelling liquids called cadaverine and putrescine. Within two to four weeks, the individual's face becomes unrecognizable. There are no known photographs of the dead woman. There is just the police sketch, which must have been done when a search failed to turn up Mr. Bernard or any other relatives or friends of the deceased. The sketch was done at some point between November 30 (day of the coroner's inquest) and December 14 (probable day of her funeral and burial).

gun:

According to a firearms expert I consulted, and my own Web browsing, the American Bulldog revolver of the 1890s was not so much a brand as a generic type of handgun. The standard British Army revolver of the 1870s was the .45 Webley. A civilian knockoff called the British Bulldog was popular. Foreign copies included the Belgian Bulldog and the American Bulldog. The American Bulldog type consisted of a variety of calibers and models, which today would be classified as a 'suicide special' or a 'Saturday night special' or even a 'throwaway' on the low end. No wonder that testimony indicates it had rust on it. Its basic model was a .32 caliber six shot revolver, which was actually a smaller handgun for the times. It had a standard grip, and a short barrel. The range of calibers and dimensions varied all the way up to the .44 that LAB used to shoot herself. Gun dealer Chick says [HD32UL] he sold LAB a .44 American Bulldog. Physician/surgeon B.F. Mertzman says [HD23LL] he estimates the round to have been in the range of .38 to .40. This putative discrepancy was later (1980s) cited as possible grounds for a framed murder, in that the bullet allegedly did not match the gun. But the round taken from her skull had been damaged during the shooting, obviously, and a 1980s review of the case did not find sufficient grounds to review or overturn the 1892 jury finding of suicide. While one can't 100% rule out the possibility of murder, the fact that she went into town to purchase a gun that most likely killed her considerably weakens any supposition of murder. That's because she herself introduced a gun into the equation, and suicide is the simplest way to explain the causative arc from that purchase, across her obvious debility and depression, to her ultimate demise. The electrician Cone [HD18UR] who first found the body describes the gun as 'large.' A point of detail is in order here. The gun itself would have been considered relatively light for the time period. However, the .44 caliber introduces a new variable. Because of the size of the round, the highly unusual cylinder was able to contain only five shots. The cylinder still looked enlarged compared to the .32 for which the generic gun was designed. So most likely what Cone saw was not a really 'large' handgun, but a somewhat grotesque .44 handgun whose swollen-looking cylinder midsection looked out of place between the standard grip and short barrel designed for the .32 models.

husband:

LAB signs in at the Hotel del Coronado as Mrs. Lottie Anderson Bernard, yet she seems to devote her anxieties to waiting for her alleged brother ('Dr. Anderson'), not her alleged husband ('Mr. Bernard')—e.g. when chief hotel clerk Gomer questions her [HD29LR] about her finances and resources. It is interesting that this probably makes LAB's alleged maiden name Anderson, the name of Lizzie's aunt in Grand Rapids. More interesting is the fact that she does not seem concerned about her husband—though the man who angrily left her on the train at Orange was most likely in fact not a 'husband,' but Lizzie's lover John Longfield. It was most likely Longfield that she kept hoping to hear from, and his failure to contact her seems a plausible motive for suicide [DM179], in the further context of her self-medication, guilt about harming her fetus, and guilt about disappointing her mother and sister.

Fibs:

Lizzie (Mrs. Katie Logan, Mrs. Lottie Bernard) lets slip a series of moments in which we glimpse her airheaded struggle with a situation that was clearly over her head. The first and most glaring is when she tells a fellow housekeeper in Los Angeles that her name is really Lizzie, then quickly corrects herself and gets even her fake name wrong (Kittie, Katie). Another such moment is, as the clerk is signing her in, when she tells him she is Miss Lottie Bernard, and quickly corrects it to Mrs.—which is caught in the clerk's writing 'Mis' instead of 'Miss' or 'Mrs.' Another moment is when, on

Monday November 28, Gomer comes to ask about her finances, and she abruptly changes her lie from 'neuralgia' to terminal stomach cancer. There is something child-like, blatant, almost comical, awkward, and transparent about all these fibs. Her capacity for self-delusion is evident from the invitation she sent herself from two prominent stage actresses of national fame.

Her instinct to fib is evident from the fact that she told Fosdick she was going into town to get her baggage, when in reality she was going to buy a gun; she didn't need to say anything; but he pressed her with good advice regarding the coming storm and her weak condition, and she had to make up something to show it was imperative that she make the trip.

Friends:

At the inquest, the Coroner asks his assistant, Stetson, if there was "No trace of her friends?" [HD35LR]. This may be an innocent phrasing, but it does raise the question—since she was alone the whole time, why this reference to 'friends'? Why not 'friend' instead of the plural? If one believes the entire inquest was rigged, a hasty affair serving the interests of Spreckels, and if the Coroner (who was absent on the morning the body was found, perhaps just as the house physician happened to be away hunting [HD31UL]) knew more than he was saying, it sounds like he may have led the witness. It is an odd question that seems to open the door to the possibility that, as my book suggests [DM], the Spreckels Machine kept tabs on LAB and knew she had accomplices.

hankies:

Often, the little details loom surprisingly large in a situation like this. There are several references to hankies in this story. At the Coroner's Inquest, Coroner asks Stetson: "What is the name on the handkerchiefs?"[89] (He means those found in the dead woman's room by Asst Coroner Stetson.) Stetson says: "Little, I think it is, I cannot quite make it out, but the last name is Anderson." Consider that nobody knew her name was not Lottie A. Bernard at this point, and a nationwide search was on for both the purported Dr. Anderson (brother), as well as the purported Mr. Bernard (husband). We know that in a week or so, the corpse would be I.D.'d as Lizzie Wyllie, and a few days later that choice would change to Kate Morgan (on flimsy pretext). So we have Stetson innocently saying the blurry first name on the faded hankie looks to him like *Little*, when in fact that looks surprisingly like *Lizzie*. The opening capital *L* and small *i* are the same, followed by a double consonant—a Victorian *zz* with a bar through each *z* could easily look like a pair of *t*'s—followed by a small *l* or a small *t* (again, the dot on the *i* could easily fade so the letter looks like an *l* with a faint gap); and the final letters *e* are the same.

Stetson says with certainty that the last name is Anderson. Remember that Lizzie's aunt in Grand Rapids is Louisa (or Louise, *q.v.*) Anderson, which happens to be the name embroidered on the hankies found in Kate Morgan's trunk at the L.A. Grants' home in Los Angeles (where I believe Kate Morgan was training Lizzie to become a competent impostor, under the name Katie Logan, preparing her for her coming role as LAB in Coronado; despite the fact that she blurts out that her real name is Lizzie); and the artifacts in the L.A. Grant trunk strongly help tie the two women (Kate Morgan and Lizzie Wyllie) together.

There is a further tantalizing mystery about the hankies in her hotel room. The simple case is that the blurred first name is Louisa (again, similar to *Little*, but less so than *Lizzie*). In that case, Stetson is holding simply a few more of the Louisa Anderson hankies Lizzie probably borrowed during huge crying spells while staying with her aunt in Grand Rapids. If in fact, however, the complete name really was *Lizzie Anderson*, this raises an intriguing possibility. We know Lizzie as Lizzie Wyllie, because that's how it was used in the popular press. Lizzie's aunt's (Lizzie's mother Elizabeth's sister) in Grand Rapids is Louisa Anderson. The fact that there were hankies embroidered both 'Lizzie Anderson' and 'Louisa Anderson' raises an interesting new dimension. Is it possible that Anderson was Louisa's maiden name? Can it be that Elizabeth Anderson married a man named Wyllie, who died sometime before 1892? And that her sister Louisa Anderson married a man whose name we do not know, but the names on the hankies were embroidered long before Elizabeth and Louisa grew to maturity and married? The long time span would account for the hankies both in the trunk in Los Angeles, and in the hotel room in Coronado, being almost unreadable. All we really need to know for our Coronado mystery is that Lizzie's hankies were found both in the trunk and in the hotel room, which makes her the dead woman in Coronado and ties her firmly in with Kate Morgan, so the two women were working together. Lizzie's outburst about her name suggests Katie Logan was Lizzie Wyllie, the gullible and pretty young runaway from Detroit in Kate Morgan's tutelage.

There is yet another hypothesis regarding the Lizzie Anderson hankies (if that's how the embroidery really read). Could it be that Lizzie's mother, Elizabeth Wyllie, had the maiden name of Elizabeth Anderson, went by Lizzie also in her youth, and simply gave some hankies embroidered with that name to her daughter? That would account for the age and fading of the hankies found in Room 302 at the Hotel Del in 1892. Again, there is nothing pointing to Kate Morgan in any of this, but each Anderson hypothesis points to Lizzie as having been the woman who died at the Hotel Del.

Jones, Joseph:

Joseph A. Jones[90] of Boston or Joseph E. Jones[91] of Boston was not called to testify at the inquest, but he mentioned[92] to a bellman at the Hotel Del that he recognized the woman who signed in before him, LAB, as having been on a train with him.

Despite the remarkable coincidence this invokes, I tend to take Jones at face value. Here is a man, Bostonian in origin, who happens to be (we assume) on a business trip. He is on a train from Denver, Colorado, to Orange, California, and late in that trip he notices a woman arguing with a man on the train.[93] Jones is sitting in the same railcar when this occurs. It is most important to note in his statement that he did not notice them until the train got near the Pacific coast[94], because this tends to corroborate my theory that Lizzie ('Katie Logan') during the 'Missing Day' made this significant detour that led somehow to the loss of her baggage claim tickets. Whether it was Kate Morgan, or Lizzie Wyllie was 'Katie Logan' in Los Angeles, is immaterial—either way, she mysteriously appeared on a westbound train from Denver to Orange, when she should have been on a southbound train from Los Angeles to San Diego.

If we take Jones at face value (despite the coincidence that he was in a rail car with 'Lottie A. Bernard' on the way from Denver to

Orange, and later signed in after she did at the Hotel del Coronado) then the woman on the train from Denver to Orange and the woman who signed in at the Hotel Del were the same person. I cannot, at this writing, imagine Jones to be either another concoction of Kate Morgan, or a plant of the Spreckels Machine to sow disrepute upon the conspirators.

Jones is an ephemeral character in this story. It's not known to which bellman he told his tale. He was not summoned to testify at the coroner's inquest—because, according to the bellman, he was averse to testifying, and thus did not reveal his information until after the inquest. Was he a man with secrets he was afraid would become known, or was he just too busy to get involved? Did those secrets have anything to do with the Beautiful Stranger, or was he merely a man in a hurry, who did not want to get bogged down in a criminal case that had no bearing on his business interests? Jones vanishes into history as ephemerally as he briefly appears, second-hand. He says the man with whom Lottie Bernard argued on the train was 'well-dressed,' which does support the notion he was John Longfield, who was known as a ladies' man in Detroit.

I believe Lottie Bernard was on her way from the L.A. Grants' house in Los Angeles to meet her fate in the San Diego area, but knew John Longfield would be on the train from Denver, so she boarded somewhere east of Orange. That could have been anywhere east of Anaheim. She pleaded with him until he stormed off the train at Orange (presumably to link up with Kate Morgan, with whom I believe he was by then sexually intimate) while LAB rode westward to Anaheim, and then changed trains to ride south to San Diego. Somehow, in that process, Longfield must have pocketed the checks (receipts) for her three trunks, which wound up in San Diego, and which she could not retrieve without the tickets. Perhaps, for some reason, he was bringing her trunks to her on the train by a huge detour, since the trunk at the L.A. Grant house (where LAB had worked and lived in as Katie Logan) belonged to Kate Morgan.

Kate Morgan:

A grifter from Iowa, often mistakenly thought of as the Beautiful Stranger who lay dead at the Hotel del Coronado 28-29 November 1892. My analysis clearly shows that she was instead the organizer of the blackmail plot, in whose failure Lizzie Wyllie died of a self-inflicted gunshot to the head.

A photograph (shown), allegedly of Kate Morgan, has circulated on the Internet. If this is Kate Morgan, she does not resemble the victim in the police sketch (see Embalming), who was Lizzie Wyllie. Lizzie's mother agreed that the dead girl's sketch represented her missing daughter. Hotel guests and employees stated that a photo they were shown of Kate Morgan (unavailable; presumably similar to the photo at right), did not resemble the Beautiful Stranger they had admired in life.

Katie Logan:

An alias that we probably all agree was invented by Kate Morgan. The traditional view is that Kate Morgan used the name Katie Logan while posing as a temporary domestic worker at contractor L. A. Grant's house in Los Angeles. My view is that Kate Morgan was training Lizzie Wyllie for the big impersonation (Lottie A. Bernard) at the Hotel Del, and Lizzie was the woman posing as Katie Logan at the L. A. Grants'. At one point, Katie Logan tells a co-worker that her real name is Lizzie.[95] It appears she blurted this out and quickly corrected herself, saying she preferred Kittie, then amended that to Katie. Presumably, the other woman, who reported this to police later, would have no reason to mistake the woman she knew as Katie for someone named Kittie, so most likely 'Kittie' is another of Lizzie's muddle-headed fumbles and clumsy fibs.

Another huge clue is the fact that, in Kate Morgan's trunk at the L.A. Grant house, was found a box labeled Louisa Anderson. That is the name of Lizzie's aunt in Grand Rapids, Michigan. Also found in the trunk were hankies with the name Louisa Anderson embroidered. But there was a photo of Kate Morgan as well, all of which proves beyond a reasonable doubt that Kate Morgan and Lizzie Wyllie were together in the plot—first, impersonating the fictitious Katie Logan in Los Angeles, and secondly impersonating Lottie A. Bernard in Coronado.

Missing Day:

Commentators have cited a 'missing 24 hours' between November 23 and 24, which is far longer than the short train ride it should have taken Lottie A. Bernard to arrive in San Diego from Los Angeles.

The resolution of the Lottie A. Bernard mystery does, for several reasons, suggest she took a time-consuming side trip, by rail, from Los Angeles to Orange, and from Orange to Anaheim, and thence to San Diego. The side trip did not require exactly 24 hours, but would have exhausted the better part of a day.

A passenger from Boston, Joseph E. Jones, was on the train that brought John back West from Iowa. In Iowa, Longfield had left a smallish sum ($25) with a bank manager, along with a tall tale that it was in case the money were needed by his school chum's ailing wife in Coronado. Lizzie had just left the L. A. Grant household on her way to San Diego. By now, she had a serious inkling that things were not all as Kate described them about John, but she did not yet blame Kate for being a liar and manipulator. Knowing that the train was to arrive in Anaheim, Lizzie traveled several hours east and met the train in Orange. From Orange to Anaheim, she pleaded and argued with a reticent John Longfield to marry her in Coronado. She was getting cold feet about Kate's plot, and thought it would be so much simpler if John were to rescue her and marry her. But John was following Kate's orders and demurred. The result was a rising argument that ended with John storming from the train in Anaheim. It was the last time he and Lizzie would ever see each other, and the mysterious passenger Jones would describe it to bellmen at the hotel a few days later—though he avoided attending the Coroner's inquest for some reason—perhaps connected with a cover-up by the Spreckels Machine.

Why did it take the woman more than a day to make the two-hour train trip from Los Angeles to San Diego? She left her employer, L.A. Grant, in Los Angeles on November 23rd, and arrives in Coronado on the afternoon of the next day. For all we know, she may have gone shopping—except that a witness, Joseph E. Jones of Boston, told a bellman at the Hotel Del that he recognized the mystery woman at the hotel as being the same woman he had seen on the train from Denver the day before, having a loud argument with a man who stormed off the train at Orange. What was Lottie A. Bernard doing on a train from east to west at a time when she logically would have been on a different train going from north to south? I have pieced together a plausible explanation—she was making a desperate bid to regain the affections of the man she loved, who was in the process of dumping her and betraying her in Kate Morgan's plot to blackmail John Spreckels. She traveled south from Los Angeles, then traveled a brief distance east to intercept John Longfield. She pleaded with him on the brief trip west to Orange, but his rejection of her sounded like a quarrel to the witness, Jones. Longfield jumped off the train at Orange and strode off into history, never to see her again. She continued her fateful journey south to San Diego and to her doom.

Pregnancy

The leading medical authority in San Diego, Dr. B. F. Mertzman, was not allowed to autopsy the dead woman, but he examined the body for about a half hour on the morning after she died, in other words about 24 hours after her body was found, and he stated with certainty,[96-97] from his experience as a physician and surgeon, that (a) she was pregnant (which puts her anywhere from about the first or second month, when vaginal changes would start becoming apparent, to around the fifth month (*q.v.*) when her pregnancy would have been obvious to observers, and nobody who met her indicated any inkling that she might be gravid); (b) she was taking what Mertzman called "terrible medicines" to induce a miscarriage; and (c) she had borne at least one child in the past.

On Saturday, Nov. 26, Lottie (Lizzie) sent bellman Harry West on an enigmatic quest for an empty pint bottle and a sponge from the hotel drugstore.[98] It has been common practice since ancient

Egyptian times for women to use a pessary, or sponge filled with poisons, to induce a miscarriage. The empty pint bottle (and this is all speculation, but quite provocative) could have been used to mix medicines. Some of the abortifacients used in ancient times in pessaries (vaginal suppositories, still used today but with modern medicines) included the herb pennyroyal, which functions as a natural contraceptive.

Sponge

See Pregnancy.

Stingaree

One of the most notorious red light districts on the West Coast, located approximately between today's Market (then H) Street and K Street (near the downtown baseball field today) and between Fifth Street (today's Fifth Avenue) and Second Street (today's Second Avenue). The Stingaree got its name from the stingray, a flat fish with a razor-sharp, poisonous quill for a tail. It likes to sleep in the warm, shallow waters after flapping to cover itself with sand. Lifeguards warn persons wading near shore make noise and splash water to wake the sleeping rays, which then scamper off. Many a wader has gotten an excruciatingly pierced foot requiring weeks of healing. Fatalities (like Steve Irwin, killed by the much larger Australian stingray than the pelagic stingray of San Diego) are rare, but they do occur.[99] The Stingaree was rife with prostitution, gambling, and drug abuse including heroin and opium. Shootings and stabbings were frequent. The saying was that "you could get stung as badly in the Stingaree as in the Bay." Ironically, City Hall and the police headquarters were located at 5th and G Streets near the heart of the district. Wyatt Earp ran four gambling establishments here when our Beautiful Stranger appeared on the scene.

Trunks:

Two sets of luggage are in play. One is a trunk (belonging to Kate Morgan) at the L.A. Grants' house in Los Angeles, and containing artifacts of both Lizzie Wyllie and Kate Morgan [HD70]. The other is a set of three trunks belonging to LAB, kept at the baggage terminal near the railroad station at the foot of D Street (today's West Broadway, and the current Santa Fe Depot occupies almost exactly the same spot as the old station). LAB arrived in San Diego probably late morning to noon on Thanksgiving Day, Thursday, November 24, 1892. Thanksgiving was not the huge holiday it is today, and businesses were open. LAB tried to collect her trunks, but the baggage bureaucrats refused to turn them over because she did not have her tickets. She (Lizzie) says her 'brother'[100] had kept the 'checks' when they separated at Orange.

This cleanly links to the observation by Joseph Jones of Boston that he witnessed an argument between the woman who checked into the Hotel Del just before him as 'Lottie A. Bernard' and an unknown man on the Denver to Orange rail line, who Jones suspected was romantically involved with the woman. The baggage clerk refused to release the three trunks to her because she did not have the claim checks—and probably out of Victorian prejudice against an attractive young woman traveling alone. In any case, it appears that Lottie A. Bernard (who I believe was Lizzie Wyllie, not Kate Morgan) was traveling with three trunks.

Kate Morgan was traveling with one trunk, which ended up at the L.A. Grant house in Los Angeles. We have the testimony of Kate (nee Farmer) Morgan's uncle in the Hanford and Visalia areas near San Francisco (Farmer), who wrote to Los Angeles Police Chief Glass to protest any notion that his niece, Kate Morgan, was in a mindset to commit suicide. Farmer says that she was in good spirits and (here's the kicker) "traveling with one flat-top trunk, two leather satchels, and a lady's gold watch."[101]

Meanwhile, the woman working for the L.A. Grants in Los Angeles, 'Katie Logan,' had a single trunk with her. This trunk stayed closed until well into December, when Los Angeles detectives finally opened it—and found a mix of possessions belonging to both Kate Morgan and Lizzie Wyllie. This is a new interpretation, because until now the contents of the trunk in Los Angeles were confusingly considered to lean toward an I.D. of 'Katie Logan' as Kate Morgan. My interpretation is that 'Katie Logan' was actually Lizzie Wyllie, whom Kate Morgan was giving a crash course in impersonations in preparation for her cameo role in the blackmail of John Spreckels, owner of the Hotel del Coronado—which would go horribly wrong.

So the matter of travel trunks boils down to this. Lizzie Wyllie had left Detroit, in the company of her lover John Longfield, with three trunks containing all her earthly possessions. Kate Morgan, meanwhile, was traveling with one trunk and most likely a lover — possibly her husband, Tom Morgan, but it is very likely she was getting romantically involved with Lizzie's paramour John Longfield—the latter, because he covers for her by sending a bogus account from Cleveland to his wife, saying 'Lizzie' was in Toronto.[102] I believe this story is false, and that, while Lizzie lay dead in San Diego, Kate Morgan was very much alive, assumed Lizzie's persona, and Kate may already have joined Longfield in Cleveland when he sent the letter to his gullible wife, to throw police and Lizzie's family off the trail. How long Kate and Longfield would have been together is anyone's guess, but I would surmise they tired of each other and he went back to his family in Detroit.

There is no way Kate Morgan's three Hanford pieces of luggage (a trunk and two leather satchels) can be twisted into being the three travel trunks stored at the baggage depot in San Diego. Therefore, we have compelling evidence that Kate Morgan was traveling with one trunk, which wound up at the L.A. Grant home in Los Angeles (with materials or props inside belonging to both Kate Morgan and Lizzie Wyllie), and that Lizzie Wyllie (who I surmise was both 'Katie Logan' and 'Lottie A. Bernard') arrived in San Diego with three trunks. By process of elimination, if Kate Morgan was traveling with one trunk, then the three trunks had to belong to the other woman in the case, Lizzie Wyllie.

Victorian culture:

She would have been just another nameless, faceless victim of random violence, had she not become an icon, a saint of Victorian melodrama and morbid sentiment (calling to mind the international hysteria over the life and passing of Little Nell, heroine of Charles Dickens' *The Little Curiosity Shop*, 1841, which was originally published in newspaper installments that were ferried across the Atlantic in mail ships, and which caused mobs on the Boston waterfront to riot as they cried "Is Little Nell dead? Is Little Nell dead?"[103] before the arriving ship could even dock with the latest episode on board).

The generic motif that so aroused the Victorian sentiment seems to center around an impeccably, heroically virtuous and angelically beautiful young female who is laid low by circumstance and the evil deeds of others, who violate her trust and sanctity, so that she finally dies in an orgiastic vision like that captured in the paintings of the Pre-Raphaelite[104] images like the famed Ophelia drowning (*Ophelia*[105] John Everett Millais, 1851-52, Tate Collection). The painting depicts a fully clothed beautiful young woman floating in water, with a dazed expression and half-closed eyes, while her pale hands are raised, palms up, in a gesture of limp and delicate surrender or supplication. Drawing upon the tragic character of Ophelia, Hamlet's love interest in the eponymous Shakespearean play, the painting has her mouthing vague snatches of happily remembered songs as her consciousness fades, and her clothing slowly fills with water and draws her under. We might consider this an absurd exaggeration of overblown sentiment, except that it is canonical as described in Act 4 Scene 7, Queen Gertrude's monologue[106] that begins "There is a willow grows aslant a brook..." Having been rejected in love by the angry and irrational Hamlet, and told to "get thee to a nunnery," the poor girl loses her mind, climbs into a tree—while crowned with an orchid garland—in a beautiful meadow (captured over five months' work by Millais, and as well remembered for its detail and beauty as the image of 19-year-old model Elizabeth Siddal), and accidentally falls to her death by drowning. To highlight the underlying realities of daily life that produced this phantasmagoria, the painter spent five months in a hut by a river, tormented by 'muscular' flies as he wryly called them; he was threatened by the local beadle with legal action for trespass; and, having painted the river scene, when he later inserted the scene of the drowning woman, he had his model posing in a warm bathtub at his apartment, but became so intent on his work that he let the candles go out under the tub, the water grew chill, and she caught a cold, for which Elizabeth Siddal sent Millais a £50 doctor bill.

While Lottie lay in state for about two weeks, thousands of local residents, dressed in their finest, came to stare at the decorously arrayed corpse in a display casket. This appears to have been culturally a women's liturgy of sorts, into which much can be read.

Many men were undoubtedly dragged along, but it can be surmised that every woman of any sentiment in the San Diego region dressed in her finest, and made the pilgrimage to Lottie Bernard's casket— probably many more than once. Not only can this be taken as an unspoken signal of a fetal women's suffrage movement, but modern readers must remember the untold mortality rate among Victorians, especially among children. In the great wheel of history, whatever high mortality rates existed prior, and went unrecorded except in the parish registers of isolated hamlets, the Industrial Revolution jammed vast numbers of people together in cities whose size had not been seen in Europe since the decline of Rome, nearly fourteen centuries earlier. All these things transpired rather suddenly in the space of a century. In Britain, the Industrial Revolution (as we call it) began with the industrialization of manufacture in the late 1700s, a process that began half a century later in the United States, primarily in 1830s New England, and fortuitously creating the industrialized North that would vanquish the largely rural Southern Confederacy in the Civil War of the 1860s. The urbanization of Great Britain is mirrored in the growth of cities like New York, Boston, and Chicago, and in any case the culture that expressed itself in the mortuary room at Johnson & Company in 1892 was a direct consequence of all that. During the urbanization, British villages suffered. Politics was affected by issues of zoning, fencing, 'rotten boroughs' with empty voting constituencies in the House of Commons, and the like. London (and other U.K. cities) became famous for appalling smogs, caused by vast amounts of coal being burned, well into the 20th Century, when gasoline and oil burning contributed further and under different circumstances. London, Europe's largest city, and, like Imperial Rome two thousand years earlier, a vast melting pot of humanity flowing from all directions of the compass of an 'Empire on which the sun never sets," became a mass of suffering humanity coated with a thin cream of middle and upper class society. One of the Victorian era's chief romanticizers was Charles Dickens, who had risen from humble origins that he reflected in many of his works (he *was* David Copperfield and Oliver Twist, the poor little apprentices who suffered at the hands of cruel overseers and petty criminals). In some ways, it can be said that Dickens fairly invented the modern Christmas, with his collection of holiday stories to which he returned time and again, topped by "A Christmas Carol," in which poor little crippled Tim and the ugly Scrooge meet in battle upon the field of morality. Dickens, creator of Little Nell and, in his 1854 *Hard Times*, the indomitable little Sissy Jupe,[107] was the greatest of London's 19th Century investigative journalists.

Victorian sentimentalism:

As we begin to understand the Victorians a bit, we become less supercilious about their sentimentalism. On the one hand, we cannot help but marvel at the breathtaking hypocrisy of keeping her corpse lying in state, on display for tens of thousands to gawk at, then holding a solemn and magnificent High Church funeral with flowers, chorale, organ music, and many tears shed—and finally consigning her to a rude box on a donkey cart, rumbling alone and without a single mourner, to her final resting place in a barely marked grave on a lonely spot outside town. On the other hand, we have only to understand the brevity and cruelty of a life before modern medicine, when infant mortality was rampant, when death touched every doorway, to get some understanding of where that maudlin weepiness came from. It was a world still ruled mostly by medieval monarchs and medieval ideas, where the light of modernity had just begun to poke through the windows, but city streets were still covered in animal droppings. Most people lived a rough life on primitive farms, but city life was in many ways even more fearful with its crime and disease. In London, Charles Dickens was not only a novelist, but the premier crime reporter of his age—and we learn from him, and from the illustrations of Gustave Doré, the breathtaking depravity and poverty of urban life in the early industrial age. If the Victorian era strikes us as one of double standards and maudlin sentimentality, we must understand some of its fundamental, underlying stresses. For one thing, it is an era of tectonic change from rural to urban life on a scale not seen since perhaps Ancient Rome. In that sense it is almost a going backward while going forward. On the one hand, it can be seen as a return to the great but precarious city, with its urban mob for whom Vespasian built his Colosseum to keep them from overturning the state (as in recent memory a bloodthirsty rabble had plunged 1790s France into anarchy). On the other hand, one heard the siren songs of a renewed enlightenment based on science and mechanistic technology that promised hope for all problems. It was an age of utopian solutions and dystopian realities. The facts on the ground did not seem to gibe with the theories of prison reformers and other social engineers (including Karl Marx, whose footprint would extend through the horrors of the Paris Commune in the 1870s and into the dark maw of the middle twentieth century). It was an era when the final expansion of European culture pushed rough-hewn pioneers to the far western shores of Manifest Destiny, adapting to conditions as they found them, but bringing and preserving the trappings of the Eastern U.S. establishment, which itself was a Puritanized imitation of the parent British culture. In this split personality, the individual and social pretense was of a homogenously white, Anglo-Saxon Protestant culture, while the reality was of a mix of old Spanish, Native American, Black, Jewish, Mormon, Roman Catholic, and other identities that were overlaid by a ruling class that was largely WASP. Every California city of any size had a Chinatown, and many had a Japantown. The split personality of this society is evident in the fact that San Diego's city hall and police headquarters were within a stone's throw of one of the West Coast's most notorious dens of vice—the Stingaree. The double standard is probably best remembered into the twentieth century in a long tradition of movies whose story had few if any non-WASP characters in it. Actors had to Anglicize their names to suit the type. African-Americans in particular were nearly invisible and nonexistent in American cinema before Sidney Poitier came unexpectedly to dinner in 1967's *Guess Who's Coming To Dinner*. There might have been, by some estimates, a few hazy exceptions, as in 1939's *Gone With The Wind*. The American mythos playing on every movie and television screen, before the collapse of the Western genre in the 1970s, tended to portray the Homeric American hero as a purely WASP cowboy—when, in reality, the Old West was populated by a vivid blend of multi-cultural and multi-racial personas. Wyatt Earp, who lived in San Diego in the early 1890s as the Lottie Bernard drama unfolded, was married to a Jewish actress. Many of the cowboys trailing cattle as far north as Oregon were actually Mexican, and some of their terminology survives in the Klamath Marsh of central Oregon in words like *reata* (lariat) and *vaquero* (which survives in the English as 'buckaroo' for cowboy).

Aside from territorial social reproductive customs (e.g., a young woman can't travel alone, but must be in the company of a male relative or a female governess—a Victorian custom, whose analog is still active in many cultures around the world today, and which supports a double standard on sexuality. Life in the nineteenth century city was at least as dangerous as today's. There were few real police forces in the modern sense. San Diego organized its first rudimentary, uniformed police patrol just three years before the story related in this book. On June 1, 1889 lawman Joseph Coyne became San Diego's first metropolitan chief of police. The city would not have its first detective until 1907.[108]

Among the dangers of the age, the term 'shanghai' comes down to us today as a vague, quaint concept—but it was a reality in many port cities around the world. Many a farm boy stopped into a tavern for a drink in Portland, Oregon; or San Francisco; or San Diego—and woke up days later with a severe drug hangover, amid the salty sea air of a ship heading across the Pacific, and with a cracking whip and hard work to drive the cobwebs of his new reality away. Likewise, in this new urban hell, 'white slavers' often kidnapped women into 'white slavery,' and locked them up in dungeons where they became broken victims of drug addiction, disease, and prostitution. It was not only morally forbidden for the young woman to travel alone—it was dangerous. The way this entire schizoid reality could function was that there were 'things of which we do not speak.' The great Italian archeologist, Rodolfo Lanciani, father of modern Roman archeology, reported on a certain find from Ostia. He described this object from the ancient Classical world in terse wording as an object that "I have in possession, which I cannot name, but I know what it is." It was a sizeable ceramic dildo attached to a Priapus figure.

The Yellow Press exploited the events at the Hotel del Coronado with breathless reportage, fueled with both spoken and unspeakable insinuations, which made this story a national sensation in 1892. The fuel for that bonfire of titillation and sentimentality derives its fuel from the dark experiences and the morbid uncertainties of people who had all lost dearly loved ones—children, siblings, parents—to the cold and capricious cadaver claw of cruel and sudden death. It was the age of the 1889 Eiffel Tower, of Jules Verne's imaginative 1865 journey to the moon and back (*From The Earth To The Moon*), of an ocean-going vessel like 1863's *Euterpe* (now *The Star of India*, berthed in San Diego as a museum) that is a fully rigged sailing ship, yet also built of iron like the Eiffel Tower and 1851's Crystal Palace in London—a new Iron Age, an age of untold promise and excitement. And yet it was also an age of terrible mortality, straddling the dawn of modern surgical asepsis science (Listerism), safer food preservation techniques, and common sanitation. It is worth noting that, when President Abraham Lincoln was shot in 1865, and as he lay mortally wounded in a house across the street from Ford's theater, several prominent doctors rushed to the scene. The first of these used his unwashed fingers to probe directly into Lincoln's brain in an effort to locate the bullet. Another surgeon probed inside Lincoln's brain with a hooked metal probe. They managed to get the bullet out, but the doctors helped kill the patient. There lingered a cultural resistance among medical practitioners against Listerism (sterile environment and tools, and thorough hand washing), not to mention their ignorance of the brain as a delicate and complex organ. By cultural I mean a long-standing tradition— old as the ancient Roman republic in resisting Hellenic (Greek) baths, and surviving through the European medieval age—that bathing is somehow decadent and immoral. The Lincoln tragedy happened only a century and a half ago. Who knows what people 150 years from now will think of the current age. One thing is for sure, though—150 years from now, ghosts will be as much a part of the culture as they are now or were in Lottie A. Bernard's time.

women, two:

Throughout this story, we must follow two separate, interweaving threads—on one hand, the movements of Kate Morgan, the other hand, those of Lizzie Wyllie.

Traditionally, the story has been that a woman named Kate Morgan, aged about 26, of Hamburg, Iowa, checked into the Hotel del Coronado on Thursday, November 24, 1892. Her reason for coming to the Hotel Del, her reason for staying and the way she acted, and the cause of her death, are all central mysteries in a morass of loose ends, questions, and strange clues that seem to lead nowhere.

The official report of the Coroner's Inquest[109] certainly did not appear on or immediately after the day of the trial. The cover sheet of that document identifies her as both Lottie Anderson Bernard (the false name she used at the Hotel Del) and 'a.k.a.' (also known as) Kate Morgan. We know that this official transcript of the jury trial of November 30, 1892 was 'mislaid'[110] for a time (duration unknown) according to a written note in the official transcript by clerk W. W. Whitson. Since the name Kate Morgan did not enter public cognizance until at earliest December 6, 1892,[111] the jury's report could not have had this title sheet on it any sooner.

The jury, in fact, had no idea, since the name change happened after their brief, hasty deliberation. At the time of her death on November 28-29, she was thought to be who she had said she was: Lottie Anderson Bernard, wife or widow therefore of a putative Mr. Bernard who had not been seen, and who would never turn up—and sister of another figment, Dr. Anderson of Indianapolis, who also never showed up, because he never existed.

൙ ൜

Epilog:

The Big Picture

Of Sugar Barons and Pineapple Kings

The key to this entire story is John Spreckels, wealthy and brilliant heir of a great sugar fortune based on Hawai'ian plantations. Kate Morgan and her co-conspirators picked not only an impossible target, but the worst moment possible for their scheme. John Spreckels was a powerful man, no doubt surrounded by security apparatus and many functionaries—the Spreckels Machine, as I call it—or The Spreckels Corporation, as it was actually known.

As our glimpse of Kate Morgan's life has shown, she wove a net of conspiracy from city to city across the United States. The attempt to blackmail John Spreckels was probably her biggest gamble, and it failed horribly. She vanishes from the pages of history as completely as she briefly emerged in November and December 1892. Timing is everything, and her timing could not have been worse.

Two corporate giants were battling it out over the future of Hawai'i—Spreckels' pro-monarchy group, and Dole's annexation group. Both had insinuated themselves at the court of King David. Both owned land and power while the native Hawai'ians became disenfranchised. As we know, the Dole faction won after King David (a guest of John Spreckels at the Del for 1890 Christmas dinner in the Crown Room) died at the Palace Hotel in San Francisco as a guest of John's father Claus (January 20, 1891); and after the deposition of the last monarch, Queen Lili'uokalani almost exactly two years later (January 17, 1893). Claus Spreckels, who had made and lost fortunes before, shifted operations from Hawai'ian sugar cane to California sugar beets. The City of Spreckels near Monterey is named after him, and top sugar brands on the West Coast include Spreckels and C&H (California & Hawai'ian). These two brands are no longer owned by their founders.

Hawai'i had been ruled for nearly a thousand years by a feudal system of chiefs of varying ranks, headed by royal chiefs (*alibi*). By 1818, following a series of civil wars, a royal chief named Kamehameha had made himself the first king of a unified Hawai'i. The chiefs resented this new royal system, but it ironically saved Hawai'i for a long time from the fate of many other Pacific lands that became European colonies. The kings modernized Hawai'i. They brought in American and European entrepreneurs and innovators, who helped introduce a constitution, a bill of rights, and some land reform. Essentially, the Hawai'ians owned property communally, which hurt them after annexation under the U.S., when they could not legally and formally prove their ownership of land. In fact, under the monarchy, the trend was for elite native, European, and U.S. individuals to own most of the land, while the native people owned tiny plots or no land. There was a strong U.S. missionary influence, which tried to eradicate Hawai'i's native culture. The last king, David Kalakaua (ruled 1874-1891) made enemies among these dour Puritans (one of whom was Sanford Dole, who would become the first and only president of a short-lived Hawai'ian Republic, and whose cousin James would later build a fortune and become known as the Pineapple King). The first blow toward annexation came in 1887, when a combined force of U.S. Marines, the Honolulu Rifles, and other Dole-related interests forced the 'Bayonet Constitution' on King David. The king lost most of his administrative powers, while the average natives lost many fundamental rights (to vote; to own property; etc.), and ownership swung definitively to a small native and foreign elite. King David, the Merrie Monarch, had restored the hula and written poetry and created a Church of Hawai'i based on the Anglican Church—which enraged Calvinist U.S. missionaries soon instrumental in destroying Hawai'i's monarchy and independence. David died a few years later (1891) under odd circumstances, at the Palace Hotel in San Francisco, a guest of Claus Spreckels. Was he a victim of U.S. corporate interests coupled with dominant U.S. Protestant churches? This unpleasant question begs to be asked, though I am not the person to write that book. David Kalakaua, a relatively progressive thinker, had been the world's first monarch to circle the globe—on a goodwill tour to gain acceptance for his monarchy, and allied himself with Britain's Queen Victoria—after whom his niece Victoria Ka'iulani was named.

ಇಲ್ಲ ಇಲ್ಲ

If there was a truly beautiful and tragic woman who deserves mention, even if remotely and indirectly connected with our 1892 Hotel del Coronado mystery, it was the final player in the Hawai'ian Monarchy—Crown Princess Victoria Ka'iulani. Born in 1875, she was half European and half Hawai'ian. Her mother was the daughter of a Royal Chief related to the legendary King Kamehameha, founder of the first royal dynasty. Her father was a Scottish financier intimately involved in Hawai'ian affairs.

As Crown Princess, the teenage girl became the final royal in line for the throne. She was just 18 at the overthrow of the Queen in 1893 ended the Monarchy.

During her childhood, the Crown Princess lived in Honolulu. During her adolescence, still in Hawa'i, she became close friends with a sickly young man from Scotland, Robert Louis Stevenson, who was to pen some of the world's immortal literature.

Neither was destined for a long life. Stevenson retired to the South Sea Islands, where he died in the 1890s. The Crown Princess was named after Queen Victoria of England, and studied in England, traveled around the world seeking the restoration of her family's dynasty and her nation's independence. Her Hawai'ian name meant 'Highest Peak of Heaven.' She met with several U.S. Presidents and spoke with passion before Congress, all to no avail. It is said that the Crown Princess died of a broken heart—at age 24, in 1899, not long after learning of the death of her dear friend the author of *Kidnapped, Treasure Island*, and other enduring classics.

ಇಲ್ಲ ಇಲ್ಲ

At the moment when Lottie A. Bernard checked into the Hotel del Coronado on Thanksgiving Day, 1892, John Spreckels was in Washington, D.C. lobbying with the President and Congress to avoid the overthrow of Hawai'i's monarchy. Claus Spreckels was at the

Iolani Palace in Honolulu on Kissinger-style shuttle diplomacy to achieve the same end. All was in vain.

It goes without saying that Spreckels had a machinery of people of all levels, from ordinary night watchmen at his plants, to chief executives, bankers, security agents, newspaper executives and reporters, and armies of workers in his employ. The Spreckels Companies (owned by John and his brother Adolph) were the largest tax paying entity in San Diego County. In this book, when I referred to the Spreckels Machine, I am using a term I invented to describe a hypothetical organization that the mega-wealthy Spreckels family would logically have used or created. It would have been effective on behalf of John Spreckels, owner of the Hotel del Coronado—notably, against the likes of con artist and blackmailer Kate Morgan and her accomplices. The Pinkerton agency would have been quite experienced and adept in dealing with blackmail scenarios.

My theory is just that at the present—a theory. I have taken the facts as we know them, including the wealth of detail gathered by the Heritage Department from local resources including those at the San Diego Historical Society, the Coronado History Association, and the San Diego State University and San Diego City Libraries, and added my own research and thinking. I seem to be the first person to look at the tale of Lottie A. Bernard in its larger context, starting with ownership of the Hotel Del by John Spreckels, and extending to his concerns at the time—saving the Spreckels sugar plantations in Hawai'i—and interpreted the glaring beacons shining like lighthouses amid wreckage and mystery. I believe this interpretation stands the test of reasonableness.

❧ ☙

If it is true that ghosts are restless shades of the dead, then is it not Lizzie Wyllie who troubles the quiet corridors of the Hotel del Coronado at night? Is it she who throws books off shelves and cries out for justice? Even her simple grave in a dusty corner of Mt. Hope Cemetery bears upon it the marker of the woman who betrayed and then impersonated her—Kate Morgan, who switched identities with the hapless, far prettier girl from Detroit, and made off with John Longfield. Does Lizzie make the curtains in Room 3327 room blow, though the windows are closed? Does she spin the tassels on the ceiling fan while guests lie innocently sleeping? Does she move their clothing and toiletry articles about, as so many people have reported? Did one just miss seeing her pale and vaporous form gliding down a dark and oddly twisting, narrow hallway, like a shadow or a shade?

Are there really ghosts? The mystery of Coronado begs the question. If ghosts are real, then the hundreds of reported incidents that continue to happen at the Hotel del Coronado would suggest there is an unquiet spirit who haunts the halls, seeking justice or at least attention. If there are not really such things as ghosts, this author feels that there is at least a kind of folk memory that survives and is passed along—in this case, the commemoration of a terrible event, the death of an innocent young woman, and her betrayal at the hands of the woman whose name is associated with the Beautiful Stranger's grave. In either case, our attention is called time and again to the plight of Lizzie Wyllie, the true victim of that night. Was it suicide, or was it murder? You judge. If a woman is betrayed and pushed beyond hope to commit suicide, who is to say it isn't murder?

As I said at the outset, there isn't a smoking gun. The many loose ends and frustrating dead ends tie together nicely and logically, once one starts with the fact that Spreckels owned the Hotel Del. The doomed 'Beautiful Stranger' registered there for a reason. Thereafter, many clues give the game away: The embroidered hankies in Room 302, bearing the names of Lizzie and Aunt Louisa; the moles on the left cheek; Katie Logan's stunning gaffe in Los Angeles (saying she was really Lizzie); the trunk in Los Angeles, containing artifacts of both Lizzie and Kate—these clues, and more, make a strong case for the solution I have laid out in this book. Equally convincing is the absolute certainty with which the poor girl's mother received the description of the corpse—certain beyond a doubt that it was her beloved daughter. Mrs. Elizabeth Wyllie, having learned the description of the woman found dead in Coronado, cried inconsolably and repeatedly cried: "It is my Lizzie, it is my Lizzie. Oh, what is to become of me now?"

The halls of the Hotel del Coronado are haunted as much by a loving mother's heart-rending cries, as by the ghost of a sweet and naïve young woman cut down in the flower of life. This very Victorian story leaves sentimental echoes in Coronado's balmy air, like a fading bloom of long-ago roses.

∽ end ∾

Appendix: Maps

These maps will help orient the reader to 1890s San Diego, as well as the travels of Kate Morgan and her accomplices.

The first map shows selected points on the transcontinental railroad system of the 1890s, particularly as it pertains to the movements of Tom and Kate Morgan, and their accomplices John Longfield and Elizabeth 'Lizzie' Wyllie.

The second map is an overview of greater San Diego, focusing on the harbor and bay, the Peninsula of San Diego (which includes the Silver Strand, South Island or Coronado incorporated 1891, the now-vanished Spanish Bight and isthmus connecting the two 'islands,' and North Island, which is now a U.S. Naval Air Station).

The third map is a general overview of San Diego, with two dots to orienting the reader to key points—the Hotel del Coronado (on Coronado Island), and the downtown San Diego area across the Bay.

The fourth and fifth maps are blown up from the inset in Map 3. The fourth map shows a closer view of Coronado and downtown San Diego. The fifth map shows the same detail, but with some of Lottie A. Bernard's key paths and wanderings highlighted.

Map 1: Transcontinental Rail System

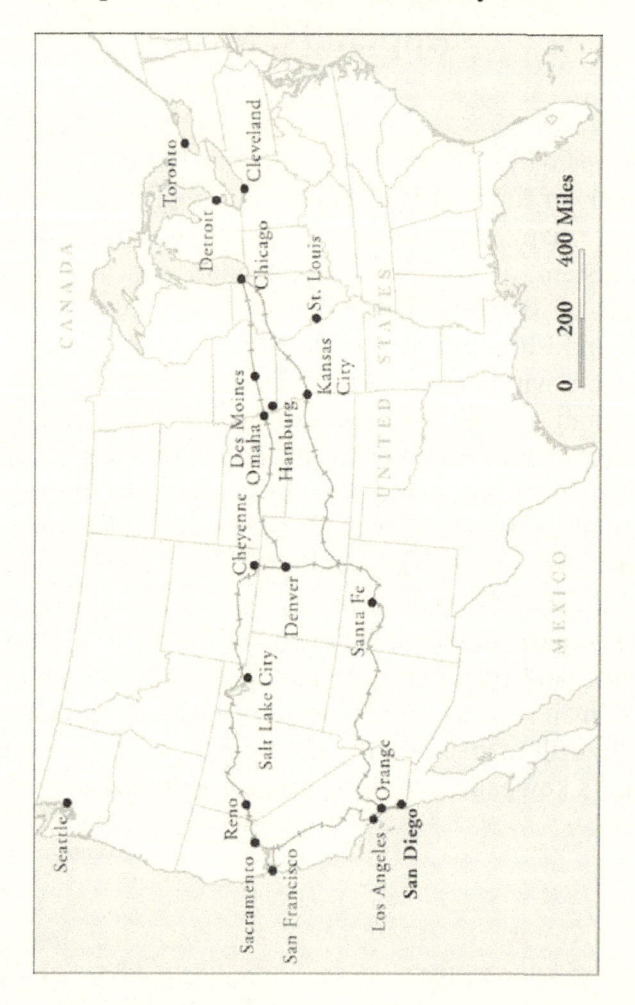

By 1892, railroads had been around for over half a century. The map above (Map 1) only shows a few selected stops and areas mentioned in this book. The country was so criss-crossed with rail lines that a complete map would look indecipherably black and veined. Here, we see selected cities mentioned in regard to Kate Morgan's mysterious aliases, or to her 'brother,' a 'doctor,' of such and such city, spanning much of the United States. Minneapolis, Indianapolis, and Detroit are among the cities she names in various schemes, as allegedly being where she or her doctor-brother are from.

There are several clusters of interest on this map.

San Francisco was the home base of the Spreckels family, and the place where the Hawai'ian king died in January 1891 as a guest of Claus Spreckels. Kate Morgan is known to have possessed business cards of several wealthy San Francisco families. Nearby are the towns of Hanford and Visalia (not shown), where Kate Morgan visited her uncle W. T. Farmer to obtain a job reference before traveling on to Los Angeles. In a hypothetical scenario, she might have altered the reference obtained from Farmer so it appears to be addressed to Katie Logan, the alter ego assumed by Lizzie Wyllie at several successive, brief temp jobs in Los Angeles area households.

Coronado (not shown) lies offshore from San Diego about a quarter mile on the San Diego Peninsula (described in subsequent maps). My theory, strongly supported by evidence, is that Kate trained Lizzie to impersonate a fictitious housekeeper (Katie Logan) to prepare her for her cameo role as the fictitious Lottie A. Bernard in Coronado the following month. In one of the most remarkable moments in this entire saga, the fictitious Katie Logan in L.A. blurts out to another housemaid that her real name is Lizzie, then quickly corrects herself and gets even her phony name wrong, saying that she goes by Kittie or Katie, since she prefers that name. A number of odd things and odd moments in the saga helped convince me of my version. For example, witnesses reported that the fictitious Lottie A. Bernard (Lizzie Wyllie) arrived in San Diego and went directly to the Hotel Brewster downtown—ostensibly to ask about her 'brother, Doctor Anderson, and his wife' (John Longfield and Kate Morgan). That is yet another indicator of her accomplices in an obvious plot.

The Iowa/Nebraska area is significant. The southwest corner of the former (Hamburg, Fremont, etc.) was home to both Kate Farmer (Morgan) and Tom Morgan. Tom settled in south-central Nebraska after the Lottie A. Bernard affair, remarried, and lived a long and prosperous life as a church deacon, postal worker, constable, and other responsible jobs. While Lottie A. Bernard was at the Hotel del Coronado, Kate Morgan sent or accompanied John Longfield, or Tom Morgan, or both, to Hamburg to induce a bank manager to hold $25 on credit in case the woman in faraway Coronado needed it.

Finally, we have a cluster of cities around the Great Lakes. Lizzie and John Longfield were from Detroit (a city mentioned in connection with one of Kate Morgan's aliases, so it is possible she and Tom met Lizzie and John there as this novel suggests. Grand Rapids was the home of Lizzie's sister Louisa, where Lizzie fled upon discovering she was (once again) pregnant out of wedlock, and no doubt having a spat with her mother; most likely the source of the monogrammed handkerchiefs mentioned in the coroner's inquest. Cleveland was where John Longfield strangely and implausibly turns up later, acting as an intermediary between Lizzie—who (he claims, implausibly) is alive and well in Toronto and will never again contact (oh, because she is dead?) her loving mother and sister—and Mrs. Longfield, who (implausibly) is acting as a somewhat dim interlocutor between the Wyllies and John Longfield.

Toronto, finally, is the alleged place where Lizzie has run off and will never again contact her loving family. That is one of the most implausible elements in the entire fabricated story I believe Kate Morgan and Longfield pulled off to cover their tracks. In my scenario, Lizzie was the housemaid missing from Los Angeles and acting as Lottie A. Bernard in Coronado. It is not a much farther stretch to suppose that Kate Morgan and John Longfield had become lovers by now, and that she was orchestrating a rather lame plot (that worked, in any case, since nobody seems to have questioned it) to cover her escape to Toronto under the guise of being Lizzie Wyllie. Kate Morgan, the woman of so many aliases, left her identity on the back steps of the Hotel del Coronado, stealing the dead woman's name and identity, as well as her lover, and made off for distant parts, while Tom Morgan (if that was him at all, by Kate's side, and not some unnamed other male lover) returned to Nebraska and started a long new life. What became of John Longfield and Kate Morgan I can only guess; maybe another researcher will find the answer. She probably dumped him and moved on again to some new frontier—her own identity now forever unusable.

Map 2: San Diego and Peninsula with Coronado

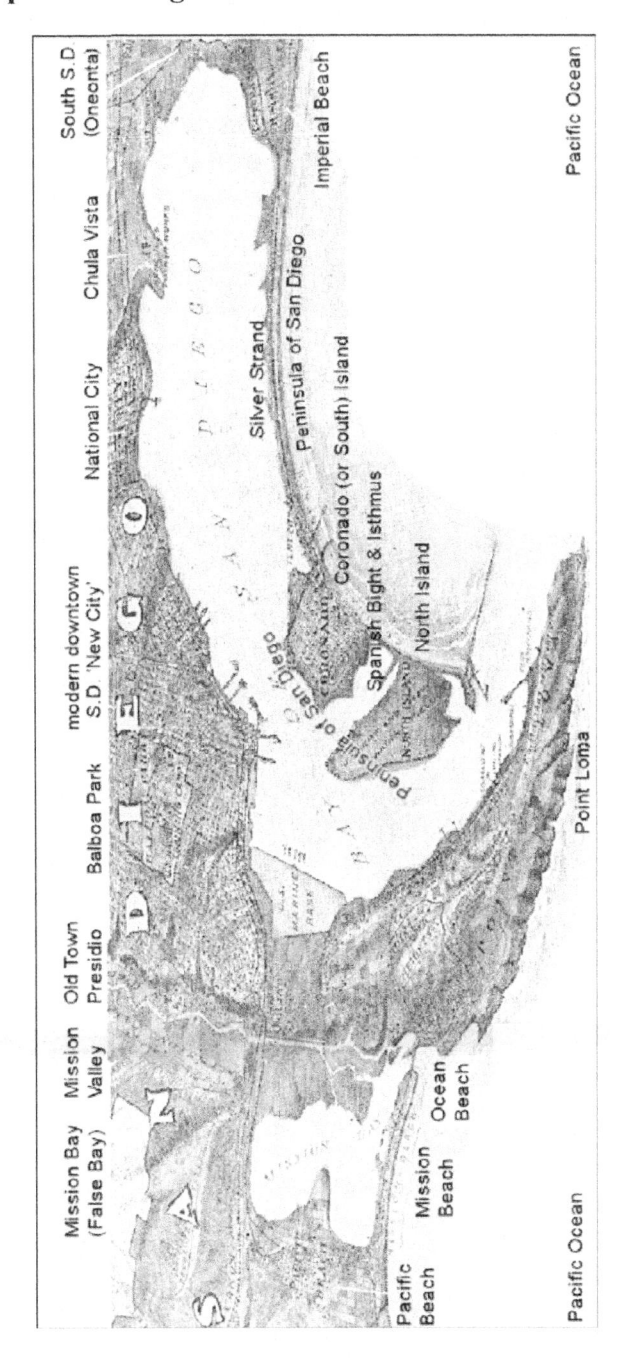

This antique aerial view adds another perspective on the two cities. San Diego Bay is the main body of water (shown on map). It is about 12 mi/19 km long, 1 mi/1.6 km–3 mi/4.8 km wide, and bordered by the Cities of Coronado, San Diego, National City, modern Chula Vista, and Imperial Beach. San Diego Harbor is the waterfront that stretches along San Diego's downtown.

Point Loma, at its tip, was where, in 1542, the first Spanish ships arrived under Juan Cabrillo, for whom the national park at the tip of Point Loma is named. He named the settlement San Miguel, but the name was changed to San Diego in 1602, when Sebastián Vizcaíno arrived with the next expedition. Point Loma was the setting of the Theosophical Society—which in Chapter 10 of my novel <u>Lethal Journey</u> I have L. Frank Baum visiting in 1892, while also meeting Lottie A. Bernard (poor Lizzie) at the Hotel del Coronado.

* * * *

The San Diego River flows westward, from the mountains and deserts, through Mission Valley, and to the sea. At one time, the river emptied into False Bay (today's Mission Bay), which may have seemed like a good harbor at first glance, but proved shallow and useless for ocean-going ships. By contrast, San Diego Bay is one of the finest natural harbors on the West Coast. The San Diego River changed course in recent centuries, and emptied into San Diego Bay. Because of silting and other concerns, the city diverted it along a channel, through Mission Bay, into the sea.

The Mission (California's first, San Diego de Alcalá) was founded by Spanish Franciscan friars in 1769, led by Father Junipero Serra. The original mission was located defensively near the Presidio (garrison) near the mouth of Mission Valley, because the native population were hostile to the invading Spaniards. Later, the Spaniards moved the mission further east along the San Diego River, to what became Grantville after the Civil War of 1861-65. Grantville, still a community of San Diego today, was a small town created as a settlement for Civil War veterans. It lay isolated in the swampy marshes around the San Diego River, amid dairy farms that covered a rural and sparsely populated Mission Valley until the latter half of the 20th Century.

The explorer Richard Henry Dana, in 1836 during the Mexican period (1821-1848), in his journal *Two Years Before The Mast*, reported that San Diego contained only the Presidio, the Mission, a small Spanish settlement known today as Old Town, and—on the beach—a shack for storing tanned hides. The mission fell into ruin and disuse, but was given to a Catholic Church organization after the Civil War by President Lincoln. It has been restored and remains under archeological excavation. Today it is an active Catholic church and basilica, and claims to be the oldest functioning church in California.

Old Town, today mainly a tourist destination, was the original Spanish, later Mexican, settlement in the safe shadow of the Presidio. This garrison, home of the first Spanish imperial governor of Alta California, has been restored as Presidio Park, overlooking the mouth of Mission Valley from a cliff on the south face of the valley entrance and river channel.

The New City, as opposed to the Old Town, came about with the arrival of a Connecticut Yankee named Alonzo Horton. He, moving in from San Francisco, saw that the great harbor was booming with ships, yet the population was centered miles inland to the north around Old Town. He bought 960 acres of barren land near the waterfront, and created what is today downtown San Diego. By then, Old Town had fallen into disuse, and hardly anyone lived there anymore. It was, for quite a time, 'out of town' as San Diego became the New City.

In the New City, Lottie A. Bernard arrived by train at the old Santa Fe depot at Kettner and D, now Broadway or West Broadway. She walked to the Brewster Hotel some blocks east, at 4th and C to ask about her two accomplices (and instead received the 'terrible medicines' mentioned by Dr. Mertzmann to induce a spontaneous abortion). She then headed back west to the ferry landing and off to Coronado to stay at the Hotel Del.

The New City is where Lottie later bought the gun with which she shot herself. The New City was where Wyatt Earp owned four gambling casinos, while he also ran horses at the Del Mar track some miles north. The New City also contained the notorious Stingaree red light district, and a small Chinatown.

Both National City and Chula Vista were newly incorporated during the late 1800s. Otay is a region in the unincorporated areas of San Diego County. South San Diego is part of the City of San Diego, also known as San Ysidro. However, the land area that meets the Silver Strand, the narrow strip of land going to Coronado, is the City of Imperial Beach (not shown on this map). The city now known as Chula Vista was a vast, privately owned preserve dedicated to the health craze of the time, known as Oneonta.

* * * *

Map 2, at lower center, shows Point Loma. This peninsula, which juts southward from the Ocean Beach and Loma Portal areas, shields the harbor entrance of San Diego Bay. By 'bay,' we mean the entire body of water enclosed within Point Loma and the Peninsula of San Diego, from Imperial Beach on the Mexican border to the south, as far north as the inner shores of Point Loma.

Not shown on the map is Ballast Point, so named because sailing vessels used to stop there and load rocks for ballast. That lies along the inner shore of Point Loma, just as you enter the harbor. Also not clearly labeled, but clearly shown, is a light-colored area of low-lying land, which was at various times property of the U.S. Army and the U.S. Marine Corps. It is now the general location of Lindbergh Field, San Diego's International Airport. This is one of the world's oldest commercial airfields, and one of the few major airports in the world that is practically located downtown.

Two modern features that did not exist in Lottie A. Bernard's time are Shelter Island and Harbor Island, both created largely from dredging operations along the bay near the airport. These dredging operations, conducted by both private and Navy operations, expanded the harbor. The Navy finished the last of these operations by 1945, eliminating the small bay, or bight, between North and South Islands.

One important feature not shown here, because it did not yet exist, is the Coronado Bay Bridge, emblematic of San Diego. The Bridge, completed 1969 and 2.2 miles long, rises nearly 300 feet above the water at its highest point. It rises from 4th Street in Coronado heading southeast, and curves around to the mainland. From the San Diego side it rises westward, starting at U.S. Interstate 5 in the Barrio Logan neighborhood.

It is useful to understand the Peninsula of San Diego, in reference to the surroundings in which Lottie A. Bernard and her contemporaries moved in the 1890s. This major geographical feature shapes San Diego's great natural harbor. It helps define San Diego, yet is not well understood even by many residents. Think of the Bay as being sheltered by two arms—one the Peninsula of San Diego which comes north, and Point Loma, a smaller peninsula that juts southward and overlaps the Peninsula of San Diego at North Island, as shown on the map. The best vantage point to see the entire city and bay is from atop Cabrillo Point, a national park situated high up on the outermost tip of Point Loma.

Originally, the peninsula consisted of the following main elements:

- **North Island** was originally an empty sand flat used for hunting jack rabbits, North Island has long been home of U. S. Naval Air Station North Island. Since about 1911, it has always been associated with military aviation—Army, Marine Corps, and, since 1917, Navy. The twin concrete hangars were featured in the 1935 James Cagney movie about U.S. Marine Corps aviation, *Devil Dogs of the Air*. Congress named North Island "the birthplace of naval aviation" in 1963. In 1927, Charles Lindbergh started from North Island on his famous flight across the U.S, across the Atlantic, and to Paris.

- **Spanish Bight**, a body of water that disappeared by 1945 as it was filled in by harbor dredging operations, especially by the U.S. Navy during World War II. A bight is what geographers call a smaller bay inside a larger bay. The strip of land joining North Island and South Island is called an isthmus. Though Spanish Bight is gone, a trace of its northern lip perhaps remains in that the mooring berths of the aircraft carriers *U.S.S. Reagan* and *U.S.S. Nimitz* are sharply angled in relation to one another, suggesting the northern lip of the vanished bight mouth. The isthmus that connected North and South Islands has vanished into the landmass of the greater peninsula.

- **Coronado Island**, or South Island. Elisha Babcock and Hampton Story used to go fishing in the bay, or come to the islands to hunt jackrabbits. Both islands (neither technically an island, but parts of a peninsula) were barren tracts overrun with brush and jackrabbits. Babcock had the soaring vision to buy the peninsula, develop it into a city, and use the sale of lots to finance a world-famous resort hotel. From that inspiration to the finished Hotel Del, and the developed community, took about four or five years (1884-1888). By 1889, San Diego was bust, Spreckels had bought out Story, and Babcock was sliding toward his ultimate bankruptcy. By 1892, Spreckels was the sole owner of the Del, and of most of the rest of Coronado and San Diego. The City of Coronado was incorporated 1891. Babcock had installed docks, ferry service, trolleys, and many other modern amenities.

- The **Silver Strand**, a long, thin strip of land stretching eight miles from Coronado in the north to Imperial Beach in the south. Became the home of the famous Tent City during the health craze starting around 1900 and lasting roughly until the Depression Era 1930s. Had a light rail system running circa 1900. Note: Coronado (incorporated as a city on South Island in 1991) had its own trolley that Lizzie rode several times—including the day she bought her gun in San Diego, with which she committed suicide at the Hotel Del.

In modern times, Spanish Bight is gone. North Island and South Island have fused into one landmass, containing North Island Naval Air Station at the northern end, and the City of Coronado at the southern end. From the City of Coronado, on Fourth Street, the soaring curve of the Coronado Bay Bridge connects the peninsula to the mainland in the City of San Diego. The Silver Strand remains, connecting Coronado with Imperial Beach. After the turn of the 20th Century (when Lottie A. Bernard lay buried and forgotten), the strand became home to the famous Tent City, part of the national health craze of the time.

Map 3: San Diego Overview

Map 3 is an overview of San Diego around 1890 or 1900, with selected details shown. The inset area refers to the next two maps.

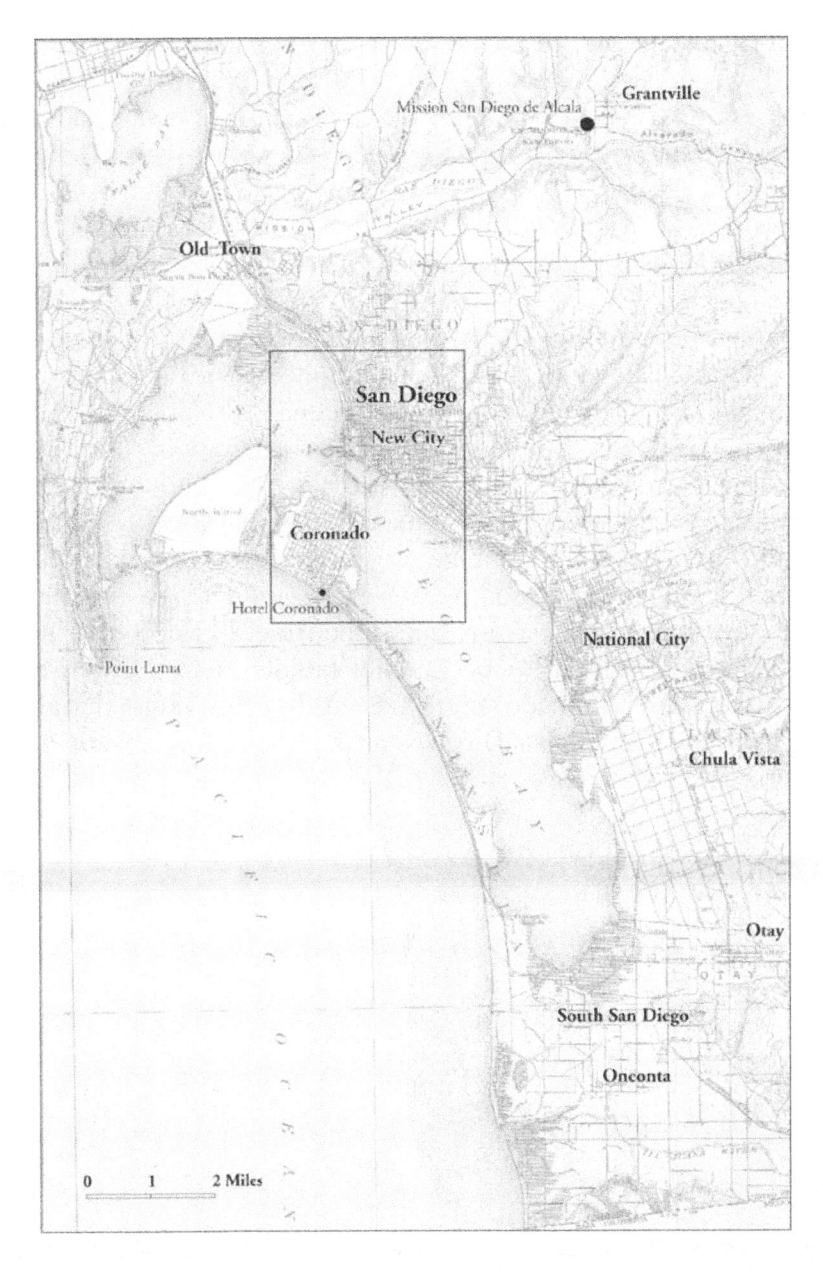

This inset focuses primarily on downtown San Diego (New City) and the City of Coronado around the time of Kate Morgan.

Coronado (2007 population 26,600) was part of the barren Peninsula of San Diego purchased 1884 by a consortium led by Elisha Babcock. Babcock and his partners developed South Island, or Coronado Island, and built the Hotel del Coronado. The grand resort was opened for business in February 1888. It is shown as the black dot on the southern beach of Coronado in Map 3, and this is where Lottie A. Bernard spent her few remaining days. The crown jewel of Coronado, the Hotel del Coronado, is where the main action of this true story takes place. Lottie A. Bernard was found shot to death on the back steps toward Ocean Boulevard on the morning of November 29, 1892.

Coronado, as it is laid out today, follows much the same street layout created by Babcock and his engineers. In the center of the island is Spreckels Park, named after the man who practically owned Coronado and San Diego for at least a generation. Opposite the Hotel Del, across Orange Avenue, today is the Glorietta Bay Inn— built after 1906 as the private mansion of John Spreckels. After the terrible earthquake in San Francisco, Spreckels moved with his wife and children to Coronado. At the corner of Orange Avenue and Adella Avenue, a block away, stands the Hotel El Cordoba, long ago the mansion of Elisha Babcock, chief builder and briefly owner of the Hotel del Coronado until ousted by Spreckels during the financial collapse in San Diego, starting 1889. We see this a little better in Maps 4 and 5.

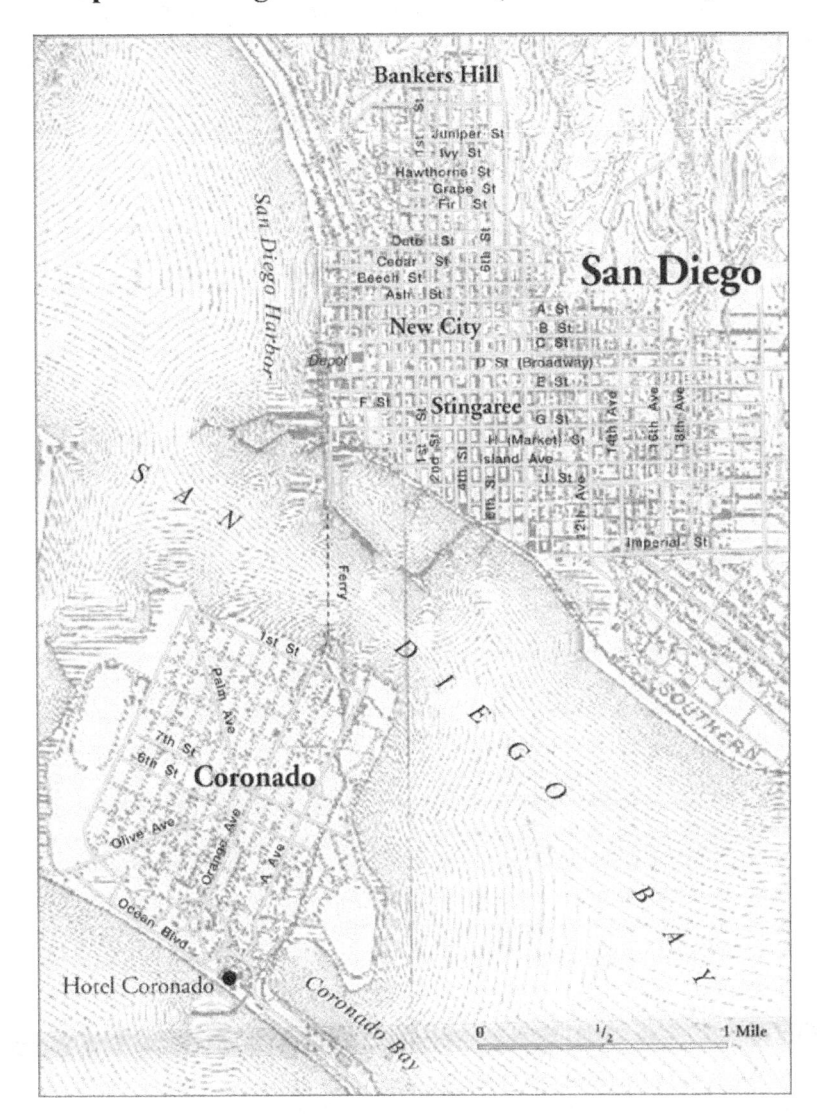

Map 4: San Diego and Coronado (3 Inset—Detail)

Map 5: San Diego and Coronado (Inset, Detail 2)

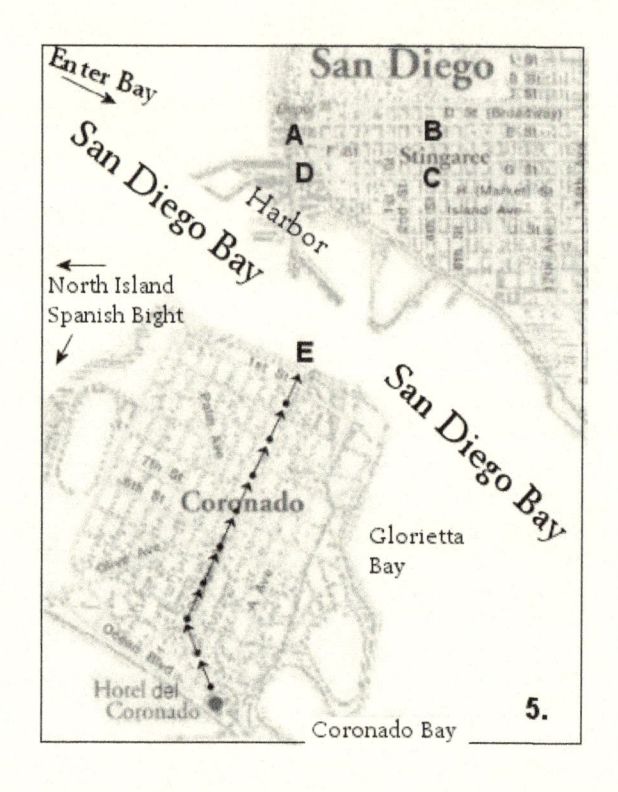

San Diego (2007 population 1.3 million): The New City is logically laid out (except that frequent deep canyons cause modern motorists to go bonkers as streets stop abruptly and start again across a chasm).

The main streets running east-west are lettered. This is important to understand in following Lottie A. Bernard's journey. In Map 2, notice Balboa Park and downtown. The dividing line (not shown) is at Ash Street, which runs east-west along the base of this enormous urban park (one of the world's largest, containing among other things the San Diego Zoo). Parallel to Ash Street, along its south side, is A Street. Beginning with Ash Street, the streets north of Ash are alphabetically named after trees (Ash, Beech, Cedar, Elm, etc.). The streets running east-west south of A Street are alphabetic (A, B, C, D, E, F, G, and a few more). In Lottie's time, today's Broadway was D Street. Also, her H Street is our modern Market Street. The notorious red light district, or Stingaree, occupied an area of some eight or ten city blocks (opinions vary) but conformed generally to today's commercially attractive and busy tourist area, the Gaslamp District. That's roughly from today's Petco Park baseball stadium north to Broadway (Lottie's D Street), and from as far west as parts of the waterfront to as far east as around Sixth or Seventh Avenues.

Running north and south, for most of the city, are numbered streets, except at the harbor front. From the water, we have Harbor Drive, Pacific Highway, Kettner Boulevard, and then these streets: India, Columbia, State, Union, and Front. From there, the north-south streets are in a fairly orderly grid, running from First into the double digits. All the numbered streets were streets in Lottie's time. With development, the first twelve streets became avenues. Where Interstate-5 is today was 18th Street in Lottie's time.

In Lottie A. Bernard's time, Wyatt Earp presided over four major gambling saloons in the Stingaree (sprawling between First and Fifth Streets, and Market and K). Lottie (Kate Morgan or Lizzie Wyllie, q.v.) trudged a relatively small area, from the railway terminal on Kettner to the Hotel Brewster, from the ferry landing to buy her gun on Fifth Street. In fact, her final journey was from the undertakers on Fifth Street (today's Fifth Avenue) to Mt. Hope Cemetery on Market Street. She is buried at Mt. Hope Cemetery, which was then outside of town, in the 3700 block of Market Street (then H Street).

Looking at Map 5 in particular, Point A indicates the area around the Santa Fe Depot (train station) where Lottie arrived in San Diego on Thanksgiving Day 1892. It was where her three trunks were kept, which she was never able to retrieve.

When she first arrived, she walked up D Street (today's Broadway) to Point B, the Hotel Brewster on 4th and D (my theory: to retrieve her abortion medicine, left there by Kate and John).

I have indicated as Point D the general area of the ferry landing(s) around G Street, where she most likely took the ferry back and forth between Coronado and San Diego. Her landing on Coronado was not the modern ferry landing, but Point E, where Centennial Park is today—some of the concrete footings of the dock are still visible. The modern ferry landing is a short walk from there.

Author 2008 photo 300ft above the Coronado Bay Bridge—see the modern San Diego waterfront at right. At the foot of the tallest buildings, center, is the Navy Pier area, within a block of the old Grand Union Depot, which was replaced 1914 by the Santa Fe Terminal. At left is the area of modern and (demolished) 19th century ferry landings. The 1892 ferry landing that Lottie A. Bernard used is gone, replaced by Centennial Park, but traces of the concrete dock remain. The 1890s ferries were steel ships, capable of loading horses and wagons, and bigger than today's ferry.)

Lizzie traveled on Orange Avenue on a trolley, which ran down the center where today we see green grass, flowers, and palm trees. At first, when the trolley tracks were removed in the early 1900s, they were replaced by a long strip of fragrant orange trees. However, the perpetual bane of Coronado Island was the jack rabbit, in limitless multitudes, who loved oranges. To rid the area of jack rabbits, it is said, the city decided to plant grass and palm trees instead.

End of First Book, Dead Move

See back pages of Second Book, Lethal Journey, for **End Notes**.

Book Two: Lethal Journey

❧ **Bonus 125th Anniversary Double Edition** ☙
Second Book of Two
Clocktower Books
San Diego

Lethal Journey

❧ A Historical Thriller ☙

By

John T. Cullen

Lethal Journey by John T. Cullen
Copyright © 2009 by John T. Cullen. All Rights Reserved.

You may not reproduce or sell the contents of this book, in whole or in part, by any means or for any purpose, in any medium known today or yet to be devised, for any reason. Severe statutory penalties apply.
Available online and in bookstores—print and digital Editions
www.sandiegoauhor.com/

Clocktower Books, Publisher
P.O. Box 600973
Grantville Station
San Diego, California 92160-0973
www.clocktowerbooks.com

Images in this book are from the 1800s, in the public domain, and easily found online. Exception: the background and rose on the cover are from the author's photos. The young woman's image is from an 1800s St. Valentine's Day card—artist unknown.

2012 Preface to Lethal Journey

Book 2, <u>Lethal Journey</u>, is the new story dramatization in the 120th Anniversary Bonus Double Edition about the famous ghost of the Hotel del Coronado near San Diego. After careful consideration, I removed the old dramatization from <u>Dead Move: Kate Morgan and the Haunting Mystery of Coronado, 2nd Edition</u>. The old dramatization seemed out of date and repetitious, since I later published this exciting thriller (novel, fiction), published separately and in this double edition.

A few words of information are in order.

(1) In the old dramatization, now gone, I ambivalently kept Tom Morgan as the dark, ruthless gambler and possible murderer. That is how he has been commonly presented in most versions of the legend that has come down to us. From the start, I had my doubts that Tom Morgan ever had anything to do with this story. I am now certain of it. I have independently concluded, from the lack of evidence showing the slightest involvement by Tom Morgan, that Kate's husband was ever in San Diego or had anything to do with her blackmail plot against Hotel del Coronado owner John D. Spreckels.

(2) In this thriller, <u>Lethal Journey</u>—adapted from my screenplay of the same title—I used the most rousing elements of both my true, factual, historical analysis and of the legend. The caveat is that <u>Lethal Journey</u>, while true to the historical facts, deviates in one aspect. For sheer excitement of the long-standing legend, I have retained the dark (noir) aspect of Tom Morgan as the villain. In real life, Tom Morgan had nothing to do with the blackmail plot at the Hotel del Coronado. Everything else in the book is true to history in my analysis. In real life, to the best that I was able to determined, Lizzie was not murdered or accidentally shot, but committed suicide out of depression. Her depression was caused both physically—by the 'terrible medicines' she had been given—and psychologically, upon realizing that she had been betrayed and abandoned by the only two persons in her immediate life that she loved and trusted—Kate Morgan and John Longfield.

(3) As I make clear in the Preface to the 3rd Edition of <u>Dead Move</u>, I am now convinced that the muddled, illogical legends associated with the famous ghost of the Hotel del Coronado are derived from a highly successful cover-up in 1892 to protect John Spreckels, who was one of the wealthiest and most powerful men in the United States. While the blackmail plot met its fated and doomed ending at his hotel, Spreckels was in the White House with family friend President Benjamin Harrison, negotiating for the future of Hawai'i. In 1890, as Spreckels took complete ownership from the hotel's co-founder and sole owner Elisha Babcock, King David Kalakaua of Hawai'i was the first royal guest. In 1891, Benjamin Harrison (Democrat) became the first U.S. president to stay as a guest—a family friend of the ultra-wealthy Spreckels clan.

Private security certainly protected folks like Spreckels from brazen yet common criminals like Kate Morgan and her gang (John Longfield and Lizzie Wyllie). The faintest scandal in Victorian society could have derailed Spreckels' efforts to save the Hawaiian monarchy, Hawaiian sovereignty, and the vast Spreckels sugar cane plantations in that sovereign South Pacific nation. As it turned out—coincidentally, but not without historical connectedness to the plot in which Lizzie Wyllie tragically perished—the Hawai'ian monarchy was overthrown just five weeks after the Beautiful Stranger died, and the ghostly legend of the Hotel del Coronado was born.

By an odd coincidence, King David visited at Christmas 1890, a guest of John Spreckels, traveled north to visit his old friend (patron) Claus Spreckels, and died as Claus' guest in San Francisco's Palace Hotel (strange timing, if not also circumstances, given the machinations of the Missionary Party and corporate republicans associated with the Dole pineapple fortune, to oust David and Spreckels and set up a pineapple territory in place of the sugar kingdom. On the other side of the coincidence coin, the Beautiful Stranger situation happened two years later in November 1892. Queen Liliukoalani was deposed in January 1893—terminating Hawai'i's monarchy and sovereignty. The former nation was made a U.S. territory, and elevated to statehood in 1959.

Second Book: Lethal Journey
Dark 1892 Thriller Closely Based on True Historical Fact

Table of Contents

Book Two: Lethal Journey	169
2012 Preface to Lethal Journey	173
1. Kate & Tom Morgan, 1888	177
2. Lizzie & John—Late Summer 1892	202
3. Kate Morgan—Late Summer 1892	213
4. Detroit—Early Fall 1892	221
5. Knocked Up & Ruined	224
6. Detroit—Kate, Lizzie, & John	230
7. Los Angeles—Mid-Autumn 1892	243
8. Conspiracy—Late Autumn 1892	255
9. San Diego—November 1892	261
10. Coronado—Thanksgiving 1892	271
11. Conspiracy's End—Legend's Start	312
Author's Notes-Lethal Journey	316
Selected Reading:	*329*
Notes:	*329*
San Diego Author John T. Cullen	331
End Notes for Dead Move	349

For End Notes to Dead Move, see end pages of this volume.
See Page 179 for Table of Contents of the novel (second book, titled Lethal Journey).

1. Kate & Tom Morgan, 1888

Two men, reeking of leather and tobacco, stood in the shade of a wooden awning at the small train station in Las Cruces, New Mexico. On this hot summer day in 1888, with tiny gusts of oven-like wind pushing through the ivy trellises around the wooden train platform, the two men looked as if they were not enjoying themselves much. On the other hand, they looked too busy to care much about their discomfort as they pored over a map together, while one of them held a packet of tear sheets with images and print on them. Wind rattled the paper every few seconds. The land all around was flat and far and baked like painted mud. Both men were tall, about the same height, and lean. Thinning hair stirred in white strands on a browned and blistered head when each removed his head gear to scratch. One man had a salt-and-pepper beard; the other, gray stubble over a mass of wrinkles around his mouth. Beard had dark brown eyes. The other was gray-eyed.

Each man, under his rumpled black suit, wore a shiny brass badge discreetly on his leather belt under a flap of his jacket. Each man's badge bore a plain, engraved personal number in the center. Fancy scrollwork, around the number, read *Union Pacific* and *Railroad Police*. On the other side of the leather belt, under the opposite jacket flap, each man wore a shiny, nickel-plated 1888 Remington New Model Pocket Army Revolver with .44 caliber Winchester rounds in the cylinder, and a short 5.5 inch barrel. Each man wore a broad-brimmed hat covered with dust from a long ride on horseback, but they had traded their riding boots for stiff-soled city shoes. The men were on the hunt, just the same, only their hunting territory was coming toward them. They heard a distant train whistle, and were eager to get on board and search for quarry. Each good arrest meant a bonus. They worked hard for their money.

"I'll send the boots out for cleaning," hollered an elderly black man in shirtsleeves and great big boots, who puffed a corncob pipe and moved at a leisurely pace as he led the two tired horses toward a barn to be wiped down and watered. Man and horses both looked husky and sun-beaten.

The bearded detective gave a little wave of thanks, as if his every motion must be spare and economical. The hand that waved wore a scuffed, fine chocolate-colored leather glove whose index finger had been removed—leaving the business end of his finger exposed, when it needed to be, on the hair-trigger of his six-shooter. Both men were Civil War veterans in their late forties. Each had killed men and faced death enough times to get that dark, lean, haunted look around the eyes that was like a permanent shadow, a veil of nightmares.

The two men rifled through their assortment of Wanted posters, trying to memorize faces and read details. They had just ridden in from Santa Fe, where they had delivered two bank robbers and collected a hefty fee aside from their regular salary. Now they were ready for a new hunt.

"These two," said Gray-Eyes as he pulled a fresh tear sheet from Beard's gloved hand. "They're new."

"Ah-yuh," said Beard. "That's a new one. Should be easy to spot if they're working as a pair."

They looked at lithographic reproductions of the profiles of a young man and woman. Under the pictures were names in bold, black print: Thomas E. Morgan and Kate Morgan, born Farmer. Under that was printed, in smaller letters, a list of charges, including that they were cardsharps. Missing was the next line that appeared in some other sheets: *Caution! Armed!*—so evidently these were light-weights. Then came the small print, citing any known details about the two. As Beard and Gray-Eyes read, the distant train whistle drew near. Already, they could hear the chuffing of the engine as the coal-burner came racing through a distant mountain range. From experience, they could assemble a small drama in their imaginations.

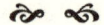

☙ ❧

T*homas Edward Morgan and his wife, Kate Morgan, were grifters who worked the Transcontinental Railroad trains. Tom was in his early 30s, while Kate was nearly ten years his junior. They hailed from the wheat belt in southwest Iowa, children of well-to-do farming and miller families. Somehow, they hadn't set well—the land apparently had no lure for them, and they preferred to travel. Once the railroad bug got you, there was no turning back.*

Typically, Kate would find a mark—some young man with a few whiskeys in him already, a gullible mind, and a fat wallet. She'd entice him into a deserted forward car, where the spider waited in his web: Tom Morgan, grinning easily under his short black hair, riffling a deck of cards. Tom would give the impression of sipping at a shot of Red Canary Straight Rye Whiskey from a colorful bottle that stood nearly full and invitingly at his elbow. "I want you to meet my brother," Kate would tell their intended victim as she ushered him into the compartment. "I hope he will like you, because he is a good judge of men, and you seem like a fine gentleman." She had the poor fool thinking, in his muddled mind, that he would somehow have his way with her in the next few days as the train clattered monotonously through the endless Continental United States. As the mark slid into his seat opposite Tom Morgan, the latter would reach into his coat for a silver etui and offer him a fresh cigar. Kate would sit in a corner and continue flirting with the man while Tom invited him to a friendly little game of poker. *"You get to know a man when you play cards with him,"* Tom would say. *"Looks like my sister here has taken a shine to you."* Then he'd riffle the deck some more, and the game was on.

ಒ ಹ

The two railroad policemen folded away their posters and stepped out to the edge of the platform, each carrying a dark and ornately decorated cloth valise. Gray-Eyes' was dark green with maroon swirls, while Beard's was dark blue with gold lines in a Romanesque motif. The train was growing louder now, and its smoke filled the sky in quick, energetic bursts. The smoke stack on the front of the dark-green locomotive was a wide cinder-catcher type, designed to prevent hot ashes from flying back and setting the cars on fire. Meanwhile, the grating in front was designed to toss aside the carcass of any stray cow unlucky enough to be wandering on the tracks. The train emitted a series of piercing steam-whistle notes, rising and falling, while the wheels chattered happily until the last mile or so, when they started to slow and the train started sounding tired. The old black man came from the stable, in that same lethargic middle-of-nowhere walk, and pulled the hose pipe around on a high wooden water tower. A trio of young Indian lads, wearing good cotton shirts and Levi Strauss work pants with suspenders, and a variety of top hats with feathers and beaded designs, pulled a wagon of coal and wood along a narrow-gauge side track nearby.

A Mexican vendor appeared on the platform with cigars, sandwiches, and fruits, while his wife and children struggled alongside with a clay coffee urn and tin cups. The train's great steel wheels screeched on the steel rails as the train chuffed slowly to a halt on air brakes. The engineers leaned from their cab, and a conductor in a dark blue uniform waved to them. The two detectives looked like traveling salesmen as they quietly boarded amid two dozen or so passengers milling about, some getting on, others getting off. A woman cried and waved her hankie as she spoke in Spanish to two brown-skinned boys with big eyes in school uniforms. A young wife waved to her Army officer husband who leaned from a window throwing kisses. Arms reached out to the Mexican, placing coins in his hand and accepting coffee, food, tobacco, even tiny paper flags with local motifs for souvenirs.

Coaled and watered within a half hour, the train emitted a shrill whistling sound. The engine pumped, and chuffed, and began its pile-driver rhythm to propel tons of steel and wood back to speed. The two detectives deposited their satchels in the railroad caboose at rear, and started a leisurely walk down the train. They kept their coats buttoned to conceal the purpose of their journey. There was no rush now. The several hundred passengers were safely imprisoned in a world of hurtling upholstery and dusty glass windows. Mesilla Valley cotton acreage passed by outside, looking like fields of snow. The sky was a cloudless darkish blue, raked by the summer sun and hot desert winds. Low mountains looked as if they had white cake-patterns baked into them. The rocking motion of the train was steady and hypnotic. The men sidled among passengers who crowded the aisle outside First Class and Second Class compartments. They moved through the bar coach and into the restaurant.

Suddenly, Beard gripped Gray-Eyes' sleeve. They froze in place, looking over the heads of a school of dark-haired children, toward a row of dining seats. Two black men in white coats served coffee and cakes to a white family seated around a long table. Beyond them, seated together in a corner, were the Morgan couple. They were unmistakable from their pictures—he with the slightly bulbous, pale head and short dark hair; she with the piercing black eyes and rather plain features. She did not have a pretty face, but she had the scintillating gaze and golden tongue of a first-class seductress. Their clothing was dark, thin for the summer, and dusty. Under a plaid blouse and ankle-length tan cotton skirt, her figure was full and robust, promising much to a gullible and slightly inebriated man looking for a place to shed his dollars. She wore a little gold locket around her neck, which she often fingered and then stuck down into her blouse for its protection. Her husband, the sibling in their brother-sister act, had the strong, wiry lean build of a Midwest farmer. He had probably been a towheaded youngster, Beard thought as he and Gray-Eyes withdrew into the shadows of the new leather accordion connectors between cars. Morgan glanced toward them for a second, then looked away.

"We'll split up," Beard said quietly. Something in that man's eyes made him nervous. The woman's were just as unsettling. Gray-Eyes nodded. They would be less conspicuous apart. The couple weren't supposed to be dangerous, and the bounty on them would be relatively small. If the detectives could apprehend them, especially in the act, with a witness and complainant, they could turn them in at the sheriff's office in some town up the road and then continue looking for bigger game.

"We're in luck," Beard said in the same low voice. "You go back to the rear and get some rest. We'll spell each other." Gray-Eyes nodded and walked leisurely off without looking around. Beard picked up a discarded, folded newspaper, and shadowed the couple as they made their way forward to an empty first-class carriage. This car did not have wood or glass dividers, but the compartments had fine, plush blue-gray seats with high backs that served like dividers. Half the coach was, in fact, a sleeper with darkened, empty bunk slots. Beard sat in a corner booth and opened his paper on the table. He watched from a distance, in window reflections, as a bottle appeared on a small window table and Tom Morgan set up his gambling ruse. Kate, meanwhile, wandered in search of just the right man with a few itches to scratch. As she passed by, Beard looked up from his newspaper and exchanged looks with her. He made himself seem distant, as if his thoughts were elsewhere. She languidly raked him with a carnal gaze. A chill ran up and down his spine. He felt as if he were being licked by a snake. He shuddered and looked away.

She passed him by because he had not radiated toward her the spark of hunger and gullibility for which she was looking. After a few minutes, he rose. Folding his newspaper under one arm, and pruning a cigar with his pocket knife, he wandered after her. The bar car was crowded with mostly men, a few women joining their husbands at window seats. Women were not allowed at the bar.

Beard watched as Kate approached a fortyish, plump man with short, graying hair parted on one side, and a checkered vest. The man was reading a Denver newspaper and tossing back shots of whiskey while fingering a coffee cup to one side and keeping a cigar going in the smoky car air. The man was florid and had little watery blue eyes as he began to notice Kate. She pretended to be looking for some acquaintance. They caught each other's eyes, and spoke to one another. She probably said she was looking for her 'brother.' After a few more words, he eagerly rose and offered her a seat opposite him at the small table. He was very solicitous, putting his cigar out and using his napkin to dust the glass counter top. He bowed slightly and said something, probably offering her a drink or coffee, and she protested, but he protested more, and she relented as he signaled for a waiter. Soon, one of the black stewards in starchy white linen vest brought a tea service for her, and another stiff drink for him.

Beard sauntered back to get Gray-Eyes. He picked up his step as soon as he was out of sight, and was fairly trotting by the time he hurried through the crowded third class coaches with their teeming families of all races. Entering the caboose, which smelled of sawdust and machine oil—no passenger comforts—he went down the row of canvas bunks hanging on steel poles. He found a bunk with Gray-Eyes' jacket curled as a pillow and still warm —but no Gray-Eyes. A Chinese porter happened by, wearing a *chignon* and round black hat, and an ankle-length blue apron. Beard pointed to the bunk. The porter pointed to the locked toilet door in a corner and grinned. Beard pounded on the door. "They're starting."

The other shouted back distantly: "I'm going to be busy here for the next few minutes. That Mexican food is going through me like a train."

"Hurry up," Beard said, laughing. "I can hear your train whistle."

"Oh shut up and go do your job."

"Join me when you're able." Beard took his time walking forward to the eerily deserted Tom Morgan coach. He passed through the bar and restaurant coaches. He'd wait for Gray-Eyes to join him. The Morgans would need a while to work their cardsharp game. The trick would be in the timing—they needed the victim as a willing witness.

Beard watched Kate sipping her tea and making pleasant conversation with her mark. Beard studied her, trying to figure out how she worked her magic. It was rather chilling, he found. She was a bit homely, but she could turn up this warm, radiant smile that made her eyes and lips sparkle. She also moved her foot close, so that the man's ankle brushed against hers. The man, for his part, was rapt. He sat forward, with his arms folded under his flabby chest in that suit, and seemed to be inhaling the very essence of her smiles and sweet words. Beard saw the ankle-action and thought to himself: *I wonder if he's wondering if she's doing it on purpose, or if she doesn't know, and he's wondering just how far she'll let him go with her, and how much it's going to cost him.*

Then, after about twenty minutes of that, they rose and she followed him out of the bar car. Then, in the corridor, she stepped ahead to guide him. He was a heavy man, and leaned a bit with one hand against the wall as he navigated in his cups. At one point, he reached out and tried to touch her rear end in its hoop skirt, but stumbled and almost fell on his face. She turned with a look of phony concern and took his arm. With this new, seemingly innocuous body contact, she lured him to the compartment where Tom sat waiting. Beard noticed a reddish bruise on one cheek, as if Morgan had given his wife a black eye recently. Morgan looked the type, Beard thought, a flinty-eyed, mean-spirited confidence artist.

Beard watched from a distance as the heavy-set man sat down opposite Tom, while Kate sat nearby and smiled at the man with that same magical, balmy look that had him eating from her hands. Tom deliberately took his time. He poured the man a shot and pushed it toward him. The victim began to lose his shyness and become part of what must have seemed like a family to him. Brother and sister, they were utterly warm, simple, charming, seductive, and friendly. Tom spread out a hand of cards and tapped the deck with his forefinger. It didn't matter what the game was. Maybe the victim didn't even know how to play cards. The ruse was that the brother must approve of the man before he would allow his sister to become more friendly with him. Beard supposed that the victim by now thought that these two odd ducks were maybe a pair of simpletons (never mind the cigars, booze, and cards) and that a license from Tom would give him entry to the paradise that Kate subliminally promised. Beard could feel it all the way across the coach, from his spy place near the connector—a radiant emanation that snared its victim in a net of coquettish nods, and glances, and smiles, and turning aside of the head in pretended shyness.

Gray-Eyes came up behind Beard and startled him. Beard said, "Just in time. The wolves are closing in on their lamb."

"Looks like the wolves have him cornered."

"They're feeding him whiskey, and I wouldn't be surprised if she's dropped some magic powder in his glass to hurry it up."

Gray-Eyes clutched his stomach. "Oh no."

"Make it quick," Beard said.

Gray-Eyes hurried away to find a toilet.

Within a few minutes, the victim began to seem torpid. First, he stopped moving and just sat like a big frozen slab of lard. His eyes grew confused and the cards tumbled from his fat white fingers. Beard knew then—Tom Morgan had slipped him a dose of something. The heavy man snapped his head upright two or three times, but finally sank into a deep slumber. Kate hurried to his side and helped him lie down on the seat. Both Morgans were all over him in an instant, going through his pockets. As Tom Morgan triumphantly held up the man's black leather wallet, Beard pulled his coat back and stepped into the middle of the cabin, displaying his badge on the left and his gun on the right. "Hold it right there, both of you. You're under arrest."

"What for?" said Kate with a big smile. "Our friend here has had too much to drink."

"With a little help from you two," Beard said.

"What is the matter with you?" Tom asked. "Are you crazy?"

"I was just about to ask you that," Beard said. He reached into his coat pocket and pulled out a chain with a shiny steel handcuff on each end. The very next instant, he knew he had terribly miscalculated.

Tom Morgan had two Deringers, one in each hand, now aimed at Beard's head and torso. Tom stood at a slight crouch, holding the pistols at slightly different angles with the practiced stance of one who was no newcomer at this. "Mister, I don't know who you are, but you're looking at the Angel of Death."

"Take it easy," said Beard as he raised his gloved hands halfway and opened them in hapless surrender.

"Now we just have minutes here, don't we? Before a porter comes through, or your friend returns. I thought you two looked suspicious. Kate, put the manacles on him."

"You are digging yourself a hole," Beard said.

"Stow the big talk. I'll kill you right here, right now, if I have to. Got nothing to lose if it comes to that."

As he spoke, Beard could feel the woman move around him. He heard the chain rattle, and felt the sharp bite of a manacle on his right wrist. "Hands behind you," she snapped. He offered his other wrist to cuff.

"Okay, Mister," said Tom Morgan. "You can avoid meeting Jesus today if you don't waste any more of my time and just do what I say."'

"Fair enough," Beard said, knowing he was licked.

"Kate," Tom said. She pushed Beard toward Tom. Morgan pocketed one gun and kept the other trained on Beard's head. The man and woman led Beard toward the door, and Beard understood what was coming next. Tom said: "You play along, you just got yourself a long, thirsty walk to the nearest town. You screw with me, and I'll throw you out there with a bullet in your head. Make up your mind."

The door swung open at Kate's push. Wind howled by, and made their hair and clothes rattle. Beard's hat flew away. Dusty grit swirled in circles that made all three persons blink. They spat harsh dust from between their teeth. As Kate and Tom watched, Beard walked straight-up, as if he were stepping onto a train platform, out into the air, and instantly disappeared in a roar of wind. A glance behind told the two that their victim had landed, rolling, somewhere on the rocks and grit. "He'll be okay," Tom said as he kicked the hat after the man and pulled the door shut. "A little banged up and worse for wear, but he'll live. I shamed him. He won't say what happened to him here. "

"He'll be looking for us, though," she said. "There is another one, too."

"Yeah, I saw them both. You got the wallet?"

They looked at the sleeper. She said: "We got his watch, his money, his gold tie clip, his cuffs, his collar pin. We've cleaned him out."

"Good. Not a minute to waste. Act natural." Leaving the sleeper where he lay, they walked slowly back to the dining coaches. Tom kept his hands in his pockets, a Deringer in each fist. Kate clung to him, and he shook her off with an elbow to the ribs. "Woman, don't dog me now."

She held her side and grimaced in pain. "One day, I'm going to throw you off a train, you son of a bitch."

"You try me, woman, and you'll join that tin horn copper."

For a minute or two of menacing silence, they walked down the corridor of an empty car that was probably expected to fill up in some city ahead. On their left were windows overlooking desert and irrigated farm land. Several of the dusty windows were slightly open. In-rushing wind freshened the hallway's stale air, but brought with it dust and pollen, and a boiled-coal smell from the locomotive. On their right were closed and darkened cabins. Far ahead were the noise and laughter of the bar car.

As Tom and Kate approached a door marked *W.C.* on the right, the toilet door opened, with the hand of Gray-Eyes on the door handle. The man had finished his business, pulled up his pants, and was about to step out. One could hear the rattling of tracks under the open-bottomed box that dumped its contents on the ties as the train flew onward.

Tom saw the man's badge and gun and brought one of his Deringers up.

The lawman, with years of experience, took this all in during an instant. Lurching back, he reached for his gun. A collection of Wanted posters fluttered from under his elbow.

Tom shot him in the chest, and the policeman keeled over backwards onto the toilet seat. Tom glanced left and right, and saw that nobody had witnessed this. He put the Derringer in his pocket. He took the key from inside the door. The man sprawled, looking away with dull eyes, dying in a pool of blood, with his long legs crumpled and his arms extended to the sides as on a cross. Grabbing the Wanted posters, Tom pulled the door shut. He locked it from outside so that the white enamel sign said *Occupied*. He threw the key and the posters out the window.

Kate pointed ahead. "We're pulling into a town."

"Good. Let's lose ourselves. We've got the guy's money, and we'll figure out something—quickly hop a train going somewhere else." He put her arm under his elbow and grinned. "You still want to throw me off a train?"

She sighed, wrapped her arm around his, and gave him a rueful smile. Together, they waited by the nearest door for the train to stop so they could vanish into the enormous, empty continent that was their playground.

                                                ❧ ☙

Tom and Kate Morgan stayed in Chicago for a time. They lived in a cheap apartment near the bay, in a third floor rear walkup with a rear landing and outside stairs. The place was a tenement, teeming night and day with screaming children, roaring drunks, and crying women. It was a veritable Babylon, with every tongue on earth being spoken.

The trains were too hot now to pull any schemes. Kate avidly followed the newspaper stories, reading them to Tom as they sat over coffee and toast for breakfast each morning.

The man Tom had forced to step off the train had landed and crushed his skull on a boulder, dying instantly. She felt a little pang in her gut as she read about this.

Elsewhere, she read about the man Tom had shot. After hours of silence, the toilet where the other railroad detective had died began to ooze a thick, dark liquid from under the door. Porters at first stepped over it and avoided it and told each other to get a mop and a bucket but nobody did, until they realized it did not stink like liquid feces but instead was cold, congealing blood. Tom and Kate were several states away before white-jacketed porters and the Chinaman broke down the door. The case was widely reported with the usual trumpeting of end-times and lax morality, but nobody really knew what had happened. The railroad issued a terse statement that the policemen had probably died in line of duty, since Wanted posters were strewn about the train tracks, but it wasn't clear who had murdered them. Nobody came forth to offer a clue.

Tom ate a ham sandwich while Kate sipped tea and read to him. Tom said: "Dammit, we have to lay low. And I need money."

"So?" Kate said. "I don't think anybody is on to us. Although it was rather stupid of you to throw the posters after the guy." As she often did, she nervously fingered the gold locket around her neck, and stuck it down her blouse for protection.

"Stupid?" Tom raged. "What choice did I have? What the hell is the matter with you? Do I see you carrying a gun? No, you depend on me to save and protect us both."

"Dear, you should have stopped to take our poster with us. Then they'd suspect all the others."

"Or, I take that one out, and they know it's us. Why don't you stick to your tea, and I'll stick to doing the thinking around here."

"Oh really, honey? And that's why we're sitting here in this dump, with breakfast but no lunch or dinner? Good job, honey."

He made a fist, as if he were going to hit her, and his eyes blazed, but bent angrily over his sandwich. "Go to hell."

She changed the subject, the way she always did when there was no reasoning with him. "So we stay off trains for a while. How long? A year? Two years?"

"I have an idea," he said. "Time for you to take another one of those temporary domestic jobs you're so good at."

"I don't have much choice, do I? I have an idea. You stay here and do all that thinking, and I'll go out to work and support us."

He reddened. "I'll support us, Kate. I'll go out and put my poker skills to use. You'll see. We'll do okay." His look appealed to her, reminding that they had been soul mates growing up in Iowa and ever since.

She sighed and put her paper down. "Oh, all right. Come here." She opened her arms with that raw sexuality she could radiate so intensely. He rushed around the table to kiss her. As they hugged, spoons and a salt shaker fell of the table. She ran her hands down his back to his buttocks. "Gimme," she said in a barely audible groan.

He uttered a groan of passion and lifted her to take her to bed. She pulled up her dress as he carried her, and with closed eyes and face turning side to side, gave him a stray thump on the chest. "Come on. "

He threw her down on the bed. She pulled up her knees and was ready for him, with her legs open. She taunted: "Are you man enough?"

He tore her underwear off along pale, smooth woman-legs. Her words rang around his ears, incomprehensible in the beating of his blood—she taunted, she begged, she cajoled.

Tossing her bloomers aside, he stared down into her as he furiously undid his belt and dropped his pants before crawling across the bed toward her. Her savage woman words rained down on him as he ran across the mattress on his knees to throw himself on her and silence her with the rage of his passion. She knew what was coming. She welcomed it. It was part of their rising to the fire, the way the sun rises from shadowy mountains in the morning and sets the sky aflame.

"Yeah!" she snarled, reaching for him with clawed fingers. Her eyes were dark orbs of desire and fury, her face a pale blur, her mouth a dark tear between wet rouge lips. He slapped her across the face, grazing a cheekbone. Stunned, she turned her face aside with the blow, but ready to take the rest of what he would give her. He tried to slap her firmly left, right, left, but she blocked his arm and pinned his wrists in her powerful hands. She spat at his face. His expression became something between rage and hunger. His eyes got huge. The corners of his mouth turned down, and his discolored teeth showed.

It was the only way she could enjoy letting a man take her. He had to defeat her, like an army climbing over ramparts in a hail of arrows. She wanted to be defeated and taken and spread open and ravaged with sex and love and passion. Her eyes fluttered as she recovered from the first blow. He squirmed around on her, grunting like a wild animal and pawing her wetness. Bracing herself, palms down, she made a bridge of her strong, firm, and ample body. She slammed her heels down repeatedly to bounce on the bed so that her bush struck his grasping palm, and wet slaps resounded through the room.

She sat astride him, still in her dress. She rode him like that for some intense minutes. He lay with his eyes closed, enjoying bliss. She felt like slapping him hard across the face in retaliation, but she knew he would go berserk and maybe forget about making love and beat her instead. In one impatient sweep, she pulled off her dress. It slid easily over her smooth, firm skin. She let it flutter away, and with it her slip. Her brassiere followed. "Grab them," she said tensely. He reached up to grasp the nurturing breasts she offered him, just for him, with thrusting nipples, and nut-dark areolas each studded with a circle of nubbins.

Her pale back was long and curving, shadowed along the *fossa* of her spine, her waist was full and firm, her buttocks were wide and creamy, her hair tumbled about as she turned her head from side to side in the rhythm of their unity. Tom pulled her gently down to nurse on her, and she grew patient as she looked at him and waited. They had been soul mates since adolescence. They had been making passionate love since long before their youthful marriage amid the grinding barrenness and intolerable boredom and then tragedy of their lives in Iowa. Nowadays, their sex was still always passionate, but the gaps between were growing ever more painful and alienating for her as Tom drank and grew moodier and more violent. He hurt her. He had murdered men, and was growing ever more dangerous, even for a woman like Kate, for whom his dangerous edge made a heady liquor. In the abandon of the love bed, that dark edge upped the ante, like when he pushed more money into one of his smoky poker games. But increasingly, except in little island moments of time like this, that intoxication grew harsh and repellent. Somewhere, deep in her soul, she knew a break was coming. Not now, not with him grasping her, mouth full, mewling under her in need as she suckled him and gently rode up and down on his hungry shaft. Not yet, but soon. She had no idea how or when, but the end seemed near. After that, she had no idea—she could not think beyond the moment. He cried out, forgetting her breasts. He held her by her sides and started thrusting in piston-quick motions. They wailed cacophonously as his savagely thrusting, bony hips slammed up at her in a frenzy, rocked her up and down. She cried out dizzily as they came together in an exhausting blur. Then they lay together, entwined, immobile, hung over from their passion and near unconsciousness as if glutted from a feast in the darkish room. As he snored on his back, she lay with her hands and chin on his chest, regarding the enigma she loved. The arch inside her thighs was gloriously sore, still trembling with the echoes of their unity. Her cheekbone, as it often did, throbbed as it swelled. She sighed deeply, and enjoyed the moment as if it were the last.

☙ ❧

Kate found temporary employment with a well-to-do family who simply adored her because she was efficient, quiet, and so very pleasant. She had done this before, when she and Tom were short of money and his gambling was driving up debts. It was a sweet system, really, and she saw great potential to milk it. Once you got in—meaning, one family used you for a week or two as a temporary domestic, usually because a prized regular girl was sick or visiting her dying mother out of town, once you had that foot in the door, there was a grapevine among other wealthy ladies in town. If you were good—and Kate, when she put her mind to it, was among the best, because she knew it would only be for a week or two, and there was money to be made—if you were good, you had no end of work. You bounced from one home to the next, always changing scenery, never bored. Kate started looking for opportunities, and she discovered a new sideline for which she had a remarkable talent. It was called blackmail, and it was a lot more lucrative and less risky than robbing strangers on trains.

Tom was in a funk. When he got like this, she usually had him cool off a while, just hang around and maybe stew over some long, slow beers in the city's many taverns while she made a little honest money as a nanny or a domestic and took whatever she could quietly steal out the back door. A silver tea service might not be missed for months until the next scheduled session when all the maids in a wealthy house gathered in that room to open the cupboards and have a polishing party—only to discover, with a shriek, that someone had made off with the ornate centerpieces. Then they might rack their brains over who had worked there the past few months, and when this might have happened, and eventually would give up, thinking maybe the pieces had never existed in the first place and it was all in their imagination. A thorough scouring of all the pawn shops and dealers for a hundred miles around might turn up some of the pieces, which had fetched twenty or fifty or a hundred dollars or more. But nobody in the pawn shop would remember who had sold them. Some young man with a slightly bulbous head and dark hair. Or was it a rather plain young woman with burning eyes?

❧ ☙

Kate thought a lot about her newly discovered talent for blackmail, but didn't tell Tom about it. Not yet. Not only was she withholding money from him, afraid he'd gamble it away, but now she withheld her thoughts. Tom was changing on her, and not for the good. The distance between them grew more out of him than from her.

The discovery came to her one day when she was dusting in a wealthy home in Chicago, and she spied a curious thing. Down the hall, in an alcove framed by bay windows, another young maid stood, also dusting. Thea was a modestly attractive girl of twenty. Kate knew of her, but had never exchanged more than a hello or goodbye with her. Thea did not appear to know Kate was watching from afar as the master of the house appeared behind her. He was a man of 50, a lawyer and partner in a big firm, with lots of money. His wife was an adorable blonde angel with beautiful blue eyes and a girlish mouth, and Kate could not imagine what her husband saw in other women. The master was not a handsome man at all, but a chubby toad with little short arms and no neck, who wore collars that rose to his ears. He had a wide, round head and was balding, and had fleshy lips that fairly reeked of his cheap appetites. His eyes fairly craned out on stalks in his hunger for forbidden fruits. His cultured wife, meanwhile, kept up a brave smile, and ushered their children through piano lessons, horseback riding, ballet, and other cultured skills, while her husband pursued depravities right under her roof.

As Kate watched, Thea kept dusting, but her pace changed. It was obvious she knew who was behind her, and what was coming next. The master came directly up behind her. He looked left and right but, in his impatience, he didn't see Kate watching from afar. He stood very close behind the girl for a few moments. She stopped dusting, and they seemed almost like one person. Kate watched him hand her a paper dollar, which she hid in her skirt. Then he stood behind her, feeling her body up and down. He handed her another bill, which she tucked away in an economy of motions. She leaned forward over a table. He lifted her skirts just enough, and pressed against her. He took her from behind in quick, rough, jerky motions. When he was done, he flung her hems down. He turned abruptly, without a smile or an endearment, buttoning his fly, and walked away as if he had just taken out the trash. Thea turned away to dab under her skirt with a cleaning cloth, and gradually resumed her work as if nothing had happened. Her expression, though unreadable even with Kate's sharp eyes, was not a pleased one. Kate loathed him, and formed a plan.

She crossed paths with him the very next day, in this household of a dozen or more women servants. Kate gave him her dazzling look, and the toad lit up. She waited for him in that very alcove, and he came up behind her. She took the dollar bill he offered, and let him feel under her dress. His hands trembled as his cold fingertips touched her warm skin. She almost choked with loathing as those chilly fingertips probed into ever more private places. He pressed another dollar on her for a minute's feeling.

This happened two or three times over the next few days. She kept the extra money from Tom. The toad became more and more enamored of her, so much so that she noticed the other maid shot her jealous looks. Finally, the toad showed her a twenty dollar bill and made sinuous motions and ravenous eyes—more mean-looking than seductive—as he blocked her into an alcove and pulled on her skirt. "Twenty I go all the way," he said. He licked his lips. She took the twenty and put it in her pocket. She took him by the lapel and swung him around. He grinned and looked happy as she pulled him around so she had him trapped in the corner with her hand still on his lapel. His leering smile vanished, replaced by a look of shock, as she spoke. "Now, buster, I have news for you. First of all, you're not getting any closer to me. Second, if I tell my husband, he'll come burn your house down and shoot you in the middle of the street like a dog. Third, I'm quitting this job right this minute, and you're going to hand me three hundred dollars cash or I go straight to your wife."

His expression went through a spectrum from shock to anger to contempt. He pushed her roughly away, though she was a half a head taller than he. "See here, bitch, how dare you talk to me like that?"

She shoved him back. "Don't try me, pal. You can either…"

He shoved her again and scoffed. "It's your word against mine. Who would believe a temporary domestic?"

"Try this on, you fool. Thea is willing to talk. Together, we can take you for twice as much." Thea knew nothing, but he wouldn't know that.

"You crooked scum." He showed snarling teeth and hateful eyes.

"You stupid, ugly old lecher. I have nothing to lose, but I can ruin you. Let's march straight to your office and get the cash, and I'm out the door."

"What if I tell the police?"

"Fine. Let's each tell our story. Your wife leaves you, and you're ruined. Come on, Frog Face, you've had your fun. Now pay up or else!"

She walked out of that house a quarter hour later with her three hundred dollars plus the twenty he'd given her initially. He would not tell his wife a thing, of that Kate was certain. He'd do as she told him, and tell his wife the temporary woman had quit, with many apologies, to care for her dying mother in—oh, make up a city, something new—Atlanta. She put the money aside where Tom wouldn't find it.

                                          ☙ ❧

Kate found another position, and spent many hours working every week. She and Tom were having sex several times a week, but life with him was becoming joyless. She put a good face on things and tried to please him, but the lack of railroad work and a few gambling losses around town made him increasingly despondent. In that state, he grew more morose and violent, until sometimes she feared him.

Her other position came to an end, and she soon found a new one. She left every morning at dawn, and came tiredly trudging up the stairs every evening after dark, to find him either gone out gambling and drinking, or passed out with his head down among bottles on the kitchen table. She was thinking about giving him her extra money, just to please him. But there weren't that many toads in the world. She always kept enough of her earnings to buy food and pay the rent, and gave him the rest as he expected and demanded. She wished they were saving some, but it wasn't her place to tell him what to do.

Months went by, and Kate realized she had missed her period. She was throwing up every morning. Tom had been terrible lately, and she expected the wonderful news would turn things around. Maybe it was time to play the trains again. That seemed to keep Tom's spirits up and his mind focused. But she was tired of that life. They had run away from what was burned into her mind as that miserable, empty farm village of Washington, Iowa, with its long, desolate winters and inbred, narrow-minded religious bigots full of pretension and self-righteousness. Tom had been her soul-mate. It was he and she together against a world that did not understand their wild freedom. Tom and Kate loathed the little people who moved about in stolid, everyday gray little lives. She was running away, too, from the memory of her Eddie dying in that desolation during his second little day of life.

ঌ ৶

Eddie lay on his back in the crib, dressed in white, and waved his little hands fitfully like any baby. He seemed lusty at first, trying to stare up into the light with unseeing eyes the color of sea foam. His crying changed from energetic to a heartbroken little mewling, as if he knew something terrible was happening. How she held him, so close to her heart! He stopped crying. He wouldn't feed. By noon on the second day of his life, he not only grew silent in her desperate embrace, while she comforted him and begged him to stay, but he grew limp and cooled in her arms. She sobbed and shrieked and threw herself on the floor holding her dead baby. She raised him to her breast, and tried pushing a milk-dripping nipple into his mouth. Tom screamed and ran out of the house in terror and despair. A neighbor woman pried the lifeless, chill little body from her naked breast after a time, and what happened from there she would never rightly remember. It was all a nightmarish haze. Tom finally came and held her, for hours it seemed, and it was the closest they two had ever been.

ঌ ৶

Always the disapproving eyes of her wealthy grandfather floated in her memory when she thought of that horrific time. He had disowned Kate not long after, when it became clear she and Tom were not cut out do farming.

Now Kate and Tom were finally going to be mother and father again. As the changes flushed through her body, filling her with new life, she started thinking of maybe settling down—all sorts of weird thoughts she wasn't used to. A little house with a white picket fence in California. Why not? They couldn't live on the run forever. Surely Tom would see that.

Kate understood she was different in how she felt in her relationships with other people. She knew she did not have much feeling about other people. This made her cling to Tom all the more, because she loved him. She could watch Tom shoot a man dead and not blink an eye. But Eddie was the tragedy of her life, the one point where she felt like other mothers. She could never let go of the little baby's memory, but carried his image with her with an obsessive love that turned to anger and rage, and enabled her to hurt people like the toad-master without a moment's hesitation.

She never expected the reaction she got when she opened the door. Tom had been drinking heavily. She found him sitting at the kitchen table with his glass and bottle, staring into nowhere. "What's the matter, honey?" she said as she hung up her purse and bonnet. As he looked up at her, with a blank, lost gaze, she could not contain herself. She sat in his lap and put her arms around his head. "Darling, I have great news to tell you."

He looked up, his eyes blinking as if he'd been napping. "What?"

"We are going to be parents."

"What do you mean?"

She hugged him. "Things are going to be different."

His reaction surprised her. He seemed numb. She wondered if he had bought some heroin from the Chinese down the street. "What is the matter, darling? Aren't you happy? We're going to have another child."

He pulled her arms down from his neck. "I don't want to go through that again."

"Oh, honey, I understand how you feel. Our poor little Eddie…"

He pushed her away so that she almost fell, and rose. "Don't speak of him again!"

"He was your son, Tom." She stumbled against the table, bracing herself with both hands. This was entirely different than she had expected. "He is an angel in heaven, but he is still your son."

Tom was cool. "I can't stand this life anymore. I'm going to cage a pair of tickets so we can take the train across country. I've got the dark itch in my fingers, and I know I can get some money off those stupid guys. How are you going to work your end of it when your gut's hanging out there like a bag of oats?"

"Honey, we can't do that forever." Seeing the frustration in his eyes, she thought of giving him her money for his tickets. She had nearly four hundred dollars set aside. But she didn't want to do any more of that. She had not yet told her of the toad, and her plan to fleece more like him. "I can work as a domestic. You could take some little jobs here and there."

"Doing what?" Tom banged his fist on the table. "What's wrong with you? We live in this slum, and you want to raise children here?" He drew closer, so that she could smell tobacco and gin on his stained teeth. His eyes were red, and she could see the mixture of rage and worry in his features. His lower lip trembled. She felt sorry for him. She started to regret not taking precautions. Maybe she should get an abortion and wait for a better day. Maybe he was right. She didn't see him haul back.

Out of the blue, Tom's fist collided with her face, and she saw stars. From there on, it was all a blur. She went down, and he stood over her. She tried pleading with him as she lay on the dirty wooden floor that smelled faintly like railroad ties, but words would not come out. His boot landed in her side. At first he was not kicking her hard, just more or less rolling her over so he could slap her face back and forth with both palms. When she pulled her knees up to protect her stomach, and held her arms over her head, he yelled himself into an ever greater rage. She could not make out what he was yelling. At one point, when his face was close to her, and words exploded from his teeth, she punched him. He blinked stupidly and fell silent. She scrambled back and punched him again. He fell on his rear, sitting side-saddle on the floor holding his jaw with one hand and bracing himself behind with the other.

She staggered to her feet and ran. She made it as far as the back door. There, he tackled her. She had the door open and could feel the cold night air, which was a relief after the stuffy, smoky kitchen that stank of cabbage and puke. He hit her, like a bolt of lightning that made her stagger out onto the creaky wooden landing. As she held on to the stair rail with both hands, she saw in his eyes the utter lack of love or feelings for her and her condition. He kicked her, and she was dimly aware of rolling, banging her head, bouncing down the wooden stairs, head over heels—amid splintering wood and people exclaiming in horror nearby—into oblivion.

Gradually, she woke into a hallucinatory state. The nausea and darkness told her, in caressing voices like nuns singing, that she was in the depths of an opium dream. Beyond that sphere of laudanum, she felt distant pain like broken furniture across a room. Her vision was blurry, and shadows moved around her. She smelled camphor and other pungent aromas, including the gnawing odor of hospital alcohol. Dimly, she thought she must still be alive, but something was badly broken and most of her body was utterly numb. She tried to signal to the shadows moving around her, but they had tied her hands and feet to the bed in which she lay, and she could not raise a hand though she tugged weakly. She could turn her head to look at her immoveable hand, and for a moment her near vision swam into focus so that she saw the hospital gauze with which they had bound her wrist to the bed post. But it was all a mystery to her, and she stared at her hand, and the wrist, and the gauze without being able to make sense of them. She tugged at the other hand, without looking, and it too seemed to be tied.

She heard a man sobbing in a nearby room, and voices comforting him. "My God, what has happened to her? She was just going out for some groceries, and I heard a terrible scream as she fell down the stairs."

A stern, older woman of authority said: "I am sorry she lost your baby, Mr. Morgan. If she lives, she will never be able to have children again."

ஐ ஜ

Kate awoke a long time later. Weeks had passed. The pain, the withdrawal from opium, had all passed. Miraculously, she had not suffered any broken bones. She sat in a high-backed wicker wheel chair with great big-spoked wheels with rubber tires. Someone had dressed her in a flannel gown, and a blanket lay across her lap. She was alone in a quiet solarium overlooking a green lawn, and the city skyline loomed beyond that in glorious sunshine. She called out, and when nobody came, she threw the blanket aside and tried to stand up. Her legs would not obey, and she uttered a convulsive scream. *Paralyzed!* In terror, she gripped the table beside her and pulled herself erect, falling on the cold floor as she did so. Sobbing, she crawled away from the wheel chair. Two nurses with white nunnish wimples came running. "Mrs. Morgan! You've fallen from your chair!" said one. They helped her to her feet.

"Am I paralyzed?"

"Why no," said the other. "You're weak from weeks lying in bed."

Kate, over the next few days, tested her legs—first one, then the other, and kept alternating, lifting them, feeling her rubbery muscles—but she was determined to get out of here, to start walking, to run for miles and miles and get her strength back.

"We thought we were going to lose you a few times."

"You had a terrible infection, and you know—" They both looked at her sadly. "You lost the baby. And you won't be able to have any more."

Kate remembered all the things she had overheard, and fell back into the wheelchair sobbing. She cried her heart out, and the two women left her alone.

※ ※

Within a few days, still feeling the tiniest bit weak, but almost back to her normal self, Kate Morgan stood in the lobby of the hospital with her bag. A nun had walked her out; had brought her bag along and set it on the floor. The nun handed her something, saying: "They brought this in with you—it fell off you when you went down the steps."

It was her gold locket, which contained her only picture of her lost child Eddie. The nuns said they were expecting Tom would come to pick her up, as he had promised someone he would. Kate looked at herself in a mirror as she put her locket back on, by its fine little gold chain. She looked gaunt, with big hollow eyes and protruding cheekbones. Her sense of loss radiated from those eyes. Twice now she had lost that precious gift, and now it would never come again. It was something she could not forgive Tom for—not this. Anything else, but not taking that away. Most women had many children, and lost a few along the way. It was normal, even though it hurt terribly. You never forgot that brief, tiny life you would have loved to nurture into a strapping son or daughter. Now she had this to bear, and she would bear it for the rest of her life. She had always dreamed of one day leading a normal life somewhere, once her demons had their fill and left her, but now she was resigned to being a shadow of a woman. She determined she could not be at the whim of the destroyer any longer. Gathering her shawl around her, and picking up her satchel, she made her way slowly and effortlessly out the door.

On the great steps overlooking the city, she was overwhelmed by the noise and the colors and the thousands of bustling people, carts, horses with clattering hooves, rumbling electric trolleys, billboards, smoking locomotives, and yelling vendors. The smell of horse manure and men's cigars and a thousand things burning, rotting, flowering, decaying, almost made her want to return to the green and silent womb of the hospital. But she pushed that morbid thought away.

To hell with Tom Morgan. To hell with her grandfather, the wealthy and stern miller back in Iowa. To hell with the toads and grabbers of this world. She had a life to live, and she would make the most of it in whatever way was hers to make it work. As she walked back to the tenements, she picked up her step. Her legs seemed to grow stronger, and the warm spring city air filled her lungs. She was 24 years old, and by God she was determined to enjoy her youth to the fullest. She resisted the urge to feel sorry for herself.

The tenements were noisy and smelly as ever. She hoped Tom wasn't there. Looking up, she saw the place seemed dark, as if nobody were home. She had only one errand here, and that was to pick up her belongings. Then she would disappear where Tom could never find her.

As she walked up the outside steps in back, she was surrounded by blurry, running, yelling children. She almost welcomed their noise in her ears. It was the music of life. She climbed up the wooden stairs to the third floor landing, from which Tom had kicked her. Someone had replaced several broken pieces of the railing. The apartment window was dark. As she turned the key in the lock and opened the door, her heart froze.

There, sitting at the table amid a litter of empty liquor bottles, was Tom Morgan, smoking. His eyes were red from drink, and he had a cold cigar butt in one dirty yellow hand. He had not washed or shaved in a week or more, from the looks of him. When he saw her, he stumbled to his feet so the wooden chair fell over backwards. "Katie, my love…"

"I have nothing to say to you."

He fell to his knees on the floor and raised his coupled hands in prayer. "My darling, my wife, I beg you, forgive me for what I have done."

"You are not the boy I fell in love with back in Iowa." She walked past him and pulled her trunk from under the bed. Surprised at her own furious strength, she sat it open on the bed and added her belongings on top of those already in the trunk—including one of Eddie that she prized above all, a wispy lock of her lost son's hair.

Tom knelt behind her and wrapped his arms around her thighs. "Katie, my darling, I can't live without you."

She struggled to get free. She waved the lock of Eddie's hair and yelled:

"This one at least I have something to remember him by. The one you just killed I don't even know if it was a boy or a girl. Get away from me." She smashed her hand across his mouth and nose, and he sat back holding his face. A noose bleed shot between his fingers. He got that ominous fury in his eyes as he rose and walked to the stove, where he rattled the empty kettle and tossed it aside, then to the sink. They had only cold water, when that was running, and there wasn't time to heat water on the stove. Cold water was just right for stopping a bloody nose. She could see the violence building in him, and yelled: "So, you dirty bastard, you want to finish the job and kill me while you still can? Because I'm leaving you, and there is nothing you can do or say to keep me with you. You don't deserve a wife. You don't even deserve a dog that you can beat and kick around."

"Katie, my love, think of our years together." He held a cold, wet towel to his face and turned, looking exhausted. "I'm sorry, Katie, I'll make it up to you, I swear."

"How can you make it up to me?" she yelled as she gathered her coat and hat and a few other belongings and threw them in the trunk. She walked to the door, stepped out onto the landing, and yelled down to the unemployed men milling below around a whiskey bottle. "I need a man to carry my trunk. Give you a quarter." There was a rumble of feet as they fought to climb over each other, up the stairs, and she pointed to one she knew, Magruder, a big quiet reliable man. "You'll get the trunk for me, and I'll tell you where to bring it when we're gone from here."

Magruder trudged up the steps, eyeballing Tom Morgan nervously. He wore a gray woolen slouch hat and a rumpled gray suit stained with sweat from many days' work when there had been work to do. He could probably hold his own against the whipcrack Morgan, but he wasn't a man who relished a fight. With his missing teeth, he kept nervously chewing his tongue and flicking its pink serpentine length among his various stumps like an eel underwater. He walked with his fists balled, keeping a nervous gaze on Tom Morgan, who stood dabbing himself on the face with the rose-stained towel.

Kate told him: "Go on, take the trunk down and I'll be after you in a minute." Ignoring Tom, she looked about to make sure she had not forgotten anything. Tom didn't get in Magruder's way—clearly that was not the fight Tom wanted to pick just now. Magruder left with the trunk, clomping down the wooden stairs. The noise of children, the wind, the city clamor, rose up as he went down. Kate turned and started for the door, but Tom blocked it. "Katie, you're my wife. I forbid you to leave."

"You can't stop me, Tom. Don't even try."

Tom closed the door, so that they were alone and shut in. "Kate, you've had your say, and now I'll have mine."

She started around him, but he gripped her arm in a steely hand. As she struggled to escape, he yanked her back. He gripped both her arms, and she cried out in pain. He reeked sourly of whiskey, and his breath was foul from sore gums and unbrushed teeth stained with cigar juice. "Kate, Kate, stop it, Kate, Kate," he said in a low, warning voice that usually meant kicks and blows were coming.

"You've already killed me," she wailed. "What more can you do but kick my poor body to death?"

"I'm not going to do anything bad to you," he slurred. But his grip on her was like a vise. She tried to wriggle free, and he dug his thumbs painfully into the nerves above the hollows of her elbows. She started to cry with pain. He pressed her toward the bed, speaking in that low, ominous voice: "Katie…Katie…look at me…I can't live without you…" He threw her down on the bed, and then stood undoing his belt. For a moment she thought he was going to rape her. But the belt came off, and the square steel buckle dangled at his knees like a weapon. "I'll kill you before I let you leave me."

Still rubbing the numbness in each arm where he had gripped her, she rolled out of the way as the belt descended on the bed. The steel buckle landed with a thump in the pillow beside her skull. With a choking shriek of terror, she rolled off the bed and into the narrow space between bed and wall, onto the dusty, dirty wooden floor. Tom started to climb over the bed. Raising her feet, with her back propped against the wall, she shoved the flimsy steel bed against him. He yelled in pain as it gouged his shins. "Damn you, woman! Just trying to reason with you. Now you're in for it!"

One of his Deringers lay on the floor in a heap of soiled clothing. She reached behind to get to the gun, sprawling awkwardly. He came crawling around the bed and grabbed her ankle. She kicked him in the head with her free foot, but he was unstoppable. She saw his full rage and fury come to the fore, clouded by days of drinking, and she hoped there was a round in the chamber as she aimed the gun at his face and pressed the trigger.

At that very moment, he jerked on her leg, and the shot went off a bit, creating a red splash in his filthy gray shirt, halfway between his neck and his shoulder joint. He grimaced, and gripped the wound.

She pulled the trigger again, but nothing more came out. She remembered it was a single-shooter. She dropped the gun, kicked him in the face with her free foot, and struggled up over the bed. He pushed himself up along the wall and started after her. She picked up the belt that lay on the floor, held it in both hands, and swung it fully around as hard as she could. She heard the crack as it connected with his head, and he went down like a sack. She stumbled to the door, sobbing, yanked it open, and ran outside without looking back or shutting the door. She half ran, half staggered down the stairs, one flight after another, until she arrived in the courtyard. The men standing around, amid a thousand yelling and running little street Arabs, were used to fights and screams and looked at her dumbly. Magruder stood by the trunk, tipped his hat, and his eelish tongue ran a few pink flicks amid the yellow reefs of his mouth.

Shortly, Kate and Magruder were on their way down the dirt alley. She held his quarter, and he carried her trunk on his shoulder as if he were an elephant of a man. Tom appeared on the balustrade high above, clutching his nicked shoulder. Streams of blood crisscrossed each other on his face from the wound on his head. "Kate, don't leave me! Please! I love you." She ignored him. Men all around sniggered, because none liked Morgan. Tom yelled all the louder: "You are my wife! I will find you, woman. Look over your shoulder every day! You are mine, and I will have you back no matter where you go." Then he could be heard brokenly wailing in his drunken state, both from his physical pain and from the loss of her as Kate walked out of his life. She would keep looking over her shoulder for the rest of her life, but now she began to think about where her path would take her next.

2. Lizzie & John–Late Summer 1892

The city of Detroit loomed large and industrial and dotted with lights as dusk fell on a hot summer afternoon. The city's downtown streets were jammed with horses, buggies, and street cars. Pedestrians in fine clothing were out for a refreshing stroll as the evening breeze replaced the sullen humidity of day. Shop windows were brightly lit and stuffed full of goods. Above the windows were endless competing signs and billboards, some twinkling with myriad little metallic disks, others with flashing colored lights. Theater marquees shone brightly. Ticket booths stayed busy as men and women lined up to buy seats.

An attractive young couple hurried along, dressed in their finest. They held hands and half ran, half walked toward a performance of Denman Thompson's popular comedy, *The Old Homestead*. The girl was Elizabeth 'Lizzie' Wyllie, aged 24, and she loved theater. Her eyes were bright with excitement. Her smile was dazzling as she looked up at her companion with love, and held hands with him. Lizzie was a beautiful young woman, always elegant in her manner and dress, and people turned their heads to look after her. Her lover was John Longfield, a good-looking tall dark-haired man with a rakish twinkle in his eye, dimpled cheeks, and a card-player's deceptive grin under a pencil mustache. He said to her "Come on, Lizzie, we'll go in the side entrance. I got tickets from my friend Steve."

Lizzie loved him and his take-charge manner. John seemed to know his way around people and situations, whereas she was—to begin with—near sighted, and on top of that not terribly good at reading people or understanding how to finagle things the way John always did. What would not be apparent to the casual eye, either, was that she was a single girl and he was a married man. In fact, he was her foreman at a large Detroit bookbindery. It wasn't clear to her whether his wife knew what he did, and she could never get him to quite spell things out about that or about their relationship. They had fallen into a mad, passionate sexual love affair a few months ago—Spring 1892—and had begun to attract attention in the work place. Lizzie's sister May, the sensible sibling, also worked there and kept telling Lizzie to be prudent and to be discreet. As far as Lizzie was concerned, she had been lonely and unhappy for some time, and she hoped…well, she knew it would be a bad thing to wish that he'd leave his wife and children for her. She'd never met the wife, but sort of pictured her as a dumpy workhorse who was afraid to stand in his way for fear of losing him and the household income. In this world, a woman alone, with children, abandoned by her husband, was at best an object of pity—what had she done to drive him away? What was wrong with her? At worst, one might speculate that perhaps she had been caught in some indecent situation and he had, in his justifiable outrage, moved away to maintain his honor and integrity in the eyes of society. Then again, plenty of people were practical and realistic, and realized that men were like the wolf or any other opportunistic predator, so the woman should not always be blamed. Lizzie was willing to settle for being his mistress, if only he would set her up in a little place of her own so she wouldn't have to live with her loving but impossibly domineering mother any longer, and share a bedroom with her loving but strong-willed sister May. All these thoughts, and the dark blot of bad memories about her previous misadventure in sex, formed a blurred and fleeting background to her sense of pleasure as she ran along the sidewalk with John. Steve could have been John's twin, complete with mustache and rakish grin, as he opened a side door and let them in. John handed him something—money, Lizzie thought—and Steve solicitously escorted them through a door, to a winding little stairwell that led up to good seats in the mezzanine.

For the next few hours, Lizzie laughed and clapped delightedly, while John kept his arm around her and absently fondled her in the dark. Sometimes, she responded by touching him. It excited her that he seemed to always be erect around her, and that made her feel hot inside. She had learned that if she let him go too far, or too long, or if she responded too ardently in these public situations, then he would lose some of that cool veneer and become too heated. That in turn might attract attention from others in the seats around them, and that would mortify Lizzie—because she was by nature always lady-like, demure, and cool. It wasn't that she was putting on an act. She was just naturally dignified like that, and people often thought she was wealthy. She had long ago accepted who she was—a myopic, beautiful factory girl with champagne tastes and a beer pocket book, as one of her old *beaux* used to say. She had always assumed one day a boy with some style and money would take a fancy to her, and she'd live in a big house with servants. In the meantime, she was quite content to go out with May now and then for a beer at the German gardens, or a walk in the Campus Martius with John. She knew nobody would approve of her relationship with her foreman, so she had kept the affair a secret. If the women at work were beginning to notice, well, so what? As long as she and John were discreet, nobody would get hurt or embarrassed. Her happy, cozy affair could play out in its own little world.

Lizzie had seen this production a dozen times, and knew its main acts by heart. The piece was a record-breaking success around the country—the story of a New England rustic who leaves his village for the big city, has many misadventures, and is only too happy to return to his simple life. The play plucked nerve strings around the nation, but Lizzie especially appreciated its sentimentality. And she had a rare eye for fine costume.

John arranged for her to meet one of the stars at a reception in the lobby afterward. About a hundred men and women crowded around for punch and snacks. The noise seemed deafening and overwhelming to Lizzie, who still felt tender with the story's magic. Actors and actresses, still in stage costume, mingled with guests. John said: "Lizzie, over here, quick, I want you to meet someone." John led a spellbound Lizzie toward Steve, who stood waiting beside a splendid actress in beautiful white gown and large silvery wig. She did not seem entirely comfortable. Steve said: "Oh, hello John—Lizzie—please meet Miss Lilly."

Lizzie said "The famous actress!" and Miss Lilly brightened.

John said to Miss Lilly: "My lady friend and I have been dying to speak with you. We enjoy your performances so much—we've seen you three times so far."

Miss Lilly said: "Why thank you. That's so nice to hear. What a beautiful young lady!"

Lizzie said: "Thank you! Your dress is absolutely fabulous. You must have a great designer and tailor to do such fine work."

Miss Lilly said: "I do, my dear. You're not only a theater fan, but a *connoisseuse* of fine dress. Are you an actress also?"

Lizzie said: "No, hardly. I have wicked stage fright, and can never remember any lines. I was thrown out of my second grade school play because I couldn't remember some dumb lines about a rabbit." Miss Lilly's dazzling features grew confused—Lizzie was not the person she'd been told she would be seeing.

John, aside, asked Steve: "Can you get me the tickets I asked about?"

Steve said: "We'll see what I can do about those tickets. Will you be stopping by the office anytime soon? I'll be waiting for you."

John said: "You'll see plenty of me."

Miss Lilly said: "I see my manager over there. I must leave you. It was such a pleasure to chat with you all. Bye!"

On the way home, John and Lizzie ambled happily under the gas lamps on the street. Both lived in central Detroit. He would put her on a streetcar, and then take a different car to his home about a mile away. "I have a present for you."

"What is it?" They stopped under a street light. He held out a little box. She opened it and gasped. On a bed of cotton lay two pretty silver earrings. "John, these are beautiful." She kissed him on the lips, briefly and excitedly, before returning her wide-eyed and open mouthed attention to the earrings. "I'll have to get my ears pierced finally."

He held one up, and she obliged by turning her head to one side with a happy look. "They will look gorgeous on you."

"Thank you so much!" Lizzie said. She put the box in her purse, and they continued walking arm in arm. "What a thrilling evening."

John said: "One of these days, darling, you'll win the lottery or I'll hit it big at cards, and we'll have a nest egg."

Lizzie clung to him. "That's a lovely dream, John. I love when you take me to the theater, and to such splendid parties."

John said: "You are a lady of class, sweetheart. I am proud to be seen with you."

Lizzie beamed and said: "Until the dream comes true, I just want to take things a moment at a time, savor the good, and put up with our poor, everyday lives as we are." She put her hand against his heart and gave him a dazzling smile. "One day, we'll belong just to each other, won't we?"

John put his hand over hers, holding it to his heart, and regarded her with unknown calculations in his eyes, saying nothing.

Not long after the theater night, Lizzie and her mother, Elizabeth Wyllie, and her sister May were in their kitchen at home. Late summer sunshine poured in through the one small window with its gray sheer curtains. It was humble, but cozy—it was all the home the three women knew, and a loving one at that.

May sat in her corner, rattling away at her sewing machine while her foot pumped underneath. Lizzie lay curled up with a book on the sofa. She wore eyeglasses and read her novel with a serious expression.

Mrs. Wyllie carefully took a hot baking sheet from the oven. "Here you go, girls, for your day off. Fudge brownies with powder sugar." She regarded Lizzie and chided lovingly: "Now she is wearing her glasses for a change. What vanity—only when she reads her fantasies."

May said: "Nose stuck in a book as usual. What are you reading, bookworm sister?"

Lizzie looked up from her book as if in a great trance. "What?"

May said: "What tragedy of love and death are you devouring?"

Lizzie said: "The newest novel by the English author Thomas Hardy. It was published last year. It's about this beautiful maiden, and titled *Tess D'Urberville, A Pure Woman Faithfully Presented*, who started out pure, but was brought low by a careless man, and the evil world in general." Lizzie sighed, shuddered, and hugged her book. "I'm almost done. What a dreamy feeling. I could just die with Tess, or I could cry all day."

May said: "I know what you mean. What is it about love sorrow that makes us weepy and we can't get enough of all that sentiment?"

Mrs. Wyllie served cookies with a pleased look, though she pretended to be grumpy. "Two young girls looking for the loves of your lives. Beautiful flowers, waiting for just the right butterfly. Watch that you don't land some handsome moth in a cheap suit, singing you lines written in heaven with the devil's own pen."

Lizzie laughed. "You mean, wearing cheap wings." She and May laughed, and even their mother cracked a reluctant grin. May said to Lizzie: "I don't read like you do, but I adore those theater plays. Like Dickens' tragic Little Nell—a fallen angel."

Mrs. Willey said: "You girls have your heads in the clouds. You're a bright girl, Lizzie, and with all your reading you could have gone to teacher's school."

May said: "Must you bring that up again, Mom?"

Lizzie said: "At my age, it's too late now. What a terrible thing that was. I would still never let a man see me with eyeglasses!" She closed her eyes and reflected back on that day of anguish.

☙ ❧

It had happened a few years ago at the teachers' college entrance exam. A young, bookish Lizzie, wearing glasses, stood among ninety other girls awaiting admission to the test hall. The corridor had that forbidding shine, and a severe wax smell, that always reminded Lizzie of those dreadful tests she rarely ever passed. Her mother had made her come here, and she was sure she would fail. Just because she was bookish didn't mean she was teacher material—Lizzie knew that, but her mother needed to have it demonstrated. Nearby stood a hundred or more boys waiting to be admitted by another door. Beyond was a single large room, with the girls' exam desks on one side, and the boys' exam desks on the other side, separated by a wide aisle.

Seeing the boys outside—as the boys and girls exchanged shy, interested looks—Lizzie furtively put her glasses away and fluffed her hair.

A bell shrilled. The doors burst open.

The exam candidates poured into the room and took their seats.

On the blackboard were the rules, clearly written, among them: *No satchels, books, or notes of any kind.*

All the other students left their satchels on the floor by the back wall.

Lizzie, who couldn't read the board, walked in and sat down, putting her satchel under her chair. Soon, the exams began.

Students were bent over their test booklets in deep and stressful concentration. Stern and scary proctors marched about like police detectives in black suits.

Lizzie was working hard on her exam.

Suddenly, a proctor pointed from a distance—at Lizzie's satchel under the chair. She was reaching down for a hankie to blow her nose. Several proctors hurried to her desk. They took her exam book away, and escorted a shocked and tearful Lizzie from the exam hall. She never did try to take the exam again, but found work, along with her sister, at Winn and Hammond Bookbinders.

⊱ ⊰

In the kitchen today with Lizzie and May, a few years later, Mrs. Wyllie said: "We all make mistakes. Life goes on. Vanity is one of the deadly sins or is it? We will be okay, we three, if we stick together, work hard, and stay out of trouble."

Mrs. Wyllie left the room with a load of wash.

Lizzie said: "I heard that our American Stephen Crane is working on a book titled *Maggie: A Girl of the Streets*. I can't wait to read it."

May said: "I just love those tragedies. Let me know if you hear of a good play."

Lizzie said: "I have a gentleman friend who has good taste in theater, and he'll take me. Maybe he'll bring you too."

May said: "Do I know this gentleman friend?"

Lizzie shrugged her shoulders and smiled secretively. "I can't tell."

May said: "Oh no, Lizzie, I know who it is. Don't go with him. He's bad news."

&

About that same time of year, late summer, John Longfield and Lizzie Wyllie walked arm in arm on gravel walks amid flowered lawns, to the tunes of distant calliope music. There was a carnival in a far corner of the park, with music and rides.

John and Lizzie stopped to smell gorgeous, colorful flowers.

Women with parasols and men in straw boater hats strolled by.

John bought Lizzie a cotton candy.

Lizzie was joyful as John helped her on a carnival ride. She had already dismissed the cautions uttered by her sister, and she had sworn May to secrecy. If her mother ever found out—there would be the dickens to pay, because Lizzie had already once made a terrible mistake of this nature, and it didn't seem possible that she would fall into the same ditch again. But, looking back on it all some months later, half a continent away, in a fairy-tale hotel and resort overlooking a stunning vista of Pacific Ocean and Coronado Beach and Cabrillo Point, Lizzie would have occasion to ponder the collision course on which she already was, unwittingly, during those innocent strolls in the park.

&

The factory hall was gloomy, with dusty air illumined through barred, jail-like windows. The hall was full of women of all ages engaged in the complex stages of case binding, from gathering the signatures to folding and stitching them on wooden frames, and building the covers around them. May and Lizzie were busy at a bench with eight other women.

A door across the floor, marked *Foreman*, opened, and John Longfield peered out.

May looked up, and caught Longfield's hungry look toward Lizzie.

Longfield closed the door.

May watched her sister rise. Lizzie wiped her hands on a cloth, and walked off to the ladies' room. Minutes later, she was on her way back. All the women noticed.

Lizzie knocked on the foreman's door. The door opened, revealing a brief glimpse of Longfield. Lizzie entered the room. The door closed, and the women at the bench with May exchanged looks. Some were darkly amused, others scandalized.

⁂

Inside the office, Longfield's naked back moved in sensual thrusting motions over a long table. Under him, Lizzie's ecstatic face looked up, enraptured. Her eyes opened and closed with each of his long, slow strokes, except to flicker now and then, to look up at him with love and ardor.

Lizzie got on top, riding him, swaying sensuously. Longfield clasped her buttocks as he thrust upward, again and again and again.

Lizzie said: "John, John, I love you so."

John said: "And I adore you, Lizzie, my darling."

Lizzie said: "Promise you'll keep me forever!"

John did not answer, but he grunted as he approached climax, and his rutting drowned out any reply he might have made.

⁂

John Longfield was one of several men playing cards at a round table in a dark, smoky den. It was in the cellar of a cheap hotel downtown. The bare stone walls had been white-washed. Only a few narrow slit-windows near the ceilings let out smoke and brought in fresh air.

A stony-faced waiter in a long white apron brought the men round after round of tall beers dripping with foam.

In the background, a crippled man with an eye patch fiddled a lilting sea chantey. A hat sat at his feet with change in it. A few bar flies hung about—older women with leathery skin and missing teeth.

The card game was hard and spirited.

John Longfield happened to be on a lucky streak. He cleaned out an angry, puffy-faced man. The loser reluctantly paid up in the form of a tin money clip with several bills folded into it, which he tossed on the table as he stormed out.

≈ ≈

In a dirty alley full of puddles and horse droppings, against the backdrop of a brick factory wall and an open gate where a horse-drawn delivery cart came rumbling out, Steve had his 'office,' as he called it. He was perennially one step ahead of the vice squad, several of whom were on his payroll and would tip him off about raids. Steve worked as a pimp, cardsharp, drug dealer, petty thief, and burglar—at the moment hanging out with three of his prostitutes.

A regular with a white mustache came down the street. He wore a black suit and bowler hat, and had a black umbrella over one arm. Names were never part of the transaction. The man never came within view under a street lamp, but stopped some distance away and pointed to one of the women. She nodded and hurried toward the man, giving raunchy come-on gestures to get him going and make it quick. The two disappeared into the shadows together, arm in arm.

John Longfield appeared. Steve walked away from his two women to meet him. Longfield pulled out the tin money clip with the bills. "Here it is, like I promised. For the earrings and the tickets, and Miss Lilly."

Steve rattled a finger over the bills as if counting. He pocketed them. "Perfect. Did she like the earrings?"

"She was ecstatic." Steve was also a fence for burglars. Lizzie did not ever need to know her expensive earrings came from a wealthy home across the city. "Thanks."

"Any time I can be of service, Johnny Boy."

John said: "You did fine. My little Lizzie loves nice clothes and jewelry. And she loves anything to do with theater. Getting Miss Lilly out there was an accomplishment."

"The timing was good. I told her I am a press agent, and a critic wanted to talk with her. Instead, you showed up with your girl. I think she got a little confused, expecting you to ask for an interview. No matter. Was your girlfriend pleased?"

"It went off perfectly," John said: "I need to keep it going. She loves me, and I do have a soft spot for the little thing."

"She's a beauty. You're a lucky man. I can arrange something else soon. How about balcony tickets for a nice romantic play?"

John said: " She'd love it!"

"Consider it done. I'll need some extra by Tuesday."

ॐ ॐ

On a hot summer day, Lizzie and May walked along a sidewalk on their way to work. The young women stayed under the shade of awnings as much as the could. The sidewalk glittered under their feet, all concrete and silica, hot enough to fry an egg.

May said: "You really mustn't see him, Lizzie."

Lizzie said: "But he makes me so dreamy."

May said: "Don't you ever learn? Don't you remember what happened when you were eighteen? "

Lizzie said: "But this is different. John may seem rough until you know him. He has such good taste in clothing, theater, all the nice things in life."

ॐ ॐ

That evening, Mrs. Wyllie was doing dishes in her kitchen. May sat in the corner at her sewing machine. Lizzie opened the door and came happily into the apartment. "Good evening!"

May froze over her sewing, and looked on darkly. Elizabeth sniffed Lizzie's breath: "Lizzie, where have you been? I smell gin, girl."

Lizzie said: "Oh, Mommy..." She started washing her hands at the sink.

Elizabeth grabbed her daughter roughly by the shoulders. "You're smoked like a sausage. You've been with men—wrong side of the tracks, by the smell of those cheap stogies."

Lizzie said: "Mother! I am 24 years old and a grown woman. It's summer, and I want to live a little."

Her mother said: "I hear you're seeing a married man."

"Not true!"

Mother put a hand on Lizzie's shoulder. "Lizzie, don't lie to me."

Lizzie shrieked: "May, you traitor!"

May shook her head and looked on silently.

Elizabeth said: "Lizzie, you dim thing! Don't you remember the hell you put us through? How you suffered? Having it and giving it up like that?"

Lizzie said: "Mind your own business, Mommy!"

Elizabeth said: "As long as you live under my roof, what you do is my business. I want no scandal in my home."

Lizzie said: "Then I'll leave!"

"Where would you go, poor factory girl who thinks she's an actress?"

Lizzie said: "Grand Rapids, for one thing."

"To my sister? You think she'd take you in?"

Lizzie said: "I'm just saying. Aunt Louisa is calm and understanding."

"Louisa Anderson has not been through the devil and back with you. She doesn't know the half."

3. Kate Morgan–Late Summer 1892

In a tiny room, on a morning in late summer 1892, Kate Morgan sat on her neatly made bed, with her head bowed and her hands raised. She stared at her palms, holding her locket on a fine chain.

The room was stripped of her personal possessions. She wore street clothing. Her maid's uniform was stuffed in her open satchel, and a distinctive wooden trunk stood closed nearby with a sense of finality and transition. It was the same trunk Magruder had carried down the stairs nearly four years earlier, the day she had last seen Tom in Chicago. She had moved around to many cities, plying her trade, and staying one step ahead of the shadowy husband she feared might still be tracking her.

Her face looked pale and transfigured as if she were staring into another world. The atmosphere around her, by contrast, was dark and brooding, filled with danger. But she was used to that. It was part of her way of living and surviving. What she could never get used to was the truth and finality of what she was staring at—her past, and its breaking point.

Kate looked unutterably sad and vulnerable in that moment.

≈ ≈

Outside the dark little bubble of her moment, had she looked up at her two windows, she would have seen a sweeping view of the city in summer bloom. Her employer's house stood atop a hill, and a good part of the best of glorious San Francisco spread before her, including the cliffs that opened like a doorway to the Pacific Ocean.

In San Francisco Bay, the harbor still bristled with a forest of ships' masts, but a number of new steam ships showed their funnels among them.

The hills were covered with houses and tree crowns, all choked in fragrant blossoms. In the distance stood the Spreckels mansion at Washington and Van Ness Streets, among smaller but fine homes. The Spreckels family, whose patriarch was the so-called Hawai'ian sugar baron, Claus Spreckels, controlled much of the Pacific sugar industry. They owned vast holdings of cane fields under the Kalakaua Dynasty. Kate's boss was an executive in Spreckels' sugar industries, and owned this beautiful home with two dozen servants on Nob Hill.

※ ※

This room would be her bedroom no longer. Kate Morgan heard footsteps approach. She heard the voice of Ida, the chief of female domestic staff, who was subordinate only to the butler. Kate pictured Ida in a long black uniform dress and white starched cap as she walked down a carpeted corridor in the maids' quarters. A heavier set of footfalls rumbled along with her—a porter wearing hobnail boots. The two stopped at Kate's door, and the rumbling ceased. Ida knocked imperiously.

Kate ignored the knocks as she sat on her bed and stared into the locket.

Ida said: "You're wanted downstairs."

Kate said icily: "I'll be out in a moment." She stared longingly at a tiny portrait. The newborn infant's eyes had a glazed look. The image was bordered in mourning black—a Victorian death photograph. Kate whispered: "Eddie." She closed the locket.

Ida rapped loudly. "You better not keep the boss waiting!"

Kate held the locket in her fist for a long moment as she closed her eyes with intense concentration.

Ida pounded on the door. "I don't have time for this."

Kate rose, assuming a stony look. Her world was as big as that locket, as big as her trunk, as small as this cramped room that had been her home—no, her place to collapse in exhaustion after a day's unrelenting work—for several weeks. As the pounding continued, she opened her eyes and saw herself in the mirror above the wash basin—a glowering, plain woman with cunning eyes, a fearless expression, and a full mouth. And what she wanted was what she was talented at extracting money from her employers. The moment had come again. She ignored Ida and clutched her locket a moment longer—as if it contained her very heart locked up in its cold metal casing.

※ ※

Kate snapped the door open and stepped out, holding her satchel. Instantly, she was in charge, just by her demeanor. She regarded the domestic with a smoldering, wounded, threatening intensity that signaled Kate felt she had nothing to lose, and was capable of anything. The older woman stepped back, blanching, and spoke in a faint and tremulous voice. Her eyes were wide, and her rudeness was gone. "Claire, the boss wants to see you in his study." Kate knew the woman had no idea why the boss wanted to see her, and walked past her as if she were an insect.

The porter stood apologetically behind Kate, eyeballing her room over her shoulder, and the object he'd been sent to fetch. Kate told him over her shoulder, without looking back: "Wait for me outside by the curb. I won't be long."

"Yes, Miss Claire." Kate heard him tromp into the room to lift her wooden trunk. Ida scurried inside, with a wide-eyed afterglance, to start fluffing the bed, which Kate had perfectly made and needed no fluffing.

As Kate walked away from her room, down a maze of carpeted hallways with oak wainscoting and leaded glass windows, she spotted someone out of the corner of her eye. Emily, a fellow domestic, stood far down a cross hall. Kate knew very little of her—only that Emily had a reputation for being an impoverished, childless widow, who lived in a seedy neighborhood and drank herself into a stupor every night. Emily gave Kate a strange, meaningful look and an odd, unholy grin. Kate wondered—did Emily know? Was she a threat? There was something loaded and dangerous about Emily's hard face.

❦ ❧

They were alone in the room together—Kate, and her employer. In the smoky, mahogany gloom of a richly appointed library, the boss stood stiffly behind his desk. Books were all around on the walls, Oriental carpets on the floors, vases, umbrellas, top hats of the upper society, all sorts of knick-knacks, many of them quite expensive. Standing before him was Kate in her street clothes, with her satchel on the floor.

The boss, a fastidious, well dressed man, said: "Damn you!"

Kate said: "No, damn yourself. You mistook an innocent smile for a young woman's careless flirtation, and pressed yourself upon me with gross physicality."

The boss said: "Oh, what nonsense. You offered yourself, and I had a moment of mental and moral weakness. I thought that somehow I could find pleasure in your carnality."

Kate said: "You'd better watch your mouth, you impertinent pecker-head. Who do you think you are, talking to a woman that way?"

Boss said: "Okay, okay—I'm sorry. Please—Miss Lomax—take your pay and go away."

Kate said: "I'll spare your wife and children the embarrassment of a public disgrace, you sanctimonious pig. Pay me my quitting wage plus three hundred, and we'll be done."

He had been ready for this. He counted out twenties with a cynical, defeated grin. He said: "Is your name really even Claire Lomax?"

Kate said: "Lay it to rest." She pocketed the money.

He stood uncomfortably, perhaps thinking of going to the police.

She walked to the door, stopped half way, and turned. She said: "Forget your pecker pride, and think of your family. Three hundred dollars is a small price to pay, rather than go to the police and have the whole city laughing at you and you lose your job, your house, your family. Think carefully." She had a last glimpse of the boss. He stood scared and sweaty in place for a long moment, and wiped a trembling hand across his brow. It was a scenario Kate had engineered often enough by now. This one had gone well. Served him right.

She slammed the door shut and strode down the hall. Her young, robust body moved with a seductive, hippy fullness that no employer with meandering eyes could miss under the dark dress. Her secret weapon was a subliminal, sensual allure that she broadcast with all her charm and guile. She was not beautiful—some might think her plain—but she was a dark-haired destroyer with fierce eyes and imposing, intelligent features.

She'd seen the look on Emily's face in that corridor, signaling some dark intention. Outside, Kate again saw Emily's pale face floating behind an upper story stairwell window. Kate tipped the porter and climbed aboard the Stanhope—a horse-drawn, open buggy with an accordion-top folded up—on whose rear boot the porter had loaded her trunk.

༺ ༻

In the gloom of a tavern—which smelled richly of beer, bread, and meat, as well as coffee and cigar smoke—Kate sipped at a mug of beer as she sat in a corner reserved for the female gender. She ate a corned beef sandwich with a gherkin on the side. She was flush, on vacation, and feeling good. She wore traveling clothes, and had a carpet bag on one side. Indianapolis was her next destination. Leaning upright against the wall beside her was the wooden trunk containing all her earthly possessions.

A piano player pounded out a raggy waltz full of rhythm and mischief. The bar brimmed with the noise of working class men in cheap black suits and stained bowlers. They told jokes and laughed raucously. The bartender juggled glasses in the air. Smoke floated in a gray-blue layer.

Emily, the older domestic from the house, entered with a businessy look and a package the size of a book, wrapped in plain white paper. Emily wore a coat over her domestic's uniform. Kate had been expecting something like this.

Spotting Kate in the corner, Emily walked toward her.

Kate pretended to ignore her. Best play it cool.

Emily said: "Claire dearie, or whatever you call yourself now that you're no longer working with us—how are you?"

"Fine, until you came in."

"I came to show you something, Claire."

"Don't scheme too much—you'll hurt your head."

"Speaking of schemes! Oh I seen how you operate. Very clever, girl. The boss ain't such a bad egg—just a bit weak for silky young skin. Likes to wander his fingers under a girl's dress for a little feel now and then."

"I wouldn't know—you tell me."

"If you say so. I got a business preppy-sition for you. Seeing as how clever you are."

Kate yawned and said: "I'm listening."

Emily put her package on the table and said: "I seen how you went after him. There's a maid here and there that will let herself be stroked for a dollar, without anything serious more. Or a look at something pink. It happens. But you, my girl, you bring it on and then whack them on the peckie. No no no! Bad boy! Pay up or else!"

"You already got a load of gin on, this time of day?"

"Deny it then. I don't care. I'm not here to make trouble. See what I got."

Kate casually hoisted her beer and eyeballed the package. With the white paper, it looked pharmaceutical. "I don't deal in stolen opiates of any kind. No cocaine, heroin, pills, or needles."

"Nothing like that, Claire. This is right up your alley. Take a look."

Unwrapping the package, Kate saw a stack of letters. "What are these?"

"Them are love notes."

Kate examined one love note, on fine paper. "They're unsigned. What good is that?"

"Does the name Spreckels mean anything to you?"

"Spreckels. The sugar people. My no-longer boss's employer."

Emily said: "That's right. I bet you never worked there. They got a huge mansion here in town, with lots of serving staff. I'm surprised you ain't gotten keen on that, but here's your chance."

Kate started reading one letter after another.

Emily said: "Twenty bucks, they're all yours."

Kate said while reading: "John Spreckels was having an affair with a young lady. He must had been quite gooey to write these."

Emily said: "Oh it was all noise. You know how men are. Promise anything for a little coussy."

Kate glowed as she held up one letter. "What do you know? Here's one from her to him. She's a domestic!"

Emily said: "Was, dearie, was. This girl, Charlotte Barnard, was a total lag, if you know what I mean. The dust was faster than her." She made slow dusting motions with a dumb face. "Mrs. Spreckels let her go. If the girl had your tits, she'd 'a gone right to the old lady with her story."

Kate kept reading. "No money in that. She'd ruin her references. Spreckels probably paid her to shut up and leave town, without his old lady getting wise."

Emily said: "Want them? Twenty bucks. I ain't offering again."

Kate said: "Where'd you get these?"

Emily said: "Charlotte. She asked me to safeguard them for her until she could burn them, but she left town and never came back."

Kate said: "You know where she went?"

Emily said: "Michigan somewheres. She won't find work in this town for a long time. You know how the grapevine goes, especially for temporary help. The slightest bad word or a dirty look, and you're finished. Like you are, here, as of now."

Kate said: "Memories are short. Takes a year or two and nobody remembers." She patted her hand on the letters. "They're nice, but they are unsigned—not even initials?"

Emily, still on the topic of blackmail, said knowingly: "Or you use a different name again."

"Don't try to be more clever than you really are, Emily."

Emily said: "The point is—it really happened. I know two girls who saw them a couple of times, slipping into his office with that look between them. Point is—he'd remember it, if you chose to bring it to his attention. You're the only one I know that has that much nerve."

Kate said: "How do I know you didn't forge the letters? I pay you, and there really was no Charlotte Barnard."

Emily said: "You can find some samples of his handwriting to compare if you want. I swear—they are the real thing."

Kate said: "Ten bucks."

Emily said: "Fifteen."

Kate said: "I'll bring the money to your apartment. Where do you live?"

Emily packed the letters away and rose. She scribbled on a card and said: "There's my address. Come up for a drink and some fun, eh?"

A swirling mist descended upon the harbor. Lights went on early, and people hurried about looking cold. Lanterns burned aboard moored ships as the fog deepened.

Kate stood in the shadows of a narrow alley, dressed in dark clothing. She kept her eye on a battered door of no particular color across the way.

As dusk fell, the first tendrils of fog crept up from the harbor.

The alley reeked of poverty. It abounded with dirty children and drunken women and sallow men whose arms bore needle tracks. This quarter was a mosaic of empty faces with idiot grins and missing teeth and vacant eyes. People moved about like shadows, like the half-dead, ghosts already.

A lamplighter came by with his wick on a stick, singing off-key. It was kind of a nice little ditty, soaked in brandy and nudged up and down the scales with schoolboy effort, but also an air of resignation amid gray beard stubble. He sang too softly to leave an echo as he passed through like a leaf falling from a tree.

A woman shouted, a door slammed, a man cursed, a dog barked, a child cried, a dove fluttered, a flying bottle shattered. And so it went.

The battered door opened and a drunken Emily staggered forth.

Kate watched as Emily lurched down the lane and into a tavern.

A ghostly shadow, Kate crossed the alley in a few blinks of the eye.

Kate groped her way up a dark, dank, smelly stairwell. She came to a door, and rattled the knob, but it was locked.

She looked left and right.

She held her purse over her elbow, and smashed a small glass pane in the door. Reaching in, she unlocked the door and entered.

She fumbled on the walls, found a gas lamp, and lit a faint yellow light. Gas whispered and sputtered softly around her as she searched.

She tossed the place, throwing things into a pile in the middle of the room. There wasn't much to search. All of Emily's meager possessions flew onto the bare floor in minutes.

In the bedroom, Kate found the letters buried amid dirty linen in a corner on the floor. Slipping the package under her arm, she headed back down the stairs. From the doorway, she peered left and right. Then, walking calmly, she disappeared into deepening night and fog.

4. Detroit—Early Fall 1892

A doorway brooded over an iron catwalk high above the work floor of Winn & Hammond, Bookbinders. The door had a sign on it, reading *General Manager*. Coarse female laughter sickered through the twilight of grimy windows, littered work benches, and hunched women. The air smelled of paper, glue, and machine oil.

Lizzie's seat was empty. The closed door marked *Foreman* spoke volumes. May Wyllie looked embarrassed while the other women, some missing teeth, most quite rough, laughed and jeered softly. They kept their heads down and their postures workmanlike.

The door above opened. The General Manager, a stern older man in starched shirt and stiff clothes, walked out with arms akimbo. He stopped to stare at the women, who promptly fell silent and bowed deeper over their work. The General Manager walked deliberately down the steel steps, one clattering step at a time, and then on the concrete toward the Foreman's door.

A vicious crone muttered: "There you go, Sister May. The whore is about to get found out, and the hound with her." Stifled laughter erupted all around the table. May rose, threw aside her work, and tore at the other woman's hair.

The General Manager rattled John Longfield's door knob. The door was locked from within. The General Manager came prepared, however—he fished a spare key from his vest pocket, and turned it in the lock. The door swung open. There they were—lovers, half naked, frozen in shock and shame, atop Longfield's desk. They were mussy-haired and sweaty, cheeks flushed with passion and now shame, as they fumbled into their clothes.

The General Manager turned and pointed to May. His voice was harsh as whip-cracks. "For starters, you are terminated. Get out! The rest of you, back to work or I'll fire you all."

The General Manager entered John's office and slammed the door.

❦ ❧

A short time later, a tearful May and sobbing Lizzie clung together as they hurried down a bleak street that was beginning to rustle with the first wind-blown, brown leaves of fall.

Not far away went a stooped, gloomy John Longfield shuffled off in another direction, carrying a leather satchel of tools.

❦ ❧

Lizzie and May sat with teary, smeared, swollen faces at the table. Mrs. Wyllie served them hot oatmeal and coffee.

Elizabeth said: "So that's it. This is what it's come to. I am alone, a widow, barely making ends meet, taking in sewing and cleaning as I can, working my fingers to the bone. Now where will the rent and food money come from?" She bent close to Lizzie and said: "You fool! Look what you have done to yourself and your poor sister! You must be totally daffy, to make the same mistake over and over again, without learning a lesson! Next you'll be knocked up and there we go through all that again!"

❦ ❧

Far away, in the evening at a foggy railway station in San Francisco, Kate Morgan stood in line at the ticket counter. She had just come from Emily's tenement flat, where she had taken away the Spreckels love notes. She looked over her shoulders several times. A porter wheeled her trunk to the baggage car.

Kate reached across the counter and put down a ticket and some dollar bills under the window. "I bought a ticket to Indianapolis recently. I want to exchange it."

The ticket agent said: "And where to, Miss?"

Kate said: "To Detroit." She choked excitedly. "Michigan."

❦ ❧

The transcontinental railroad was a marvel of its age, as was the telegraph. Kate Morgan, dressed nicely for travel, sat on a wooden train bench in third class. She cut an apple with a paring knife, eating slowly, bite for bite, while she once again compared one of sugar mogul John Spreckels' and domestic Charlotte Barnard's love letters with samples of Spreckels' handwriting that she had obtained.

Meanwhile, the train rumbled its stately, rhythmic *clackity-clack*. Kate had many hours to spare before she would reach Michigan, but she'd already seen enough to convince her the letters were real. She considered the vast fortune owned by the Spreckels family, and the possibilities for the largest score she had yet made, and might ever make if she had the nerve. As she examined herself, and clutched the locket at her neck, she knew she did have the nerve. She had nothing to lose, and everything to gain.

These trains had a class system. In first class coaches, better-off families sat on upholstered, spacious seats. White-jacketed waiters served them appetizing treats. In second class coaches, passengers sat jammed together in separate compartments with upholstered seats. Kate preferred the anonymity and crowding of third class. The working poor rode on hard wooden benches.

Kate ate a sandwich from wax paper on her lap as she read. She savored pungent innuendos and verbal frolicking suggesting Mr. Spreckels'd had quite a sexual romp. How nice being able to afford such fun with a poor but beautiful girl, scrubbing her hands and knees raw at the dirt in his house. *Oh, yes, Mr. Spreckels, what if you had a little come-uppance for a change?*

Kate sipped hot coffee from a thermos as she schemed. She envisioned a Robin Hood scheme, stealing from the wealthy to enrich the poor, meaning herself. She had next to nothing, except her previous master's little blood money for her silence, so he could keep tormenting and fondling innocent young women. There had to be an angle. There always was an angle. What was the angle, the hinge, on which her strategy upon Mr. Spreckels would turn? Visiting his latest victim would help her figure that out. She hugged herself and shuddered at the thrill of coming into several thousand dollars—her largest haul to date, if she could pull it off. Surely Spreckels must value his privacy and good name that much. A plan began to take amorphous shape. Spreckels would value his good name, and she would see that he feared for it. It was just a matter of putting the right playing cards on the table for this game to begin. And it must be soon if she were to capitalize on Charlotte Barnard's folly. Passing countryside turned from Western mountains and deserts to Central plains, and eventually Eastern forests starting to turn Fall colors.

5. Knocked Up & Ruined

Not long into autumn, May Wyllie stood forebodingly before the bathroom door in her mother's house. Her face radiated worry. She knocked again, and whispered: "Lizzie?"

The door opened, revealing her sister, who stood with her hands folded before her as if in penance, shaking her head. Her eyes were full of anguish. May raised her hands to her face in horror. Her poor sister! Not again! A tear ran down each of Lizzie's cheeks—the first of many.

Arm in arm, the sisters took the first of many walks to counter the numbing shock that overtook Lizzie. Mother didn't know yet, but you couldn't hide something like this from her for long.

The streets of the city became barren as summer turned into autumn, and the two sisters went for forlorn walks, thinking of ways to find money to help their mother and keep up the household. Lizzie was much in despair over John's on again, off again attentions. Sometimes it seemed as if he were going to leave his wife and children, and at other times it seemed he was abandoning Lizzie. May could only comfort Lizzie and warn her of any further contact with their former boss.

"The game has changed now, Lizzie."

"I know, I know, I have been a fool again. But I still hope."

"You hope what?"

"That he will leave her for me. I'm younger and far prettier, for one thing. And I am willing to work."

"You're carrying his child. You won't work with a little one depending on you to be there every second."

"I couldn't bear to give it up again," Lizzie said with tears springing forth. "I would rather die."

Leaves whirled around the young women's long dresses as they walked along gray and industrial streets.

As the days grew shorter, lights stayed on in houses and lingered into the early evenings.

The very air looked gray and sad, foreboding and gloomy.

Everything had a hard, mean look, even the gleaming surfaces of a black carriage pulled by a single horse. An old man smoking a pipe sat on top, in a torn wool coat. The coach lights glimmered faintly in little brass lanterns with red glass windows as the carriage clip-clopped out of sight. It reminded Lizzie of a last, fading glimmer of hope.

☙ ❧

Kate Morgan walked along a country lane in Michigan, having crossed the country by train. She was relieved to be away from the Transcontinental Railroads on which she and Tom had shared such mischief.

It was early fall, and there was still a little green in the trees, but the light was sad and beautiful, and many of the leaves had dried into the colors of apples—bright yellows and somber reds and purples.

She arrived at a brick mansion with ivied walls and a magnificent front.

Walking around the back, she came to a servants' entrance and knocked. A pretty young woman in maid's uniform came to the door. "Yes?"

Kate said: "I'm looking for Charlotte Barnard."

Charlotte Barnard said: "That's me."

Kate said: "My name is Lucy Crawford. I just came from San Francisco."

Charlotte Barnard looked horrified. "Is it something I done?"

Kate said: "No, no, I came to give you this." She handed over a love note. "Emily says she waited a time, then burned them all—but she forgot that one."

Charlotte snatched the love note and stared at it open-mouthed. "Oh my God. I thought I was done with this. Now I'll burn this one and it's all behind me."

Kate said: "Charlotte, I can't stay long because I am taking a position in Detroit, and have to show up there tomorrow. Apparently, Mr. Spreckels got in hot water with his old lady over a little fling with you."

Charlotte Barnard cried: "My new employer must hear nothing about it. Nothing! Or I'm ruined!"

Kate said: "Hush, dear. There won't be a word. Does Spreckels know where to find you?"

"Oh God, I hope not."

Kate said: "Wonderful. I'm a bit curious. Such a wealthy man. What was he like?"

Charlotte looked furtively around. She seemed nervous, but eager to learn what she could from Kate, just as Kate was eager to learn from her about

Spreckels. "Why do you want to know?"

Kate said: "Just nosey as the dickens."

Charlotte Barnard grinned: "I have a little time. Would you like to come in for tea?"

"I've been walking for a few hours, and I could use something hot."

Charlotte Barnard said: "We have hot soup in the kitchen. And bread. Come on in, and I'll give you a mouthful and an earful. All the gossip. They are an interesting family. Now about John Spreckels..."

                        ❦ ❧

In Detroit, streets were piled deeply with golden and dark apple-red leaves. Trees looked twisted and barren. Days were short—gray and rainy, except for a few stand-out sunny days.

Mrs. Elizabeth Wyllie had found out about Lizzie's new out-of-wedlock pregnancy. An argument was on in the apartment, where light seeped wanly through the kitchen window. Mrs. Wyllie walked up and down yelling amid her few pieces of shabby furniture May tried to step between her mother and sister. Lizzie sniffled into one of several hankies with the monogram *Lizzie Anderson*. They were her mother's. Elizabeth said: "I can't stand it any more. You got yourself knocked up again, Lizzie. How could you be so stupid?"

May said: "Easy, Mom. She's fragile."

Elizabeth said: "Fragile! Am I a brown bear? She wasn't fragile to be carrying on with that wolf in his lair!"

Lizzie said: "I can't stand it any longer! He loves me and I love him."

Elizabeth said: "If that man loves you, Lizzie, then I am a Christmas tree. Are you daffy? He's a married man with children, out of work, and broke. What can he possibly do for you? He has ruined you, all for his craven lust and selfishness."

Lizzie held her fists over her ears. "I can't think! I can't think! You drive me crazy!"

"I drive you crazy?" Her mother sniffed. "Hah. I'll soon be committed."

May said: "Have you heard from him lately?"

Lizzie sniffled, wiping a wrist across her face. "Not a peep so far this week."

May said: "He's dumped you, girl. Showed you the street. We'll see about that."

Leaves swirled thickly in damp, chill air the color of smoke, and people wore thick clothing. In an arched brick portal, framed in ivy, May stood before a chastened John Longfield. "I'll not let you just throw her away, Mr. Longfield."

John said: "I care greatly about your sister. I'll do what a man must do."

May said: "Oh, and what's that, Mr. Longfield? Leave your wife and children? And you have no job, no money to feed them?"

John said: "May, please, it's already all so difficult."

May said: "It'll be far worse if I go to your wife and pour out the truth. Your poor wife, Mr. Longfield. Think about her and your children."

John cringed. "You wouldn't do that to me."

May said: "See, it's always about you. You could implore me not to do that to her. Lizzie is knocked up, Mr. Longfield, by you."

"I know. She's told me. You've told me."

"So what are you going to do?"

"That's the question, isn't it? What would you do, May?"

"I have no idea. I didn't get myself into such a mess."

"I'm puzzling over it, trust me, until my brain hurts."

May said: "You created this puzzle for yourself."

John said: "Lizzie created hers too. She got herself into it."

May said: "Don't give me that, you son of a bitch. You ruined my sister. You can walk away, a bounder, a hound, but my poor sweet sister—who is naive and innocent and lacks common sense, as much as she is elegant and beautiful and has a head full of airy dreams about being an actress, when she can't remember a cake recipe, much less lines on stage— you used this poor dear girl like a common whore and now you don't know what to do. Well, Mr. Longfield, short of tossing yourself under a train, you'd better come up with something good. And soon."

May turned and strode away, leaving a troubled John Longfield to consider his options.

Lizzie sat in third class on a train chuffing through early autumn Michigan countryside. Its severe beauty was enough to make you cry.

It was like reading one of those fallen angel books. She looked anxiously about, and occasionally pulled out a hankie to sniffle into it. Eventually, she passed a sign that read: *Grand Rapids 5 Mi*. From the train station it was a blurry, tearful trip to Aunt Louisa's house. She rode on a wagon pulled by a horse, driven by an older man wearing a red cap. The wagon was from the train station, and held her three trunks. Lizzie rode up to a private residence in a working class but clean neighborhood. She ran up the steps and knocked on the door, while the porter brought her trunks to the porch, one by one. Lizzie tipped him and he departed, touching his cap.

The door opened and a woman resembling Lizzie's mother opened. Louisa Anderson brightened and opened her arms lovingly. "Lizzie, my sweet, favorite niece. Oh how good to see you, baby."

They embraced, and Lizzie started crying again

"Come on in, sweetheart," said Aunt Louisa. She put her arm around Lizzie and guided her into the dark, spacious comfort of her house. As she did so, Louisa, a spinster, called for a male friend who was doing work in the house to fetch Lizzie's three trunks.

Louisa sat on the couch while Lizzie sat opposite her. Louisa's male friend, having taken the trunks upstairs to a spare bedroom, stirred his coffee. He was a powerful but gentle looking man in his forties, in a worn herringbone suit, white shirt, and burgundy silk necktie worn shiny.

Lizzie sobbed wetly into a hankie embroidered *Lizzie Anderson*.

The man said: "Poor girl—she's beside herself."

Aunt Louisa said: "Lizzie darling, is that your last hankie? Your mother's old hankies yet—she does love you, even if she throws you out—but sends you away with her personal hankies."

"Well, it's not like she threw me out—I actually left on my own."

"Oh, I know, darling, but she does have a temper. She must have been impossible. I'm sure I know what it's all about, and we'll talk about it when you catch a hold of yourself." She extended a hand for the hankie, which looked soppy and ready to be washed. "Here," Louisa said. "I'll give you some of mine."

Louisa went to a cupboard and took out a half dozen embroidered hankies, which she put on the table near Lizzie. She took the wet one away to wash. The fresh hankies were stitched *Louisa Anderson*. Her mother and aunt had received a combined gift set as little girls.

Aunt Louisa returned from the laundry chute in the kitchen. "You're welcome to stay here as long as you like. So your mother is upset with you? Oh, you'll tell me, won't you? And you came for refuge in my house. When you're able to speak, you can pour out the whole sad drama to me. Whatever it is, I won't think any the less of you. My sister will get over her fuss, and your dear sweet sister May is such a steady mate that you'll always have her support."

6. Detroit—Kate, Lizzie, & John

Kate Morgan stepped from the servants' entrance of a splendid mansion in a better neighborhood of Detroit. The day was done. She was among several other female domestics who bid each other good night.

Kate wore a coat over her domestic's garb, and strode briskly down a tree-lined, cobblestone street that was damp from rain and littered with bright yellow and dull russet leaves. After a few blocks, on a main cross street, she boarded an electric trolley. She sat among a crowd of people employed much like she was. She felt anonymous, though she still looked around fearfully from time to time. As she and her fellow passengers rocked about, she thought about her grand scheme. How could she pull off a job on Spreckels? It must be carefully planned, effective, and safe. No doubt, the more important the man, the more he would worry for his reputation. Suppose a big man like that got a girl in trouble. Wouldn't other companies cancel their orders from him? What would his wife think? What if he had daughters? It must be humiliating. She felt a bit like Archimedes, who'd said something like "Give me a big enough lever, and I can move the world." The love notes were her lever, but were they lever enough? The trolley hummed on its tracks along pleasantly littered streets, among the cozy-lit windows of good homes, and into a shabbier part of Detroit. There, she got off and walked deeper and deeper into the heart of the working people's quarter. On the way to her rented room in a boarding house for women domestics of virtue, she spotted a random tavern and decided her tired whistle could use a cool, tasty, sudsy beer.

☙ ❧

May Wyllie and John Longfield stood huddled in the same covered archway where she had confronted him a day earlier. She had summoned him again. John said: "How is she, May?"

May said: "She's with our Aunt Louisa in Grand Rapids. My poor mother gets crazier by the day."

John said: "I'm a stupid bastard. If you want me to throw myself off a bridge, I'll gladly do it if it will help."

"We need to have it taken care of. She can't go through all that again."

John said: "I have no money or means to help, May—I'm sorry. I cherish your sister very much. I'll do anything I can."

May said: "Can I trust you then, Mr. Longfield? Will you do one thing right for us all?"

John said: "On my heart, I swear it. On my dead mother's grave."

May said: "I know a woman in Cleveland, who is very good at helping girls in trouble. She's a school-taught nurse, clean, and knows what she is doing. She'll finish in less than hour if all goes well. Lizzie needs a man with her on the trip. Can you take her there and watch out for her?"

"On my soul, May. Have you got the money for it? I sure don't."

May reluctantly held up a wad of money in a gilded clip. "My savings. I took up a collection from my girl friends. Promise me you will use it to help my sister." She handed it over. "Lizzie was nearly destroyed last time, having the baby and then giving it up because that's what they made her do. She couldn't go through that again, and she is nowhere near ready to have a child, especially unmarried, no money, and on her own. It's our only chance to save her life and her reputation."

John took the money clip. "On my life, May. I'll be on the train to Grand Rapids first thing to get Lizzie. I pray all goes well. I'll leave the poor angel alone."

"If you screw up, Mr. Longfield, you'll have me to deal with."

"I know it, May. I promise I'll be good."

ಎ ಲ

In a Detroit tavern, men and women sang rowdy songs amid beer and good cheer as Kate walked to a side counter of the bar. Waiting her turn, she ordered food and drink. She looked around at the pool players and card players and dark players. She bought a beer, and a German sausage on a roll with spicy mustard. Then she found herself a little table in a corner and dug in with hunger and thirst.

She began to notice a man playing cards at a nearby table. He kept peeling bills off of a gilded clip, and he was losing. Kate watched in detached amusement as the man looked increasingly desperate. He was a handsome, if disreputable looking fellow, with a nice face, a pencil mustache, and heavy beard shadow. He had seductive, boyish, dark blue eyes and strong but soft white hands. Kate looked his lean, well-proportioned body up and down in his wool, herringbone suit. He lost—again and again. And he'd had a few beers too many, but he was holding his liquor well. She liked that in a man. He didn't seem like the violent type, and he looked like he needed a hand.

Kate finished her sandwich and washed it down with a rich, heady mug of beer with a thick mustache of white foam on it. She felt tired from her day's work, but eating and drinking and being around people made her feel better again. She liked being among people, though she did not form relationships with them, unless it was through the filter of her disguises and ruses, by which she could control the situation. This man interested her, and she daydreamed about having him in bed with her.

The man angrily rose and tossed his cards aside. Unlike Tom, this one looked sort of helpless and harmless in his anger. He stomped to the bar. He ordered a beer and stood darkly sucking on it, wrapping himself around it as if nursing his wounded feelings. Several times, he glanced resentfully at the red-haired man who had cleaned him out. Red was already taking yet another man's money while grinning smugly and taunting him softly. Kate felt her pulse quicken as she read her blue-eyed man's mind. She watched as Blue-Eyes sneaked out the back door. She quickly grew more and more interested. From the trapped look in his eyes, she had an idea what the beaten young man was planning.

Shortly, Red rose and picked up his coat. He bid his fellow card players good night and headed for the door. Kate thought he looked smug and mean-eyed as he shoved the door open on his way out. Kate rose with her beer and sidled over to the window. Pulling the curtain slightly aside, she peered out. Red walked past the window toward the trolley station, whistling, with his head held high. Blue-Eyes moved stealthily after him.

Kate drained her beer, wiped her wrist across her mouth, grabbed her purse, and sidled out the door.

Red walked happily toward the lights of a distant street and trolley stop. His path ran along a sidewalk that made a wide curve around a dark church yard full of shadowy bushes.

Kate moved after him like a shadow among shadows. In a few seconds, she spotted her man hunkering under the shadows of the purplish blocks of the church wall. It was clear he planned to jump the red-haired man in a few seconds as he rounded the curve, but he looked desperate and unsure of himself. This was no fearless Tom Morgan with guns, and he endeared himself to her instantly. Blue-Eyes hunkered under a large tree, veiled in darkness.

Blue-Eyes looked at her as if caught with his pants down. She almost laughed at his bunny-like face of pale terror. He'd already missed his chance. Red was several seconds past on his way to the trolley station.

Kate walked up to blue-eyes, staying on the sidewalk. "I saw you lose your money. I know what you're about to do."

He said: "Lady, I need that money back. It's life or death."

"Let me help you out." She hailed the red haired man: "Sir!" Kate's new companion ducked back down.

Red turned. "Yes?" His face flickered through a range of expressions and possibilities.

Kate said: "I think you lost something here in the bushes."

Red licked his lips with nervous hunger. "I did, did I?"

Kate said: "Something mighty nice, for a very small price."

Red said: "I'll have to come look at it then."

Kate said: "You'll be a happy man, and I'll be a happy gal—we could even split a beer afterward."

Red came back down the sidewalk. "A sweet way to end a lovely night!" Face radiant with expectation, he put his arm around Kate's waist. She touched the hardness in his pants, and he moaned. Together, they stepped into the bushes and darkness under the great tree. She heard the ragged sawing of his excited breath. He moaned with anticipation. He leaned eagerly down to put his lips on Kate's mouth. Just the right moment, she thought as she cold-cocked him with a hard fist. He staggered backward with fluttering eyes.

Blue-Eyes rose up from behind and hit him with a brick, dropping him cold. He pulled Red's body deeper into the bushes.

Kate said: "Don't kill him. Just grab the money. He'll stay put a while." From her copious experience with men, Red would not report that he was mugged by a prostitute in the bushes outside a church. His shame would overcome his moral outrage. Pecker pride was a man's Achilles Heel.

Her new partner in crime emerged, counting his wad of money.

Kate stretched forth her palm and said: "My share."

He stared at her, open-mouthed.

Kate said: "Don't even think of stiffing me. I helped you get your money back, that you lost in there. I want my cut. Or I'll start screaming bloody murder. And if the guy's dead..."

He said: "Aw hell, he's alive. Just out cold. Here, thank you, I wasn't thinking—I'll give you five. How's that?"

Kate said: "Ten, or I start piping like a steam ship."

He meekly handed over the money.

"What's your name?"

"John Longfield. What's yours?"

"Kate Morgan." As they conversed, they walked into the street. Soon she felt comfortable with this John Longfield. She put her arm around his arm. "I have a feeling we'll do well together, don't you? I'm thirsty. How about sharing a beer?"

"Sounds good to me." He winked. "I'll buy. I made a few bucks on this deal. He cleaned a few others out." John put his arm around her waist. "You won't sock me, will you?"

It dawned on her—she'd made a mistake, and used her real name. *Oh well,* she thought, *I'll bed this stray cat one night, we'll have our fun, and I'll never see him again.* She laughed. "Only if you deserve it." She welcomed the sensuous touch of his hand, which timidly probed the curve of her waist, feeling the sturdiness of her torso. His fingertips probed as far as he dared down the softness of her belly. Then he ran his palm over the generous curve of her thigh and buttock. She pushed his hand away, but kept an arm around his waist. He felt hard and muscular. Her one hand lingered on the ridge of his hip, and with her other fingers brushed over the rocky flatness of his rippling abdomen. Kate said: "Let's find a cozy little crib, and you can tell me all about yourself."

※ ※

A few hours later, John Longfield and Kate Morgan were in bed in a shabby hotel. John had paid for their beers, as promised, and he'd paid for the night here. Kate felt a languid sense of generosity and wanted to repay him with something sweet. She did not want him to know about her room not far away, nor could she bring him there. Here, where nobody asked questions, a blanket covered them on a fresh but rude bed. The sheets were clean, but stiff. Their smell had an alkaline bite of cheap soap. John and Kate were naked. Their clothes hung thrown over a chair. Their bare shoulders and faces were sweaty from sex. He noticed she wore a gold locket on a chain around her neck. He was still on top, as they exchanged languid kisses. She was a lively mare of a woman. "You wear me out, my sweet." He palmed her thigh. "And I love it." He rolled over beside her.

Kate loved his boyish, irresponsible grin. "My handsome playboy." She planted a string of kisses across his features. "I'm tired, honey, and I have to be at work early." She'd had experience with boys very early, even before Tom, but had never cheated on him, not even in their last few years together, when he'd been terrible to her. Since she'd left him, she'd had an occasional quick fling. Tom had been the love of her life, and she never expected to trust a man again or get involved, and had no intention of it with this one, but she knew she would be a little taken with this one and maybe let him under her skin a bit, as long as he didn't hit her or drink too much. Men were men—there was no changing them. Evolution had worked for women, but men had remained monkeys. She took his sex in her hand and played with it tenderly.

John said: "Where do you work?"

Kate said: "I am a substitute maid. I work all over. A day here, a week there. If a maid has to visit her dying mother, or a maid is out sick, they hire me for the short term." She felt him grow hard in her hand again. Did this boy have a full coal tender, always ready to roll and toot? What surprised her was that she didn't want him to conquer her. She wanted to take him, safely control him, enjoy him at arms' length. She sighed deeply, shuddering, realizing how much she needed a man, and here he was.

John pressed himself upon her once more. She put him into her, and they rocked together with eyes closed. John said: "I want you, oh God I want you."

Kate said: "I want you too, sweetheart. I've been pretty lonely, working for those stiff-neck phonies up in the good part of town." She chortled softly. "They have no idea about the good parts of town." She reached down under the covers and palmed his behind. "But I do."

John groaned and gasped as she expertly rocked him to climax. They moaned together, holding each other. His climax excited her over the top.

He whispered: "Where did you learn these tricks? Where do you come from, woman? Where do they make women like you?"

"You really want to know?"

John nodded as they lay quietly, side by side, in the soft light..

Kate said: "I was born in Hamburg, Iowa, named Katie Farmer. My mother died when I was young. I grew up restless, before the trains came through. I was a wild kid, the devil to my poor widowed dad and my grandfather. I am from a wealthy miller's family."

John said: "With all that money, why did you leave them?"

Kate said: "I never could sit still or behave. On a freezing cold day, one of the worst winters in many years, I married a young fellow named Thomas Morgan. He had the same wild streak I did, and we understood each other well, soul to soul. My grandfather, Joe Chandler—he knew I was hard of heart and harder of head. The Transcontinental Railroad came in, which was good for the millers to send their flour far and wide, but Tom and I, we caught the travel bug and ran off to see the world. Once we saw those wonderful trains going far and wide, we couldn't stop ourselves. We did some nasty tricks on people to stay flush." She giggled.

"And this man of yours?"

"He turned mean, beat me bloody, threw me down the stairs. I can never have children again. So I left him, and I haven't seen him in several years. I hope I never lay eyes on him again."

"Ah. So you have no children then." It was as much a question as a polite comment. Kate was silent for a while. He stroked her face with his fingers, kissed her gently, and enjoyed being with her. That softened her up, and she cuddled close to him. She touched her locket and said tenderly, breaking up in tears a bit: "Tom and I had a fine little boy. My little Eddie. He lived just two days, the poor little angel. I don't know why he was taken. He lived long enough to have a little name all his own—Eddie. That's all he got—two nights and one day of grim, icy gray winter, and then he was taken. Tom and I went a long time before I became pregnant again, and then he got drunk and threw me down the stairs. I can't have children now. After that I left him. And I still look over my shoulder every day. I'm afraid of him." She started crying.

John comforted her with kisses and tender words. She held onto him tightly. "You be good to me."

"I will," John promised. He felt himself growing hard again.

Kate said: "I've been on my own ever since. I've figured out how to take care of myself. That's all it is. Taking care of yourself in a world that takes your babies. There's a rich family named Spreckels in San Francisco where I worked. They had thirteen children. Only five lived. They lost eight—so what kind of world is this?"

John said: "I know, I know. A tough one. And you have to know how to get through the day and not let the other dogs run off with your bone. You figure losing Eddie made you tough?"

Kate said: "Oh no, the other way around. I was plenty tough. That made me understand what it was to feel something. It softened me a bit. I thank Eddie for it every day. I always had a hard time feeling for other people. Now I cry when I think of that." She sniffled.

A while later, Kate and John lay drowsily in each other's arms. They nuzzled slowly on their way to sleep.

John said: "Wake me when you get up."

"Are you going to work too?"

"Lost my job. I'm fixing a problem for a friend."

"And what's that, sweetie?"

"This friend of mine knocked a lady up, and I'm taking her to a doctor to get her problem fixed."

"She is pregnant?"

"Yeah. In a manner of speaking."

"How far along?" She knew, from the sound of his voice, what it was about, and she thought of her Spreckels plan.

"Can't be more than two months. Three at most."

"Level with me, Lothario. She's your piece, right?"

"Was. I wish I could shake her. I promised her sister I would take her to this woman for an abortion, but then I lost the money—I was just trying to multiply it, so to speak, so I could double it, take care of Lizzie, and still have a pile. But I ran out of luck, until you helped me, bless your soul."

"Maybe we can help each other out. By the pale of your finger, I see you're hiding a wedding ring."

"You're sharp. Actually, since I lost my job, I pawned it, along with Lizzie's earrings. My old lady's no sweat."

"I know what you mean. There's my old man dangling around someplace. So Lizzie is the name of your problem, is it?"

"One of them."

"Oh yes, the wife and kids. Well, honey, you can warm my bed for however long I am in town. I'll be no trouble to you. I'm barren as an Iowa field in winter, I don't carry disease, and I am hot as fire."

John mounted her again and said: "Oh God bless you. I do love you so. Give me some more of that. I can't stay away."

"Have all you want. There's plenty more for you—all you need." As they headed to climax, Kate held him and thrust back with all her bodily might while she goaded him: "Come on, give it to me. Give me all you've got. More! Harder! Show me you're a man. Rip me now, in me hard. No shame. Just do me down and dirty so I feel you deep…"

ぞ ぐ

Next morning, in a gray dawn light, Kate dressed. She looked tired but happy. She had her hair up in both hands, and hairpins in her mouth. "John!"

John stirred and moaned faintly. Then he sat up, rubbing his eyes. "My God, is it morning already? You wore me out last night."

"I'll wear you out plenty more, don't worry. Go get the girl, bring her to town. Get her a fancy place that she'll like."

John said: "Lizzie is so particular! She's neat and dainty like a great lady, even though she's just a fired little factory girl."

Kate threw down a few bills. "Here—get a dollar-a-day place downtown. That should impress her. I'll tell you more this evening. I have something in store for that girl—for us three, actually."

‧ ❧

John Longfield took the train to get Lizzie Wyllie at her aunt's house in Grand Rapids. Aunt Louisa sent them off with mixed feelings, confused about whether this oddly good-looking yet somehow devious looking man had come to fetch her for a wedding, or something else. Seeing Lizzie's radiant face, she grew baffled and tentative, and resolved to talk more with her sister, now that Elizabeth might have calmed down a bit. She would send a telegram to Elizabeth and May.

Lizzie and John rode to the train station in the same wagon with the same three trunks. The same red-cap was driving the same horse that had brought Lizzie here just a few days earlier. Lizzie put her arm through John's arm, and snuggled close.

He patted her hand. "I came back to get you. Told you I would, didn't I?"

Lizzie said: "I never lost faith in you."

John said: "Your sister May and I had a talk, Lizzie. She wants me to help get you fixed up. And then we'll figure what to do next."

Lizzie'd had time to think. "I can't go through the whole thing of having the baby and giving it up again. I would rather have our child and raise it by myself, if I have to, if you'll just provide for us and come see me once or twice a week."

"I would gladly see you every day, Lizzie, but I have no job right now and I'm having trouble making ends meet."

Lizzie said slowly: "Then you want me to get rid of it."

"Well, we can think about what to do. There is a kind woman I spoke with, Kate Morgan, who wants to help us. I'm in this with you, Lizzie."

"Oh, thank you!" She gripped his arm. "Sometimes I just want you for myself. Then I realize—what am I doing? What am I thinking? It would be so unfair to you, and your wife, and your children. Then I think—you could just keep me on the side. I'd be no trouble. I could find work again, and keep a small place, and we'd have a little love nest. You'd like that, wouldn't you?"

John said: "You are the sweetest little birdie I did ever hear sing." He knew he had no tact or feeling for these things, but his wooden comments had all the same effect on her as eloquent speech.

Lizzie said: "Hold me tight to you."

John put his arm around her and held her close.

She laughed and cried at the same time. "I'm sorry. I have all these crazy ups and downs in my condition. I'll do whatever you want me to." She took off her earrings. "Remember these? I'm going to give them back to you, in case you need money."

He examined the tiny holes in her earlobes. "Do they hurt?"

She shook her head. "Not at all. I'll have to get them re-pierced if I don't find some posts to put in soon."

He reddened. "Darling, why don't you keep them? You look so beautiful in them." He looked genuinely upset.

She laughed and hugged him. "It's just stuff. We can always get more stuff. As long as we are together, you are all the stuff that I need."

֎ ֍

Once John and Lizzie were back in Detroit, he took her to a fine hotel he had chosen. He ushered Lizzie into a sparkling hotel room with clean sheets and curtains. A bellhop followed, wheeling her three trunks. The man thoughtfully lined them up along one wall in a corner, for convenient access. John tipped the man and thanked him as he left.

Alone with John, Lizzie hugged herself and looked around. She twirled around the room, glancing at all the little touches. "This is nice."

John said: "Something special for you. For a special gal."

Lizzie sat down on the bed and patted the bed by her thigh. John sat down beside her. "I missed you so," Lizzie said as she reached for him. They struggled from their clothes, kissing ardently. She pulled the covers apart, and

John kissed Lizzie as she pulled him down on her. "I've been so lonely without you."

John said: "I've been lonely without you too. You're so nice to be with."

Lizzie said: "I want you so...come here...love me!" She pulled him toward her, and his ardor grew instantly. She was far more cultured and elegant than Kate, even if she was a poor factory girl. John knew he was a rough cut who belonged with the likes of Kate. But this beautiful young woman wanted him and who was he to deny her? Especially, with this commanding and self-assured Kate Morgan in charge. Kate could do all the thinking now, and that was okay with John.

☙ ❧

That evening, John and Kate sat in a corner by a brick wall. The large noisy tavern had many people talking and shouting. "Can you talk her into it?" Kate asked.

"I think she'll go along. She doesn't have much choice. I don't want to hurt her, Kate."

"I don't either. You'll have to trust me. We'll all be a lot richer, including her. Just a few days of discomfort, and she'll be rid of her problem, you'll be rid of yours, and everyone will live happily ever after."

"Is this going to be dangerous, Kate?"

"Don't worry. You let me handle things."

"You swear?"

She held two fingers over her heart and put on her most radiant, convincing face. "Honest Injun."

A little bit reluctantly, he set aside any nagging little doubts he still had. "Okay then—I trust you."

She gripped his wrist on the table, and leaned close with that piercing, forceful, irresistibly hypnotic gaze. "You can't just trust me, John. You have to be with me totally, a hundred percent, or this won't work."

He swallowed hard, trying to think it all through, though everything just stayed a big muddle in his mind. "I do," he said, reassured by her firm stare and her iron grip. She was stronger than any woman he'd ever met.

Kate released his arm and picked up her beer. "We'll get her out of town, where nobody will recognize her."

"You're the brain of the outfit, boss."

"Where have you stuck her?"

"First class hotel, in a nice sunny room—like you said. So what's next?"

Kate said: "We'll head for Los Angeles, with a stop in Iowa to deposit a little money. I'll fill you in on the plan as we go along. We'll kill two birds with one stone. We'll fix Lizzie right up so her baby problem goes away. Your baby problem goes away. Same time, we'll make a pile of dough."

John said: "Honestly, I'd like Lizzie to go away too. I have enough trouble on my hands, trying to feed my wife and kids. She's nice, but I'm tired of her. I'm just crazy about you."

"Don't think about leaving your family for me. I wouldn't let you."

"Maybe I can change your mind, woman."

Kate shook her head. "You'll have a snoot full of me soon enough. I can be hard on a man."

"I've never met a woman like you." He added reluctantly: "I know you know what's best. You do mean the best for me, for us, even for Lizzie."

"Sure." Kate nodded. "There's this wealthy man in San Francisco named John Spreckels. He has been buying up everything in San Diego since the financial boom there collapsed in 1889. He owns a splendid resort hotel in Coronado. I have some love letters Mr. Spreckels foolishly gave to a maid he was sweet on. I want Lizzie to play the maid. We'll tell Spreckels he got her pregnant, and order him to pay up, or else. It's really simple."

John said: "Lizzie couldn't play a maid. She can hardly play herself. Her head is full of theater posters, fancy clothes, all what she can't afford."

Kate said: "I'll train her to impersonate. I can start her in Los Angeles. I'll show her the ropes."

"So it's pay-up-or-else for this Spreckels goon? Sounds like blackmail."

Kate said: "If Mr. Spreckels doesn't wire a large amount of money to a distant bank, where we can grab it and run, then Lizzie will have her miscarriage right in his hotel lobby. You want to call that blackmail—I call it goose mail—goosing him to behave like a man."

John said: "Well, I'm sure you know best, Kate, being so sure about this and all. Sounds like he should gladly pay to avoid the embarrassment."

Kate said: "The best part is—he's too far away to investigate. There won't be time. He'll be quick to pay us off in exchange for a signed release from Charlotte Barnard."

"How you going to do that?" He stared at her owlishly.

She stared back. "I already wrote the letter." She burst out laughing. He blinked, realizing he was always slow keeping up with Kate, and then he too laughed. They were both at it, with shaking shoulders, staring at each other and giggling. When he calmed down, John asked: "What kind of sum are you talking?"

Kate said: "A lot—enough for each of us to live well for years. When you get tired of me, you can go back to your wife and kids."

John pulled at her dress and said: "You won't tire me out. "

Kate pushed his hand away: "Not now. Not here. Go take care of Lizzie. She needs you. She must never guess about you and me. We'll get Lizzie fixed and send her home with her cut. Then you and I can play all we want. But never, ever sit next to me in public or in her sight. Never touch me. Never give me that look. Save it for Lizzie." She patted his hand. "It'll be over soon, and Lizzie will be a busy girl."

7. Los Angeles—Mid-Autumn 1892

John and Lizzie sat side by side in second class on a drizzly October day. Kate sat opposite them, dark and cold, her gaze out the window.

Beautiful wide-open American countryside rolled endlessly by outside. Rain and mud slowly gave way to the wide open skies and rolling prairies of the Midwest. Lizzie clung to John like a school girl.

Kate kept driving her plan home, one small piece at a time that Lizzie could digest: "Lizzie, this man Spreckels is a very bad man. He mashed a girl named Charlotte Barnard, and ruined her career in San Francisco."

Lizzie said: "Yes?" She had her hands folded between her knees.

Kate said: "You're not going to think about him. He'll get what he deserves. He has millions of dollars, and won't miss a few thousand."

Lizzie said: "That much!"

Kate said: "I have a great plan, but you won't really need to do anything much. I'll show you how to behave. You just pretend to be Charlotte Barnard—or actually, Lottie Bernard. Mr. Spreckels will be hundreds of miles away in San Francisco. You'll be down in San Diego. You'll never see him. He'll quickly decide the best thing is to pay up and we'll leave town within a day or two. I've seen it work before."

Lizzie said: "You've done this before?"

Kate caught herself, and said with a veiled look: "I knew someone who was good at it, and I learned a few tricks from her."

Lizzie said: "And you'll teach me? I'm bright enough—just a little slow at learning. I make up for it in looks and style." John rolled his eyes, laughing kindly.

Kate said: "I'll teach you how to impersonate a maid. That's simple, right? All you do is keep your beautiful face shut, and dust. Got that?"

Lizzie made dusting motions. "Just keep dusting, huh? I think I can do that." She giggled.

Kate said: "You speak only when spoken to, and say as little as possible. Avoid small talk with the other girls. Keep to yourself. It will all be over in a few weeks, and then you'll have a lot of money."

Lizzie said: "I'll try my very best."

Kate took Lizzie's hands in both of her hands and said: "No, Lizzie, 'try' is not good enough. You have to be determined that it's going to work. It's like I told John—you have to be a hundred percent or it won't work right."

Lizzie said: "I promise. I'll give it a hundred percent." She held one of Kate's hands, and one of John's in her other hand. She looked radiantly happy in that union of love and friendship. Her lover and her friend both let her be like that for a happy minute or two. Then Kate got back to business. Kate said: "I made up a name for you. I'm going to call you Katie Logan. Can you remember that?"

Lizzie said: "Sure, that's easy."

Kate said: "I like your confidence. Now start thinking that you're Katie Logan in your head. Get used to the name. I made it easy for you to remember. I used my first name, Kate, and a family name that's close to mine, Logan instead of Morgan."

ತಿ ಎ

John, Kate, and Lizzie arrived on the West Coast on a sunny, balmy day in early November 1892. As they walked through the Los Angeles train station, Kate said: "Lizzie, I'm sending your trunks on to San Diego. Here are the three baggage claim checks." She offered three pieces of paper, but Lizzie said: "I'm afraid I might lose them."

Kate said: "Here, John, you hold them for her."

John said: "Sure—for my sweetheart, anything." He put the tickets in his wallet. He took out the silver earrings. "See? I still have them. Holding them for my sweetheart, and I swear I always will."

Lizzie tugged bravely at her earlobes, which were closing up.

Kate said: "Lizzie, you sure you won't lose your nerve? You can't come running to me or John. You have to stay on the job and not get fired."

Lizzie said: "I've been a hard-working girl for years. I know how to keep my nose to the grindstone. "

Kate said: "Great. Well, then, let's go find a hotel. You two lovers should spend at least one night together before our adventure starts. I'll see you in the morning, Lizzie."

In a darkened hotel room, John and Lizzie made love, and then lay together in sweaty lethargy. John said: "That Kate is a thinker, huh?"

Lizzie said: "She'll save me from ruination. You and I will have a lot of money to make a new life together." She touched his nose, trying to push home her point. He always became evasive about staying with her. It made her uneasy deep down, but she always pushed the thought away. If he did not love her, then she was ruined for sure. It was to scary to be possible.

He sensed her feelings and said: "Don't worry so much. Don't think too far ahead. Just think about how you're going to manage this impersonation thing in the next couple of weeks."

Lizzie sighed and lay back in a blind rush of desperation and hope. She had no choice but to trust John and this kind stranger, Kate Morgan.

John put his arm around her. Comforted, she said: "Katie Logan, Katie Logan, Katie Logan..." She laughed. "See? I have it down pat."

John mumbled a reassurance, gave her a gentle shake, and started snoring. She turned over and spooned her back against his front. His warmth made her drowsy and pushed her worries away as she drifted off.

☙ ❧

In the early morning, Lizzie and Kate stood near a wealthy home. Kate handed Lizzie an envelope. "Here is a letter of recommendation I got my Uncle Will Farmer to write for me. He's an important grower in Hanford and Visalia. I've changed the name on the letter to Katie Logan for you." She added: "Your employer is Mrs. R. M Widney. I'll send my own trunk along for storage. Pretend it's yours, since your three trunks will be at the baggage depot in San Diego."

Lizzie said: "I promise I will do very well. I like how you've planned everything out to the last detail."

Kate said: "Where are your glasses?"

Lizzie stared at her—then, reluctantly, produced a pair of wire-rimmed glasses from her purse.

Kate said: "Be sure you have them so you're not blind as a bat and mix things up." She fluffed Lizzie's clothing. "Make sure you look presentable. But then you're a clothes horse. Be brave. Just keep your mouth shut and keep dusting. They don't expect conversation or entertainment from you. For all they care, a domestic is just another piece of furniture. In some homes, husband and wife have their most private arguments right in front of you, as if you were an ottoman or a sofa."

Lizzie laughed and said: "This will be an adventure."

Kate said: "You'll get used to being someone other than you, and in a few weeks you'll be ready for your dramatic stage entrance in Coronado."

Lizzie said: "I love acting and actresses."

Kate said: "I know you do. But honey, for God's sake, these will be roles without speaking parts." She gave Lizzie a brief hug. "Good luck!" With that, she walked away.

☙ ❧

Lizzie took a deep breath and then walked up to the main door. She knocked, and a voice called for her to enter. For a moment, she felt apprehensive. A kind lady sat at a desk in the parlor as Lizzie entered. Mrs. Widney said: "Hello, dear. You must be Katie Logan."

Lizzie looked stunned for an instant, then caught herself and said: "Yes." She was in for it now. She was in the swim, and there was no turning back. She felt strangely calm, knowing that Kate Morgan had thought everything through.

The lady rose, smiling graciously, and pointed to a hallway. Mrs. Widney said: "My regular upstairs girl is on vacation. You seem entirely acceptable, my dear. Your reference letters from Mr. Farmer is very strong. Our interview need not continue. Go down that hallway and introduce yourself to the Head of Staff."

Lizzie spent a week with the Widneys, and became totally immersed in her work and in the strange sensation of being someone other than herself. Kate was right. It was fun, it was exciting, it was interesting—and easy. She felt as if she finally had an opportunity at acting, and found she was very good at it.

☙ ❧

As during last week with the Widneys, Lizzie entered service at the Hughes home, carrying only a satchel. She turned to tip a porter, who delivered Kate's trunk. A haughty man in butler uniform appeared in the entrance. "Miss Katie Logan?"

Lizzie said: "Yes!"

Butler said: "Welcome to the Hughes home. You come highly recommended by the Widneys. I am reassured by your reference letters from Mr. Farmer and Mrs. Widney. We'll need your services for about a week while our regular maid is on vacation."

❦ ❦

The following week, with a porter struggling (again) behind her with Kate Morgan's trunk, Lizzie entered the servants' entrance of the L. A. Grants' home at 917 South Hill Street, Los Angeles. It was mid-November 1892. She was used to her impersonation by now, and very glad to have some employment and the income. Being on short term meant that you got paid weekly, and she relished the idea of having some cash around. She met Mr. Grant, a contractor, and Mrs. Grant. They liked Lizzie very much from the first. Mrs. Grant told her at the start: "We've had glowing reports about you from the Widneys and the Hugheses, Katie, as well as Mr. Farmer's letter. What a refined and lovely young woman you are."

Lizzie said: "Thank you. I'll do my best for you."

Mr. Grant said: "I'm sure you will. And with Thanksgiving coming later this month, I'm sure you will have fun helping prepare a wonderful dinner."

Lizzie said: "I look forward to it. Thank you."

She began to feel more pregnant. One day, as she swept a carpeted parlor with a rolling sweeper, Lizzie held her stomach and ran from the room. After vomiting in the bathroom, she returned to her work and grimaced with stomach cramps. Just then, another maid walked through, carrying a stack of towels, and saw her grimace. "Hello, Katie. Everything okay?"

Lizzie said: "Yes. A little touch of something—I ate something funny last night."

"That'll do it every time."

After the maid left, Lizzie broke down crying. She took out her hankie and quietly sobbed for a while. Then she reminded herself that Kate Morgan was helping her in so many ways. She dreamed of living with John Longfield, and what a wonderful time they would have together.

The very next day, Lizzie and the other maid grabbed lunch in the kitchen on a short break. As they ate, they jabbered in random conversation. The other maid said: "...so I had this Uncle Wilbur who never liked his name, and all the kids called him Willie..."

Lizzie said: "...Some names are like that. My mother's name is Elizabeth, which is also my real name, which is why everyone calls me Lizzie..."

The other maid sat gaping at her with eyes wide open.

Lizzie froze, realizing she had made a huge mistake. "I'm joking, of course. Actually, I like the name Kitty. I mean, Katie. That's what I prefer people to call me—Katie Logan."

The other maid had not yet resumed chewing, but stared at Lizzie puzzled and unconvinced. "I see. How interesting." It was an incident she would tell a Los Angeles newspaper reporter a few weeks later, but Lizzie would not know that.

The incident so shook Lizzie that she did finally contact Kate Morgan, and they met on a street corner in Los Angeles. Lizzie said: "I'm lonely. I can't do this anymore. I miss John, and I feel like a hollow person, being someone other than myself."

Kate said: "You've done swell. You feel ready to go to Coronado?"

"Yes. Let's get it all over with." She began to cry. "I want John to come spend a day with me. Why has he not been here to see me?"

Kate said: "I sent him to my home town in Iowa—to talk with my old high school friend Allen, who is the banker there, so you'll have bank credit available if you need it at the Hotel del Coronado."

Lizzie said: "Can I see my John?"

Kate said: "Of course. He'll be on the train from Denver Thanksgiving Day, and he'll go to San Diego with me. If you want, you can meet him at the Hotel Brewster in San Diego before you go to Coronado."

Lizzie dried her tears with one of her embroidered hankies. "I want to see him before that. I want to see him now."

"But honey, he's not even in California." Kate scribbled on a piece of paper and said: "The whole thing will be over in a few days, and we'll all have our money, and you'll have your man. Try to keep your act together for a few more days. Can you do that?"

Lizzie nodded. "I'm sorry. I'll pull myself together. I'm putting my complete trust in you, Kate. My life."

"I won't let you down, sweetheart." She handed Lizzie the piece of paper. "Here is the address of the Hotel Brewster at Fourth and C in San Diego. I wrote it all down for you. Go there and ask for Dr. and Mrs. M. C. Anderson. That's John and me. You're going to the Brewster to pick up the medicine to fix your problem."

Lizzie took the paper and hugged her impulsively.

Kate said: "You've been very brave. You'll have a lot of money, both of you. He'll figure out how to take care of his dumpy wife and kids so you two can make a new life together."

Lizzie dabbed at her eyes with her hankie. "Oh God, that would be divine. You think he still loves me?"

Kate said: "He loves you very much and wants to marry you. He told me so last week before he left for Iowa. He also went to Cleveland to set up a General Delivery address so his wife will think he's looking for work there. He won't even give her a real address where she can reach him."

Lizzie said: "Sounds like he'll leave her then, after all."

"He can't love her much if he won't tell her where he's staying."

Lizzie said: "Will you be there in San Diego?"

"I have to stay out of sight, Lizzie. You'll be watched by Spreckels' people. We can't afford a flub. I'm giving it five days, no more. It won't be weeks like it's been here."

Lizzie uttered a gush of relief. "Oh, good."

Kate said: "I'll send my demand to Spreckels in San Francisco by telegram. Thanksgiving is around the corner, and I expect he'll be with his family. That's a Thursday. Too far away to look in on us, and right where we want him, remembering how dear his wife and children are to him. You start taking your medicines on Thursday. Take a dose Friday, and another on Saturday. That should do the trick. Watch how it goes. If you don't have bleeding and contractions, take a fourth dose on Sunday. That will surely do the trick. If I don't give you the signal, you have your abortion right in the main lobby of his hotel. John and I will take you away, saying he is Doctor Anderson, and everything will be swell."

Lizzie said: "But no money."

Kate said: "Not in that case. But I don't think that will happen. I'll send my threat, and he'll pay up quickly to be rid of us."

Lizzie said: "Sounds scary."

"Just don't think about it," Kate said. "You'll be sick a few days, and you'll miscarry. You'll soon get better, I promise. John would kill me if anything happened to you."

"I would feel much better if I knew you were right near me. Please!"

Kate said: "Very well, then let's do this. John and I will join you at the hotel late Thursday or early Friday. We will check in as Dr. and Mrs. M. C. Anderson. You can remember that name—it's your aunt in Grand Rapids,

Louisa Anderson. M is for money, and C is for can-do. You can do this, and you will have your money. We will be staying right there in the hotel with you, but you must not let on, and you must not talk to us, because I expect Spreckels' detectives will be watching you."

Lizzie said: "And—?"

Kate said: "They'll be watching if you are acting alone, or if you have accomplices—us. We want them to think you really are Charlotte Barnard, and pay out the money. If they see you have accomplices, they'll know it's a false paternity charge, and they'll have the police arrest us all. Have courage, Lizzie—trust me—it will all turn out for the best."

                              ❧ ☙

In the early morning on November 23, Lizzie rose at the Grants' house. She dressed, went downstairs, and mingled with the other help over coffee and breakfast in the kitchen. Then she wandered into the garden by the servants' quarters. Mrs. Grant, who really liked her, waved. "Oh, there you are, Katie. So nice to see you. I want to be sure you will help Cook stuff the turkey this evening."

Lizzie whirled, looking pained. "Oh, Mrs. Grant, you are so good to me. I have to run an errand. I'm afraid it is a personal matter. I will be gone all afternoon, with your permission, but I promised to be back before dark."

Mrs. Grant said sternly: "Of course, my dear. You do what you must. But promise you'll be here to help, and I'll make sure you get a nice plate tomorrow, and some pie."

Lizzie said: "I do promise! I do so promise! Thank you!"

                              ❧ ☙

Lightly dressed, and carrying only a hand satchel, Lizzie wandered up and down the station platform in Los Angeles. It was late Wednesday, Nov. 23, 1892. She had already missed her promised return to help the cook stuff the turkey, and she regretted having lied to Mrs. Grant, who was so nice to her, but she was on a mission that even Kate Morgan had not sanctioned. She was going to meet John Longfield and propose that he make a commitment to marry her.

She took the train south, and got off in Santa Ana. At the ticket booths, she bought a fare east to Barstow. As she waited on the platform, she ate a sandwich and a banana, and drank coffee.

She took the train to Barstow. She rode through the night, a forlorn figure. In Barstow, Lizzie sat alone on the platform, in the dark, as November 24, 1892 rolled around—Thanksgiving Day. She knew she cut a solitary and desolate figure in the middle of nowhere, a ruined woman, gambling desperately with all her life on the two people who could save her—Kate Morgan and John Longfield. She was tired, but she was so tense that her body felt as if shot through with electricity, so she dozed only fitfully.

Night turned to morning, and still she sat there. As dawn broke, she bought coffee and buttered marmalade rolls from the station snack window when it finally opened. With her stomach somewhat full, she dozed again. And she walked up and down the platform.

At last! Midmorning, the train from Denver pulled in, and she boarded. As the train chugged southwest toward Orange and Santa Ana, Lizzie walked down the aisles of rocking coaches looking for John. Reluctantly, she put her glasses on. When she spotted Longfield, who did not see her at first, she hid her glasses in her purse, and ran to him. "John!"

"My God! Lizzie! What on earth?"

She sat by him. "I am so glad to see you." She grasped his hand, and put her cheek on his shoulder. "I have missed you so, my love."

John said awkwardly: "This is quite a surprise."

"Are you glad to see me?"

"Yes, of course. Just tired. Been traveling for days."

Lizzie took off her jacket and rolled it up. "I understand. Here is a pillow for you."

"Thanks. What a surprise."

Lizzie said: "Do you have the three baggage receipts for my trunks?"

"Yes." He started to reach into his pocket for them, but Lizzie shook her head and said: "Keep them until we get to San Diego. It's a few hours yet. I'll take care of you. You sleep, and we'll travel to San Diego together."

Looking oddly at her, John put his head on her jacket by the window, and fell asleep. Lizzie sat patiently watching the landscape roll by, lost in her thoughts and dreams. She dozed a bit herself, being overly tired.

At some point, someone said: "We're almost there." People began to take down their luggage, close their sandwich boxes, get ready to disembark. Lizzie shook John. A sign passed: *Orange 10 Miles*. Lizzie said: "We're almost on the West Coast, darling. Wake up."

John stirred. He yawned and wiped his eyes. He blinked repeatedly as he saw her, as if he could not believe he was seeing her there.

Lizzie thought she read coldness and resentment in his gaze, but pushed the feeling away because it couldn't be. It mustn't be. It would mean the end of the world. She said: "Kate told me you and she will sign into the Hotel del Coronado as Dr. and Mrs. Anderson."

"That's new to me, Lizzie. Don't go changing the plan now."

"I'm not changing the plan, John. Kate did. She's in charge."

"Yeah, that's right. Well..." He waggled a finger. "Lizzie, I'm not going to San Diego with you."

"You're not?" She felt thunderstruck.

"We can't be seen together. Remember Kate said that?"

"Oh yes." She remembered, but something wasn't right here. They sat in silence for a few minutes. "Kate said you went to Cleveland."

"That's right. Cleveland."

"To mail your wife some news," Lizzie prodded. *I hope you sent her a letter saying you want a divorce,* she thought. He seemed so odd coldly distant...unloving... Lizzie grew alarmed again. She was tired, and scared, and trusting—could he not understand that she needed some reassurance?

"I don't want her to know where I am."

She put her hands together in his lap, over his hands. "You don't love her anymore." It was a statement, a question, a plea. She needed him to love her. Enough of the pretense. She wanted him for herself. It had to be that way. She was carrying his child, which she was willing to abort for him according to Kate Morgan's plan, so that Lizzie and John could be together. So why was he now being evasive? Did he not love her? Her heart would break if he did not love her.

John ignored her hands and said: "What? What makes you say I don't love her? I love you, Lizzie. I told you not to think too much ahead." He pulled his hands away as if out of a bear trap.

"If you love me, then leave her and marry me." She crossed her hands over her aching and scared heart, sitting bolt upright like a scared rabbit.

"I have children, Lizzie. I'm tired—stop joking around. "

Lizzie said: "I was hoping—"

"Nothing is simple or easy, Lizzie."

"You're just tired, John. I'm tired. Neither of us is making any sense."

"You know that I like you very much—"

Lizzie said: "You like me very much. You like donuts or beer very much. What does it mean? I am willing to give you my life. I am carrying your child. Do you love me as I love you?"

John said: "One of my children is sick, I am told, and people say my wife is looking haggard. I worry about them. Yes, I worry about you too. I love you. I love all of you. I have no time to love myself with all this damned loving."

Lizzie said: "So you really have no thoughts of being with me. It's the money you want. I am your pregnant mistress, a ruined woman, and you tell me you are worried about your wife and children. Am I supposed to give a damn about everyone else in the world at this point?"

John said: "Lizzie, you'll drive us both crazy with this talk. We agreed to just think about the next few days, get through this thing at the hotel."

A sallow man in a black suit became aware of their conversation as their voices rose. He watched the developing spat with the bored attentiveness of a traveler trapped in the moment. He would tell a bellman some time later, who would tell newspaper reporters.

As the train approached Orange, Lizzie was in tears. She could not afford to lose him. She was desperate. "I am sorry. I'll do whatever you want me to. Please, John—"

John felt himself grow inarticulate. "You drive me crazy babbling so."

Lizzie sobbed. "I'm sorry. I know you are going to leave me. Please don't do it, because I will die. Don't leave me. Please."

"I'm sorry I got myself into this. I can't sleep nights for worry."

Lizzie said: "About me? Or about yourself?"

John yelled: "About you. About me. About my wife. About each of my kids, whom I love." The train ground to a stop, and John rose.

Lizzie tugged at his jacket, but he darted down the aisle. Lizzie wailed: "Please! Don't leave me! I'm sorry."

John bounded off the train like a man in a panic and ran, dodging left and right through the thick crowd. He vanished in two or three minutes.

The sallow man, whose name was Joseph Jones, rose and followed Lizzie off the train. He too was headed for the Hotel del Coronado that day. He would be amazed to see her again in the lobby of the Hotel del Coronado as they both registered. He would avoid direct involvement in the great mystery that was about to grip the entire United States through breathless hour by hour telegraphic reports to the Yellow Press. But he would tell reporters about the man and woman he'd seen on the train. For over a century, people would be puzzled how a girl who was on her way south from Los Angeles to San Diego could simultaneously be on a train headed west from Denver to the coast at Orange and Santa Ana. That it would take her an entire day to make a two-hour train trip from Los Angeles to San Diego, from the time she left the Grants to her signing in at the Hotel del Coronado the following afternoon would be remembered as a mystery within a mystery—the so-called Missing Day. The case that was about to break would be a national sensation for weeks, and an enigma full of tantalizing and contradictory clues for many generations.

8. Conspiracy—Late Autumn 1892

The old Spreckels Mansion in San Francisco resided on well-kept, green grounds on a slope overlooking the bay and harbor entrance leading to the Pacific Ocean. In the working wing of the building, a messenger hurried down office corridors that clattered with typing. Male secretaries and female typists came and went through office doors, but many offices were empty because of the Thanksgiving holiday. The messenger moved along Mahogany Row, the executive section, to a door with the name *Mr. John Spreckels* on it. Another door had a sign reading *Mr. Spreckels' Secretary*.

The messenger knocked on the secretarial door. A demure, well-dressed female receptionist in her 40s opened the door. Seeing the messenger's uniform and satchel, she let him into a carpeted office suite. The messenger had been here before, and knocked on the main door. An older man's gruff voice called out inside: "Yes, come in."

Inside the room, the messenger found a balding man of about 60 working at a desk. Joshua Babbitt had been one of the Spreckels' chief adjutants for many years. The messenger handed over a sealed envelope. "Priority telegram, Sir—highly personal for Mr. Spreckels."

"Thanks," said the secretary, handing him a tip. The messenger nodded and left, and the secretary opened the telegram. His eyes bulged and his jaw dropped as he read the message from a Lottie Bernard in San Diego. This woman claimed to have worked for John Spreckels as a domestic. Her tone was unseemly and familiar. She wrote that she had a stack of incriminating love letters. Not only that, but she said she was pregnant with John Spreckels' child, and required a large sum of money to discreetly raise the child and cause Mr. Spreckels no further anxiety. In other words, she was blackmailing him under threat of causing him a terrible embarrassment—at his hotel in Coronado, at the worst possible moment. Did this woman realize that John Spreckels was at that moment sitting opposite President Benjamin Harrison in the White House, in tense negotiations for the future of the Spreckels sugar plantations in Hawai'i, the future of that nation itself, and to a considerable extent the future of capitalism in the United States? Was she just naïve, or a genius who understood the growing hunger of corporate America to create overseas empires in Central and South America as well as Hawai'i? Not to mention the decaying Spanish empire around the world? Her timing just had to be a diabolical coincidence. There was also the possibility that Spreckels' enemies were planting a scandal, framing John, to hurt his father, and deal a fatal blow to their chances of holding on to Hawai'i. *Dreadful. Just dreadful.* Babbitt rose and hurried to a mahogany door leading into the private offices of John Spreckels; his brother Adolph; and their father Claus, head of the dynasty of Sugar Barons. Those offices were, at the moment, quiet and nearly empty. Even the air was almost devoid of its constant pall of cigar smoke, and servants had opened the windows to let in fresh air. John was in Washington D.C. lobbying the President and Congress. Claus, the dynasty's founder, was in Honolulu for desperate, last-minute shuttle diplomacy to stave off an imminent coup against Queen Lili'uokalani and her government. Adolph was away on business somewhere. That left an Executive Vice President and Chief of Operations, Peter Maurice, in charge of the Spreckels business empire.

Maurice and Babbitt stood together reading. "The nerve!" said Secretary Babbitt.

"She must be crazy," EVP Maurice said: "Not a word of this to anyone."

"Of course, Mr. Maurice, understood. Anything I can do to help out?"

Maurice thought for a moment, rattling the telegram in one hand to help focus his anger into strategy. "Get me the cipher code book. This is an outrage. How dare this woman? I'll immediately telegraph Mr. Spreckels and the Pinkertons in Washington, D. C."

"And the hotel in Coronado?"

"Let's let Mr. Spreckels decide how he wants to handle this. I will advise him to let the Pinkertons handle this from the start, since this is one of their specialties—high-stakes blackmail."

※ ※

In the Oval Office, President Benjamin Harrison and John Spreckels were conferring. Harrison was a white-haired, bearded man of quiet disposition and slight frame. Spreckels, in his thirties and just graying slightly, was handsome and carried himself with the natural ease and dignity of one born into financial princeliness. He was just concluding a line of persuasive argument: "Mr. President, I hope to bring together some of our party in Congress to effect a consensus."

President Harrison said: "Mr. Spreckels, certainly I oppose any sort of imperialistic move to annex a sovereign nation. Much as Hawai'i looks tempting, going that far would make us look bad."

"I have no illusions," Spreckels said. "They'll do it in increments so the world won't notice. It's the snake strategy. I've watched a boa constrictor crush its victim, and then devour it slowly, one heaving gulp at a time." President Harrison grimaced. Both men were Republicans, supporters of industry and big business. They felt comfortable with each other as they teased and argued back and forth. The problem, as Spreckels saw it, was that his father's rivals had more support in the Republican-dominated Senate, and even in the Democratically led House of the 52nd Congress. Spreckels said: "The Missionary Party and the Dole interests are creating popular sentiment in the national press here in the United States. They are portraying the Hawai'ian people and their beautiful crown princess as monkeys and cannibals, to turn the American people against them, and to cause our people to support annexation."

President Harrison said: "I agree, it's a nasty business. But Mr. Spreckels, allow me to play Devil's Advocate for a moment. The question before us is—should I, as President, intervene in a matter between corporate rivals? After all, your father owns most of the cane fields in that nation. He controls the government through his friendship with the royal family. He has amassed a great fortune in sugar—a virtual monopoly—while other U.S. corporations seek to gain a foothold and generate profits. That is the narrow line I must tread here. The Dole faction will argue that what's good for business is good for America, and that preserving the Spreckels monopoly on sugar is not in our nation's best interests."

Spreckels said more heatedly: "Mr. Dole and his pineapple monopoly are thriving, so it seems clear to me that they don't need to overthrow the legitimate government of Hawai'i..."

Someone knocked on the door, and President Harrison said: "Come in."

A male secretary stepped in. "Mr. President, excuse me. There is an extremely urgent visitor for Mr. Spreckels, on a personal matter."

Spreckels immediately blanched, thinking there might have been a death in the family. President Harrison told Spreckels with kind sympathy: "Go on—I'll go have lunch. We can reconvene this afternoon. We still have much to talk about."

Spreckels rose. "My deepest apologies, Mr. President." He followed the secretary out of the room and into the hallway outside.

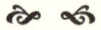

※ ※

As John Spreckels stepped out of the President's office, the male secretary waved close a man in a business suit. The man waited until the secretary stepped away, then introduced himself. "My name is Desmond Pinkerton. I'm a second cousin and employee of Alan Pinkerton, the founder of our agency. I'm here on a mission of special urgency, requested by your offices in San Francisco in the absence of you and your father. They received a telegram, addressed to you personally, which is being treated with the utmost sensitivity and secrecy, I assure you. It will be best if you read this telegraphic transcript of what they received in San Francisco." With that, he handed over a sealed document, which Spreckels tore open and read. In seconds, Spreckels had grasped the situation. "This is blackmail, pure and simple," he told Pinkerton as he felt blood pounding in his temples. He remembered Charlotte Barnard all too well. A beautiful young woman, and very discreet, except that his wife hated her instinctively. His wife, Lillie, suspected he had affairs here and there. They were an adventurous family, all the Spreckelses, but you had to play it smart. Lillie had fired the girl for ineptitude, and John had paid her off generously. How was it possible she was now blackmailing him?

Pinkerton nodded. "Of course."

Spreckels said: "I'm overloaded with important matters. I can hardly add this to my list of urgent concerns. And yet this woman wants to ruin my reputation, and she could destroy the work I am here to do."

"Of course, Mr. Spreckels. This distraction needs to be handled by competent service. We are quite experienced in dealing with situations like this. If you want to employ me, I will trouble you very little with it. I have only one concern."

Spreckels said: "What is it?"

"This young woman has checked in at your hotel in Coronado. She claims to be the mother of your child, if you will forgive me for voicing such an outrage."

Spreckels turned red and trembled, with a look of distress and shame. "I should have known."

Pinkerton nodded. "The name she gives is Lottie A. Bernard. Does this name have any resonance with you?"

Spreckels said: "Oh the devil, yes, I might as well come clean to you, though

I'll deny anything—"

"No need to worry. I give you the seal of the confessional. I will take your secrets to my grave. We are Pinkertons, after all."

"I work hard, and I love my family. As you can imagine, a man of my standing is surrounded by temptation, and I am generally very disciplined. I don't make a habit of womanizing. But, as it happened, circumstances being what they were for a brief time, I had an unfortunate and thoughtless liaison with a domestic named Charlotte Barnard earlier this year. It was a foolish mistake on my part."

"Did you exchange any letters with her, as this woman claims?"

"Love notes, I am ashamed to say. I never signed them, but they are in my handwriting."

Pinkerton said: "The woman says she is willing to sell them to you, in effect. Would you consider paying the sum she asks?"

Spreckels said: "What a nuisance! I paid her off and sent her packing. She didn't strike me as a copperhead."

"People can be two-faced. Or desperate."

"What if she keeps a few letters and comes back with it later? She could sell them to a newspaper—"

"We can plant some rumors. Trust me, we are very good at this. I'll assume she has more duplicity planned, and we'll tactically and strategically anticipate her and outflank her. There are a number of what-ifs here, and we can anticipate most of them. The key is to neutralize her, pay her off again, and blacken her reputation so she cannot credibly cause any more scandal."

Spreckels said: "Thanks! Please deal with this for me. I will pay whatever fees you require, gladly."

"Is it possible you really did impregnate this woman? Think carefully."

Spreckels deliberated. "Depends on how far along she is. I last saw Charlotte late this summer. Unfortunately, yes, it's possible. The timing would be just right. It's November, and she'd be about four months along."

"Let's not draw any conclusions," Pinkerton said with calm assurance. "If she has any accomplices down there in Coronado, it's a closed case—she would be a fake. We are quite used to dealing with these situations."

Spreckels said: "What do you suggest?"

Pinkerton said: "Our rule of thumb is quite simple and usually effective. If the girl is acting alone, pay her and get her out of your hair. If she has accomplices, then she clearly is a simple blackmailer. We'll have a different approach, and it has to be done carefully—discredit them, counter their lies with lies of our own, so that they lose all credibility. We usually spread stories that they are grifters, cardsharps, gypsies, that sort of thing. They'll seem quite repulsive when our stories get into the popular press."

Spreckels looked relieved. "You'll handle it then? You feel you can?"

Pinkerton nodded. "We'll have our local talent in San Diego shadow this woman, see how far along she is, and make a judgment on that if possible. We'll see if she has accomplices—if not, pay her off, get the documents from her, search her room and her belongings for any other letters, and be done with it. If she has accomplices, we bring in the police and round up the whole gang. We then orchestrate a clean-up so that anything they say will make them sound worse than they already are. If any other notes surface, we'll bring in experts who will testify they are fakes."

Spreckels said: "Very well then. My man in San Francisco was right to bring you in. I can't afford an embarrassment at this moment. Even my own agents in San Diego must not know anything about this."

Pinkerton said: "I will have telegrams go out instantly. We are already hard at work, and will resolve the matter for you very quickly."

9. San Diego—November 1892

Around noon on Thanksgiving Day—November 24, 1892—Lizzie Wyllie arrived in San Diego. Still reeling from her disastrous meeting with John Longfield on the train from Denver to the coast, she was a pale face sitting at the window as the southbound train from Santa Ana huffed and chuffed into San Diego's 1887 California Southern Railway train station. The small but ornate wooden station, which was square and had on top a disproportionately large clock tower, was full of people coming and going. San Diego had blossomed into a city of over 45,000 during the brief boom of the 1880s. The economy collapsed back to fewer than 20,000 souls trying to eke out a living after the panic of 1889. Speculation had driven the real estate and financial markets through the roof—most notably, that the Santa Fe Railroad was about to push through a direct artery of the Transcontinental Railroad, which proved to be untrue. Also, initial enthusiasm about French efforts to build a canal through Panama had also killed the idea of San Diego as an important cargo hub—though by 1892, after more than 20,000 worker deaths, total failure of the French venture was imminent, due to poor planning, virulent tropical diseases, and seemingly impossible geological and hydrological problems. San Diego's real estate and financial ventures collapsed overnight, and one could buy land for pennies on the dollar—if one wanted to live in this beautiful but isolated and impoverished place. Much of the Spanish and Mexican Old Town at the mouth of Mission Valley had burned down in the early 1870s, about the same time that Connecticut newcomer Alonzo Horton developed his New City on nearly 1,000 acres of beachfront land on San Diego Bay. The military saw San Diego's harbor as one of the finest natural harbors on the Pacific Coast. Entrepreneurs Hampton Story and Elisha Babcock had developed Coronado Island. They'd built the Hotel del Coronado in 1887 as a fabulous red-turreted fantasy resort, opening in February 1888. After the collapse of '89, John Spreckels bought up everything in sight—North Island and South Island, the newspapers, the utilities, the light rail, banks, even the open flume that brought water from the East County mountains to this arid coastal city. The Depression of 1893 was yet to strike, and San Diego, in 1892, was still a shattered ghost of its glorious past decade, sleeping in the sunlight.

This was the moment in time, and the place, in which Lizzie Wyllie got off the train and pretended to be the imaginary person named Lottie Anderson

Bernard. It was the start of her lethal adventure at the Hotel del Coronado.

Still shaken from the ill-omened meeting with her lover John Longfield, she went from the train station next door to the baggage terminal. At a window, she addressed a red-faced older man in a gray smock and dark blue cap. "Sir, I have come to collect my three trunks."

The baggage agent said gruffly without looking at her: "Got your checks?"

Lizzie said: "No, my husband has them, and he got off in Santa Ana."

The rude man said: "Have him come pick them up then."

Lizzie said: "I don't know how to contact him, and I need my dresses and shoes and things. Everything I own is in those trunks."

"You have no business here." It was the social custom that a young single women must travel with either her husband, a male relative, or an older female chaperone. The baggage man regarded her as if she were a woman of ill repute. "Someone with you?"

Lizzie said: "I'm not traveling alone by my choice. Look, my name is—"

"I don't care what your name is. Rules are rules, girlie. No checks, no baggage. Now get lost." He slammed the window shut on her. Distraught, she turned away.

Lizzie remembered that Kate Morgan had said she could meet her and John at a hotel. She found the address in her purse, written in Kate's handwriting. After asking directions of a woman waiting for a train, Lizzie walked east on C Street. Her walk took her into Alonzo Horton's New City. Some of the buildings she passed, like the back of Horton's grand hotel, reminded her of the big buildings in a real city. This felt like a backward little town trying to become a great city like Detroit or Chicago. The streets were neatly named, with letters running east-west and numbers running north-south.

At Fourth and C, Lizzie saw the splendid, wood-and-stucco Hotel Brewster, several stories high, which occupied the entire city block. It was a large modern hotel offering clean rooms, safety, and comfort to traveling businessmen. In the spacious lobby, she made her way across shining wood floors and area rugs to the front desk. There she addressed a male concierge. "Sir, I am looking for my brother and his wife."

The concierge, a tall, dark-haired young man in a black suit, asked: "Are they guests here, Miss?"

"They said they'd be here—Dr. M.C. Anderson and his wife Louisa."

"Let me see if they checked in." He spent a minute or two looking at the guest register on the marble counter top. "No, I'm sorry, there is nobody by that name registered here. I didn't think they sounded familiar."

Lizzie felt stung—puzzled, and mortified. What next? Was everything meant to go wrong? Seeing her consternation, the man said, "Wait here a moment," and went to speak with a tall, dark-haired woman at a counter nearby. She seemed to be an authority figure in her black silk dress, with a severe looking silver and mother-of-pearl brooch over one breast. The dark woman approached with the concierge. Lizzie regarded the woman with an instinctive mix of hope and dread. The woman had a strong, deep voice. "Are you looking for a Dr. Anderson and his wife?"

Lizzie said: "Yes!"

"What is your name?"

Lizzie said: "Mrs. Lottie Anderson Bernard."

"Follow me." She led Lizzie into an office marked *Assistant Manager*. She closed the door. "Sit down, please." The woman seemed a bit scary to Lizzie, sort of veiled and dark-minded. Her features were handsome, if one could say as much, not unpleasant. She was attractive without losing a certain forbidding air. Or maybe it was a touch of evil. Lizzie knew she did not read people well, especially without her glasses. She sat down before the desk, and the tall woman went to a cupboard. She took out a small package and placed it before Lizzie. Then she sat down behind the desk. "Examine it and see if it is what you came for."

Lizzie opened it with trembling fingers and found a little cardboard box. In it was a vial of medicine with a note rolled around it and held by an elastic. The note read: *If the pain gets too bad, see the doctor.* It was signed simply *Druggist*.

Lizzie said: "What is this?"

The tall woman said: "Dr. and Mrs. Anderson came to see me and left that for you. They said you would know what to do with it. Your medicine. I know nothing more. I don't know who those two people really were. They paid me a small sum, to be sure and give you this package when you came asking for them." She nodded, looking at the box. "There's my end of the bargain."

Lizzie slipped the box into her purse. In a shaky voice, she said: "I was hoping to speak with them. She said to ask for them here."

The tall woman shook her head vehemently, and rose. "We're done, I'm afraid. This feels like shady business, and I want no more part of it. Good day, Lottie, and best of luck to you." Her expression was pitying.

☙ ❧

In an office in the Pinkerton building in San Diego sat two long-term, trusted Pinkerton employees. They had a wooden desk between them, and a filing cabinet and other amenities around them in the second floor office that would be the operating headquarters for the case.

Senior Special Detective Jeb Collins was briefing subordinate Special Detective Sam Dolbee on the case. Dolbee lived and worked in San Diego, while Collins was an expert who had been rushed down from Los Angeles. "We are the only two men in San Diego who will be fully inside on the case. The client's name will remain secret from the rest of our Pinkerton people, from the local police, and even from Spreckels' personal detectives at the banks and hotels."

Detective Sam Dolbee finishing reading the case file as he listened. "That's quite a situation." He closed the folder and handed it back.

Senior Detective Collins put the case file in a large safe and locked its door. Dolbee said: "You say she is at the Hotel del Coronado?"

Collins said: "Yes. Just got the information via telegram from Washington, and confirmed it by telephone with the hotel desk. It seems clear that she's at his hotel to blackmail him."

"What's the procedure typically?" Dolbee asked.

"It's simple. We need to find out if she is really pregnant, and acting alone and in desperation, or if she is just a criminal. The way we determine that is if we find accomplices involved."

Dolbee nodded. "Seems reasonable."

Collins continued: "Spreckels doesn't want his personal army involved. I gather he owns all of Coronado, most of San Diego, and much of San Diego County." Dolbee well knew that the city was still a backwater with no detective force of their own—they'd only recently started up a small uniformed police department. The mayor's office and the police headquarters were in a brownstone overlooking the edge of the Stingaree, the second biggest and craziest red light district on the West Coast after the one in Frisco. The U.S. Frontier had just been declared officially gone by the national census of 1890. The approximately twenty lawless blocks were a remaining patch of the great Wild West, and its most famous inhabitant was none other than Wyatt Earp. The retired Frontier lawman now ran four gambling saloons, and raced fine horses in Del Mar.

Dolbee suggested: "I would ask Wyatt Earp to help lend a hand. He's a little shady, but he's still a lawman at heart, and he might work with us if we need."

Collins nodded. "I'll buy that. Can you get a hold of him quickly? Will he be discreet?"

"Sure. I know the guy. I now how he works. He's quiet, and doesn't miss a thing. We just need to ask him to look out for any signs of unusual activity involving the Hotel del Coronado. Strange people moving through the Stingaree, without seeming to belong. Sooner or later, every shady character in the region filters through his casinos."

"That's right," Collins said heartily. "Amateurs just give themselves away. They skulk around with a dark cloud over their heads like a billboard."

"Any other instructions?" Dolbee asked.

" I'll direct the other agents without telling them the full picture. Time is short. We need to shadow her every move at the Hotel del Coronado for signs of accomplices. I'm having other staff watch the train station and the hotels, and any other logical points of passage for signs of anything unusual. We'll make this room our headquarters, and then as quickly as possible figure out all we can about her. Nobody is to set foot in here but you and me. If she's knocked up legit, we pay her and run her out of town. If she's part of a gang, we lock them up, keep the press away, and spread rumors about them so nobody will believe anything they say, just in case the story gets out. If we can, make a deal—freedom to leave town rather than jail time if they clam up."

Dolbee said: "I'll get to the Hotel Del quick as I can."

"Just a minute." Collins rose and walked to a large black steel safe. "I've been given some cash for field operations. There is no time to lose, and we can use whatever sum we need. Spreckels will pay any price." He spun the dials and unlocked the safe. There, amid stacks of important papers, sat a tidy block of paper money in various denominations. He took a few fives off the top and handed them to Dolbee. "This will keep you flush as you get started. If you need bribe money or anything, just let me know. Spreckels will pay anything to keep this hushed up."

John and Kate stayed in a small, cheap hotel near the waterfront in San Diego, on India near Date. They had registered as Douglas and Claire Lomax. Kate put their lone large open suitcase under the window for easy access. They had little baggage between them. Kate's trunk still sat in the L. A. Grant house in Los Angeles. The trunk would be safe there. She could send for it later, pretending to be Katie Logan, and apologize that her mother was dying and it had proven impossible for her to return.

John and Kate sat on the bed, eating ham and cheese sandwiches with pickles and beer. They both felt relaxed and content, letting Lizzie take the brunt of risk.

John said: "It's a bit boring, this waiting."

Kate produced a few dollars. "Johnny, I know you want to go have yourself a beer and watch the ladies. Just stay away from the card tables."

He took the money, counted it, kissed it, and put it in his trouser pocket. "Bless you, my darling. What a golden woman you are."

Kate said: "Relax. Have a beer or two. Clear your mind. Let me do the thinking. Stay low, don't attract any attention." She grinned. "I'm going to go have my hair done. It helps me think."

ॐ ॐ

On her way to the hairdresser, Kate walked by the Hotel Brewster. She walked along the building on its Fifth Street side, and tossed a small pebble at a first-floor window. The window opened, and the tall woman in dark clothing leaned out.

Kate said: "Did she come by?"

"Yes. I gave her the medicine as you said." Her voice was low and full.

"Did she seem okay? How was she taking things?"

The tall woman said: "She seemed pitiful. She looked tired and nervous, and she almost cried when I told her you two aren't here."

Kate handed her a five dollar bill. "Thanks. Here is the rest. Our business is finished."

The tall woman folded her money quickly and closed the window.

Kate headed south on Fifth Street, looking for the hairdresser shop to which someone at the hotel had referred her. Along the way, she noticed a mustachioed man leaning on a porch, chewing a toothpick and casually watching the street. He wore a six-shooter under his jacket. His eyes caught Kate's attention—they had the razor-sharp glint of a lawman's penetrating gaze, but she saw no badge. He looked like a tough customer, and made Kate a bit nervous. The law was no friend of hers.

Kate walked into the hairdresser's and got herself situated in a hair trimming chair attended by a buxom woman in her forties, who never stopped talking.

Kate tried to ignore her, and watched people outside through the window. She saw the mustachioed man loitering about as if he were looking for someone. Kate had a touch of paranoia about Tom Morgan, and this man stirred ominous, sinister feelings in her. The hair cutter noticed her looking, and said: "You're interested in that buckaroo over there, eh?"

"Just curious," Kate said.

"You know who that is?" She waited a second, stopped clipping and combing, and then said with a flourish: "That's Wyatt Earp."

Kate was genuinely surprised. "No." Her instinctive alarm deepened.

"Yes. He runs several gambling saloons and race horses here in town. His place is over in the Stingaree, if you know the Yuma Building."

"Not really. I'm new in town."

"Well, you'd do well to stay away from there. Avoid the streets between 1st and 6th, and between H and K. So are you going to be in town long?"

"I'm just here on business with my husband."

"Oh? What business is your husband in?"

"He imports and exports beer."

"Oh? You mean like in business establishments?"

"Yes, exactly."

"Where does the beer come from?"

"Usually not far away. Mostly local. Sometimes fancy, from far away."

"Sounds exciting."

"He does get excited about it."

"Your husband must do a brisk business."

"He does." Kate thought to herself, stifling a laugh as she thought, *He imports it all right—from the table, to the toilet. Why does this busybody need to ask?* She changed the subject. "So Wyatt Earp is now a gambling man?"

"He calls himself a Capitalist," she said as she continued snipping and clipping Kate's thick hair. "I think he works both sides of the law, personally. A lot of coppers do. Just look at them crooks over in the Stingaree, with City Hall and the Police Headquarters overlooking the whole crazy sing-along by night and by day."

After about an hour, when Kate's hair was done—tightly curled, with a slight burned smell from the curling irons, and fragrant with pomade—she took a walk down into the Stingaree to see for herself. It was the equal of any large city red light district she had ever seen. The main body of it seemed to be a long rectangle about four blocks east-west and about eight blocks north-south. There was even a small Chinatown containing laundries, opium dens, and cat houses.

The main action was in the Stingaree itself, though. On Fourth, Fifth, and Sixth Streets, Kate saw house upon house of prostitution, gambling, drinking, and any other vice you could name. The women were not allowed to leave their district, so the madams hired a corps of young men on high-wheel bicycles to come racing at all hours of the day and night with the finest wines and baskets of catered steak, lobster, and just about any fine food imaginable. Kate was curious about Earp, and found the Yuma Building on Fifth Street. It was a tall, narrow building with an ornate façade in several noisy colors. She recognized the man from a distance, by his great mustachio and sharp-eyed gaze. As she spotted him, she saw he was being tailed by a dark-suited man in a Bowler hat. The Bowler man didn't look like someone who belonged in the Stingaree. If anything, he had the hard chops and cold eyes of a detective.

Kate hung back and watched the two men. All around her were flying bottles and screaming women, caterers racing by on bicycles, gunmen riding in or out on their horses, women coming and going in carriages, and often a distant pop of gunfire and the laughter and shrieking of drugged and drunken men and women.

Earp stepped up into his gambling saloon on Fifth Street. The Bowler man, having apparently had his fill of observing Earp, took the closing door as his cue to turn and walk north on Fifth, back to the civilized part of town. Many streets here had been paved during the boom years, and each city block had a tall metal tower with a bank of electric lights high up to mimic sunlight (or at least the full moon) at night. Kate followed half a block behind. He crossed a street, and walked through an alley opening on a wide street, which he crossed. Kate stopped on the opposite sidewalk, because the Bowler had stepped inside the city's clearly marked Pinkerton headquarters. She frowned and thought: *Why is Earp being followed by these people? Could this be about me and Lizzie?* She had never pulled off a scheme this elaborate, and she began to wonder if she'd bitten off more than she could chew. But she'd always managed to charm and talk her way out of a situation, so maybe she could do it again here if necessary. She prepared herself to bolt at the first sign that Spreckels wasn't just easily sending the money.

When Kate returned to the hotel room, she found John sleeping. She took off her hat and started to nervously undress. John stirred in his sleep and muttered drunkenly. Kate said: "I thought you'd be out somewhere."

John groaned and sat up, smelling boozy. "I got side tracked at a pretty little bar, and thought I would have those beers like you said. I don't feel ready to gamble. When I feel that itch in my fingers, I'll wander over into the Stingaree and rake up a pile of dough."

Kate said: "You better sober up. I think we're in deep water here."

John said: "Why?"

Kate said: "This is a small town. I have a feeling the Spreckels people are more clever and determined than I imagined. I get these gut feelings, and right now my gut is starting to feel like a trapped animal." She explained about Earp and the man she'd followed, adding: "I'm going to think what to do next. If the money doesn't come quickly, we may just have to cut and run."

"And Lizzie?"

"We take her along if we can." She had no intention of being captured by the police or the Pinkertons if things went wrong—not to save Lizzie, nor to save John. She could not tell him this, of course. She remembered, too, that she had made one fatal mistake. She, the mistress of false names, had given John and Lizzie her real name. Now she could not simply abandon them—because they knew who she was, and it would only be a matter of time before the police were looking for her. If that happened, she could never use her real name again.

❧ ☙

Tom Morgan was holed up in the Eagle Hotel, a tiny building on the eastern outskirts of sleepy Salem, Oregon. He'd pulled off a job with some boys up near Portland, waylaying a Wells Fargo shipment. There was supposed to be gold on board, but it turned out to be a few measly little bags of silver coins. But it was nearly a grand, and Tom managed to drive the other two boys off at gunpoint and elope with the coins, so he was flush for a little while. About once a month, he would telegraph an old friend of his back in his home town of Hamburg, Iowa, a fellow named Allen, who had known both Tom and Kate. His friend was quietly watching out for the possible reappearance in her home town of Kate Morgan, to whom Tom was still legally married. He'd curbed his drinking lately, out of regrets for losing her. He longed for her. He missed the old days when they'd ridden the trains, gambling and conning men for their money. Tom knew he wasn't any prize, but he hoped somehow that they could be together again. His years with her had been the best of his life, and he'd been a fool not to know it.

To Tom's surprise, a telegram arrived within the hour from Hamburg. It was signed Allen, and said:

Kate in San Diego STOP + possibly at a hotel, not sure which STOP + Deposited $25 credit at bank here STOP + may claim it next few days STOP + All I know thus far + STOP.

Tom's heart skipped a beat. This was what he'd been waiting for the past few years—a chance to get on his knees and beg his wife to come back to him. He loved her very much and pined for her. Packing his suitcase in a great hurry, he rushed for the train station. He'd be in San Diego within a day or two. Oh God, he'd see his Katie Farmer again and he'd beg her to come back to him. What great times they'd had together! What great times they could have again together! Within an hour, he was on a train heading south along the California coast. When nobody was looking, he polished his twin Deringers and prepared himself inwardly for mortal combat with any man who would stand in his way. He was a desperate man, but a righteous one. The Law and the Bible were very clear on this. Kate was his lawfully wedded wife, his property, his chattel, and he had the God-given right and obligation to retrieve her, to protect her, to keep her by his side.

10. Coronado—Thanksgiving 1892

Lizzie left the Hotel Brewster after her upsetting meeting with the tall, dark woman. She took the ferry across the bay, which was a nice, sunny, breezy ride. Having been unable to retrieve her trunks, she carried only her satchel with a few things in it. She rode across the length of Coronado Island on the steam trolley, rolling down the center of Orange Avenue along the store fronts and decorative palm trees. Less than a mile and a half from the ferry landing, she stepped off the trolley before a magnificent white hotel with brick-red conical roofs and white turrets. The Hotel del Coronado lifted her spirits. The sunshine and fresh air restored her a bit. She slipped back into her wishful dream, in which John came to get her and they lived happily ever after. The hotel was a Victorian confection with no two walls, windows, turrets, or other features matching any other.

Lizzie entered the hotel's cool, shady lobby and walked to the desk. She put her satchel down and leaned her elbows on the desk. A young clerk saw her and came to help her. He looked a bit puzzled and uneasy about admitting an attractive, elegantly dressed young woman who was traveling without luggage, alone and unchaperoned. He went to consult with a frowning chief clerk, and then returned. After a brief conversation, the young man signed the guest register for her. The pen paused in his hand a second. He had started to write *Miss*. "Can you spell that for me?"

Lizzie enunciated: "Mrs. Lottie Anderson Bernard."

"Will Mr. Bernard be checking in today also?" he asked as he changed the *Miss* to *Mrs*.

Lizzie said: "No, but I expect my brother and his wife, Dr. and Mrs. M. C. Anderson, to check in later today."

"Very good, Mrs. Bernard. The bellman will see you to your room."

Another young man in his early 20s stepped forward, wearing the standard uniform of bellmen—a modified Crimean War officer's uniform with pillbox hat, all in burgundy, with gilded braiding. "My name is Harry West. I manage the third floor. Any luggage today, or does Mr. Bernard have it with him?"

There was an instant spark of platonic friendship between them. Harry wore a wedding ring and seemed innocently just a pleasant man eager to be helpful. Earning or not earning a tip did not affect his naturally pleasant personality.

Lizzie said: "I'm afraid he does. I feel awkward without my shoes, my dresses, my makeup…"

"I'm sure he will be along shortly," said Harry diplomatically. They rose in a brass elevator cage. "You'll be in Room 302, Ma'am."

Lizzie said: "I am not expecting my husband today, but my brother and his wife will be checking sometime later. I've left instructions at the desk to notify me when they come."

"We'll keep an eye out, Mrs. Bernard. Don't you worry." On the third floor, Harry West led her out on a glassed-in balcony overlooking the central courtyard, then into a corridor above a stairwell, and immediately there was Room 302. Harry opened the door and showed her in. "Baths are at the end of the hall. Towels are in the closet. Please feel free at any time to ring me if you have any needs. There are shops below, including a druggist and a real estate office."

Lizzie said: "Thank you, Harry. There's one thing you could do for me."

Harry said: "Of course."

Lizzie pressed a healthy tip on him and said: "Bring me a large, empty bottle from the pharmacy, and a sponge please."

He looked amazed at the huge tip. "Certainly, but this is not necessary—a whole day's wages..."

Lizzie said: "Take it, please, with my good will. It does me good to know you are around and I can call on you. I suffer from the neuralgia, you know, and my doctor sent me to recuperate in this wonderful climate."

☙ ❧

Harry West went down to the lobby and spoke with the Chief Clerk. A. S. Gomer said: "Have you tended to the peculiar woman everyone is talking about?"

Harry said: "I have. She tips magnificently and seems very nice."

Gomer said: "You don't think the fact she came alone, with no baggage, and looks like an actress, has any shady or immoral leanings to it?"

Harry shook his head. "Like I said, she seems to be a fine lady."

Gomer said: "These days, with the economy so bad, we'll take almost anybody. It appears she'll be paying day by day, which could be a bad sign in itself. " He shook his head, with a suspicious look.

Harry said: "She's running a tab, just so you know. I'm getting her a few items from the pharmacy. For her neuralgia."

A Pinkerton man approached the desk and addressed Gomer. He identified himself as Sam Dolbee as he displayed a badge. "You the manager?"

"Chief Clerk, sir. I double as manager sometimes."

Dolbee said: "Listen carefully. This must remain confidential. I am working on a situation for the management. You will talk to nobody about me, or anything I am working on, got that?"

"Yes!" Gomer's eyes widened. He gripped the desk with white knuckles.

"When I say confidential, I mean put big steel staples in your lips, or I will take you outside and do it to you myself."

A. S. Gomer said: "Yes sir! Whatever you need."

Dolbee said: "Let me see the guest register." He read the names and other information on the current day's page. After making some notes, he went to the hotel telephone and cranked the magneto. This put him in touch with an operator across the bay in San Diego, who in turn connected him with his boss Jeb Collins' office in the Pinkerton building.

Dolbee told Collins: "She signed in as Mrs. Lottie A. Bernard."

"Good. That checks with our information, so it's her."

"She gives her city of origin as Detroit."

"Good. I'll get the Detroit and Michigan people working on leads."

Dolbee added: "She expects her brother, a Dr. M. C. Anderson, and his wife Louisa to arrive any time."

"Hmmm. Sounds like accomplices."

"I agree."

"I get a feeling she's a phony. We'll have our Pinkerton offices check all the Bernards and Andersons in Greater Detroit, and any relatives they may have elsewhere in Michigan."

"Right." Dolbee rang off. He had another lead to check.

Dolbee knocked on a door on the third floor—Room 372. A sallow, middle-aged man opened the door. "Yes?"

"Mr. Joseph A. Jones?"

"Yes?"

"I'm with hotel security, doing a little routine investigation. Nothing to be alarmed about. Standard stuff. It's for the safety and well-being of our guests. I saw that you signed in right after a young lady—"

"Oh yes, the beautiful odd duck."

Dolbee whipped out his pad and said: "Now why do you call her that?"

Joseph A. Jones said: "By an amazing coincidence, I saw her on the train from Denver early this morning. She was having an argument with some cardsharp looking scoundrel."

Dolbee scribbled avidly. "Can you describe the man?"

"See here, I don't want to get involved in anything. I'm a businessman on a tight schedule. I have to be on a train out of state in two days, and I can't afford to get hung up in any local police work."

"Don't you worry, Mr. Jones. I'm not with the police. This is a private security matter. I'll say nothing about you to anyone. Just putting some information together. Now what can you tell me?" As Jones gave a good description of the man on the train, Dolbee was pleased—already, pieces were starting to fall into place.

☙ ❧

In an atmosphere of dread, Lizzie slowly undressed. She stood naked by the night table. Her dress lay on the bed beside her. She felt a terrible unease about doing this, but she knew she had no choice but to trust Kate Morgan. Maybe John had just been having a bad day.

Her window overlooked the sunny intersection of Orange Avenue and two smaller side streets. Her room faced away from the ocean, east toward downtown Coronado, all three blocks of it. The room would get morning sun, but be in shade most of the day. She gazed out and forced herself to relax, to drift as best possible into a haze of positive thoughts.

Lizzie uncorked the bottle Harry West had brought. She poured it a third full of water from the wash jug on the bureau. She put the sponge into the ceramic bowl that came with the water jug. She opened the medicine box from the

Hotel Brewster, and poured a fourth of the powder into the bottle. She corked the bottle and shook it well. Carefully opening it, she poured the resulting reddish, cloudy liquid into the sponge, in the ceramic wash bowl on the bureau, until the sponge had a wet spot in its center. She cringed a bit, alarmed by its blood-like color, as she pressed lightly to spread the liquid out. Then she poured a little more. She sat back in a chair and slowly and carefully pushed the sponge inside herself. It was a pessary, used since ancient Egyptian times for dosing the lower extremities of women. It could relieve constipation and menstrual cramps, or induce a deliberate miscarriage.

She also took quinine pills, which Kate said would help the process along, and chased the pills with a whiskey Harry West had brought at her request. There was also a small bottle of laudanum for pain—also known as tincture of opium, a powerful herbal mix of opium and alcohol—but she discovered someone had already taken most of it, and that was just another of many little knife pricks of betrayal.

When she was done, she dressed herself, and rested a while on the bed. She hoped that, at any minute, Harry would knock on the door and tell her that her brother and sister-in-law had arrived. But nobody came. The silence was oppressive, even ominous, as evening closed in. When it was dark outside, she went down to the front desk and spoke with Chief Clerk A. S. Gomer. "Hello—has my brother, Dr. Anderson, arrived or sent a message?"

"No, Mrs. Bernard. I am sorry, he has not."

"I—oh well, I am going to bed early tonight. It's been a long trip. I'm tired and want to go sight seeing tomorrow. I also have to figure out how to get my luggage from the depot, if my brother is delayed."

He looked at her, pityingly, looking a bit distrustful, and confused about these shadowy men in her life. "Good night, Mrs. Bernard. Sleep well. I will be on duty here tomorrow morning. Maybe I can call you a carriage then."

ॐ ॐ

Kate Morgan returned to the hotel room that afternoon. She lay curled up next to John Longfield, and fell into a deep slumber. Hours later, it seemed, she was startled awake by an unknown noise. The space by her side was cold. John was gone. She jumped out of bed and saw her purse lying open on the floor. "Oh, damn you!" What next? He had taken her money, but she knew where to find him. It reminded her of how they'd met—he'd been gambling with someone else's money. This situation was getting too complicated, too fast. She had never worked with anyone, besides her stint with Tom Morgan, and never this many people and this many loose ends. The situation threatened to come undone, and she didn't like it one bit. First, she must retrieve her incorrigible boyfriend. Why did men always seem to do things like this?

She got dressed and walked toward the Stingaree with all of its bedlam and mayhem. She heard distant gunshots and men whooping. Women shrilled suggestively, probably drunk. More gunshots, more laughter…

Kate came to the Yuma Building on Fifth Street, where she'd last seen Earp. His name was posted in a window, followed by the word *Capitalist*. In another window was a sign—*Gambling*. Kate entered.

She walked into a dark, noisy bar. The bartender told a lusty joke as he served up a brace of sudsy beers. Men laughed and talked—and ogled her.

Kate passed into a bigger room, whose door was marked *Cards*, and closed the door. The atmosphere was quiet and full of smoky concentration. Men puffing on cigars sat around tables poring over their cards. There he was—John Longfield, drinking, losing at poker, and red-faced. Before Kate could rescue him, John said: "You rigged that!" He threw his cards down and lurched to his feet, making fists.

Kate rushed toward him, but too late. Three plainclothes security men, their holstered guns in reach, rushed in and grabbed John by the scruff. One waved a cosh, but didn't use it on John's head. There was a scuffle and a sound of smacking flesh as the security men quickly led John out a back door marked *Office*.

Kate followed, and entered Wyatt Earp's office without knocking. She froze at the door, with the handle in one hand. Nobody noticed her as she stood gaping. Wyatt Earp, still wearing his six-shooter, filled a pan with water at a small sink. He said: "No more liquor for our friend here."

The men pressed John down into a chair near the window. Earp poured water over a spluttering John's head, soaking him. "No more gambling here, bucko, ever again. You're a drunk and a sore loser. We look for guys like you and toss you on your ear."

John sputtered: "That guy was cheating."

"Yeah, maybe he does that now and then, but he makes money for the house. You're just an idiot who pisses his money away " Just then, Wyatt Earp spotted Kate. "Pardon me, Ma'am, my language—"

Kate said: "I've heard worse. I came to pick up my husband and take him home. If you see him in your saloons again, show him the door."

John looked at Kate with big red eyes and mussy hair as he sat dripping. At Earp's signal, the security men backed away. Kate said to John: "You go home right now and I'll see you there. Don't you dare go left or right, but straight to our room and wait there for me." She said to Earp: "Can I bend your ear a moment?"

Earp waved his men out, and they accompanied John out the door.

Earp and Kate were alone. Kate said: "You were watching the Brewster the other day. I was out getting my hair done and saw you."

Wyatt Earp said: "There is almost nothing around the New City that I don't learn about. Why is this of any importance to you?"

Kate said: "We all have our reasons, Mr. Earp. I have a bit of information for you. By the way, I'm surprised and glad to meet the famous lawman. I had no idea it was you."

He seemed good-natured enough, though shrewd and suspicious. "So what can I help you with?"

Kate said: "Well, to begin with, I thought you'd like to know Pinkerton has a tail on you."

He frowned. "How would you know? Are you with Pinkerton?"

"No, I came looking for my husband." She thought quickly and made up a fib. "I saw you outside the Brewster, and the man following you. I was having my hair done, and saw my good-for-nothing husband go by. As I was looking for Doug, I saw the man following you. He went into the Pinkerton building."

Wyatt Earp said: "I have news for you. Now that you came here, the same people will start tailing you. I know about them."

"What do you know about them?"

"Nothing to tell," he lied, and they both knew it. He eyeballed her strangely, though his smile never faded. Just a refocusing of light, in those sharp-as-glass eyes, by the instincts of an experienced lawman.

"So now you got yourself into the game. Where are you staying, anyway?"

"Coronado," Kate lied. "Why should I be concerned, Mr. Earp?"

Wyatt Earp relented and said: "I play my cards close to the chest. Something big is going on in town. The cops and the Pinkertons always come to me. This is one of those times, but I have no idea what that would be. Are you involved in whatever it is?" He regarded her closely.

Kate slipped into her most innocent persona. "Not at all. Just trying to stay out of trouble, collect my drunken husband, and get him home before he gets into trouble. Thanks for not roughing him up too much."

Wyatt Earp said: "I don't like roughing men up, Mrs.—"

"Katie Lomax. "

"And what do you do, Mrs. Lomax?"

"I am a domestic servant in rich people's homes. My husband was a book binder, but he recently lost his job."

Wyatt Earp had a twinkle in his eyes: "Not a book maker, eh?"

"You are a great man, and funny! So it's nothing my husband got himself involved in then?"

"Your husband, involved in something so big that it's got a whole mess of Pinkertons running around town?" Wyatt Earp laughed at the thought. "Nahhh. We are small fry in Mr. Spreckels' grand schemes, whatever those may be."

"Oh, the rich guy," Kate said.

"I think it's about him, because the Hotel del Coronado has come up in conversation, and he owns it. I'm not one to serve any rich man. I'm out to protect my own interests. I don't owe a thing to any man. I have four gambling establishments and I partner on some fine racing horses at Del Mar. What I'm afraid of is Mr. Spreckels is going to clean up the Stingaree, now that he owns most of San Diego and all of Coronado, and those temperance people hate gambling as much as they hate drink. So I keep an eye out for anything that affects me."

The door opened, and the beautiful former actress Josephine Marcus entered, age 31, carrying a basket of wash. Despite her dowdy clothes, torn apron, and a kerchief around her dark hair, she looked exotic and stunning, as in lithos Kate had seen in gossipy magazines. Josie held a large wicker basket full of laundry in both hands. "I'm sorry to interrupt, folks. Wyatt, love, do you have anything for this basket? Ah Wong is taking a load to the laundry."

Wyatt Earp said to his wife: "No, love, thanks." He told Kate: "Mrs. Lomax, meet my wife, Josie Marcus. Josie, Mrs. Lomax." Then he told Josie: "We were just helping her husband with a problem."

Josie Earp said: "From the look of that floor, you gave him a bath. Did he have fleas?"

"You are so lovely and famous. I've read about you." She'd seen a famous glamour shot of Josie, wrapped in mystery, and titillating..

Josie Marcus said: "Those days are long behind me."

Kate said: "I have a friend who would love to meet you—but she's not in town just now." She was thinking of Lizzie, who loved theater.

Josie Marcus said: "I still get letters from admirers from my Tombstone days. Excuse me. I have to hurry! Nice meeting you!" She sidled out the door, turning to maneuver the large laundry basket. To Kate, the actress looked perfectly happy in her new role as housewife.

Earp said: "Good luck, Mrs. Lomax. Keep your eye on Mr. Lomax so he stays out of trouble."

"Thank you, Mr. Earp. It has been a lot of fun meeting you and your lovely wife." Kate's spine crawled as she left. She felt his eyes boring into her back.

෭෮ ෮෨

Lizzie came down to the desk and got the chief clerk's attention. "Good morning, Mr. Gomer. Any word from my brother?"

"Nothing yet, Mrs. Bernard, I am sorry."

"There's also my other problem. My brother ran off with the claim tickets for my luggage up north the other day. I have no clothes, no shoes, no jewelry to wear. I'll have to cross the bay to speak with someone at the baggage terminal."

"I wish I could help you there. I understand they are sticklers for the rules. Maybe you should wait until your brother arrives with the tickets so you don't waste a trip."

She sighed deeply. "I'll check with you again to see if Dr. Anderson has arrived. I'll have something to eat, and then go for a walk."

"Relaxation—that's the key with the neuralgia. We see a lot of it here at the resort. Enjoy your day, Mrs. Bernard."

Lizzie ate a leisurely breakfast in the Coronet dining area near the main lobby. She had coffee, English muffin, eggs scrambled, bacon, tomatoes, and cereal with cream. As much as she enjoyed it, she was beginning to feel an aching heaviness in her lower torso, which told her the medicine was beginning to take effect. Being pregnant already changed much in one's body, but this was all the more strange and different. It affected how she sat, how she walked, or even bent forward to grab the table salt.

After lunch, Lizzie walked along the beach. The sun streamed down on her, and she closed her eyes and looked up at it as if it were a medicinal shower.

She came to Star Stables, and saw a frisky stallion. Walking closer, she asked a groom about it, and he directed her to a cashier's office. She rented the horse, had it saddled, and climbed aboard. No sooner was she astride the saddle, than the horse bucked and would not do her bidding. For a moment, she was afraid to fall off backwards and get kicked. As she cried out, along came teenage stable-hand Charlie Stevens. He took the animal firmly in hand. "They haven't gelded him yet," he apologized. "They should not have given you this one."

Lizzie said: "Please help me. I want to get off." He held the reins in one hand, and offered his other hand. "Thank you, Charlie," she said as she dismounted. "Whew!"

"Are you visiting from out of town?"

"I'm staying at the resort for my neuralgia," Lizzie said: "Do you have a carriage? And someone to drive it?"

Charlie grinned. "That would be me, Ma'am, if you will permit me. I will gladly take you on a tour of the area." At her bidding, he harnessed the wayward horse to a carriage. It submitted meekly, glad to be under firm hand. Lizzie sat in the carriage while Charlie trotted them out for a tour of Coronado. As he would later tell a newspaper reporter, on that day Lizzie looked robust and in the pink of health despite the medicines she was already taking.

Back in her room that evening, Lizzie took another dose of pills, and redid her pessary. Before going to bed, she wandered down into the lobby, which sported large chandeliers lit by electric power. She stopped to ask the front desk clerks about her brother, but there was still no word. She held her stomach in discomfort as she rode the elevator out of sight.

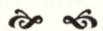

&

As was her frequent habit, in the morning Lizzie stopped at the front desk. It was becoming like the refrain in a song. Lizzie said: "Has Dr. Anderson sent any word for me yet?"

As always, the clerks shook their heads solemnly.

Lizzie went for a walk along the beach. She still wore the clothes she had come with, and they were starting to look shabby. Elegant women carrying parasols turned to stare at her with haughty, withering glances. She walked to the water's edge and looked south at a distant ship. How strange and disembodied she felt! How much like a dream all this was! She watched a seagull fly past.

Nearby stood a charming looking man in his 30s, with a mustache. He wore dark trousers and a white shirt open at the neck, with no collar or tie. He was barefoot, and struck her as funny because his feet looked pink and uncomfortable. Lizzie laughed as she picked up a pebble and threw it out over the water. The pebble skipped several times before vanishing.

The man said: "Bravo! Five skips."

Lizzie said: "Oh, hi," in an easy, familiar way, as if they knew each other. He sauntered closer. He seemed harmless and friendly at the first glance.

"Are you laughing at me?"

"Your feet. They look as if they are squinting at the sunlight. They wish they were back in their shoes.

He laughed. Looking down, he wiggled his toes. "You're right." He and she both laughed. Lizzie felt good to have something to laugh about, and someone to laugh with. He said: "Are you here on holiday?"

Lizzie said: "I'm here to recover from a bout of the neuralgia. The doctor says I am the worrying type, and he sent me here to rest."

He said: "Me too. I live in Chicago but I'm thinking of moving here with my family. I came to explore the Theosophical Society."

Lizzie said: "What's that?" She skipped more pebbles as they spoke.

He pointed west to the long, misty pile of Point Loma and Cabrillo Point sticking out darkly into the sea. "They are building their society up there on the point. I have a nervous ailment that I'm told this climate and their spiritualist theories may help. My name is Frank." He stuck out his hand. "And you are—?"

"My name is Lottie. I am staying here at the hotel." She was going to add *with my husband and my brother and his wife*, but what was the point in fibbing? It was beginning to dawn on her that neither John nor Kate had any intention of contacting her until the game was over. She must stay here and soldier on, waiting for word, and if no word came, it meant Spreckels wasn't paying up. Then she would take the last of her medicines and collapse in a lake of blood in the middle of his hotel lobby. And they would either save her, or she would die, and she no longer entirely cared which solution it was. Either way, she would be freed of the terrible burdens she had borne. And she felt terrible at the suffering this would impose on the life growing within her. It would all be over in a few days, one way or another.

ತಿ ∞

The great epiphany came to her as she stood like a child, skipping pebbles on the sea, and talking with this pleasant, innocent man who reminded her suddenly what it was like to speak with a decent human being once again. She almost told him her real name, but realized maybe she wasn't really herself anymore. All of this came to her in a sudden flash of insight. The sun shone, the sea smelled fresh, the wind was frisky like that puppy she saw playing with children in the tide nearby, and she felt lightened. She realized what must now happen, what she must do—only, not now; tomorrow. It could be put off in honor of this beautiful day and her enjoyment of it. "So what do you do, Frank?"

"Why—I am a professional failure, a fool, and a burden to my wife."

Lizzie said: "You sound a lot like me, except I have no spouse. I have nobody. I am all alone in the world." She thought again of the child she had once given up, and the changes taking place in her body. She thought about spiritualism, of which she had heard, and looked southeast at the sun hanging reddish-yellow over distant water. She understood now. Beauty, like happiness, could be seen but not touched, like that light rippling over water, ephemeral as light and shadow.

The way the sea washed gently up on the earth, pulled by the moon, and washed out in its rhythms twice daily, Lizzie herself felt like the earth and the sea, containing but not owning life or beauty. She had nothing to do in this moment but let nature show its full beauty, with Lizzie and the great hotel and the beautiful sea and this wonderful man and all these people parts of that greater, unified whole as the wonderful moments flickered by, *the golden atoms of the day* as she'd read once in a romantic poem.

In giving up control, or the illusion of control, she gained total power. And what was power? She held up her hand, opening it, as if power was just wind that blew between her fingers. Everything seemed so clear now, if slightly out of phase due to the medicines, and maybe she needed to eat something. But she felt content.

"You poor young lady."

Lizzie smiled comfortably. "So what does a professional failure do?"

Frank said: "I've tried everything from acting to writing, from raising fancy poultry to running a theater. My chickens died, the theater failed, my scripts burned, and my health collapsed." Lizzie held her hand over her mouth. They laughed again together. Soon they were both howling with laughter and slapping each other on the back. It was all in the moment. People looked at them, turning from conversations to crane their necks and see what the laughter was, and the world seemed to be smiling with the slightly shabby, very pretty girl who seemed so free, and the shoeless man. Finally, Lizzie and he caught their breath. They strolled along the beach.

Frank said: "It does a man good to laugh at himself. And to be laughed at by a beautiful woman."

"I wasn't laughing at you. I was laughing at your story. It all seems to blend so well—the chickens, the burning pages, the theater..."

"And you, Lottie? What do you do?"

"I am a rain cloud."

"What?"

"I cry very easily, so sad have I lately been. But you don't want to hear of my troubles, nor would I want to share them with anyone."

Frank said: "You are a very smart young lady. That was a clever conceit about the tears and the rain cloud."

"That's very sweet of you to say. I wonder, Frank, if people all around the world said pleasant things to each other, and made each other laugh, if it would be a cure for neuralgia and all of humanity's ills."

"I bet it would work. Well, I am trying to think of a children's book to write. I have some ideas."

Lizzie said: "Like what?"

"I lived in the Dakota Territory not long ago, and it was amazing to see how a tornado could sweep up people and animals and wagons and fly them through the air and then set them down a mile away. Sometimes in smithereens, sometimes unscathed. It might be a fun adventure to write a story about some people who are animals, and animals who are people, that get swept away to an imaginary land in the ozone, and have adventures. A little bit like Alice in Wonderland. I could call it Thunderland. Make a good theater play also."

Lizzie said: "I love theater. Did you meet any famous actresses during your theater years?"

"Why yes—quite a few. Their fame and fortune didn't rub off on me."

"Now Frank. Talk about a rain cloud. You seem to always make such a misery of yourself. Be positive."

"I'm sorry. Do I do that? Thanks for pointing that out to me."

"I believe that if you force yourself to smile, you will believe you are happy. Of course that's easy for an old rain cloud to say."

Frank said: "You are a very wise old rain cloud."

"Belatedly."

"What troubles you so, Lottie? I sense that, under all that sunshine and beauty, you carry a heavy stone on your heart."

"You're right, Frank. I've made some poor decisions, and now I have to carry the rocks."

"And you don't want to unburden yourself of them? We've scarcely met, but

I already think of you as a dear friend."

Lizzie said: "No, it's just as well that I keep my mistakes to myself. But I do appreciate your kind companionship. You are a married man, and nothing untoward must pass between us."

"Oh heavens, my intentions are pure."

"I sense that about you. A woman would see through me instantly, but a man has a certain innocence. And I think I am really a very nice girl, who has trusted other people too much. Enough of that. It sounds like you want to write a children's story."

Frank said: "I think that's what it wants to be."

"Tell me a bit more about your ideas. It makes me feel so light and happy to forget my own troubles."

So L. Frank Baum proceeded to tell her the earliest inklings he had of what would become a great classic, *The Wonderful Wizard of Oz*, to be published in 1900, and on whose sequels he would work at the Hotel del Coronado. But that lay in the future, when all the footsteps of this day, and many of the people who made them, would be long washed away by the tide.

☙ ❧

While Lizzie and Frank chatted on the beach, Pinkerton detective Sam Dolbee was going through Lizzie's belongings in her room. He had obtained a key from A. S. Gomer, and now looked like a gray shadow, bent over the Detroit woman's meager belongings.

In a dim, shadowy light, he saw the medicine box on the table. He ran his fingertip over her medicine vial, delicately, as if he were afraid the dully gleaming glass would cut him. The liquid inside looked a muddy red color, like congealing blood. The white label, with its red border lines, was marked in blue ink using a dipping pen in a blocky penmanship whose author could be male or female. A note in plainer pen lay near the vial. The note read: *If the pain gets too bad, see the doctor.* It was signed simply *Druggist.* No official markings like *Rx.* He left everything exactly as he found it, barely brushing his fingertip over surfaces as he gazed with critical, inquisitive eyes.

His gaze stabbed around the room, with its three windows facing Orange Avenue. The room had a fireplace, bed, table, chair, and a bureau whose drawers were all empty—nothing else. He found nothing under the bureau. He pawed through her satchel. He ran his hands under the mattress, but found nothing. He ran his fingers over the window and door frames, finding nothing but dust. If she had the love letters of which she had written in her blackmail note to Spreckels, they were well hidden. He could find no sign of them, and time was running out. She must not find him in her room. It was imperative that she (and any possible accomplices) be watched without knowing they were under observation. That would make it easier to catch any slip-ups she (or they) made.

Just before he left the room, tiptoeing out as quietly as he had entered, and leaving no sign of his presence, he did find several faded hankies embroidered with a name that was hard to make out—Lizzie Anderson. He made a note of the name. He would telephone his superior Jeb Collins, in San Diego, and tell him to quickly start a search around Detroit for anyone named Anderson or Lizzie Anderson, and all the variants on that name and their relatives in other cities in Michigan. Detroit was the city she gave on the hotel's register as her origin. Like so many other particulars of the case, the local police and the coroner would learn nothing from him. They did not even know the two Pinkerton Special Agents were on the case. The client they served was not the truth, nor the better good of humanity, but John Spreckels.

☙ ❦

Frank and Lizzie sauntered along the beach, chatting and laughing at little jokes. Frank said: "It's getting late, and I have to get back to Point Loma for dinner with the Theosophists." He pointed to the peninsula sticking out into the ocean to their west, framing the harbor entrance.

Lizzie said: "You don't know how much it's helped me to have your company this afternoon."

"I must tell you the same, since I'm alone here on business. You are so sad, Lottie. Despite your beauty and your many smiles, your eyes look haunted. Won't you unburden yourself? I'm a good listener."

"It's best I don't, Frank. It's just as well. Humor me. "

"Is it some illness far worse than your neuralgia?"

"Now that you say it, it's love."

"That can be a terrible sickness."

"When you've been betrayed and abandoned, yes. Not only by your *beau*, but by your friends."

Frank looked at his watch as it grew darker. "I have to run, much as it pains me. Will you be here tomorrow?"

Lizzie extended a hand and smiled sadly. "I can't see you, Frank. Not that I fear that you plan to mash me or anything." They both laughed. "I just think it's best that I spend the day resting and reading."

They shook hands and parted, going their separate ways.

Alone in her room, Lizzie took more medicine. She settled on her bed to read, and soon fell asleep clutching her stomach as the pain grew worse.

*   *

On Sunday morning, Lizzie awoke with stabbing pains. With a drawn-out, low wail moan, she staggered to the table and swallowed more pills. She chased them with water. Sitting down hard, she rang for bellman Harry West.

Harry arrived quickly at the open door. "How are you today, Mrs. Bernard. Oh, you don't look so well."

"I don't feel well." She handed him a dollar. "Can you bring me a cocktail and some wine?"

He took the money reluctantly. "It's a bit early in the day, isn't it?"

"I need something. And I plan to take a bath and wash my clothes. I still have not gotten my baggage checks, nor have I heard from my brother and his wife. Will you draw hot water for me?"

"Whatever you say. But do you think it's a good idea, getting yourself wet, and your hair wet too—it might make your illness worse."

"I think a bath will be relaxing, and I have to wash my clothes. I have never before, in my entire life, had to wear the same clothes three days in a row. "

"I'll be back with some towels in a little while. I'll heat water and run down to get your drinks."

A while later, Lizzie sat alone in the steamy bath room, washing her clothes while sipping wine. The door was locked, and nobody knocked to bother her. Lizzie wrung out her skirt, her blouse, and her undies and stockings, and hung them up on a clothes line the hotel had strung along one tiled wall for the benefit and comfort of female guests.

It took effort to climb into the tub, holding her drink. The warmth wrapped around her aching lower torso, and comforted her achy thighs. She rested and soaked in the tub. The wine brought a blush to her cheeks, and she felt drowsy.

She grew light-headed. The glass started to slip from her hand, and she was barely able to lean over and put it on the floor. The glass keeled over, without breaking, and made a blood-colored puddle on the floor's tiny, patterned white tiles. She spit up something reddish-purple, maybe a mix of blood and wine. She wasn't sure. Her body felt paralyzed, and for a moment it seemed a dark force was pulling her under. It felt like quicksand working on her. Consciousness ebbed and returned in waves like the tides out at the beach. This dark sea, however, felt like a dozen arms, like a painting she had seen in a magazine, of nightmarish evil water nymphs, pulling her down to a watery death. Recalling her epiphany on the beach, she struggled inwardly. *Please. It's not time yet. I'm not ready today.* Darkness rose up, and next thing she knew, she wasn't breathing—her face was in the water.

She lifted her head like a drowning person, cried out, and clutched the side of the bath. The water in the tub sloshed hard and noisily around her from the panicked motion. She clung to the tub with her head and hair hanging down the outside. The floor was covered with water. She retched, and a string of blood-red vomit and undigested food fell to the tiles.

She half climbed, half fell from the tub. Slipping on the wet floor, she wrapped herself in a heavy white robe Harry had provided. She staggered out of the bathroom, down the hall, toward her room. She braced herself against the wall with one arm, while the other flailed and she half stumbled several times on rubbery knees. Harry happened to be passing by (or hovering concernedly about) and he helped her to the room. His face portrayed shock.

In her room, Lizzie sat gravely ill on the chair while Harry toweled her hair dry. "Thank you, Harry."

Harry said: "You're far more ill than you said."

"It's just a bad case of neuralgia."

"I'll clean up the bath room and get your clothing. Don't you worry."

"It's good of you to care so much. Can you bring me some hot broth?"

☙ ❦

Lizzie was alone, and felt a bit better, after eating the bouillon Harry brought her, along with bits of buttered French bread and black coffee. Wearing a fresh hotel bathrobe, she sat at the table. She chewed idly on a pencil and played with some scraps of paper. On one scrap she doodled pictures, and wrote: *Frank Frank Frank Frank*—pining for his company. As she remembered the pleasant man she'd met on the beach, she said out loud: "Frank Frank Frank Frank—oh, if only my John were more a man like you. Everything would be so totally different."

The pain ebbed and flowed. She went down to see the legitimate pharmacist in the basement shops to buy a quantity of laudanum. He sold her a bottle with a red skull and crossbones symbol of terrible danger on it. He asked her about her pain, and urged her to see a doctor. She had no intention of doing so.

Back in the room she took a spoonful, and welcomed the numbness it brought. She thought of this whole mess that Kate had convinced her to be involved in. She had no desire to hurt John Spreckels, who had done her no harm. She scribbled: *I hardly know that man—I have only heard of him.* To Kate, wherever she might be, she said: "I thought I could trust you, and you never showed up. You and John both. And I don't have the evil in me to harm this great and powerful man I don't even know." She started to rise, but fell from the chair. On her hands and knees, she crawled to the closet. In the shadows, she lifted a wooden floor board. She pulled out the love letters Kate had given her. She was to give these to a messenger who would come in exchange for the money that would be wired to a bank. She would do the right thing now, and burn these things. But she felt too weak. She left the letters strewn on the wooden closet floor, and pushed the closet door shut. She half crept, half walked and fell, to the bed. There, wracked by spasms of pain, Lizzie held her stomach and lay in a fetal position.

A while later, she woke when Harry West brought her a bowl of oatmeal and some wine. She sat up and felt happy to see him and the food. "I thought you might like these. You look a little better, Mrs. Bernard."

"Thank you, Harry. What would I do without you?" Slowly, she walked to the table, sat on the chair, and took the spoon he handed her. The oatmeal had milk and brown sugar in it, and some sliced apples. "Oh, this is divine. Thank you."

Harry West said: "Anything else before I leave for home?"

Lizzie said: "Thanks, Harry. Run along to your wife and children. Come see me tomorrow."

"I will." He gave her shoulder a light squeeze, in answer to her plaintive tone. After he left, she ate, and then sipped the wine. She gathered the letters for now, and put them back in their hiding place. She amused herself, writing imaginary invitations to Lottie Bernard from famous actresses. Lizzie read out loud as she wrote: "Miss Louise Leslie Carter, star of the stage and theater, wishes to invite you to a pleasant stay at the famous Hotel del Coronado." She paused with dreamy smile and wrote as she said: "Miss Lillian Russell requests the honor of your company on a visit to the Hotel del Coronado." She paused, then continued: "Mr. Denman Thompson, author of the famous play 'The Old Homestead'..."

Lizzie paused at a lack for words. She had a coughing spell and crawled to the bed, debilitated. Light burned low in the fireplace as night wrapped itself around her.

* *

In the gray dawn light on Monday, Lizzie lay sleeping on her bed. Daylight was just beginning to penetrate the darkness, driving night away. Outside, it was a cold and drizzly day. A great sea storm was coming, and the atmosphere was charged with strange electricities as if sensing the storm raging inside her. Someone knocked on the door.

Lizzie slept on.

A rough hand rattled the door handle—not a hand intending kindness.

Still Lizzie slept.

A key turned in the lock. It was a sharp, slicing sound, like someone cutting with a knife. The man whose hands were on the door paused. The door opened, and Lizzie started up from her sleep. She could not reach her glasses. Her vision was blurry, and she couldn't move, as a man intruded in the room and stood by the bed. He smelled cold and smoky, like tobacco and cheap soap. She tried to sit up, but he roughly shoved her back. The intruder said: "We know you are here under an alias."

Lizzie swallowed hard, could not speak. She squinted at his dark, blurry outline. He said: "Who are your accomplices? We know you are working with a man and a woman."

Lizzie reached for a water glass. It fell and shattered.

He was relentless, in a cold tone as even and sharp as a knife blade. "The game is over, Lizzie. Yes, we know your name. You can sign this paper—" She heard a sheet of paper rattle. "—And we will pay you something to leave town. What do you say? It's your only hope. I won't be back to ask you again."

Lizzie tried to nod, but only managed a shake of her head that he took for a no.

"Very well then. I'll give you twenty-four hours. If you have not changed your mind by then, we will arrest you. Nobody will pay you the blackmail money, and we won't allow you to ruin our client's good name. Trust me, we have dealt with vermin like you many times, and the outcome is always terrible for your kind. Think about sitting in a cold, smelly, dirty prison cell for the rest of your life. That's the only future in store for you." The intruder made a blurry, hazy exit, sort of jerky, like a reflection in a rain puddle that kept coming apart in slices, and then slid biliously back together, only to balloon and break apart again. Lizzie coughed up watery blood and yellowish bile as she fell back into unconsciousness.

❧ ☙

Kate Morgan and John Longfield sat together talking in their hotel room. They were affectionate with one other, but the atmosphere was tense. Kate said: "It's Monday. We were going to give it five days. Time's up tomorrow. I have a crawling sensation."

John said: "You want to get Lizzie and pull her out? Can you imagine if something went wrong, and she told the coppers about us?"

Kate said: "You're right. Let's not waste another minute. I don't relish ending up in prison for many years. Let's go across to Coronado and get her out. We'll take her to a doctor, and she can have her miscarriage. Then at least your problem is solved. I will find another day to scalp Mr. Spreckels, or someone like him." She thought about it. "On the other hand, Johnny, you stay here, out of sight. I'll go out and run some errands, and get a message to her. It's best if we stay as low as possible."

"You always know best," John said.

"I'll be back after dark," Kate said. She put on her hat and shawl, and started for the door. She needed a walk, and some time to think. What was the best way to end this without leaving a trail for the police? She must be very careful. At least she would not have clumsy John dashing her plans. And she really could not leave Lizzie behind. "Stay here," she admonished him, and let herself out. Before she left, she instructed him: "I'm going to send a note across, telling her to meet me and you secretly after midnight on the back steps. It will be rainy. We can leave together without being seen. You lay low here, and don't do anything without me. Got that?"

"I got it, darling. You can rely on me."

Kate closed the door and hurried off down the corridor.

John pulled a bag full of beer bottles out from under the bed. He lit a cigar, gave a sigh of satisfaction, and opened the first bottle.

The damp, gray air that met Kate Morgan was far from the balmy, sunny normal climate of San Diego. It was a wall of gray maritime moisture, like a thick fog blanketing everything. In the distance reared the black clouds of a terrible sea storm that was about to hit that night. People said it was expected to be a storm of the century.

❧ ☙

Lizzie lay in her room at the Hotel del Coronado, suffering intensely. Gray light filtered into the room from the heavy marine layer outside. The room was chilly, and the little fireplace was full of cold ash. Her medications were strewn on the table, along with the scraps of paper and her hankies. Her satchel hung on a hook behind the door.

She heard Harry West outside, even before he knocked. Lizzie could not force herself to answer, nor stir. Harry used his pass key to let himself in. "Mrs. Bernard—are you okay?"

Lizzie turned weakly, and whispered. "Thank God, Harry. Bring me something hot."

Harry ran from the room. A while later, he returned with a tray of hot steaming tea and cereal with milk. "You have to eat. Can you sit up?"

Lizzie nodded and sat up. As she ate from the tray he placed on her lap, she asked: "Do you have some matches?"

He fumbled in his pockets. "Yeah, I think I have a few in my pocket. Will this do?" He showed her three or four wooden matches.

"Those will do." She nodded and took them.

Someone knocked on the door. She said "Enter," fearing that terrible man and his threats was returning.

Chief Clerk Gomer came in, looking serious. "Good morning, Mrs. Bernard. Please pardon my intrusion. It's freezing in here." He shuddered. "Shall I have Harry light your fire for you?"

Lizzie said: "No..."

"Mrs. Bernard, Harry has told me how ill you are. This is nothing to fool around with. I suggest calling the house physician."

Lizzie panicked at the idea of a doctor figuring out what she was doing to herself, so she fibbed. "No, there is no use. I am terminally ill with stomach cancer. I was hoping my brother would come, but he seems to be delayed. I am dying, Mr. Gomer, and wish to be left alone."

A. S. Gomer looked shocked. "Mrs. Bernard, if there is anything—."

Lizzie said: "There is nothing. I am told I only have days to live." It sounded silly even to her own ears. And yet—

Gomer told Harry: "Light a fire. Don't charge her for the service." To Lizzie he said: "Mrs. Bernard, I must ask if you will be able to pay the credit charges you have accumulated. They amount to more than twenty dollars by now."

Lizzie nodded. "Yes, there is money on account for me at the bank in Washington, Iowa. You have only to telegraph them, and they will forward a Western Union wire draft."

"Thank you," Gomer said, and left.

Harry meanwhile started a little fire, using scraps of paper and kindling in a basket beside the fireplace. He stirred the fire with the poker that stood in a corner. "This will warm you up a bit."

"Thanks, Harry."

Alone in the room, Lizzie lay sleeping.

She woke to pull a chamber pot from under the bed to retch in it. She fell back asleep, with her hand dangling off the bed and her fingers loosely holding the handle of the soiled white ceramic pot.

As the morning wore on, she slowly rose and went to the closet. She gathered up the love notes of Spreckels and Charlotte Barnard. She fanned the coals to get the fire going solidly. Effortfully, she started tearing the letters up one by one and fed them to the fire. The room grew warmer and brighter. Harry stopped by to check on her, and saw her burning the documents, as he would soon testify.

ର୍ଚ ଝ

Kate Morgan was on her way down to the ferry landing. As she came down D Street, she approached the California Southern Railway's train station. She stopped in at the telegraph office, as she did every day, to see if there was anything for Charlotte Barnard. She would simply walk by the postal boxes, and see if there was a slip of paper behind the little glass window. She knew the box was being watched, and would not actually go near it. Her plan, if she saw something inside, was to telegraph her old school friend Allen in Iowa and see if Spreckels had wired the money, as they had arranged last month. By now, she realized the hopes of that were scant to none. The box was empty. She borrowed some writing materials at a table set aside for customers, and wrote a note for Lizzie, pretending it was from John: *Lizzie, the game is up. I will come by this evening to get you. Look for me, and if all else fails, meet me on the back stairs outside after midnight. I love you always—John L..*

Her intention was to send John to fetch her under cover of night, and let him take the risk of being caught.

As she sealed the envelope and tucked it in her pocket, and started to exit the telegraph office, she almost had a heart attack.

There, tacked to the wooden door, was a picture of her husband, Tom Morgan. He looked exactly as he had when she last saw him—the thick head, the receding dark hair, the pleasant face with slightly crazy eyes. Underneath the photograph was a note: *Kate, if you read this, contact me at the Hotel Brewster. I have much to tell you. Love you forever, Tom.*

Shaken, she looked left and right and hurried out into the street. What a damned complication! She no longer loved Tom, nor did she believe he had changed. It would be as before—lovey dovey one day, then drinking and beatings the next. She could never forgive him for kicking her down the stairs, killing their unborn child, and leaving her barren. Reviewing that incident alone in her thoughts, she firmly and absolutely made up her mind. She would never go back to him. But dammit—he was the last thing she needed right now. What luck, to spot his note. Now at least he would not surprise her if he spotted her on the street of this small town. She must be extra vigilant. Pulling the brim of her black straw hat low, she hurried across the street to a lunch counter, and ordered a little beer to sip while she deliberated what to do next. In this dim gray light, people moved about like hazy shadows. Lights burned, and animals slunk away seeking shelter. The barometric pressure was dropping, and a chill drizzle hung in the air along with a sour scent of wood smoke. The train that pulled out of the station looked like a long, dark smoke-wraith threaded with rows of blurry yellow lanterns. Its hard chuffing and the slam of its gear shafts made steel scream on steel. It was almost as if the train were struggling to escape, which mirrored the cold panic Kate Morgan felt. Her collapsing plans enclosed her like a trapped animal in a cage. Kate's main thought now was to get Lizzie out of there, and herself and John and Lizzie out of San Diego. She would get Lizzie to a doctor, and make her promise never to tell what she had been involved in—yes, that was it, Lizzie and John would be glad to get out of San Diego safe and secure, with no police troubles. Spreckels would most likely keep the matter secret. And Kate had to figure out how to escape back into the vastness of the continental United States, maybe lie low for a year or two, work as a domestic, until all this blew over. That was her state of mind as she finished her beer, and walked down to the ferry. She asked around until she found a reputable looking young man and woman headed for the Hotel del Coronado. She asked them if they would deliver her note, which was addressed to Mrs. Lottie A. Bernard, directly to her room, which Kate by now had learned was Number 302 on the third floor. The young couple were very nice, realizing the importance that Kate put on it, and promised to slide it directly under Lizzie's door.

Kate watched the ferry—a large gray ship capable of carrying horses and buggies in addition to passengers—leave the dock on its fifteen-minute steam-powered journey across roughly a quarter mile of San Diego Bay, from the landing near G Street to the foot of Orange Avenue in Coronado.

※ ※

Tom Morgan walked the streets of San Diego, looking for his wife. Passion burned in his chest and gorge as he thought of her in bed with him. Here he was, close to her at last, in this small city. He had sometimes wept with despair and remorse at losing her because of his faults. At other times, he could just as easily weep with rage at what she had done to him, abandoning him, and she being his lawfully wedded wife! They had been two souls together, with the world against them, and now they would be together again, by whatever it took to make it happen.

He'd take a few drinks to calm himself, and try to think constructively. He kept pretty much sober except for a bracing whiskey or two at times like this. The best idea, he thought, had been the pictures—having his photo taken and posting copies in prominent spots around town. That should get her attention. Meanwhile, he spent every waking hour walking around looking for her.

Tom's path soon took him, in a day or so, to the Stingaree. There, he visited Wyatt Earp's dining and gambling establishments and ate a nice steak dinner with cold beer. Lighting a fresh cigar, he took a walk through the card rooms, but had no interest in gambling just now. His mind was on Kate.

In this hopeful, virtuous frame of mind, he met the great lawman and his beautiful actress wife. He introduced himself simply as Tom, a visitor from Nebraska, and Earp was very cordial. Tom had visited some of Earp's former stomping grounds like Dodge City, Kansas, and Tombstone, Arizona. Earp put a hand on his shoulder and invited him to the bar for a whisky, which Tom gladly accepted. "So what brings you to town?" Wyatt asked by way of conversation, while the bartender set their shot glasses before them.

"On me," Wyatt said. He and Tom clinked glasses and downed the drinks.

"Thank you, Sir," said Tom. Tom knew the man was studying him attentively behind that easy-going front and that imposing mustachio. No matter—whatever Earp hoped to learn about him, he hoped to learn what he could. They set their glasses aside. Tom said: "I've come to San Diego in search of my poor wife." He offered Wyatt a sanitized tale about how they had an argument a few years ago, and she had some other troubles, and left him. Now he had had time to think over his sins, and regret the times he spoke sharply to her, and wished to find her and get before her on his knees and beg her to come back.

"What does she look like?" Wyatt asked innocently. Tom, just as innocently, described Kate while ordering a second round on himself. Wyatt lifted his drink and froze. "Why, that describes a Mrs....." He downed his drink. "Now what was her name?"

Tom shot his down and set his glass aside, feeling a hot tingle both from the whisky and from Wyatt's frowning effort to recall a woman he had recently met.

"There was a woman who said her name was Claire something. She came to get her drunken idiot husband. That wouldn't be her. Naw."

"I'm clutching at straws," Tom said. "Any idea where they're staying?"

"Oh, some hotel downtown. Now wait a moment. It seems to me she mentioned something about Coronado at one point."

"The island across the bay?" Tom asked.

"I remember her name now. It was Claire Lomax, and she lied to me. She wasn't staying in Coronado."

"A lie, eh? That sounds more like my Katie already."

"For reasons of my own, I did some leg work. I learned she and that man are staying at a hotel near India and Date. I'll give you directions."

Tom thanked him and bought another round. Wyatt Earp explained about the wonderful resort that Elisha Babcock and Hampton Story had built during the boom years. The two men had developed Coronado from a forlorn wilderness full of jack rabbits into an upscale city that was incorporated in 1891. Spreckels had bought them out, like so much else. Wyatt worried that Spreckels and the do-gooders were going to clean up San Diego, get rid of the Stingaree, and drive out all of Wyatt's business.

Tom left the saloon elatedly, and fortified with a few drinks. Thinking of the man she was with, Tom checked his Deringers, one in each vest pocket. They were Colt No. 2 'New Deringers,' single-shot, .41 caliber. Tom had a satisfied feeling that he would be back together that very day with the woman he loved and adored.

❦ ❧

Lizzie Wyllie lay dozing, alone in the room, early Monday afternoon. A noise at the door woke her. A man and woman with pleasant voices laughed and called out "Western Union Express!" It took Lizzie a minute or two to rise and falter toward the door, and by then the couple were gone. She saw a small envelope on the floor, the kind telegrams came in. She picked it up and went to the light at the window to open it.

My God, she thought, *finally something from Kate and John!*

When she read the note, she dropped her hands in bitter disappointment at the irony. She was past tears. All this for nothing! She could have stayed in Michigan and had an abortion instead of all this posing and lying and dirtiness, just to wind up half-dead and miserable, with nothing to show for it. What drove it home was that she recognized the handwriting—it wasn't John's. It was Kate Morgan's, who was being dishonest as always. Why was she writing for John? Had John left town already to go back to his wife? Was anyone really even coming for her tonight? Should she try to leave now, rather than wait for the noose to tighten—or was Kate really going to come with John to get her? Or maybe Kate was sending John, and then bugging out on both of them to leave them in the lurch. Lizzie's thinking wasn't clear enough to make heads or tails of her dilemma.

All she had now was a final, depressed resolve. She had made a botch of her life, and was destroying the poor thing growing inside of her. She determined she was going to kill herself, the baby, and the man who had betrayed her. And Kate Morgan, if possible. It wasn't revenge—it was justice. It was preventing these depraved people from hurting anyone else. The great irony was that, had she kept the baby, the child would have been the one person who would be with her always. The world had taken the first one from her, and now she was again betrayed. To do what she had decided yesterday, on the beach with Frank, she would make one final trip across the Bay into San Diego. She dropped Kate's note into the fire, where it folded up like an autumn leaf, blackening as if in proof of Kate's evil, and consumed in a brightening of the yellow-orange flame.

With its rising smoke fled the last ounce of trust Lizzie had in Kate, and the last shred of love she felt for John. She loved her mother and sister too much to return to them in this ruined state. They would be better off without her.

❧ ☙

In the early afternoon, Lizzie set out on her journey. She was so sick she could hardly walk. For the first time, she went by the front desk without asking for the imaginary doctor and his imaginary wife—Kate and John, who had never come for her, and the devil might care if they ever did.

The light was gray and dismal outside, as a weak Lizzie walked slowly to the street and waited for a trolley. The conductor had to help her on board. The steam-powered trolley rolled slowly through a darkening Coronado. Storm clouds were rolling in. The air was disturbed, and horses acted skittish. Dogs and cats slunk for cover.

It was a rough crossing on the great steel boat that carried people and horse carriages. The water was choppy. It was windy and chilly, and people were bundled up. Lizzie shivered in her shawl.

As the boat rocked with an ominous threat of violence to come, she saw a huge black wall of storm clouds approaching from the southwest.

On the San Diego side, a man helped Lizzie up onto the dock. She paid a man with a carriage to take her up D Street. She half drowsed as the horse's hooves steadily clip-clopped on the concrete pavement littered with horse manure. He let her off on Fifth Street. She knew exactly what she wanted to do here.

❧ ☙

Tom Morgan took only about twenty minutes to reach the inexpensive hotel where Wyatt Earp had told him Kate and her companion were staying. He walked calmly into the lobby and spoke to an elderly concierge who looked up, over half-rim glasses, from the newspaper he was reading. "Good day, Sir. Need a room before it rains?"

No thanks," Tom said carefully. "I'm looking for some friends of mine, whom I would like to invite to dinner. She's a dark-haired, strong looking woman with a pleasant face and striking eyes. He's a handsome man with a mustache, about so high—?" Tom raised his hand to his shoulder.

The concierge nodded. "Sounds like Mr. and Mrs. Lomax. The Lomaxes." He turned and looked at the key board. "Doug and Claire Lomax, in Room 15 upstairs. Would you like me to show you up there?"

"No, thanks, no need to trouble yourself."

"On the second floor then," said the concierge, pointing to a wooden staircase wending out of sight from the carpeted and ornately furnished, rather cluttered little lobby.

"Thank you very kindly," Tom said. He debated—should he wait in the shadows? Afraid to miss her and lose her again, he bounded up the stairs, ready for anything. His guns were ready. He feared no man. Walking down the narrow, carpeted hallway, he came to the reddish, shellacked door of Room 15. He put his ear to the door and listened for a minute or two. He wondered if they were in. He didn't hear Kate's voice, nor a man's. Then he heard a faint clinking sound, like glass on glass. A smell of beer and cigar smoke wafted through the key hole. That did it. Tom knocked.

"Yeah?" said a man's voice.

"Mr. Lomax? I have a message for you."

"Gimme a second."

Tom heard a crashing, stumbling sound. Feet shuffled on a linoleum floor. A chain lock rattled, and the door opened a few inches. An unshaven man in his 30s stared out with bloodshot eyes. "Yeah?"

"I have some money for you, Mr. Lomax."

"Hold it a moment." The chain rattled as he released it, and he opened the door. "You from Western Union?"

"Something like that." Tom stepped inside. "Where's Kate?"

"What?"

Tom had sized him up—a tough guy, but a city type, without a farm boy's brawn and sinew. Tom shoved him lightly away from the door, and slipped the door shut behind him. "If you have a gun," Tom said, "don't pull it out. I've got two guns, and I'll plug you before you can roll those drunken eyes twice in your skull. Where is she?"

"Who?"

Tom slapped him across the face, and the man fell down against the bed in the middle of the room. "I'm not going to ask you twice." He pulled out one of his Deringers. "If you lie to me, or lead me on, I'll put lead in your skull. Do you understand me, fool?"

The man staggered to a table covered with beer bottles and slumped in the chair. This man wasn't going to fight anyone. He mumbled something slurry in a disgruntled, fuzzy voice.

Tom held the Deringer and lifted the man erect by his soiled shirt back with his free hand. "One more time, before I throw you out the window. Where is Kate, my wife?"

John Longfield held up his hands defensively. He slurred: "Meeting 'm in back Hotel del Coronado after midnight."

"Who is them?'

"Claire and Lizzie. Kate, I mean, and Lizzie."

"This must be another of Kate's schemes. Who's she blackmailing now?"

"Spreckels."

"The rich guy? She's lost her mind for sure." Tom saw he must save Kate from herself. "Are you sure about this? What is your name?"

"John Longfield. Doug Lomax, husband of Claire Lomax. You?"

"Tom Morgan, her real husband. I've come to get her back. When is she coming back to this room?" He released his grip on the man's shirt, and John Longfield slumped with lolling head.

"Isn't," Longfield slurred. Gesturing drunkenly, he pulled his watch from his pocket and showed it to Tom. "Midnight, hotel."

The thought of this drunk's hands on Kate nearly made Tom shoot him, but Tom thought of the concierge and the mess that would cause. Prudently, he pocketed his Deringer. "You got any whiskey?"

Longfield pointed to a dark area under the bed. Tom reached underneath and pulled out a bottle of Red Canary. "That's good stuff. Let's split a glass before I go."

"Delighted," John said, lolling around.

Tom poured himself a glass and pushed the bottle across. "Help yourself."

Longfield grabbed the bottle and upended it in a generous swig.

"That's right," Tom said. He rose and pushed his untouched glass to Longfield. "You should have a few more."

Tom let himself out of the room. His last view of Longfield was as the man poured himself another shot, and almost missed the glass. He wouldn't be going anywhere with Kate tonight. As far as Tom was concerned, he hoped Longfield would drink himself into a coma this evening so he wouldn't warn Kate.

Tom went down the stairs, thanked the concierge, and left the building. He knew where the ferry landing was. He would head there later this evening. First, he must go to his hotel room, have a bit to eat, rest a little, and then pack his belongings.

After giving the note to the young couple who would deliver it to Lizzie, Kate walked back toward Date Street. Her path took her by the railroad station, and there she saw two men who looked like detectives looking at a police sketch—of Lizzie. The town was swarming with people paid to secretly protect John Spreckels, and he could easily pay an army if need be. Instead of numbers, he had brains on his side, the best in the business. Time to get out of town, and not a moment too soon.

When Kate arrived at the hotel room, John Longfield lay on the bed, passed out. The table was covered with empty beer bottles and an upended whiskey bottle. Looked like he'd tied one on. One side of his face had a welt on it, and his eye socket was turning purple.

She shook him. "John! John! Wake up. We've got to get out of town."

"Tom Morgan," John said in a slurry voice with his head hanging to one side and his cheeks rubbery. His eyes fluttered.

"Oh my God," Kate said. "Was Tom here? Did he hit you?"

John couldn't raise his head, but he brought up one hand, the fingers in the shape of a gun. "Had Deringer."

"That's Tom," she said. "Did you tell him anything?"

"Told him midnight at the Del."

"How could you?"

"Had Deringer." John lifted the two fingers again, face down on the table. She started to protest, but he raised himself up and said more lucidly: "I was afraid he was going to stay here waiting for you, so I told him that to get him out of here."

"You should have said we were meeting her in New York in Times Square," Kate yelled, throwing her purse at the wall. She stormed down the hall to the bathroom so she wouldn't do something to him. She made up her mind that she was going to lose John Longfield at the first opportunity. But she still needed him for the moment. And she was pretty soft on him.

When she returned to the room, he lay sprawled and snoring on the bed. She gently put a coverlet over him. He had never raised a hand to her, not even while plastered, and she like that about him.

Kate agitatedly walked up and down the room. What to do now? It would be too risky to try and reach the Hotel del Coronado before Tom did. She was frightened enough of him to not want to go in the first place, knowing he was there. With any luck, Tom would be stuck on the island all night. Ferry service ended in the early evening, and she hoped it would shut down a little earlier in anticipation of the storm. He would go there, look for Kate, and not find her. He might see Lizzie outside but would not recognize her. She thought: *Maybe I can escape from Tom if I go to Canada.*

☙ ❧

Lottie A. Bernard entered Chick's Gun Shop on Fifth Street in San Diego, and walked stiffly to the counter. Several onlookers watched, and they would testify. Mrs. Bernard spoke with Chick in a conversation that lasted a few minutes. Chick handed her an unloaded gun. She held it, gave it back, and asked if it would be hard to use. Chick showed her how to point it, and how to pull the trigger. With the cylinder empty, he aimed at the floor and pulled the trigger for her several times. She nodded and pushed a handful of dollar bills across the counter.

At her request, Chick loaded five rounds into the cylinder, and put the gun into a shoe box. She had purchased a rather ungainly weapon, a cheap throw-away with rust on it, known as an American Bulldog. That wasn't a brand name, but a type. It was a cheap knock-off of the British Bulldog, the much-imitated civilian version of the British Army's Webley service revolver. The usual Bulldog was a .32 caliber with a six shot cylinder, but this .45 version had an usual five-round cylinder because the rounds were longer than the gun's design called for. It made for a deceptively large looking cannon of a gun. Chick wrapped the box in brown gift paper and tied it with sturdy string. He slid it across the counter to her with words of thanks. She picked up her package from the counter, and hobbled out the door.

A bystander commented to Chick: "That woman is going to hurt herself with that thing."

Chick shrugged. A sale was a sale. What she did was no business of his.

☙ ❧

Waiting for John to sober up, Kate walked through the Stingaree on a mission—to learn how much the Pinkertons actually knew about her, if anything. She walked through the red light district, retracing her steps of a few days ago when she'd trailed the Bowler Pinkerton agent. Her mind raced with plans and counter-plans. She walked obliviously through the bedlam of drunks, gamblers, prostitutes, Chinese laundrymen and tong assassins, delivery boys on bicycles, gunslingers, Mexican cowboys in sombreros toting steel, madams leering from open windows, and all the rest of the colorful Stingaree. It was getting cold and drizzly. She pulled her shawl tightly around her shoulders, with her arms wrapped protectively around herself under that, as if to protect and isolate herself from the mayhem all around. Not that it would help if a bottle or knife happened to come flying her way. She kept her hat low over her forehead as she passed through that same alley again. She stood across from the Pinkerton building, a two-story Spanish-Mexican mission-style building with a flat roof and yellowish stucco surfaces. As Kate stood watching the building, she saw a slow but constant stream of people come and go. It was a hive of activity, and Kate understood why. She could be sure that almost none of the people coming and going had any real grasp of the case they were part of. Spreckels' people would use extreme discretion. The left hand would not know what the right was doing.

A woman agent disguised in maid's dress was just coming out in the company of a Pinkerton agent who shifted his walking stick from one hand to the other as he pulled out his watch fob, and as he looked at the time, Kate saw a Pinkerton badge by the watch, confirming they were agents. Kate stepped into a general store nearby, found a section with uniforms, and emerged not long after wearing a starchy little white domestic's cap on her head. She had worn such things often enough. With feigned surety and casualness, she crossed the street and entered the Pinkerton building.

Kate walked along a smoky corridor where she heard people's voices in conversation and typewriters clattering. She ducked into someone's empty office, picked up a box of papers, and made herself look as if she were on official business as she walked through the building. She looked around and then ascended a winding stairway at the end of a corridor. Emerging on the second floor, she walked calmly but purposefully as if she belonged there. A man nodded to her, and she nodded back with an efficient little smile she hoped was agent-like.

Kate saw a door marked *Supervisor*, which was partly open. On the wall just outside this door was a cork board with papers tacked to it. Some were Wanted posters, others telegrams or notes. She heard men talking inside the room. "Hotel del Coronado," she heard, and other snatches of conversation wafted out: "money" and "girl" and "Room 302." She heard enough to know they were working her case in that very room. Standing at the cork board, as if doing some legitimate task, Kate spied a blackboard in a wooden frame inside the room. It was on wheels, and on it was chalked writing—telling her this was the planning and staging room for the Spreckels case. She'd found the Lottie A. Bernard headquarters.

Two men in heated conversation came out, one of them smoking a cigar. Kate reached up to the cork bulletin board and rattled one of the papers as if on business. The two men, who looked like high officials, walked past her with furrowed brows and preoccupied looks, and continued their conversation as they strode away. "Another day or two, that's all we need," one said to the other.

Kate thought: *You are so right about that!* She looked left and right. A young female with rolls of paper under her arms passed but didn't pay attention to the domestic standing by the cork board. Kate ducked into the office and pushed the door shut.

Seeing a large black steel safe, she noticed its door was not quite locked. In their haste and argument, the two Pinkertons had left it ajar. She pulled the heavy door open, glanced at the piled papers, and saw the money. She quickly scooped what looked like a thousand dollars in tens and twenties into her pockets. Her heart beat fast and hard now that she had a payoff.

She rifled through papers piled on a desk and a table. She saw diagrams of the Hotel Del, with Lizzie's room circled. She saw surveillance sketches of Lizzie...*Too much!* They had pictures of Lizzie talking with some shoeless man on the beach. Lizzie being ferried around town, smiling, by a boy in a carriage. Lizzie having tea and a bun in the hotel restaurant.

Kate blanched at seeing a sketch of herself, talking with Wyatt Earp outside the Yuma Building. She closed her eyes and shuddered deeply. She fingered the locket at her neck. The noose was already tightening. And there was a copy of Tom Morgan's photo from the telegraph office. They had photographs and sketches, of other people she didn't recognize, so they had not quite put the case together yet. The detective she'd overheard estimated they were two days from solving their case. *I'll be out of town by then*, Kate thought, *vanished without a trace, like a ghost.*

She heard voices drawing near, so she ducked behind the door with her heart pounding and the arteries in her neck drumming into her throbbing ears. What if they were to walk in now and catch her here? It would all be over—she'd get decades in prison, or worse. She stiffened and prepared for the worst. But the voices passed outside and receded down the corridor. She released a huge lungful of pent air. Slowly, her heart and ears and neck stopped feeling constricted, and the pounding died away.

In this silence, standing at the heart of the Pinkerton case, she pulled the blackboard closer. She piled all their papers up high on a table and on chairs. Nearby stood an ashtray, beside a humidor and smoking supplies, including matches. Kate lit a large, pungent cigar, got it going nicely, and buried it in the papers. The crisp smell of burning paper told her the fire was pulling nicely.

She opened a supply cabinet and saw a bottle of rubber cement. That would be nicely and highly flammable. She opened it and set it right near the papers. Smoky flames were just starting to lightly rise as she slipped outside. She locked the door from outside and threw the key into a dark corner as she sauntered to the stairs.

As she headed down the stairs, she pulled on the little red lever of an electrically operated fire alarm system. Bells began ringing all over the building. People looked puzzled as they stepped out of offices and stood around looking at each other.

The weight of the money felt good in her pockets. It took Kate about two minutes to step out the front door and start across the street, which was shrouded in fast-moving waves of drizzle and fog. As she stepped onto the opposite curb, she heard shouts and yells on the second floor. The fire would not hurt or kill anyone, but would incinerate the Pinkertons' evidence in an accident apparently caused by a careless smoker.

It mattered little in several ways as time marched on. The Pinkertons would orchestrate a cover-up designed to protect John Spreckels from any hint of scandal. The Hawai'ian monarchy would be overthrown by U.S. and European corporate opportunists just six weeks later, led by Pineapple King Sanford Dole. The redoubtable Claus Spreckels would lose his sugar cane plantations and all interest in the Hawai'ian state as a government hostile to him took over, under U.S. management and protected by the U.S. Marines. Claus would move his operations to the region around Monterey, California, where a town named Spreckels would grow up, and a new era in his sugar empire would dawn—fueled by sugar beets instead of cane. People like Spreckels always landed on their feet.

☙ ❧

Kate returned to the hotel room to find John Longfield sitting on the bed, holding his head. He had made some coffee, and the room was filled with its good aroma. "If you pull another stunt like that, I'm throwing you out," she told him.

"I'm sorry." He held his head and winced. "Never again."

"That's what they all say. Here, I brought us something to eat." She had picked up a light dinner of sandwiches in wax paper bags in a restaurant along the way. "We're pulling out, John. The Pinkertons are on our heels, and my husband is in town looking for me."

"And Lizzie?"

"I don't know. I've set them back a bit, but we don't have a minute to lose. We have to try to get Lizzie out tomorrow. Tom will go to the hotel and not recognize her and he won't see me. He may come back here looking for me…" She stopped and calculated. "Yes, he'll know during the middle of the night that I won't be there. He'll be in a rage because he'll figure I tricked him. He won't recognize Lizzie, so they'll pass each other in the night. Tom will take the first ferry back in the morning. The peninsular road will probably be flooded. I don't think he'll be able to rent a horse from anyone to ride the twenty miles or whatever it is along the beach. He'll come straight here, but we'll be gone, and I'll leave a false forwarding address. We've still got to get my trunk out of Los Angeles."

"And Lizzie's trunks are here in town. I have the baggage claim checks."

"Don't you dare go anywhere near that depot right now. We have to wait for it all to cool off. And besides, her trunks are high and dry there for the time being. Where would we put them?"

John nibbled at his sandwich and sipped coffee, slurping and blinking. "When do we leave here?"

"In the morning. We'll wait, out of sight. When we see him get off the ferry and head for our hotel, we'll get on board when it's safe. We'll cross over to Coronado, get Lizzie, and take the beach train back into town the long way. Or maybe I'll hire a carriage to take us north to Del Mar to catch the train, avoiding San Diego altogether." She sighed deeply. "I'm tired. Let's get a good night's sleep, and be well rested in the morning. Promise me, John, please, that you'll behave yourself from here on."

"I'm sorry. I will be good, I swear it."

"Yeah, like you swore to spend May's money on Lizzie's abortion, and a thousand other things. You are enough to drive a woman crazy." She rubbed her hand in his hair. "But you are far more loveable than Tom."

Tom checked out of the Hotel Brewster and walked, with his bag in hand, down to the ferry dock. He just caught the last ferry across. It was a gray and blustery crossing as darkness fell early. Drizzle and fog moved this way and that in a growing, knife-like wind. Icy, gritty gusts slashed left and right in unpredictable turns. Tom huddled, thinking, on a bench in the large common hall on the top deck. He planned to rent a horse and buggy tomorrow morning, once he had Kate with him, and ride with her to the train station. There was little for him to do in San Diego. He'd talk her into moving to Chicago or someplace with excitement and action. This was no place for her either—just a quiet backwater except for that teeming red light district that belonged in a city ten times the size of San Diego. Whatever this crazy scheme of hers, she might come away with a nice sum of money. He couldn't wait to have her in bed with him. The ferry churned and rocked on the foamy Bay waters as the lights of Coronado drew near.

A monstrous storm cloud like a black wall, an animal with claws, at least a mile high and hundreds of miles wide, rolled toward landfall in Southern California as night fell. Lizzie had her purse, and the gun in it, as she stood with other guests on a balcony to see the storm approach. It seemed a fitting end to a stormy saga and a depressing tragedy. Harry West spoke with her briefly before he went home—he asked about her, and warned her that nobody really knew how this new hotel would endure such a terrible storm. Windows on the sea side were being boarded up, and guests were being moved to the street side just in case. With myriad little lanterns and many windows, the great white building with its brick-red turrets looked like a newly launched ship about to test itself in one of the century's worst storms.

Scared but intrigued hotel guests huddled together on balconies for a view, as if at a racing event. Dressed in warm coats and hats, they sipped hot drinks and looked toward the monster bearing down on them. Then, as night fell, people went off to eat. They were bored with waiting. The barometric pressure dropped, and Lizzie's head felt light. She took the last of her laudanum, welcoming its herbal bite and then the numbness. There was no way back; no way forward. Her guts felt as if they were on fire.

The balconies were empty, as the wind began to howl. Shotguns of sleet and hail slammed against the windows and their wooden coverings on the sea side. The storm grew ever more furious. From time to time, one heard the pop of a window here or there, sucked out and burst by low pressure, or gripped by the cooling and contraction of the building. Dropping glass tinkled along the hotel's outside walls and rattled on concrete walks. Even as the shards fell, they were spun and twirled by the lashing rain.

Lizzie kept her shawl around her shoulders as she wandered around the common areas of the great hotel. She went to her room to doze for a few hours. Not long before midnight, she rose and dressed. She wore her sealskin jacket and the shawl over that. What a shame that she had never gotten any of her nice clothes out of the trunks. No matter now.

A shadowy female shape, hunched in pain, she walked slowly down the deserted hallways. The hotel was sparsely populated because of its remoteness and the economic disaster that had devastated San Diego since 1889. She walked down to the first floor and saw that its carpeted emptiness was silent as in a church by night. She continued down the stairs, into the corridors under the ground, and up a flight of stairs to the rear of the hotel. The storm raged outside. Wind howled like an army at war, complete with the artillery flashes of lightning and the boom of thunder. She came to the open door and tried peering outside. She doubted if John cared enough about her to come in this mess to get her. After all, Kate had to fake notes from him to Lizzie. She felt the sting of cold, and the biting pangs in her belly, and thought it was the fetus clawing at her in pain and protest. What fear she felt relented to angry resignation. She didn't cry—she was past all that. She was drained of emotion, and scarce on reason. She had her glasses in her purse, but didn't bother wearing them. If he were looking for her, let him find her, instead of always the other way around. She was done with that.

            ❧ ☙

Hearing sweet, strong chimes—as the metal works and steel hammers of a clock rang quarter to midnight, in that little ditty of Big Ben notes—Tom Morgan rose from the deep, comfortable arm chair in which he had been sitting for some time. It was located in the guts of the Hotel del Coronado, in an area near the main lobby from where he could watch people coming and going. He had dozed a little when the hallway fell silent and nobody came along. Now he was awake. The new-fangled electric lights burned soft and steady as you pleased, and made for an oddly comforting, safe feeling. Not that Tom wanted to feel comfortable or safe. He wanted Kate, and she had not appeared. He was beginning to get angry. Was she pulling a terrible trick on him? Was she getting back at him somehow? In the silence, his mind began to launch conspiracies, one after the other. No, she wouldn't be that cruel. Then again, Kate had a streak, maybe cruel, certainly unfeeling. She could walk over corpses without blinking, as the Germans around Hamburg, Iowa would say in their accents. What about this damned guy she was with? That drunken slob did look like a city con man. Maybe the plan was to have him come instead and shoot Tom in the back. He felt his vest pockets and made sure his Deringers were ready and loaded. In that rain outside, he must keep his pistols dry.

Tom Morgan walked cautiously and quietly through the subterranean corridors of the hotel. There! A woman's ghostly figure walked through the bowels of the hotel. It could only be Kate!

She disappeared around a bend in the underground passage, where store windows gleamed dully in the night. He came to a small flight of steps leading upward to an open door. No sight of her. Was she leading him on? Did she have that drunkard lying in wait to kill him? His paranoia fueled rage as he knotted his fist around a Deringer.

Wind and rain blew in relentlessly. The gale outside howled. He walked up the stairs and out to the edge of the rain. He felt betrayed, sent here on a fool's errand. Kate had seen his photographs, and decided to send him in one direction while she and her worthless lover-boy vanished in the opposite direction. She'd be halfway to Los Angeles by now. He almost cried with the terrible, overpowering rage that gripped him.

Standing in the open French doors, he saw the woman again.

Kate! So was it a trick, or wasn't it?

She stood outside, at the bottom of the steps below leading down to the beach sand. She was looking out toward the black, roiling sea. White crests by the hundred ran like wild horses panicked by constant lightning. Low pressure lifted the sea in a monstrous curve like a pregnant woman's belly. Unthinkable powers raged and thundered, moving boulders under the water as if they were pebbles, rattling like gravel. The world was coming apart. The hotel would surely be torn apart any moment now like paper in mad hands.

Tom stared at the woman. From behind, sopping in the rain, she looked just like Kate. It must be her. Maybe the head, the height, the hair were a little different—or she looked different because he had not seen her in years, or he didn't remember her as she was, but he was overcome by a mix of overwhelming emotions as he started to open her mouth to call her name. "Kate!"

☙ ❧

Somewhere behind Lizzie, inside the hotel, one of the clocks struck twelve times. The long, slow tolling of hammer on gong, heavy steel on heavy steel, sounded like a summons to a funeral—her own. It was midnight—the time Kate had said to meet her and John behind the hotel. Lizzie stood trembling on the steps outside, holding her purse in both hands. In the purse was the heavy gun. Wind whipped her this way and that. Her hair was plastered wetly around her skull. The wind seemed to want to tear off what little clothing she had. It moved her around in little steps. Her clothing was soaked, and she trembled with a chill. She felt utterly drained of any hope, any emotion, even of thought. She rode a nightmare of pure instinct.

Long seething white breakers came thundering up the shore like express trains, crashing against boulders. The ground shook under her feet.

Lightning flashed as the storm grew ever more powerful. Maenads howled in the night, and lightning gave sickly flashes that were followed by growls of thunder. The storm grew ever more terrifying on her numbed senses and chilled body. This must be the doorway to Hell.

She dropped her purse as she held the gun in both trembling hands. Her hair blew back and forth across her face, and buckets of rain slammed against her from all sides. The rain seemed sinuous and alive as it wrapped itself around her in violent seduction.

Lightning made claw marks in the sky and tortured her figure with cold light. Standing on a small flight of concrete steps near the beach sand, with the sea just a few yards away, she raised the gun in both hands. She had figured out that she would put the gun high up in the roof in back of her mouth and aim at the center of her brain. That was the surest and quickest way to end everything for herself and the child. Already she could taste metal, like blood, and smell machine oil. Her hands trembled as she tried to tighten her grip and position her finger on the trigger.

Lightning and thunder crescendoed.

She heard a man's voice. John! So he'd come after all. What was he shouting? She lowered the gun and turned.

☙ ❧

Yelling "Kate! Oh my God! My darling Kate!" Tom bounded across the walkway toward a spooky, sopping figure with rain-flat hair who stood looking toward the sea. "Kate!" As he reached the top of the steps, she turned.

The face looking up at him was pale as a fish's belly, with the same sickly, slimy gray color. Her cheeks might even be covered in fine scales, for all he knew, or were those droplets of water? Her eye sockets were bony, her eyes and mouth nocturnal holes. Her mouth hung open and her features rippled with exaggerated, inhuman emotions. This was a monster in a nightmare. Was she a thing that had come out of the sea? He stood frozen with fear and wonder. No, it was Kate for sure.

She raised a gun at him with both hands, and the muzzle flashed. He heard the pop and felt something whiz by his head. She wanted to kill him. Why, Kate? He couldn't be sure—the face looked distorted and grotesque with emotions in a lightning flash. Her gaze was large and luminous, almost supernatural. Her eyes were so wide he saw white all around the pupils. Thunder growled warnings and threats.

She'd lured him here to kill him.

That did it. Tom felt slammed by adrenalin, and cross-current emotions as if he were drunk. He reached into his vest pocket in one sweeping motion, took out a Deringer, and went down the steps in a second, maybe two. She fired again, but her gun was a piece of junk that fizzled and failed to shoot properly. He put the muzzle of his Deringer to her right temple and squeezed the trigger. In the muzzle flash, muffled by rain and wind, he saw that it was not Kate at all, but some crazed dark-haired girl who looked a bit like her. Tom pocketed his gun and ran. He had not meant to kill the girl, but she had tried to shoot him—why? He would never understand.

With that, Tom Morgan disappeared into the night and into history.

He left behind him Lizzie Wyllie, now dead, the supposed Lottie Bernard. Rain and wind whipped her lifeless figure as she lay face up. Her face looked indistinct—veiled in shadow, one side blackened with powder residue, the other pale as a porcelain angel's, enigmatic but peaceful. The gun lay on the step under a blackened, dangling hand that would never grasp again. The storm buffeted her body with passionate lust. Gradually, the residue washed away, leaving a pale, sleeping angel.

∂∂ ∂∂

The storm abated before dawn. Only a mute fog remained, penetrating everywhere. Electric lights glowed like luminous cotton balls, and the eaves dripped noisily all around. Here and there lay broken glass, but the great resort hotel had survived its first typhoon.

The body lay as she had fallen during the night. An electrician named Cone moved wraithlike through the fog on his morning rounds to attend to the lights,. He stopped when he saw what he at first thought was a mannequin lying on her back on the steps. Then he saw the gun by her right hand, the empty gaze, the gory hole in her right temple. He bent down with horror written on his face, and lightly slapped her cheek. "Ma'am! Lady! You have to wake up. Please wake up. Oh my God, you're not sleeping. You're—oh my God, oh my God..."

Cone ran to fetch help, and a saga was launched that would take the nation by storm, and be remembered for generations.

∂∂ ∂∂

11. Conspiracy's End—Legend's Start

Kate and John heard the near-hysterical rumors and gossip about the beautiful woman found dead across the bay, and knew it was Lizzie. They need not bother crossing. Poor Lizzie would now tell no tales, and Kate was eager to get far away from Tom. John grew misty-eyed, but Kate comforted him: "She's an angel in heaven now, Johnny."

Days later, Kate and John sat together in Third Class as a train clattered eastward. She had plenty of money from the Pinkerton safe, but would not tell him about it. She always bought him cigars and a little beer at train stops, and he seemed contented. They enjoyed a mild midmorning sunshine under blue skies in the California desert. The black locomotive lustily pulled dozens of passenger and cargo cars while emitting a long plume of dark gray smoke.

John, dressed in his dark suit and slouch hat, sat dozing against Kate. She wore a wide-brimmed straw hat and a tan outfit with black trim and buttons. Feeling his strong body against her, she did some careful calculations. She thought ahead, planning to lose him, but for a while she would continue enjoying him. She'd keep him under her thumb, feeding him sex candy, until she was safely far away from Southern California. Her main concern now was that her trunk was still at the Grants' house in Los Angeles. Actually, she reflected, her main concern was that she'd been so close to Tom. More than anything, she needed to put distance between herself and Tom, the more the better, so she could stop looking over her shoulder so much. Maybe she would disappear into Canada.

Kate read the newspapers and was able to follow the story in San Diego minutely, as it was telegraphed in breathless relays to all parts of the United States. The main source of information were the Spreckels-owned and controlled newspapers in San Diego, and Kate knew they were doctoring information to protect the owner of the Hotel del Coronado.

When the body was found by an electrician, the coroner's people came across within two hours to collect it. She was still thought to be Mrs. Lottie A. Bernard. Her stay had been a mysterious one, with many questions being asked, but it took a week or two to realize Lottie A. Bernard was a fiction. Then, for a period of some days, there was absolute certainty she had been a gorgeous and stylish runaway from Detroit named Lizzie Wyllie, whose grieving mother and sister identified her for certain from a coroner's description and a police sketch circulating throughout the country. Kate only barely recognized her—the beautiful hair had been cropped after death, and the corpse had been embalmed after some amount of deterioration. To Kate's relief, the identity kept changing as new leads poured in. For a time, police thought she was a Katie Logan who had worked for the Grants in Los Angeles. Alas, that meant never being able to get her trunk out. But the next bit of news made up for all of that.

Finally, someone notified San Diego police it might have been Kate Morgan. As Kate read this, in a train station near Omaha, she glowed with joy. Here was her opportunity to escape responsibility for the botched blackmail attempt. On the one hand, the national media made a circus of her name, which she could never use again. On the other hand, as it now seemed she was officially dead, she could reincarnate herself in any of her many aliases, and live a new life free as a bird. The Spreckels Machine were only too glad to spread dark rumors to tarnish Kate and Tom Morgan in a cover-up. If someone had a brain, Kate thought, they could put the clues together. Mrs. Wyllie swore it was her daughter, dead and lost to her. The press reported that Katie Logan had babbled to someone that her real name was Lizzie. The hankies in her room said *Lizzie Anderson*, but the coroner misread it as *Little Anderson*. The hankies in Kate's trunk in Los Angeles were embroidered *Louisa Anderson*, but it appeared the fools in charge of the world were so busy creating elusive fantasies that nobody thought the case through. Gradually, Kate began breathing easier. In a way, it was like threatening the Toad she'd rat on him, and getting paid off, as with all the other stupid men she'd blackmailed. She was going to get away with this, and she'd learned some valuable lessons. She'd never work with others again, nor use any name more than once.

Poor Lizzie lay in state like a dead princess at Johnson & Company Mortuary in San Diego, while breathless rumors and stories about her swirled across the nation. No doubt fueled by Pinkerton's and Spreckels' sources, the rumors told of her shady dealings, her hushed sex scandals involving the high and mighty, her husband's disgraceful cardsharping, and so on. Even as Lizzie became ever more disgraced as a Ruined Woman, a perverse romantic sense raised her to the saintly status of Fallen Angel. A Ruined Woman could be a whore or an adulteress, and fie on her—but, in the romantic version, she could be an innocent angel brought low by the evils of men and the world. Apparently, as Kate saw in the newspaper accounts, the women of San Diego, and of the nation, felt the latter was the case. San Diego's women, dressed in their finest, thronged by the thousands to visit their Fallen Angel every day and converse endlessly as if visiting with relatives. In the end, after a solemn high church funeral, she was sent off on a donkey cart, in a plain wooden box, driven by some old man who'd been given a coin to get drunk on later. She was dropped in a hole at Mount Hope Cemetery, without a marker, and forgotten as quickly as the dirt started hitting her coffin.

கூ ஒ

Kate mulled her options as they rode east toward Cleveland. As she remarked to John, "If Kate Morgan lies dead in San Diego, and if I never use my name again, I can put this whole thing behind me."

"What name would you use?" John asked innocently, smoking a cigarette, legs crossed, just making conversation.

She looked at him and realized she would never tell him. She had not even made up a new name, but she would never again make the mistake of sharing it with an accomplice. "Maybe I'll go by Lizzie Wyllie for a while." He looked startled, she grinned as if it were just a joke, and he shrugged carelessly and looked out the window while enjoying his smoke.

John and Kate changed trains regularly over several days. At one point, John said: "Poor Lizzie. What will I tell her mother? Her sister?"

She said: "We'll be in Cleveland soon. You'll mail your wife that you are still looking for work, as you did before we left for California with Lizzie. Make sure nobody can find your address in Cleveland. We'll stay there together for a little while, and you can have me all to yourself. Tell her you think you'll have work soon, and, oh by the way, you heard about Lizzie—the rumors are all false. There is nothing to it. She...has...let's see...she has run away. She is living happily in Toronto and never plans to visit Detroit again, nor does she ever want to see her family again."

"Nobody'll believe it. Everyone knows she loved her mother and sister, and they loved her."

"Lizzie will never return to them, so it doesn't matter. It's nice to think that Lizzie still lives, in her fashion—in some ghostly way, in her mother's and sister's faith and hopes. It will give them hope, even if it's a cruel hope that ends in disappointment." Kate grinned. " I died on the beach that night in the great storm—and am a ghost now, a ghost of me, but people will say I am the ghost of the Hotel del Coronado, when it's really Lizzie."

"That's pretty rich." John put his arm around her. *Poor Lizzie*, he thought. *Nice Kate.*

She told John: "Soon, you'll go back to your wife and kids. You'll put all this behind you. You'll tell them Lizzie went her way, and lives in Toronto, and you will go back to your life and be happy."

John laid a furtive hand on her thigh. "I can't get enough of you."

She patted his hand. "It'll wear off. Love and sex always do." She nuzzled a kiss behind his ear. "You flatter me though. I'll stay with you in Cleveland for a bit. We'll have fun together. You won't get lonely or bored, and I'll keep you out of trouble. When the dust has settled, you'll go back to Detroit, and I will get on a train and vanish."

John said: "Like a ghost."

❧ END ☙

Author's Notes~Lethal Journey

I have published a nonfictional, scholarly analysis of the so-called Kate Morgan story, titled <u>Dead Move: Kate Morgan and the Haunting Mystery of Coronado</u>—that is the first of two books in this volume. The second book in this volume is a novel, <u>Lethal Journey</u>—an 1892 noir period piece, a gaslight mystery, closely based on <u>Dead Move</u> in almost every regard except one.

In <u>Dead Move</u>, I lay out my theory about what really happened. It is very close to the gripping drama in this book in most points, but not all. One major difference is that, while Tom Morgan as a character has no importance in my nonfiction analysis, legend has made of him the larger than life villain you find in this novel. Legend has it that Kate Morgan died at the hotel, not Lizzie. As you can see in this book and in my other book, I believe it was Lizzie Wyllie who died at the Hotel del Coronado on that fateful night in November 1892. I have thoroughly documented and detailed my theory in <u>Dead Move</u>.

That title, by the way, came to me courtesy a friend of mine, who was a manager at the hotel. I worked at the hotel as a part-time shuttle driver for several years, and one day in 2006 I asked him, jokingly, if he'd experienced any ghostly activities lately. He said a lady had only a few days earlier checked in, and light-heartedly asked to be put in Room 3327. People often do this, to challenge the ghost legend. That was once Room 302, in which Lottie A. Bernard was staying at the time of her death.

The hotel's policy, in modern times, has been to only rent that room out if it is the last room available, or if a guest specifically asks for it. In either case, the desk clerks are to tell the guest that the room is said to be haunted, and to proceed with that caution in mind. The lady called the front desk after midnight, as many people before her have, and demanded to immediately be moved to another room as far from there as possible. As my friend explained to me, moving guests and their luggage to another room, without re-registering them, is called a 'dead move' in hotel parlance. I thought it was a fitting element for a gripping title. The most famous dead move occurred in 1983, in connection with another haunted room (3519) that is sometimes connected with the Kate Morgan (or Lizzie Wyllie) ghost story. Vice President George H. W. Bush was staying at the hotel, and one of his Secret Service officers was housed in Room

3519. The agent called the front desk in the middle of the night, asking them to tell the people above him to stop loudly talking and walking around. They informed him he was directly under the roof, and only pigeons could be walking around. This strong and fearless public servant demanded an immediate dead move. I imagine he was already outside the room with his gun and luggage as the bellhops came running.

☙ ❧

The terrible storm that so dramatically underscores the ending really happened, exactly as I describe it—said to be the storm of the century.
On that terrible night, the drama of Lottie A. Bernard did really reach its dark finale with the sound of gunfire. There are some major differences, however, between this novel and my nonfiction Dead Move. The nonfiction book sets forth my theory in earnest, with no embellishments.

The primary purpose of Lethal Journey is to entertain. Accordingly, I have blended the best elements of my analysis with the murky legends of tradition. As I discovered in writing Dead Move, the true story is far more gripping than the legend of Kate and Tom Morgan. With Lethal Journey, I am able to ratchet the suspense as high as it will go. The reader should be aware that I do not believe some elements of the legend, and I had to add a few embroideries—but Lethal Journey is largely faithful to Dead Move.

The biggest difference is that Tom Morgan plays no significant role in Dead Move, whereas, in Lethal Journey, he is the murderous villain that legend has made him out to be. Wyatt and Josephine Earp really did live in the Stingaree, exactly as depicted. The dark lady at the Hotel Brewster is a fiction, though the Brewster really existed, and witnesses placed Lottie A. Bernard at that hotel. Other fictional elements include the Desmond Pinkerton, Secretary Babbitt, Peter Maurice, and Special Agents Dolbee and Collins.

On the other hand again, for example, Charlie Stevens of Star Stables really did take Lottie Bernard for a tour of the city, and Harry West attended her exactly as shown here. She really did, for example, ask for an empty bottle and a sponge, and I am the first to suggest it was to make a pessary.

All these facts started tying together so obviously, once I had started assembling the many loose threads, tantalizing clues, and baffling dead ends of the true story as researched and related in the Heritage Department's official nonfiction book about the case. A.S. Gomer was the Chief Clerk, as mentioned.

John Spreckels really owned the Hotel del Coronado, and he was indeed with President Benjamin Harrison on a mission to save the Hawai'ian monarchy when Kate Morgan and her accomplices tried to blackmail him.

The blackmail is part of my theory, strongly supported in Dead Move. The story of the trunks (Kate's in Los Angeles, Lizzie's three in San Diego) is true. So are the families we know Katie Logan worked for in Los Angeles.

Katie Logan is truly documented as having told another maid at the Grants' house that her real name was Lizzie, and that she then corrected herself, stumbling, first saying she preferred Kittie, and then Katie.

Most importantly, in Dead Move I strongly explain that her death was a suicide. She really did write all those things on scraps of paper before she died—the invitations from famous actresses; the words *I hardly know that man, I have only heard of him*, which must refer to John Spreckels; and the enigmatic *Frank Frank Frank Frank*.

Regarding the latter, I took the liberty, with fun and delight, of having her meet L. Frank Baum. Why not? Baum did not, as far as I know, appear at the Hotel Del until after the publication and great success of The Wonderful Wizard of Oz in 1900. However, it is entirely possible that he visited San Diego in the decade previous, though it is unlikely he really met Lizzie. But you never know.

The words *the golden atoms of the day* were penned in the early 1600s by the Cavalier poet Thomas Carew as part of his poem *A Song*—here, the stanza:

> ...Ask me no more whither doth stray
> The golden atoms of the day;
> For in pure love heaven did prepare
> Those powders to enrich your hair...

෴

Street names, some mentioned in the book, have not changed much in modern downtown San Diego. From the southern end of Balboa Park, on the park's western side, just north of A Street, the east-west streets run alphabetically as trees from Ash through Walnut. They are crossed by the numbered streets rising from downtown into Bankers' Hill.

The downtown streets begin at a line running east-west near the southern end of Balboa Park. They run east-west as the letters A through L. A Street runs parallel to, and just south of, Ash Street. At the south end of downtown, L Street is today a small piece running about four blocks, from near the Convention Center to Petco Park.

The numbered streets run north-south, starting east of Harbor Drive, Pacific Highway, and Kettner Boulevard. In Lizzie's day, the numbers were all designated as streets. Today, 1st through 12th are avenues, and the higher numbers are still streets. Where 18th Street should be is now Interstate 5, running north-south.

In Lizzie's day, today's Broadway was D Street, and today's Market Street was H Street. When Lizzie arrived in San Diego, she got off the train at the old California Southern Railroad Station on Kettner (pictured, at C Street). She walked east on C to the Hotel Brewster at 4th and C. The modern Union Station (opened as the Santa Fe Depot in 1915) stands on the same spot where, during the boom years, in 1887, the old station was built at which Lizzie arrived.

෴

Of the many fascinating twists to this story, one of the most remarkable is the so-called Mystery of the Missing Day. Katie Logan, the house maid —reported missing in Los Angeles, and usually thought to be

Kate Morgan under and alias, although there is powerful reason to think she was really Lizzie (she told another maid her name was really Lizzie)—bade the L. A. Grant family goodbye in the afternoon of Wednesday, November 23, 1892. The (also fake) Lottie A. Bernard shows up almost exactly 24 hours later at the Hotel del Coronado. Then, as now, the trip would take about two hours by train.

So where was she that whole time? Witnesses did report seeing her at the Hotel Brewster shortly before she arrived at the Hotel Del. Still, why care what she did during the missing day? Well, a witness named Joseph A. or Joseph E. Jones, who signed in right after her at the Hotel Del, told reporters he had seen her that morning on a train coming from Denver. He had noticed a man and woman having a commotion, resulting in many tearful apologies and entreaties from her, and his bolting off the train in a fit of anger. Jones, who was not subpoenaed to appear at the Coroner's Inquest, and who stated he wanted to avoid publicity, had no reason to lie. So how could she be on a train headed south from L.A. to San Diego, and simultaneously appear on a train headed west from Denver to Orange? Why go to so much trouble to make the huge detour suggested in my books? It can only have been out of her desperation and love for John Longfield—who saw Kate Morgan's blackmail scheme as a way to get rid of both Lizzie and the problem of her unwanted pregnancy. Longfield no doubt was motivated to go his extra mile (rather than cut and run back to Cleveland and Detroit) because Kate Morgan controlled him with what must have been her irresistible and wild sexuality. All these people disappear into history, but we can assume that Kate soon enough went her way after Lizzie's death, and John had no choice but to return to his wife and children in Detroit, after planting, for Kate, the implausible cover that Lizzie was alive and well in Toronto, and never planned to see her sister and mother again.

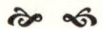

A nother matter deserves closer scrutiny: the incomprehensible behavior of thousands of San Diegans—and, in fact, millions of Americans who breathlessly followed every rumor, every tidbit of truth, every scandalous insinuation of this saga from day to day in the nation's great newspapers, from New York to Los Angeles, from Chicago to New Orleans. Rumor and spectacle are understandably titillating, but why the vast circus of morbid sentimentality? Once we understand the Victorian mind a bit better, it all makes more sense.

Our mysterious, deceased 1892 beauty was on display for weeks in a San Diego mortuary while police orchestrated a nationwide search for her husband (who did not exist) and her brother (who was a lie) until, finally, they realized that the gorgeous and stylish Lottie A. Bernard herself was a total fiction. She had been found dead at the rear of the Hotel del Coronado after a 'sea storm of the century,' with a gun at her side and a bullet in her head, and nobody had any idea of who she was, why she had chosen this particular hotel, and why she had died there. All across the United States, newspapers great and small daily published the latest breathless telegraphic dispatches from San Diego. The stories were part fact, part rumor, and part dramas clattering in the purple prose of journalistic imaginations from typewriters inked with Yellow Press propaganda.

People who claimed to have known her contacted police—from Los Angeles, from Pasadena, from Detroit, from San Francisco, from Omaha, from all over the country. Various identifications were tried, of which the most promising was that of young Lizzie Wyllie, a beautiful young runaway from Detroit, pregnant by her married lover, a Ruined Woman in the most delicious Victorian tradition, and just as much a Fallen Angel—a pure and sublime female ideal, the embodiment of goodness, brought low by a coarse world and gross men (and women of low character).

Dark rumors swirled around her—that her husband, Tom Morgan, was a gambler who used her charms on Transcontinental Railroad cars to lure unsuspecting men into robbery and possibly even murder. She lay in state like the fictional dead princess in Maurice Ravel's famous 1902 piano composition *Pavane pour une Infante défunte*. Moderns wonder at this morbid spectacle, until one understands its roots. Among the Victorians, this grave sentimentality was a feature of their character—I think, a way of coping with the tensions of a universe of contradictions, in which one said one thing but did another, a world precariously balancing on a tightrope between an agrarian past and an urban future. London, the world's largest city at the time—possibly the largest city in the world since ancient Rome—was the clockwork and symbol of a newly industrialized civilization. At its apex, in turn, was a Queen and Empress, Victoria, after whose long (nearly 64 year) reign a world era would be named. She ruled from 1837 to 1901. In the 24th year of her reign, 1861, her young husband, Prince Albert, 42, died of typhoid fever, due to poor sanitation (and ignorance) in the royal residences. Deaths from preventable diseases were common among royals across Europe, which gives an indication of the mortality suffered by ordinary people and especially their children. The remaining forty years of Victoria's life and reign could be characterized as a cult of grief, in which she only wore black, and isolated herself in her royal estates. Prince Albert was enshrined at Windsor Castle until he and

Victoria, after her death in 1901, were entombed in the royal mausoleum at Frogmore nearby. She dedicated monuments to him in London, like Royal Albert Hall and the Albert Memorial. Her life, thus, both flowed with, and to some extent set the tone for, the morbid sentimentality of the age. The mixture of emotional currents associated with Victoria (dark sentimentality, prudery, etc.) spread around the English-speaking world, including far-away places like San Diego. The classic White Anglo-Saxon Protestant Anglophile in the U.S. often referred to England as 'the mother country' (forgetting the long animosity of New England WASP farmer against this motherland, leading up to the American Revolution). Wealthy U.S. industrialists married their daughters off to penniless but titled English aristocrats (e.g., Consuelo Vanderbilt as Duchess of Marlborough).

During the 19th Century, displaced agrarian people thronged great new urban centers that were serviced by gas and electric lighting, central heating, paved roads, mass transportation, and complex water and sewage systems. As science and technology blossomed (the first modern gas-lamp in London is said to have been lit in 1816), sanitation, food preservation, and medicine struggled to catch up. The streets were still littered with horse droppings. In 1900, the average American lived about 49 years. Child mortality was crushing in its ubiquity and its tragedy. Death saturated every household. It was as yet a universe barely illuminated by modern understandings of theology and science. Death and judgment were, for most people, in the next room rather than somewhere in a distant future. For all the average person understood, the universe had been created only a few thousand years earlier. The farm itself represented a bloody, smelly, muddy universe of constantly evident birth and death in the keeping of animals and growing of crops (the Neolithic miracle of divine rebirth in grain)—all of this today sanitized from modern city life but, back then, a short walk or a quick ride away, and ever in the memories of people whose parents or grandparents might never even have seen a large city. And the city was, of course, wrapped in a pall of industrial smoke that made it seem like a Gothic purgatory.

෪ ෬

The dead girl in San Diego was the embodiment of a Victorian fetish. I say girl rather than woman, because she would be utterly pure in and of herself, and only defiled by gross people and circumstances beyond the self-control of her innocence.

The Fallen Angel was a Victorian trope represented in the work of many great artists, writers, musicians, and their schools. The Pre-Raphaelites were famous for their sentimental representations of historical myth, like Alfred Lord Tennyson's *The Lady of Shallott* (1833). The movement was a rebellion against the lurid, formal neo-Classicism of the French school of the late Bourbon monarchy.

The Pre-Raphaelites sought to replace faux Romanism in the arts with an earthier, more Nordic-Keltic-Arthurian ambience—hence, ladies drowning sorrowfully in inches of water, surrounded by lilies, or dying in castle beds surrounded by weeping Druids and so forth. John William Waterhouse, William Holman Hunt, and Dante Gabriel Rossetti were among the artists pouring forth these dark canvases whose tragedies were echoed in the streets and halls of 1892 San Diego. Charles Dickens (who also wrote of boy heroes like Tiny Tim in *A Christmas Carol*, and *David Copperfield* and *Oliver Twist*) created little heroines like Amy in *Little Dorrit* and Sissy Jupe in *Hard Times*. Little Nell Trent in his 1840s' *The Old Curiosity Shop* weakens and dies, and crowds on Boston docks cause such a riot (yelling "is she dead?") that the captain of the ship bringing the latest installment of the journal hails them from off-shore, via megaphone, to tell them "She has died!" rather than risk having his ship swamped by a stampeding mob. In the United States, Stephen Crane (who would die in 1900 at age 28 of tuberculosis, one of the age's various horrid killers) created *Maggie, A Girl of the Streets* in 1893. The list of such artists and their creations is long. (It may even echo in many hard-boiled 20th Century novels, where the female lead is often objectified simply as 'the girl').

It was the age of Poe, who died young and tragically, and spent his life in drugs and drink, mourning the passing of his wife and cousin, and concocting dread tales (*The Pit and the Pendulum*) and poetry (*Ulalume*). It was the age of Byron, who eloped with his half-sister Augusta, and of Shelley, who drowned at Leghorn and was burned in Viking manner on the shore. It was the age of Mary Shelley, who lost all but one of her children in childhood, and died after a sad and stressful life at age 53—but not before, on a dark and stormy night in 1816 (the Year Without a Summer, owing to the explosion of Mount Tambora in Indonesia) she invented Frankenstein at a nocturnal party thrown by Lord Byron. That same night in the Villa Diodati, Lord Byron's physician, Dr. John Polidori (who died a few years later, 1821, probably a suicide) invented the modern vampire (Lord Ruthven). Later in the century (1897), Bram Stoker published his definitive Dracula.

ॐ ॐ

Another real-life tragic heroine deserves mention, in connection with the Spreckels family and the events in Hawai'i concurrent with the story at the Hotel del Coronado that is told in the novel you have just read. In fact, we begin with another tragic hero of the age, the Scottish author Robert Louis Stevenson (1850-1894) of famous works like *Treasure Island, The Strange Case of Dr. Jekyll and Mr. Hyde, Kidnapped*, and others. Frail and beset with serious ailments, he sought a better climate in the South Pacific, and would ultimately die at 44 in the Samoan Islands. In the 1880s, he landed in Honolulu and befriended the beautiful and legendary Crown Princess Victoria Ka'iulani (1875-1899). She was the daughter of a Royal Hawai'ian mother and a Scottish financier, and designated heir to the childless King David. Traditionally, the Hawai'ian people had been ruled not by a central monarch, but by a powerful network of Royal Chiefs. All property was held in the name of these Royal Chiefs, and they elected their successors. Then, against their objections, amid mayhem and civil war in the 1780s, a powerful leader named Kamehameha the Great unified Hawai'i with himself as King. He and his successors adopted many European traditions, and managed to save their nation's sovereignty because it began to look a lot like a true nation in the Eurocentric sense. King David (1836-1891), for a time managed to resist the powerful U.S. missionaries who, together with U.S. corporate interests, tried to banish local customs, make people wear restrictive dark clothing, and—egad!—stop all that happy singing. King David, known as the Merrie Monarch, restored the hula dance and gave people back many of their rights and customs. He was the world's first monarch to travel around the globe, and was recognized by most of the world's monarchies including that of Queen Victoria in London. During the late 1800s, a German immigrant named Claus Spreckels made several fortunes in the U.S., culminating in the purchase of vast tracts of Hawai'ian cane sugar. He was a friend of King David, and became known as the Sugar Baron. The so-called Missionary Party, and their allies the Honolulu Bayonets and U.S. corporate interests—exemplified by Spreckels' rival, the so-called Pineapple King James Dole, cousin of missionary and future 'president' of a short-lived 'republic' of Hawai'i, Sanford Dole—conspired for years against King David's government. In 1887 they led a coup that installed the so-called Bayonet Constitution, depriving the king of much power. At the same time, they managed to dispossess the vast majority of Hawai'ians, on the theory that they had no right to their land because they did not have Western-style deeds of ownership. They also portrayed the native people as ignorant and brainless cannibals with bones in their noses (this, in the U.S. media and reactionary pulpits of the time), which helped allay any popular American objections to the eventual takeover.

King David became the first king to stay at the Hotel del Coronado. He dined in the Crown Room at Christmas 1890, a guest of John Spreckels, and then traveled north to San Francisco, presumably in Spreckels' yacht *Lurline*. He visited with his old friend Claus Spreckels (*père*) but died rather mysteriously at the Palace Hotel in January 1891. He was succeeded by his sister, Queen Lili'uokalani, who would be overthrown by U.S. and European corporate and missionary interests in January 1893. The succession would have gone to the Crown Princess, except the sovereign Kingdom of Hawai'i was no more.

The premature death of Crown Princess Victoria Ka'iulani's old friend Stevenson in 1894 was yet another blow, coming upon the death of the King in 1891, and the overthrow, treason trials, and other torments inflicted upon the doomed royal family at the hands of the European and American business owners, the Dole pineapple empire, and the Bible missionaries of which James Dole's cousin Sanford was the leader and the future ruler before annexation to the U.S. in 1898. Presidents Benjamin Harrison, a Democrat, and Grover Cleveland, a Republican, both tried to intervene on behalf of the monarchy, but without success (and very likely without sufficient energy or will). Crown Princess Victoria was at the time studying at a college near London, and returned hastily after the coup staged with U.S. Marines and Honolulu Rifles. Her work, petitioning the U.S. Presidents and Congress, and her efforts on behalf of many of her former subjects, now living in poverty and homeless, wore her down. When she traveled around the United States, her enemies in the Missionary Party widely portrayed her as a clown, a degenerate, a cannibal, and a heathen (her family had been Christian for generations). She was a cultured young woman who had been educated at the finest schools in Great Britain. She excelled in Latin, science, history, and sports. She spoke with the same refined accent spoken at Queen Victoria's court, and was far above the louts who constantly savaged her. Worn out, and hurt by other deaths in her family, she succumbed to stress and illness, and passed away in 1899 at age 24. She had been engaged to marry a young Hawai'ian prince. She has been called the Peacock Princess because she loved her birds. It is said that when word spread of her death, the peacocks on her estate began screaming so loudly and incessantly in their grief, that servants finally had to go out and shoot all of the birds.

Such stories are background to our tale of Lottie A. Bernard, her true life of crime, and how she became a ghost. Some will continue to think of her as Kate Morgan, while others will be convinced by my theory that she was Lizzie Wyllie (pronounced like Wylie, of which it is a variant).

Dressed in their finest, the city's womanhood came daily to spend hours with the dead woman's embalmed corpse at Johnson & Company Mortuary. She was the incarnation of that sentimental and tragic Victorian saint, the Fallen Angel. For a few weeks, the distant and shabby outpost of San Diego possessed that Holy Grail of all Victorian fantasies—a genuine tragic Fallen Angel.

Embodying the artistic and literary ideal of Tess of the d'Urbervilles, Little Nell, Maggie of the Streets, and a thousand other fictitious women, she had become flesh and died for the world to see. She was an unintended consequence of Kate Morgan's machinations, which have become enshrined in legend, although legend generally has Kate as victim and Tom as her murderer. I have taken a different tack in my 2008 analysis *Dead Move: Kate Morgan and the Haunting Mystery of Coronado, Second Edition (Nonfiction)*.

I based my carefully reasoned analysis on my own research and on the official research published [*Beautiful Stranger: The Ghost of Kate Morgan and the Hotel del Coronado* (HdC Heritage Department, 2002, 102 pp., ISBN 091625173X).] by the Heritage Department of the Hotel del Coronado, which they derived from copious reliable sources like the San Diego Public Library, the Coronado History Association, the San Diego Historical Society, the San Diego State University Library collections, and more. In my analysis, the presence or absence of Tom Morgan has no bearing on the plot Kate Morgan hatched, involving Lizzie Wyllie and Lizzie's married lover John Longfield.

In this novel, my goal has been to entertain you. I have combined the most exciting aspects of the traditional legend with the most logical revelations of my research. The result is a dark, crackling yarn that has me, as always, very excited by this great story. It is both a great San Diego tale, and a universal saga for men and women of all places and all times.

Police contacted Kate Morgan's grandfather asking how to dispose of the remains, and he wired back simply: "Bury her and send me the bill." He was obviously long disenchanted by her behavior.

When the ladies (and the gentlemen) of San Diego had finished adoring their Dead Princess, their Fallen Angel in her coffin, they organized a High Service funeral in the finest Episcopalian tradition. There was a great church service with flowers, a choir, priests in vestments with incense and liturgy, and all the city's gentry in gowns and black suits. There were tears, eulogies, and poetry readings.

When the ceremonies were over, she was forgotten that very day. After noon, her body was put in a plain wooden coffin on a wagon pulled by a donkey and driven (we assume) by a boy or an old man who got a coin for his services. Not a single mourner accompanied her on her final short journey to Mount Hope Cemetery on Market Street, outside the city limits at that time. She made her last trip alone, and was put in an unmarked (though numbered) grave without further ceremony or mention.

There the story would have ended except that, even today, people say the dead woman's ghost prowls the great hotel where she died. We might assume she is trying to tell us the truth about herself and what really happened—and that is probably very much like the story in this book.

From my nonfiction analysis in *Dead Move*:

> The halls of the Hotel del Coronado are haunted as much by a loving mother's heart-rending cries, as by the ghost of a sweet and naïve young woman cut down in the flower of life. This very Victorian story leaves sentimental echoes in Coronado's balmy air, like a fading bloom of long-ago roses.

John T. Cullen
San Diego
January 11, 2009

About The Cover of <u>Lethal Journey</u>. The Hotel del Coronado's official Heritage Department book mentions, among many loose ends, a report that a handsome stranger visited the Wyllie home in Detroit a few times—no doubt John Longfield, whose relationship with Lizzie her sister May knew, but would have kept from their mother, Elizabeth. Longfield became a Detroit Police suspect after Lizzie's disappearance, and was found to have eloped with her. On one visit, he 'jocosely' made a statement May Wyllie later told to police, about picking roses in California—hence, the San Diegan rose on the front cover: "While you are freezing your feet in Detroit, I will be picking roses in California." The other rose in the image is not Lizzie Wyllie, but an unknown model for a Victorian postcard. Even in that guileless image, dangerous passion and unspecified tragedy seem to hover around her angelic features. Or is it just a weary sort of sadness? The picture, like the age that produced it, and the century that gave us Lizzie Wyllie, seems enigmatic when we look more closely.

Selected Reading:

Beautiful Stranger: The Ghost of Kate Morgan and the Hotel del Coronado
by Heritage Department, Hotel del Coronado
(Hotel del Coronado, 2002, 2005, etc.)

San Diego: California's Cornerstone
by Engstrand, Iris (Ph.D.):
(Sunbelt, 1980)

San Diego's Gaslamp Quarter
by The San Diego Gaslamp Quarter Association & The San Diego Historical Society:
(Arcadia, 2003)

The Story of New San Diego and of its Founder, Alonzo E. Horton
by McPhail, Elizabeth C.:
(San Diego Historical Society, 1979)

Website of the San Diego History Center:
http://www.sandiegohistory.org/

Website of the Coronado Historical Association:
http://coronadohistory.org/

Website of the San Diego Police Historical Association
http://www.sdpolicemuseum.com/

Notes:

1. Note about Wikipedia: The 'Kate Morgan' entry at Wikipedia perpetuates the erroneous myth that the dead woman found at the Hotel del Coronado was Kate Morgan. I have independently concluded, without reference to any of this online material, that Tom Morgan appears not to have been involved in the crime. I have no comment on the Iowa background—interesting to some, but it has no direct bearing on the overall outcome of my research. The dead woman was not Kate Morgan, but Elizabeth 'Lizzie' Wyllie—as I have minutely and accurately detailed in this book.

2. The Legend of Kate Morgan: The Search for the Ghost of the Hotel del Coronado. By Alan M. May (ELK Publishing 1987, 1991) This book created a great deal of new misinformation, on top of the already baffling disinformation resulting from the 1892 cover-up of what really happened. Mr. May's book rekindled interest in the long-dormant story, which had been doctored into incomprehensibility by Spreckels' agents in 1892, and further suppressed by the hotel management over many decades. It should be noted that the Spreckels family owned the Hotel del Coronado until around 1948, after which time it was owned by various unrelated individuals or corporations. The Heritage Department appears to have published its excellent book Beautiful Stranger: The Ghost of Kate Morgan and the Hotel del Coronado in 2001 to counteract the misinformation of Alan May's sensational 1987 book. Mr. May's book caused local authorities to briefly reopen the investigation of 1892, but they quickly closed it, citing a lack of substantive new evidence in Mr. May's book. Mr. May died before actual publication in 1987. Mr. May claimed, among other things, to be descended from Kate Morgan (utterly unlikely), and that he, Alan May, regularly had dinner with the ghost in her former room at the Hotel del Coronado. The latter item, alone, should be enough to help the critical thinker and sensible reader draw their own conclusions.

3. The only two books I would recommend for reading about this true crime story are Beautiful Stranger: The Ghost of Kate Morgan and the Hotel del Coronado (official publication by the HdC Heritage Department) and Dead Move: Kate Morgan and the Haunting Mystery of Coronado (my analysis of the case, which you are reading, first published in 2008). While the hotel's otherwise excellent book continues to support the misleading idea that Kate Morgan was the victim, my book shows the victim was Lizzie Wyllie, and Kate Morgan was her mentor, accomplice, and ultimately worst betrayer.

About Clocktower Books:

Internet and Digital Publishing Pioneer Since 1996

Clocktower Books is a recognized publisher of the Internatial Thriller Writers (ITW), and John T. Cullen is an Active Member of ITW.

Clocktower Books has been noted by many resources, especially in the early days of the World Wide Web. These include the Wayback Machine, Encyclopedia Britannica Online in a 1998 article about Clocktower Fiction, the Encyclopedia of Science Fiction (for our acclaimed online magazine Deep Outside/Far Sector SFFH which ran for a decade 1998-2007); and more.

Clocktower Books has published books and shorter works by over one hundred authors, including several still on the roster in 2017. Among them, listed here in random order, are Renée B. Horowitz, Dennis Latham, Robin Marchesi, Deborah Cannon, and more.

John T. Cullen, publisher of Clocktower Books, has released over forty books, stories, articles, and more (fiction, nonfiction, poetry) under the names John T. Cullen, John Argo (his 1996 name for speculative fiction), and Jean-Thomas Cullen (his actual birth name of European origin).

In the following pages we present some current titles by John T. Cullen, John Argo, and Jean-Thomas Cullen.

Following that are some historical notes about Clocktower Books and about this novel (*This Shoal of Space*).

Adrenalin Rocket by Y. B. Suttle

Here's a thriller (2017) unlike anything you've ever read. Think of the dark comedy movie After Hours (Martin Scorsese, all-star cast) which is considered one of the funniest (and craziest) films ever made. We agree. Think of Linda Fiorentino in *The Last Seduction*, Jack Lemmon in *The Out-of-Towners*, and how about Thomas Pynchon's classic novel *The Crying of Lot 49*.

Adrenalin Rocket is the love story of Martin Brown and Chloë Setreal, and how Martin became Odysseus in his wild and dangerous journey to reach the Penelope of his epic quest. JTC used the pseudonym Y. B. Suttle on a whim. The question remains: why be subtle when you can be blatantly & darkly humorous?

ADRENALIN ROCKET

RUN FOR YOUR LIFE: A LOVE STORY YANAPOP

a novel by

John Argo

Valley of Seven Castles: A Progressive Thriller

Set in tomorrow's Europe, in a world gone global and run as one big feudal state by a thousand zillionaire families, here is the world's first progressive thriller. A U.S. Army deserter running from a crime he didn't commit, and a young California woman who sold herself into a modern form of five-year slavery to pay her mother's final hospital bills, are on the run. With them they carry the plans for a new warplane fuselage that must not fall into the wrong hands. Chasing them from Paris to Luxembourg is the Chinese billionaire who murdered a young Luxembourg engineer in London and wants his toy back. In the spirit of John Buchan's 1915 *The Thirty-Nine Steps* as well as Alfred Hitchcock's 1935 movie version *The 39 Steps*, plus a big surprise (see Thrillerology in the novel). Add to that the pace of the 2002 thriller movie The Bourne Identity starring Matt Damon and Franka Potente, based on a 1970 thriller novel by Robert Ludlum, and you have a first-class read.
(cover image next page)

Valley of Seven Castles
A Luxembourg Thriller by John T. Cullen

PROGRESSIVE THRILLERS SERIES

John Argo and Clocktower Books Present

Stunning and poetic far-future history (2016) by John Argo in the tradition of Cordwainer Smith's Classic Norstrilia and other tales of the Instrumentality.

Nonfiction by John T. Cullen: Coronado Mystery
Two in One—Dead Move & Lethal Journey

John T. Cullen, a San Diego author and scholar (BA, BBA, MSBA) applies his journalistic and historical expertise to solve a long-standing true crime. During Thanksgiving Week 1892, a stylish young woman (about 24) officially called The Beautiful Stranger by the Hotel del Coronado near San Diego, checked in under a false name and died a violent, mysterious death a few days later. Her case became a national sensation full of notoriety overnight because of allegations of affairs with men in high places. It was a Victorian scandal of epic proportions, resulting in the famous ghost legend at the hotel. John T. Cullen, basing his research entirely on true history (no ghosts were harmed), provides the first ever plausible explanation of what really happened—including a coverup of global proportions. See also Lethal Journey, the noir gaslight mystery thriller he wrote to dramatize Dead Move, on which Lethal Journey is closely based.

(cover image next page)

The nonfiction analysis (*Dead Move: Kate Morgan and the Haunting Mystery of Coronado*) is contained in the dual edition (two books in one) *Coronado Mystery*.

The dual edition also contains the full text of the novel *Lethal Journey* (see next page).

Thriller by John T. Cullen: Lethal Journey

Closely based on his nonfictional scholarly analysis of the 1892 true crime (*Dead Move*) here is a dramatization treated as a gaslight era noir suspense thriller.

Ray Bradbury Loved This One:

Ray Bradbury wrote a personal fan mail note to John T. Cullen in January 2008, praising this little gem, a novel that is a tribute both to Charles Dickens' classic A Christmas Carol, and to Ray Bradbury's dark but playful fantasies.

We Made History

Lots More Where These Came From…

Please visit the website of Clocktower Books for a full listing of our exciting fiction and nonfiction books, articles, and short works by a variety of talented authors.

www.clocktowerbooks.com

Written in Fall 1990, This Shoal of Space became an artifact of world history when first published on the Internet in 1996. It achieved several historical firsts.

Above all, this novel was one of the first complete novels ever published online, written by John T. Cullen and published by Clocktower Fiction (which became Clocktower Books). We make this claim according to very strict criteria for these several novels and shorter works: (1) proprietary, not public domain, which rules out Project Gutenberg and similar endeavors; (2) complete, not teasers or sample chapters; (3) published online, not on portable media like floppies or CD-ROM; (4) published in HTML, to be read online rather than downloaded; although we also provided a complete TXT file for download because so many of our readers around the world could not wait for the weekly serial chapters and wanted to know right away how these suspenseful novels reached their climax and denouement.

First was the suspense novel *Neon Blue*, published in weekly serial chapters at our *Neon Blue Fiction* suspense website starting April 1996.

Second was this novel, originally released as *Heartbreaker* by John Argo, but retitled *This Shoal of Space* in 1998. It appeared on our SFFH site The Haunted Village. Both sites were subsumed under our omnibus imprint Clocktower Fiction, created December 1996.

In 1998, we followed with the John T. Cullen political thriller *The Generals of October* (also titled *CON2*, or *Autumn of the Republic*), about a Second Constitutional Convention in the near future, held in a time of national crisis in accord with Article V of the U.S. Constitution, and leading to a civil war before reason and order can be restored. We also released shorter fiction by John Argo during that early period before e-commerce and commercial publishers (including us) started to release works for sale (e.g., Nuvomedia Rocket eBooks). These works were a sensation in the early days of the World Wide Web, praised by thousands of avid readers around the world. All were bestsellers on early retail sites like Barnes-Noble.com, Rocket eBooks, and Fictionwise. For complete information on these novels and stories, please visit our museum pages at museum.clocktowerbooks.com.

This Shoal of Space was an early Virtual Reality (VR) novel. Although a handful of earlier works by other authors presaged this subgenre of SF (e.g., Ray Bradbury's *The Veldt*, 1950), this is the first novel involving networked micro-computers, as PCs were originally called. This novel predated late-1990s landmark movies *The Matrix* and *Dark City,* among other dramatic and literary works that explored Virtual Reality (VR).

Reviews

An article about Clocktower Fiction (later Clocktower Books) and its genre websites (The Haunted Village, Neon Blue Fiction) was published by Britannica.com (the online version of Encyclopedia) in 1998. The online magazine The Haunted Village was the world's oldest digital-only, professional magazine of sf/f/h listed in the 1999 Writer's Market. Fragments of this early history are available on **Internet Archive: Wayback Machine** (http://www.archive.org/web/web.php) although, sadly, much has also been lost. We are still working to recapture from many sources the ephemera of our early WWW presence. Please consult our museum pages at museum.clocktowerbooks.com. *Heartbreaker* (retitled *This Shoal of Space*) received many positive reviews. Early WWW reviewer Tracy Eastgate wrote:

"Five Stars. Outstanding, A definite must read... a powerful book"—Tracy Eastgate, *Under The Covers Reviews*.
Personal e-mail to the author, from Ms. Eastgate: "I want to pay you a compliment. Rarely does a book EVER get under my skin or in my subconcious enough to cause dreams of any sort, but I'll tell you what, by time this morning came, I wasn't sure I wanted to go back to sleep or not ... lol ... I actually had mild nightmares last night ... I love it!!!! ... this is an absolutely awesome book."

End Notes for Dead Move

[1] *Beautiful Stranger: The Ghost of Kate Morgan and the Hotel del Coronado*, ISBN 978-0916251737 available in the gift shop, in most San Diego area bookstores, and online.
[2] Official Hotel del Coronado website—www.hoteldel.com/
[3] In competition with at least one other famous, disputed legend—that in 1920, the visiting Prince of Wales (one day King Edward VIII) met his future wife, Wallis Simpson, at the hotel while she was living in Coronado as the wife of a young U.S. Navy officer stationed a mile away at North Island. That legend now debunked.
[4] San Diego Historical Society website
[5] HD28MR (notation convention: Heritage Dept. book, page 28, middle right)
[6] Photo: http://www.sandiegohistory.org/journal/56april/images/page19.jpg
Article: http://www.sandiegohistory.org/journal/56april/palace.htm
[7] SD Historical Society, http://www.sandiegohistory.org/journal/56july/cattle.htm
[8] *History of San Diego 1542-1908* by William Smythe, San Diego Historical Society, http://www.sandiegohistory.org/books/smythe/7-4.htm
[9] More info about the peninsula is in the Maps section at book's end
[10] HD7UL (Heritage Dept. page 7, upper left)
[11] HD8LL (Heritage Dept. page 8, lower left)
[12] HD54 (Heritage Dept. entire page 54)
[13] HD54
[14] HD8
[15] HD42UR
[16] HD24UL
[17] In those days, San Diego's numbered streets were streets. Today, from 1st to 12th, they are avenues. Starting with 13th, they are still today streets.
[18] D Avenue was today's Broadway. Yesteryear's lettered avenues are today's lettered streets.
[19] HD11

[20] http://www.measuringworth.com/uscompare/ estimates $571.43 using the Consumer Price Index as a measure to compare 1892 and 2007 (115 years).
[21] HD12LL
[22] HD 63LL
[23] HD 39LR.
[24] In 1892, the Coronado Beach as we know it in the 2000s had not yet been created, and the hotel sat very close to the ocean.
[25] Probably a typical example of imaginative reasoning and inaccurate reporting. At the inquest, Cone says there was blood on the step [HD18UR]. The gardener Koeppen also saw blood [HD20ML]. Deputy Coroner Stetson saw blood around and underneath the gun [HD34LL]. See Part 3, Day 1, in this book for a conjecture on how blood could have gotten there after being washed away by a fierce rain storm.
[26] At the inquest, Deputy Coroner Stetson describes it as a 'valise' [HD34RM]
[27] HD40-41
[28] While Frank Heath did not know where she went from his shop [HD22LL], W. P. Walters, witness in Chick's Gun Shop, said he saw her leave to go to the Combination, another retail store, which sounds like a clothing store, and we know she was 'well-dressed' and seemed to like clothing. It seems odd that a depressed woman about to commit suicide, who could hardly walk, would saunter around town looking at clothes. Walters says (he was told by another man) she also went across the street to Schiller & Murtha's dry good store. Walters watched her for a time. [HD33LL-HD33UR].
[29] HD41UL
[30] Stetson testified at the inquest on the previous day that there were handkerchiefs with an unreadable name embroidered, which thought might be "Little Anderson." [HD34LR].
[31] HD29RM.
[32] HD42UL
[33] HD42LL
[34] HD71-72
[35] HD43
[36] HD74UL
[37] *Chronological List of San Diego City Officials*, San Diego Historical Society website.
[38] University of Iowa, http://sdrc.lib.uiowa.edu/lucile/publishers/winn/WINN.HTM
[39] HD69-70
[40] HD73
[41] HD45-46
[42] HD73-74
[43] HD46-47.
[44] HD74UR
[45] HD47-48
[46] HD65-66

[47] HD73
[48] HD48-49
[49] HD66-67
[50] HD70-71
[51] HD75
[52] HD49-50
[53] HD50
[54] HD50
[55] HD67-68
[56] HD51
[57] HD68-69
[58] A baffling observation that clearly seems to be an alibi—either to cover why the couple are not together, or to cover why Tom is not at home in Iowa. Why, if Victorians frowned on women traveling alone, did her uncle not question this?
[59] Those relatives could not identify the body one way or another. They had not seen her since she was a small child, so relatives from Pasadena were supposed to come to identify the body—but there is no record they ever showed up. Had Lizzie Wyllie (the first i.d. on the body after the Lottie A. Bernard persona became suspect) been alive, there can be absolutely no doubt the police would have found her, or she would have notified police she was alive. This strongly supports the notion that Lizzie was in fact dead, which makes her, *de facto,* the strongest candidate for the role of the dead woman at the Hotel del Coronado.
[60] 35HDLL
[61] It was extremely dangerous for anyone to travel alone in that era. Consider the thousands of innocent men shanghaied in the bars of Portland, Oregon in those days alone. And if a woman was raped, Victorians regarded her as a 'fallen woman'—so, society protected her not only from rape, but from social stigma.
[62] This housekeeper, in another wild urban legend connected to the saga) is said to have committed suicide in the "heavily haunted" Room 3519, not the same as Lottie Bernard/Lizzie's Room 3327. (Room numbers were different then, and Lizzie's room was 302.)
[63] HD24UL
[64] HD29UR
[65] HD11
[66] HD12LL
[67] HD46UR
[68] HD36
[69] HD42LL
[70] http://www.mchsmuseum.com/clausspreckels.html Monterey County Historical Society website
[71] *Encyclopedia of San Francisco*: http://www.sfhistoryencyclopedia.com/
[72] HD69-70
[73] HD73
[74] HD73LL
[75] HD45-46

[76] HD46LL-UR
[77] HD73-74
[78] HD46-47
[79] HD74UR
[80] HD47-48
[81] HD65-66
[82] HD48-49
[83] HD70
[84] HD49-50
[85] HD50
[86] HD50
[87] http://en.wikipedia.org/wiki/Embalming
[88] http://en.wikipedia.org/wiki/Embalming
[89] BS34LL
[90] HD54
[91] HD2UR
[92] HD54
[93] HD43LL
[94] HC43LL
[95] HD66UL
[96] HD42LL
[97] HD41-42 Interviewed by *The San Diego Union*, Dec. 1, the unnamed doctor is almost certainly B. F. Mertzman, given that he repeats statements attributed to Mertzman (e.g., it being ridiculous to think she had cancer, but most likely show herself while pregnant, abandoned, and in a lovers' spat.)
[98] HD27UL
[99] *The Stingray* by Russell, Findlay, posted by Cal Tech Library (http://calteches.library.caltech.edu/149/01/Russell.pdf)
[100] HD28LR
[101] HD70ML, HD68UR
[102] HD74LL
[103] http://en.wikipedia.org/wiki/Dickens#Characters
[104] http://en.wikipedia.org/wiki/Pre-Raphaelite_Brotherhood
[105] http://en.wikipedia.org/wiki/Ophelia_%28painting%29
[106] http://en.wikipedia.org/wiki/Ophelia_%28character%29
[107] http://en.wikipedia.org/wiki/Hard_Times
[108] Official San Diego City website, Police Department history, www.sandiego.gov/police/
[109] HD15UL
[110] HD36
[111] HD 47L

Made in the USA
Las Vegas, NV
27 April 2025